Medieval Germany and
its Neighbours
900–1250

Medieval Germany and its Neighbours 900–1250

K.J. Leyser

THE HAMBLEDON
PRESS

Published by The Hambledon Press
35 Gloucester Avenue, London NW1 7AX

ISBN 0 907628 08 7 (Cased)
     0 907628 09 5 (Paper)

History Series Volume 12

British Library Cataloguing in Publication Data

Leyser, Karl J.
    Medieval Germany and its neighbours.
    900-1250 – (History series; 12)
    1. Germany – History
    I. Title
    943'.02   DD137

Printed and bound in Great Britain by
Robert Hartnoll Ltd., Bodmin, Cornwall

CONTENTS

ACKNOWLEDGEMENTS

The articles collected here, with the exception of Chapter 10 which appears for the first time, were originally published in the following places and are reprinted by the kind permission of the original publishers.

1   The core of this chapter was first given as a talk on
       BBC Radio 3 in 1980.

2   English Historical Review, LXXXIII (1968), 1-32.

3   History, L (1965), 1-25.

4   E. H. R., XCVI (1981), 721-53.

5   *The Relations between East and West in the Middle Ages*,
       edited by Derek Baker (Edinburgh University Press, 1973), 29-63.

6   *Trends in Medieval Political Thought*, edited with introduction
       by Beryl Smalley (Blackwells, 1965), 42-64.

7   World Copyright: The Past and Present Society, Corpus Christi
       College, Oxford, England. This article first appeared in
       Past and Present A Journal of Historical Studies, no. 41
       (Dec. 1968), 25-53.

8   Transactions of the Royal Historical Society, 5th Series,
       vol. 10 (1960), 61-83.

9   E. H. R., XC (1975), 481-506.

11   The Listener, August 16, 1973.

To my Mother

INTRODUCTION

The papers gathered here were not designedly written to some master plan but the history of early and high medieval Germany stands in the centre and there is, to my astonishment, a certain thematic consistency and coherence about them. The inner workings of early medieval societies cannot be understood without also studying their links, religious, cultural, economic and political, with their neighbours. This is the main business of these essays. The worlds beyond the frontiers of early medieval kingdoms and principalities mattered to them for their own internal stabilisation and for the precarious margin of wealth available for distribution without which it was difficult, if not impossible to maintain any kind of royal or princely regime. The very struggle for frontiers created permanencies within and without on either side of them, senses of identity and difference which outlasted their begetters and the political structures that first embodied them.

To begin with we look at the bare conditions of existence in the tenth century and some of the beliefs and values by which they were endured or made endurable. 'The Tenth-Century Condition', originally a Third Programme talk, is here published for the first time. The beginnings of the Ottonian Empire are dealt with next in the studies of Henry I and the making of his equestrian host and the battle at the Lech in 955 which gave to Otto I his hegemony and to him and his following the opportunities to intensify their wars of subjection waged against the Slav peoples beyond the Elbe and their chances to contract further valuable alliances elsewhere in Europe. It also enlarged Otto's access to the poles of tenth-century civilisation in the Mediterranean, above all Byzantium. Larger and more lavish embassies arrived from the East. The study of byzantine-western relations in the tenth and early eleventh centuries is of central importance to shed light on the nascent self-confidence of the

ix

INTRODUCTION

Latins, on the gradual and obscure shift of relativities and scales of measurement which had begun with Charlemagne's intervention in Rome. The contacts of Otto I with the Caliphate of Cordoba and its christian subject community mattered perhaps a little less but they too left their mark on the Saxon king, his entourage and writers like Hrotsvitha of Gandersheim and Liudprand of Cremona. They brought to life a new intolerance, a closing of ranks among the Latins under Otto's rule. This topic must await a future collection of papers together with a study of Otto's links with Wessex. Here too I hope to have something new to offer in due course.

The dynamics of kinship and the stern and yet inadequate management of German noble society by its rulers are caught in two papers: 'The German aristocracy from the ninth to the early twelfth century' and 'Ottonian government'. Both reveal war and fighting as necessary ingredients and functions in the modest institutional framework of the early medieval *Reich*. Many nobles were poor, there was little else for them to do, so they saw to it that their betters, princes, bishops and kings, had quarrels and they willingly followed them to Italy to gain their imperial crown and elsewhere, Poland, Hungary and occasionally Denmark, Flanders or Burgundy. Yet the crisis of this stately world with its imposing hierarchies and their seemingly well-ordered relationships came from within, the great Saxon revolt against the Salian king Henry IV which erupted in 1073 and the struggle for the vertebrae of his kingship and of Gregory VII's pontificate which Henry himself unleashed in 1076. Not the failures of the old order but its success, the wealth it had created and accumulated, the grandeur, pride, artistic splendour and resonance of an all-too-aristocratic and king-dominated church first aroused criticism, discontent, mounting anger and in the end the impatient scorn of the radical reformers and purists, headed by Hildebrand. It was criticism from within its own ranks, in a stabler and more secure world which fuelled the church's and the papacy's movement of reform backed though it was at key points by new social forces, revolts and urban upheavals.

The catastrophic challenge to the achievements of the episcopal and monastic church of the Ottonian and Salian *Reich* is treated here in two papers, 'The Polemics of the Papal Revolution' which surveys the war of ideas fanned by the sentences of condemnation, excommunication and mutual deposition. In a wholly different vein the study devoted to the Anglo-Norman-Imperial alliance concluded between the last Salian emperor, Henry V and his father-in-law, Henry I, deals with the later phase of the conflict when it had narrowed down to the matter of investitures and the services and dues kings could expect as of right from bishops and abbots. Here we enter upon new features in the German polity and the German kingdom's relations with its neighbours, a change in the character of these relations set against those of the early middle ages. Kings still exchanged presents, intermarried and promised each other their friendship but they also wanted to mobilise their allies more directly and purposefully than ever before for the sake of their hard-faced purposes. Henry I and Henry V intended to use each other in their dealings with the papacy and later also France and they did. Kingdoms as political societies became more mature, more populous and they commanded larger internal resources than they had been able to muster in the tenth century. A bigger quotient and volume of commodities were now exchanged by way of commerce rather than diplomacy and war. Rulers still needed one another for reasons of prestige but the parameter of their calculations and the ends of their alliances and hostilities grew larger, more ambitious and explicit or, at least we seem to know more about them from the narrative sources than before. Something like 'foreign policies' emerge.

The twelfth century must nonetheless be understood as much for its continuities, the persistent strength of traditions and inherited attitudes as for its modernities and innovations. The dichotomy is illustrated in Henry II's dealings with Frederick Barbarossa over a relic, the hand of St. James and especially in the 'Reflections on twelfth-century kings and kingship', here published for the first time in which changing modes of seeing and describing kings at their work in Western, Central and Southern Europe are compared with those current in early medieval historiography. Here also the *Reich* is set against new and more recent royal regimes, especially those of Norman foundation. To all these themes the enlarged version of a broadcast talk on Frederick II, first published in *The Listener*, forms an epilogue.

The internal and external workings of the medieval *Reich* and its society are selectively covered in these papers and researches of some twenty years and they contain examples of the narrative, descriptive and analytical treatment of problems. They do not sum up all the work I have done and hope to do. Looking at them I am conscious of my debts of gratitude to masters, mentors and scholars who have honoured me with their friendship and encouragement. I would like to express it above all to Philip Whitting of St. Paul's School who first set me on the road towards the study of history as a passion, a necessity and a calling with the urge to teach it. I thank the editor of the English Historical Review, my colleague Angus Macintyre and Longmans, the Publishers, Professor Keith Robbins, the editor of History and the Historical Association, for allowing me to re-print the relevant pieces here. I am equally indebted to Trevor Aston, the editor of *Past and Present*, the Edinburgh University Press, Basil Blackwell, Oxford, and the Royal Historical Society. A portion of the paper on Ottonian government was first read before a conference at Tours in 1977 under the auspices of the German Historical Institute in Paris. I am grateful to Professor Karl Ferdinand Werner, the director, who invited me to take part in this large gathering of French and German scholars. Finally I would like to thank Martin Sheppard and the Hambledon Press for publishing these papers and so making it possible to offer them as an *ensemble*. If they are not the continuous and balanced history of medieval Germany that is still so badly needed, they yet highlight certain problems and events of which that history is compounded and without which it cannot be understood. Sometimes the beams of a searchlight can capture what might not be noticed even in full daylight.

Magdalen College, Oxford
January 14, 1982

Otto III and homaging, gift-bearing nations, led by Roma, then Gallia,
Germania, Sclavinia. The emperor, with staff and orb, is attended by
two clerical and two lay dignitaries. The latter inevitably appear as
warriors. Late tenth-century Gospel Book created at the Reichenau,
now in the Bavarian State Library in Munich (Clm 4453).

Photograph by Mr. K.P. Gingell, Islip, to whom I should like to express
my gratitude here.

1

THE TENTH-CENTURY CONDITION

We have just entered a new decade in a mood of pessimism and forebodings. For the historian of the early middle ages it is tempting to think back a millenium if only to give scale, dimension and a larger relativity to these forebodings. What was the world like in 980 and what was it like to have to live in it or at any rate that part of it with which we can most readily identify, the British Isles, Western, Central and Southern Europe. First of all there are some sombre similarities. A large section of the world's population lives near and beyond the threshold of starvation or at any rate permanent malnutrition. Famine, or rather cycles of dearth, famine and disease were endemic in the tenth century, an inbuilt feature of its economy. We meet them everywhere, here at home, at intervals of roughly ten years and sometimes less. They did not hit the whole of Western Europe with this frequency but no region was exempt from them either. In some years the calamity was universal, in others one country alone suffered. The reasons for the difficulties or near-impossibility to correct local shortages differed from these reasons now. They lay in poor communications. It was in many instances not feasible to transport large quantities of grain long distances overland, even if it had been possible to buy it from an area of surplus. As so often economic imbalances were accompanied by sheer waste. Occasionally privileged people could go where the food was when the food could not be brought to them. Sea and river transport helped and seaports were to have an important advantage. They could survive even if they had, like Genoa, little agrarian hinterland.

For inland-populations famines were disastrous and hit the vital nerves of their existence. Followed by disease, their consequences could stretch over years and undermine the resilience and even military security of an area. Here is an example. The scene is the Lower Rhine, the year 1006 when a

Danish band of pirates sailed up the Waal and reached the toll-station and merchant settlement of Tiel, the main exit-port for the traffic to England. The inhabitants of the riparian landscape fled taking only their money with them. The pirates sacked Tiel and carried a great store of victuals to their ships. The count of this region on whom the burden of defence lay, was old and could hardly walk any more. The task of trying to intercept or contain the raiders fell to two younger colleagues. Their host shadowed the Danes along the banks of the river but when they landed and offered battle the counts would not accept it because many of their men had been levied from the land, — they were peasants — inexperienced in war and still badly impoverished by a crop failure last year, so that they could not risk a battle. A harvest missed thus might mean defencelessness a year later and sure enough there had been a major and widespread famine in 1005. We read of it in all the chronicles including the Anglo-Saxon ones: 'This was the year of the great famine throughout England, the most severe in living memory'. Even its accessibility by sea and river could not have helped Tiel then. In France also many died and there are reports of cannibalism. Hunger and dearth afflicted also the aristocracy in this society so that they might be compelled to sell valuables and land to have nourishment.

They caused widespread dislocation. People moved where they hoped they might survive or out of sheer despair. Villages emptied. The Saxon historian Widukind of Corvey — he wrote in the 960-ties — tells us that a Slav tribe near Meissen was in 906 reduced to such penury that it had to take service with other nations in order to survive. Here the cause of dearth had been two Magyar armies who had used the Slavs' settlements as a base for their operations against Saxony. The crisis of this border people's subsistence was not unlike those described by anthropologists as endemic in the economy of certain African tribes. The late Max Gluckmann in his *Politics, Law and Ritual in Tribal Society* mentioned the inhabitants of the Middle-Zambesi who moved to their kinsfolk on the plateau when their crops perished through flooding.

Mortality from famine and disease in its wake could be wide-spread and serious. How then did peasants get by? Their lords, especially the churches, bishoprics and abbeys, as a rule and as a matter of policy accumulated surpluses and used some of them in charity and alms at all times but especially during these emergencies. Giving bread to their starving agrarian dependants who normally produced their surplus for them, was not only a religious duty fulfilled, a means of salvation for the givers, it was also common prudence. It preserved their labour force intact for the coming years. A bishop of Liège, for instance, was able to buy and store grain during a severe famine which hit France and Germany in 1042 and he distributed it to the tenants of the see. Not only that but he had also two pennies per week given to these men so that they would not have to sell their plough-oxen for food. The charity thus helped to preserve capital and labour services. The archbishop of Cologne in 1005 distributed grain on a huge scale to the starving crowds that flocked into his city and elsewhere. The abbot of a monastery in South Holland made sure that his own dependants should be the sole recipients of his alms in the same emergency. The serfs of other convents must turn to their masters to be fed. Much charity was thus self-interested and a kind of policing, of strengthening lordship, dependance and hierarchy. Sometimes it was coupled with public works, especially building, where the displaced population had to give a hand. Great lay princes too fed hunger- and disease-stricken throngs, like the Capetian duke Hugh who in 945 nourished the sufferers from a wasting disease who had crowded into Paris to implore the help of the Virgin at Notre Dame. They came largely from the surrounding districts under his power and control.

The sudden rush of refugees to a centre of wealth was a crisis also for its lords. Sometimes treasures had to be minted or sold to buy supplies at scarcity prices. Usually monastic communities could weather the shortage for themselves but their starving and dying tenants might easily exhaust their stores before a new and better harvest could be gathered. It was far from certain whether supplies would last and survival by the charity of lordship could not be counted on even where it was available. We know this from a letter of the monks of Tegernsee in Bavaria in which they turned to their bishop for help. The year was once again the terrible 1005.

As has already been said, alms-giving and feeding the poor were not only responses to shortages and exceptional dearth. No, they happened at all times and often on a massive scale, hundreds of poor being fed by great lords, kings and queens. In this way some of the surpluses which they had rendered to their masters were returned to them and in this way they might even share in the proceeds of tributes and success in war a little. Where urban markets had not yet gained enough volume to absorb all the corn not consumed by its producers and their lords' households, there was little else that could be done with it. The circular economy served to enforce and to enlarge the social distance between those who gave and spent and those who received. Kings liked to have their praises sung by the poor to whom they had given bounty.

This leads us to the hierarchies of power, crowned rulers, dukes, margraves, counts, ealdormen, bishops and abbots presiding over a ubiquity of aristocratic lordship and clientage. Theirs was a society ruled by gifts and gift-giving at all levels, not least of all in diplomacy and what we would call now international relations. For government too was largely a matter of communications. Kings ruled by moving about ceaselessly and ordering things on the spot: justice, its execution, force and rewards were dispensed on these journeys. Their range defined the limits of power and influence. We can recognize their problems and trace the growth of better, more regular and permanent communications between the centre and localities, especially in tenth-century England with its great assemblies and their legislative pronouncements, the rising communities of shires and hundreds. Here and there on the continent we have a few royal letters and mandates drafted and written by the small clerical elites most kings and queens, especially the Ottonian emperors and empresses liked to keep near their persons. We are tempted to see in them the remote ancestors of bureaucracies, of things we know only too well, but there were dimensions in tenth-century government which would escape us altogether if we looked only to these faintly familiar tokens of order and chains of command. The hierarchies of the tenth century, before the age of reform in the eleventh, coped with the world as it was by an intensified faith in a world as it ought to be, governed by God and his authorised representatives which, to a degree, they felt they were. This 'ought-world' was very real to them. It filled out their horizons and manifested itself at all the most solemn moments, for instance when kings were crowned or wore their crowns at the great Christian festivals each year, Easter, Whitsun and Christmas and at certain other commemorative occasions, or when they and dukes visited monasteries and were fetched inside by solemn processions of chanting monks, imitating the coming of Christ or when royal princesses became nuns to vow themselves for the well-being and safety of their homelands. Last but not least, when the relics of an important saint arrived in the neighbourhood to be solemnly received, to bring cures, better harvests and relief from their individual troubles to worshippers. All these ceremonies and their gestures made visible and therefore understandable, abstract ideas about the higher ends of human governance to unread and illiterate multitudes, including nobles: ideas of justice, equity, mercy, the protection of the weak, the threat of punishment awaiting the wicked. Justice between quarrelling and feuding families of nobles was in fact terribly hard, if not impossible, to achieve but it could be prayed for and revered in the rituals which framed the deliberations of councils and assemblies with their disagreements, rivalries and jockeying for position.

The world as it ought to be, the resolute statement of divine dispensation and wisdom, reached the men and women of the tenth century also through their works of art. These we can in part still share with them: the Evangeliaries, Lectionaries, Benedictionals, Sacramentaries, Psalters, their bindings, ivories, jewellery and sculpture which were created at Winchester, Cologne, the Reichenau, Regensburg and in Saxony, to name only the greatest *scriptoria* and workshops. It was an unquestionably aristocratic art revelling in the uses of precious materials, gold and purple dyes. Its solemnity, seriousness and dignity were not remote for the privileged circle of clerks and lay patrons who stood close to, could gaze at and use these treasures. It was moreover an overwhelmingly religious art devoted to the life of Christ, his deeds and miracles. This should not surprise us even though we know that the palaces of rulers also contained cycles of secular paintings illustrating their victories and the feats of their forbears. Expectations of life in the tenth century were short, between thirty and forty years for men, a little longer for women, at any rate of the aristocracy, if they survived childbearing. You would spend so much longer in the other world than in this one. It was better to familiarise oneself with God's ways here and now. This gave their reality, immediacy and homiletic urgency to the forms developed by the Ottonian and Winchester artists. Here we have parted company with the tenth century: the three or so decades added to our life-expectations have changed our relations with the hereafter.

Kings, dukes, margraves, bishops and abbots, moreover, were not the sole authorised representatives of divine power. We must not forget the saints, their ubiquitous presence and action, vouchsafed by their relics and cults. The saints were men's most important intermediaries at the court of heaven and the nobles knew all about how important it was to have advocates and friends in high places at the earthly courts they frequented. We seem to be in a realm of manipulated beliefs and attitudes but not quite or, at least, the matter was not as simple as that. The saints were very much part of the hierarchies of power and their power was deemed to be near at hand and hovering about, always ready to be invoked to tilt the existing balance. They formed a court of appeal by which it was possible now and again to outflank more earthly jurisdictions and they certainly looked after their own. Let me explain what I mean by a few examples.

The agrarian dependants of the Abbey of St. Maximin by Trier had to suffer much ill-treatment at the hands of a certain Adalbert although the mother of the duke of Lotharingia, the abbey's lord, sought to restrain him. Adalbert held a manor of the monks as a fief and at one time no less than sixty men from it came to the monastery to seek the patron saint's help. They kept vigil outside while twelve of their number were admitted into the abbey church where they prayed all night before the altars. In the morning the lady and the malefactor, attended by his following, came to mass. All the sixty villagers were there, flung themselves to the ground before the chief altar and called on St. Maximin to protect them and free them from Adalbert's tyranny. They staged what would in our language be called a demonstration and their clamour lasted for at least half an hour. Adalbert began to swear, by the virtue of St. Maximin too, that the men were liars and then he gripped the hilt of his sword and swore by it that they would rue their presumption. He had not yet finished when his belt slipped — by divine power — and his sword fell to the floor in the sight of all. The bully lost face and this was only a portent for soon afterwards he became incapable of bearing arms and lost his fief. Thus, the miracle writer concluded, St. Maximin saved his servants.

Saints could do things which kings and dukes could not accomplish, like coercing a powerful man to restore his ill-gotten gains to the monks. Here is a tale to illustrate this theme. It comes from the miracles of the patron saint of Gorze, near Metz, St. Gorgonius. A count named Boso, brother of a West-Frankish king, had seized one of the monastery's more important estates and a senior monk was sent to ask for its restitution. The count would not budge and the monk, quite fearlessly, said that if he did not return it the convent would begin judicial proceedings by complaining to higher authority. The count jeered: "To whom? The king? (probably Henry I). I don't think anything of him. The duke of Lotharingia? (where Gorze lay). Why, he is as my lowest servant to me". The monk then said: "If we lack earthly help we shall turn to reinforcement from on high". The count now threatened violence but his wife restrained him and the monk — we know who he was — returned to his abbey safely. Almost at once Boso fell seriously ill and felt that St. Gorgonius had more power in heaven than he, the count, had here. It was all visualised in terms of a crass judicial conflict. Boso returned the land and became the monks' protector there, a by no means unprofitable position to hold.

We do not of course know how often a malefactor did not fall ill when he treated monks with disdain but on the whole the efforts to instil the fear to God into men of Boso's cast were successful. Life was too insecure not to make one's peace with heaven while there was yet time and most lay nobles felt the need to atone for their misdeeds sooner or later by gifts or acts of restitution, at any rate during their last mortal hours and in their wills. Notice the dynamics of these beliefs, their sudden irruption into the working world of force and fraud and the distinct element of popular participation which the great were wise enough to respect and fear, however aristocratic their outlook and their contempt for rustics might be. Notice also the restraining influence of their women. Noblewomen had a touch of literacy and could usually read the psalter. It was their role to make amends for the sins of their men. On the whole bishops and abbots in the tenth century were in control of cults and saw to it that the right incidents were recorded and yet their control was far from absolute. There could always be sudden, unexpected phenomena and spontaneous developments. Belief in the power of the saints thus formed a reservoir of protest, something that could be mobilised as a threat and a warning.

In general the later tenth century was an age of optimism and of returning hope. Europe had been under siege, threatened and in part devastated by raiders, the nomadic Magyars, the Saracens and here and there still Vikings but it was now not only recovering but growing within. New centres of population, the beginnings of towns, emerge so that the church was caught unawares by them as it was to be again during the Industrial Revolution. Relics of saints had to be despatched almost in a hurry to canalize devotions and set up new cults. In Germany this happened, for instance at Soest in Westfalia, at Goslar and a bit later at Nürnberg. We know also that the tenth century experienced fewer famines than the ninth had done and that communications and exchanges were improving. The turning point for all this was not dramatic and spectacular but a slow growth of resources of every kind, yet if we need look for one, the Battle at the Lech in 955 when the Magyars were defeated by the East-Frankish king, Otto I, will serve. Only a few years before this triumph, there appeared the most important eschatological text of the middle ages, the treatise on Anti-Christ written by Adso, a monk and later abbot of Montier-en-Der in the diocese of Chalons sur Marne. Here, seemingly, we find no optimism. To put it briefly and bluntly, the coming of Anti-Christ is depicted as a torment that combined the savageries of a totalitarian regime with the horrors of a nuclear catastrophe and it was seen as an inescapable doom hanging over mankind. Adso had written his tract at the request of a queen, a sister of Otto I's, married to the West-Frankish king, Louis IV. Why did she want to know? Like many other medieval letters Adso's bore an address of convenience. Queen Gerberga was not the only one who wanted to know who Anti-Christ was, where he came from, what he would do and when he would do it. Just here Adso was on the whole reassuring to his patroness. It would not happen until all the kingdoms had defected from the Roman Empire, he wrote, citing St. Paul, and as he saw it, the Roman Empire continued in the Frankish kings and had not wholly perished. As long as they lasted the world would go on. Now lines of kings failed frequently enough and indeed Gerberga's male offspring, the last Carolingians, died out in the early eleventh century but Adso had chosen his words carefully and also coupled his historical fiction with a prophecy: there would be a great Frankish king and Roman emperor who would eventually go to Jerusalem and lay down his sceptre and crown on the Mount of Olives. 'This shall be the end and consummation of the Romans' and Christians' empire'. Adso's message was: not for a long time yet. For this comforting thought we might almost envy the tenth century.

2

Henry I and the beginnings of the Saxon empire

To understand what the tenth-century Saxons meant by 'empire' we must consult their greatest historian, Widukind of Corvey. In his epitaph and lament for Henry, their first native king, he wrote: 'He left to his son a great and spacious *Reich* which had not been bequeathed to him by his forefathers, but he himself had won it and it was given to him by God alone.'[1] In this passage, it has been rightly thought, Widukind tried to present a substitute for Henry's defective title to kingship. The man who had refused to be an anointed king had nonetheless enjoyed God's grace.[2] But here, as in many other places, the Corvey historian described the aspirations not only of Henry but also of his following, the *principes, prefecti* and *milites* of Saxony. The advancement and enrichment of Henry's nobles and the enforcement of a *pax* which secured and upheld their *imperium* gained by victory in war were the very secular ideas which put fire and life into Widukind's history. They prescribed his ways of looking at and organizing his materials.[3] Henry was praiseworthy to him because he sought to promote his Saxon followers and raise them to new positions of consideration and advantage, enhancing their standing in the East-Frankish kingdom and even beyond its frontiers. Widukind owed something of his secularity and his means of expressing it to Einhard and more still to Roman antiquity. He preferred his rather warlike ideas of peace and *imperium* to those which he might have found in St. Augustine and the Frankish homilists of the ninth century who preached the duties of kingship in more or less Augustinian terms.[4] Even when he came to describe how Otto I's *comitatus* lamented his death by reciting his deeds to one another, the emperor's great ecclesiastical foundations and the destruction of heathen sanctuaries are mentioned after his victories

---

1. *Die Sachsengeschichte des Widukind von Korvei*, i. c. 41, ed. H.-E. Lohmann and P. Hirsch, S[criptores] R[erum] G[ermanicarum] (Hanover, 1935), p. 60: 'magnum latumque imperium, non a patribus sibi relictum, sed per semet ipsum adquisitum et a solo Deo concessum.'
2. H. Beumann, *Widukind von Korvei* (Weimar, 1950), pp. 244 ff.
3. Beumann, pp. 87 ff. and 210 ff.
4. J. M. Wallace-Hadrill, 'The *Via Regia* of the Carolingian Age', *Trends in Medieval Political Thought*, ed. B. Smalley (Oxford, 1965), pp. 29 ff.

against Magyars, Saracens, Danes, Slavs and the subjection of Italy.[1]

Not all the writers of the tenth century looked upon the enterprises of the Liudolfing dynasty and its followers in this heroic, hard-faced, let alone exclusively Saxon, way. But Widukind's fellow-authors no less than he took their *magnum latumque imperium* for granted. By 973 it existed and questions were raised more about its character, purpose and future than about this fact. The author of the older life of Mathilda, Henry I's queen, Hrotsvitha in her *Gesta Ottonis* and later Brun of Querfurt in his *Life of St. Adalbert*, to name only a few, were thinking about a legacy and the tasks it imposed. Widukind, however, not only tried to tell his audience what the Ottonian empire was but also how it had been gained by the *virtus* and *fortuna* of his heroes, the Liudolfing house, the Saxon lords and, in the third place, their *milites*. It is here that we find it hardest to interpret him. His outlook and values and his literary personality have come to be understood much better, thanks to the German school of ideological analysis.[2] But the events to which he applied them and for which he is all too often our only source remain obscure and this is especially true for the reign of Henry I, the first seventeen years of the Saxon arrival in the East-Frankish kingdom. There are very few strictly contemporary literary remains from this period, and archaeology, which has done so much to qualify, blur and dilute Widukind's famous description of the Saxon fortresses and their occupants, still cannot date and compare the pottery found inside them.[3] We are left therefore with Widukind's eulogies and not only his alone, for most of his generation of Ottonian historiography, Liudprand of Cremona, Adalbert of St. Maximin, Ruotger and Hrotsvitha of Gandersheim celebrated Henry I as the bringer of peace and the enlarger of his kingdom.[4]

The conditions which gave some meaning to all this courtly praise – and Henry had his critics as well as his friends amongst the

---

1. Widukind, iii. 75, p. 153. No armed encounter between Otto I and the 'Saracens' is known. An expedition against Fraxinetum was planned but, as Widukind himself knew, never made. Cordovan embassies to his court and their presents which he mentioned (iii. 56, p. 135) counted however as marks of respect and superiority.

2. Besides Beumann see K. Hauck, 'Widukind von Korvei', *Die Deutsche Literatur des Mittelalters, Verfasserlexikon*, ed. K. Langosch, (Berlin, 1953), iv. 946–58.

3. S. Krüger, 'Einige Bemerkungen zur Werla-Forschung', *Deutsche Königspfalzen*, (Veröffentlichungen des Max-Planck-Instituts für Geschichte 11/2, Göttingen, 1965), ii. 235–7.

4. Liudprand, *Antapodosis*, iii. c. 21, *Liudprandi Opera*, ed. J. Becker, S.R.G. (Hanover and Leipzig, 1915), p. 82. For Adalbert see *Reginonis Abbatis Prumiensis Chronicon cum continuatione Treverensi*, ed. F. Kurze (Hanover, 1890), p. 159: 'Heinricus rex, precipuus pacis sectator strenuusque paganorum insecutor, post plures fortiter et viriliter actas victorias dilatatis undique sui regni terminis. . . .' His emphases differ from Widukind's. For Ruotger see his *Vita Brunonis*, cc. 2, 3, ed. I. Ott, S.R.G., Nova Series, x (Weimar, 1951), p. 4. Hrotsvitha, *Gesta Ottonis*, lines 7–21 in *Hrotsvithae Opera*, ed. P. Winterfeld, S.R.G. (Berlin and Zürich, 1965 reprint), p. 205.

later Ottonian historians and biographers – need not necessarily be connected with his reign at all but with that of his greater and even more famous son, Otto I. It was really his survival and victory in the prolonged feuds which divided his own and the leading Frankish, Bavarian and Lotharingian houses from 937 to 941 that created the new regime and within the next few years enabled the Liudolfings to gain a footing and acquire vast landed wealth in Franconia, the South and the West. The network of family-connections which they were then able to form made it possible for the Saxon kings to dominate the scene as long as they endured. Part of this victory Otto owed to himself, his hardness and nerve, more still perhaps to luck, battles which were won by others for him or by his own *milites* without him.[1] To Liudprand and Hrotsvitha again these triumphs seemed to be the work of God and clearly showed Otto's divine election to a kingship that was bitterly contested even in his own house.[2] But the king's early struggles, the almost ceaseless wars against the Slavs, and the renewed conflict with the Magyars in 938, could not have been fought and won without an effective Saxon *exercitus*. This was the pre-condition for all the opportunities open to the Liudolfing rulers and their closer adherents. Without a host that was superior to the East-Elbian tribes, at least equal to the forces which the Frankish, Lotharingian and Bavarian *duces* could muster and trained also to meet the Hungarian raiders, no Saxon hegemony in the *Reich* would have been possible. We must return to what Widukind had to say about Henry I's armies, and here at least he placed temptingly within our reach an explanation for the rising honours and the new importance of the Saxons in a still largely Frankish-thinking world. The consequences of military success in the tenth century were swift and its aura could work wonders. The news of the Magyars' rout at Riade in 933 travelled a long way: not only the Salzburg Annals, usually a source unfriendly to the Liudolfings, but also Flodoard of Reims reported it, the latter with much exaggeration.[3] When Henry returned to the West his goodwill was more sought after than ever and in 934 he could send two dukes, the Conradine Eberhard and Giselbert of Lotharingia together with a number of Lotharingian bishops, on diplomatic errands to the West-Frankish king, Rudolf, on behalf of his ally, Herbert of Vermandois.[4] Widukind's 'regum maximus Europae' and 'rerum

1. The battles of Andernach and Birten in 939.
2. Liudprand, *Antapodosis*, iv. c. 29, p. 125: 'Vides igitur, quemadmodum super regem tribulantes Dominus manum miserit, quem in viis suis ambulasse cognovit.' Hrotsvitha, lines 228–36, p. 211.
3. *Annales Iuvavenses maximi*, ed. H. Bresslau, M[onumenta] G[ermaniae] H[istorica] Scriptorum xxx, ii. 743 and *Les Annales de Flodoard*, ed. P. Lauer, Collection de Textes pour servir à l'étude et à l'enseignement de l'histoire (Paris, 1905), p. 55, *sub anno* 933.
4. Flodoard, *Annales*, p. 59. H. Sproemberg, 'Die lothringische Politik Ottos des Grossen', in his *Beiträge zur Belgisch-Niederländischen Geschichte* (Berlin, 1959), p. 140.

dominus' was ready for a pilgrimage to Rome in 935, and perhaps more than a pilgrimage, when he suffered a stroke and was paralysed.

Between 924/6 and 933, to follow the *res gestae Saxonicae*, Henry I accomplished something like a military revolution in his stemland.[1] Having negotiated a peace with the Magyars and accepted their demand for annual tributes he set about the two tasks of strengthening and preparing *urbes* against the Hungarian raiders and of creating a force capable of meeting them in the field. In Widukind's narrative neither had Saxony viable fortresses nor could the king in the crisis of the great raids of 924 and (?) 926 rely on his host in a pitched battle against the 'saeva gens', the Magyars.[2] Scholars have often treated these two activities, the castle-building and the creation of mobile forces, as one or at least as closely-related problems. Here only the history of the Saxon *exercitus* in the early tenth century is to be looked at again. Much ink has flowed over Henry I's *urbes*, but empires cannot be founded by defensive measures alone. The quality of the host the Ottonian kings could muster at home was even more important than their fortresses in deciding the future role of the Saxons in the *Reich*. The group of people whom Widukind called the *principes militum*, the dukes, margraves and counts of his stemland, are relatively well-known, but their subordinates are not. Who were the Saxon *milites* of the tenth century, from what layers of Saxon society were they recruited and how were they organized for their wars? To throw the castles and the *exercitus* together is also misleading, as will be seen, although Widukind himself is responsible for the way this has been done. 'It surpasses our powers to say,' he wrote, 'with what sagacity King Henry, after he had accepted the Hungarians' peace-terms for nine years, watched over the defence

---

1. The date and scope of Henry's armistice with the Hungarians remain disputed. After G. Waitz, *Jahrbücher des Deutschen Reichs unter König Heinrich I* (Leipzig, 1885 and Darmstadt, 1963), pp. 77 ff. it was generally thought to have been concluded in 924 and to safeguard Saxony alone. But in 1933 M. Lintzel argued with force that the agreement belonged to the year 926 and applied to other regions of the *Reich* as well. Only Arnulf of Bavaria made his own terms with the Hungarians a year later. See M. Lintzel, 'Die Schlacht von Riade und die Anfänge des deutschen Staates', *Sachsen und Anhalt*, ix (1933), 27–51 and also in his *Ausgewählte Schriften* (Berlin, 1961), ii. 92–111. C. Erdmann, 'Die Burgenordnung Heinrich's I', *D[eutsches] A[rchiv für Erforschung des Mittelalters]*, vi (1943), 77 ff. enlarged on Lintzel's views and 926 has taken possession of the narrative in R. Holtzmann, *Geschichte der sächsischen Kaiserzeit* (Munich, 1943), p. 84 and B. Gebhardt, *Handbuch der deutschen Geschichte* (Stuttgart, 1954), i. 169. But against this see K. Reindel, 'Herzog Arnulf und das *Regnum Bavariae*', *Zeitschrift für bayerische Landesgeschichte*, xvii (1954), 242 reprinted in *Die Entstehung des deutschen Reiches, Wege der Forschung*, i (Darmstadt, 1956), 275 and also G. Baaken, 'Königtum Burgen und Königsfreie', *Vorträge undForschungen*, vi (Konstanzer Arbeitskreis für mittelalterliche Geschichte, Konstanz, Stuttgart, n.d.), 69, For 926 speaks Henry's renewal, in March 927, of the older Herford privileges which had been burnt in a Magyar raid. Would the nuns have waited three years to have this done? However important for our understanding of Henry I's reign the date and extent of his armistice may be, the evidence is too faint to allow a firm conclusion in favour of 926. For Henry's diploma for Herford (= DH I, 13) see *M.G.H., Die Urkunden der deutschen Könige und Kaiser* (Hanover, 1879–84), i. 50.

2. Widukind, i. 32, p. 45.

of the land and the assault on the barbarian tribes (the Slavs beyond the Elbe and Saale) although it should not be passed over in complete silence. First of all he picked every ninth man from the *agrarii milites* and made him live in the fortresses to build shelters for his fellows (*confamiliares*) and to receive and store a third of all the produce there. The remaining eight were to sow and reap and collect the crops of the ninth. . . .'[1] All assemblies were to be held in these *urbes* and, having said this, Widukind moved on without a break to describe an expedition against the Hevelli of Brandenburg. 'Having accustomed the free men' (he used the word *cives*), 'to this rule and practice, he suddenly fell upon the Slavs called Hevelli and wore them out in many combats.'[2] It is this transitional phrase which makes it possible to see in the *agrarii milites* the warriors whom Henry had to have trained for fighting pitched battles against the Magyars. When Widukind returned to them in the next chapter but two, he presented his readers with a very different military situation: the king now had an army 'iam . . . equestri prelio probatum' and this explained why he could resolve to fight it out rather than pay any more tribute.[3] In the Corvey historian's account of the spring campaign of 933 only Saxons and Thuringians took the field and his story of the events leading up to the victory at Riade contains another useful hint about their host.[4] The king who knew the Hungarians' tactics was afraid that they would take to flight as soon as they saw the *miles armatus* – the better-armed, shielded and hauberked horsemen of his army. To forestall this he devised a deceptive manoeuvre by sending a swarm of Thuringians with only a few heavily-armed horsemen ahead to lure the enemy into battle with the mass of the *miles armatus*.[5] By contrast Widukind described these Thuringians as *inermes*, 'unarmed', yet to perform their task they too must have

1. Widukind, i. 35, pp. 48 ff.: 'Igitur Heinricus rex, accepta pace ab Ungariis ad novem annos, quanta prudentia vigilaverit in munienda patria et in expugnando barbaras nationes, supra nostram est virtutem edicere, licet omnimodis non oporteat taceri. Et primum quidem ex agrariis militibus nonum quemque eligens in urbibus habitare fecit, ut ceteris confamiliaribus suis octo habitacula extrueret, frugum omnium tertiam partem exciperet servaretque. Caeteri vero octo seminarent et meterent frugesque colligerent nono et suis eas locis reconderent. . . .'

2. *Ibid.* 'Tali lege ac disciplina cum cives assuefaceret, repente irruit super Sclavos qui dicuntur Hevelli, et multis eos preliis fatigans. . . .'

3. Widukind, i. 38, p. 55: 'Rex autem cum iam militem haberet equestri prelio probatum, contra antiquos hostes, videlicet Ungarios, presumpsit inire certamen.'

4. Flodoard thought that the Bavarians and other 'subject peoples' took part at Riade and this might explain the mention of the battle in the Salzburg Annals (*cf.* above, p. 3, n. 3). But it remains doubtful whether they joined Henry's host. More than one Hungarian swarm was afield in 933 and more than one force set out to intercept them. The 'ceterae gentes subjectae' of Flodoard's, *Annales* (p. 55) were most probably Slavs.

5. Widukind, i. 38, p. 57: 'Rex vero veritus est . . . ut hostes viso milite armato fugae statim indulsissent; misit legionem Thuringorum cum raro milite armato, ut inermes prosequerentur et usque ad exercitum protraherentur.' On Hungarian ways of fighting see below, pp. 53 ff.

been mounted. From all this it is at least clear where he had seen the shortcomings of the Saxon host in 924/26. Henry could not trust his horsemen because they lacked certain skills and not enough of them were equipped as a *miles armatus* should be.

The historians who have identified the castle-building *agrarii milites* with the well-armed and mounted warriors at whose sight the Hungarians turned and fled in 933 fall into two schools.[1] One assumed that they were royal *ministeriales* for it was thought that the king could only order his own dependants to build fortresses and not those of his nobles.[2] The other, more recently, has sought to prove that they were *Königsfreie*, 'royal freemen', a class of *liberi* who inhabited royal lands, owed rents to the king and played some part in the military and settlement policies of the Frankish conquest.[3] The reality was more complex and defies such sweeping explanations. It is true that a general obligation of military service for the free and even for the *liti*, the half-free peasants, existed in tenth-century Saxony, especially along her eastern frontiers, the marches against the Slavs. But there are strong grounds for clearly distinguishing Widukind's *miles armatus* from his *agrarii milites* and for doubting whether they were recruited from the same strata in Saxon society.

We are fortunate in possessing a long run of imperial and royal mandates and diplomata for Corvey, Widukind's own house, from the second quarter of the ninth century onwards. Despite forgeries and falsifications they invite us to study the make-up of her military forces without relying too much on her great historian. Widukind could, if he cared to do so, draw on knowledge that was familiar and near at hand and it will be seen that his *agrarii milites* had local roots. Corvey with her vast possessions scattered across the whole of Saxony and her intimate ties with the native and Frankish nobility was not only a missionary and cultural but also a military bastion of the Carolingian new order there. The monastery however had been granted exemption from military service by Louis the Pious:

1. W. Giesebrecht, *Geschichte der deutschen Kaiserzeit* (Leipzig, 1881), i. 811 ff. who thought however that Widukind's description of the *agrarii milites* only applied to the marches of Saxony. Waitz, *Jahrbücher*, p. 98, n. 6; D. Schäfer, 'Die *agrarii milites* des Widukind', *Sitzungsberichte der königlich preussischen Akademie der Wissenschaften*, xxvii (1905), 569–77; E. Sander, 'Die Heeresorganisation Heinrichs I', *Historisches Jahrbuch*, lix (1939), 1–26; Baaken, *ubi supra*, p. 21. H. Delbrück, *Geschichte der Kriegskunst* (reprint, Berlin, 1964), iii. 112 rejected the whole of Widukind's bk. i. c. 35 as legend.

2. R. Köpke, 'Widukind von Korvei', *Ottonische Studien* (Berlin, 1867), i. 95 ff.; Waitz, *Jahrbücher, loc. cit.*, Giesebrecht, *loc. cit.*, and especially Schäfer, *ubi supra*, p. 576 citing Waitz; E. Stengel, 'Ueber den Ursprung der Ministerialität', *Papsttum und Kaisertum*, ed. A. Brackmann (Munich, 1926), p. 173 and revised in his *Abhandlungen und Untersuchungen zur mittelalterlichen Geschichte* (Köln-Graz, 1960), i. 74. Stengel thought, however, that they could be the *ministeriales* of other lords than the king as did Erdmann, *ubi supra*, pp. 86 ff. and n. 2.

3. H. Dannenbauer, 'Freigrafschaften und Freigerichte', in his *Grundlagen der mittelalterlichen Welt* (Stuttgart, 1958), p. 321 and esp. Baaken, *ubi supra*, p. 14, n. 1.

neither her freemen nor her *liti* were to be levied by the counts.[1] But this did not mean that they escaped service for, from the very start, the purpose of these privileges was to give the abbot the sole control over the armed strength of his lay dependants. Nor did the Carolingian kings wish to deprive themselves of the military resources which their stronghold on the upper Weser could muster. Corvey's exemption was justified in one imperial diploma by her abbot's tasks as a permanent royal *missus* in Saxony. The services of the Corvey levies were reserved for his own use and when he went on the king's *legatio*. In the last quarter of the ninth century when Danish raids struck further and further up the great river-valleys of the East-Frankish kingdom it became ever more important for an abbey to be able to collect its fighting men and prevent their being sent to distant parts, leaving the house defenceless. But in Corvey's case, the wide spread of her possessions and dependants made it difficult to enforce this immunity. In May 887, the last days of Charles III's regime, the exemption from military service which the abbots had already found troublesome to safeguard was breached in an imperial diploma which professed to confirm it. Its opening clauses rehearsed the rights conferred by Louis the Pious: the men of the abbey, of whatever condition, should be quit. But these were bad times and not all of them could be spared. The abbot might retain thirty nobles for his own service and the royal legation, more still if this led him beyond the frontiers. The rest must go to the host as long as the emergency, a bad run of Viking raids, lasted.[2] Only a few months later, hot on the heels of the coup d'état which raised Arnolf to the East-Frankish kingship, Corvey and the nunnery of Herford together secured a new exemption which restored the abbot's exclusive right to the military services of his noble vassals and also allowed him to keep at home as many of his plebeian retainers, 'vasalli inferioris conditionis', as he needed for the monastery's good and the royal legation.[3] Were these vassals of lower

1. R. Wilmans, *Die Kaiserurkunden der Provinz Westfalen* (Münster, 1867), i. 28 (No. 10), Louis the Pious's precept addressed to Bishop Badurad of Paderborn which singled out the levy of military service on the free men and the *lati* amongst the excesses which the counts had committed against the abbey's dependants.

2. M.G.H., *Die Urkunden der deutschen Karolinger*, ii: *Die Urkunden Karls III*, ed. P. Kehr (Berlin, 1937), no. 158, p. 257: '. . . sed quoniam eiusdem loci abbates missaticum regium peragere soliti erant, concedimus eis, ut triginta homines nobiles ab aliis profectionibus secum immunes habeant et, si extra patriam est legatio peragenda, plures nobiles ad hoc opus paratos teneant, reliqui vero cum suo populo in hostem proficiscantur, et hoc quandiu tanta bellorum pericula imminent.' According to the editor the correction 'triginta' instead of 'viginti' and the suspect 'plures' need not be later interpolations but could have been second thoughts in the chancery itself.

3. Our earliest source for Arnolf's diploma (DA 3), is the mid-tenth-century collection of Corvey charters in the Staatsarchiv Münster, MS. VII, 5201, p. 309 from which the relevant clause is here cited: 'Sed nec prefatus abbas eiusque successores aliquando in hostem ire cogantur. Sed sicut antea eis a predecessoribus nostris concessum fuit omnes suos uasallos nobiles secum in patria ab expeditionibus uacantes habeant, Inferioris uero

rank not Widukind's *agrarii milites* and both of them *ministeriales* or their prototypes?

Arnolf's diploma, whether we possess it in its genuine or in an adulterated version, is an important statement of Corvey's early military organization.[1] But unfortunately it reveals more about the social standing of her warriors than their respective military roles. Amongst the unnamed witnesses of a Werden charter, dated between 900 and 911, a group of 'nobiles viri' were distinguished from 'ignobiles liti et liberi'.[2] The distinction between the noble vassals and those of lower condition was much the same. In the very next confirmation of Corvey's immunity, granted to her in 900 in Louis the Child's name, the division was made once again. Neither the men of the church, the *liti* and *coloni*, nor the abbot and his men should be forced to go on expeditions.[3] The latter evidently corresponded to the noble vassals in Arnolf's diploma while the *liti* and *coloni* stood for the group which had been liable for some service outside the abbot's command: the 'vasalli inferioris conditionis'. Not too much must be read into the use of the word 'vasallus' instead of 'homo'. The abbot of Corvey in the ninth century had an aristocratic *militia* available for service as well as peasant levies. Their status and their uses differed.

After 900 the military exemption clauses disappeared altogether

---

conditionis quantis opus habuerint ad legationem nostram et ad monasterii utilitatem prout necessitas flagitat peragendum.' The capital 'I' appears also in the thirteenth-century Herford copy of the DA 3 in Staatsarchiv Münster MS VII, 5208, p. 20ᵛ, printed in H. A. Erhard, *Regesta Historiae Westfaliae*, i *Codex Diplomaticus*, no. xxxiii (Münster, 1847), p. 26. I am indebted to Professor D. J. Prinz, director of the archive, for his kind advice and photographs of the DA 3 from these MSS.

1. The genuineness of the DA 3 has been much in dispute. P. Kehr in his edition of Arnolf's diplomata, *M.G.H., Die Urkunden der deutschen Karolinger* (Berlin, 1955), iii. 5 ff. concluded that the words 'nobiles' after 'uasallos' and the whole clause beginning with 'Inferioris conditionis' were amongst others interpolated. The genuine text thus confirmed and restored only the exemption of 'vassals'. This would accord well with a later letter of Arnolf's, DA 155 of June 897 (pp. 235 ff.) in which all powers in Saxony were ordered not to extort more service from the abbot's vassals than was just. The reason for the interpolation would then have been to bring as many of the monastery's dependants as possible under the heading of 'vassals'. Stengel in the revised version of his article on the origins of the *ministeriales* (see *supra* p16, n. 2) took the view that the whole of the DA 3 as we now have it was perfectly sound. He was inclined to identify the 'uasalli . . . inferioris conditionis' with Widukind's *agrarii milites* and to plead for them both as forerunners of the *ministeriales*, and yet in a footnote (*Papsttum*, p. 173, n. 1 and *Abhandlungen*, p. 74, n. 30) he held that the epithet *agrarii* ruled out vassallic status. The capital 'I' of 'inferioris' in the mid-tenth-century MS faintly suggests that something like 'homines' rather than 'uasallos' was implied or intended or left out in the second half of the sentence. The other suspect portions of the diploma dealt with tithes.

2. R. Kötzschke, (ed.) *Die Urbare der Abtei Werden* (Bonn, 1906), i. 33:'. . . et multi alii nobiles viri (after 11 named ones) et ignobiles liti et liberi.'

3. *M.G.H., Die Urk. d. d. Karolinger* (Berlin, 1960), iv, 103:'. . . homines eiusdem ecclesie liti et coloni et rectores ipsius monasterii in expeditionem cum suis hominibus ire non cogantur.' The use of 'homines' instead of 'vasalli' is worth noting because it returns to the wording of Charles III's diploma, enlarging on its 'homines . . . cuiuscumque conditionis'. Cf. *supra*, p17.

from the surviving royal grants and confirmations for Widukind's monastery, nor is there any further mention of the abbot's *legatio* for which there was perhaps no room after 919.[1] But in 940 Corvey secured a new diploma which brought her immunity up to date. Under this privilege the abbot could compel the men of three different *pagi*, normally under the jurisdiction of four named counts, to repair his fortress and to take shelter there. These powers extended to both sides of the Weser and not only over his own but also over the dependants of other lords.[2] Otto I's grant of the *burgbann* to Corvey is the first of its kind in Saxony.[3] A similar privilege bestowed on the Alsatian monastery of Weissenburg in 965 is worth comparing with it because here all the classes of dependants whom the abbot could constrain to fortify and guard his castle are listed: *liti, coloni, fiscales* and *censuales*, whether they belonged to the abbey's agrarian *familia* or to that of a neighbouring royal *fidelis*.[4] Otto I's diploma described this grant as a restoration of ancient rights and whatever the claims of Weissenburg may have been, the system itself was well-established in Frankish practice. To go back no further, there is in the Edict of Pîtres (864) a very detailed survey of the military obligations resting on free men which ended with those who could not go to the host for want of means. They had to build fortresses, bridges and causeways, keep watch in the *civitates* or in the march and turn out for the defence of their native districts.[5] The duties of these poorer freemen came very close to those of Widukind's *agrarii milites*. As he described them they were peasants belonging to a dependant *familia*; they and their *confamiliares* had to do castle-work with as little damage to their normal agrarian routines as possible. The term *agrarius miles* may have been the Corvey historian's own; at least a close classical model for it remains unknown.[6]

1. The subject, however, was not forgotten in Corvey as can be seen from the work of the mid-tenth-century copyist in MS. Münster Staatsarchiv VII, 5201 who (p. 291) headed the diploma of Charles III: 'de expeditione hostili.'

2. Otto I's diploma, DO I 27, in *M.G.H., Die Urk. d. deutschen Könige und Kaiser*, i. 113 ff.

3. For similar grants to Magdeburg in 965 and to Gandersheim in 980 see DO I 300, p. 415 and DO II 214 in *M.G.H., Die Urk. d. deutschen Könige und Kaiser*, II. i. 241 ff.

4. DO I 287, pp. 401 ff.

5. *Edictum Pistense*, c. 27, *M.G.H., Capitularia Regum Francorum* (Hanover, 1897), ii. 321 ff.

6. H. Büttner, 'Zur Burgenordnung Heinrich's I', *Blätter für deutsche Landesgeschichte*, xcii (1956), 4 n. 13 thought that Widukind coined the term *agrarii milites* in order to distinguish these men from those whom he usually called *milites*. Students of Stubbs's *Select Charters* cannot help remembering Robert of Torigny's account of Henry II's scutage in 1159: 'Rex igitur Henricus . . . nolens vexare agrarios milites nec burgensium nec rusticorum multitudinem. . . .' W. Stubbs, *Select Charters*, 9th edn. (Oxford, 1913), p. 152. Here the *agrarii milites* are something very different and obviously not simply *rustici* and it would be very hazardous to promote Saxon peasants to the status of Anglo-Norman knights on the strength of this passage. Another example comes from the Anchin continuation of Sigebert of Gembloux *sub anno* 1172: 'In Italia homines agrarii marchisi de Montferrat cum quibusdam militibus, terras suas et possessiones relinquentes cum uxoribus et filiis, . . .', *M.G.H. Scriptores* (= *SS*) vi. 413. The careful distinction between *agrarii homines* and *milites* is striking.

But behind it his fellow-monks had no difficulty in recognizing the *liti, coloni* and *ignobiles liberi* of the monastery, performing their labour-services and guard duties. It is unlikely that Henry I introduced the burdens of fortress-building newly into his stemland in response to the Hungarian raids. There were castles in ninth-century Saxony and it is probable that the Frankish invaders had built some of them with labour levied from the surrounding countryside. The Hersfeld tithe-surveys of 880–899 show fortresses in north-eastern Thuringia with hamlets and villages attached to them.[1]

Corvey's contribution to Henry I's hosts remains unknown. Widukind does not tell us much about the *exercitus* and the *milites* who in 928 attacked the Daleminzi, the tribe between the Mulde and Elbe round Meissen, but it is possible to detect once more the difference between the mass of warriors and a small élite of *armati* on horseback in the army which defeated the Redarii of Northern Brandenburg at the battle of Lenzen in 929.[2] The Slavs had very few horsemen; the Saxons forced a decision with only fifty. This was perhaps not the whole number of *armati* in their host. Two counts, both great-grandfathers of Thietmar of Merseburg, fell, and it is likely that they, other great nobles and the two leaders, Count Bernhard and Count Thietmar, had small followings of this kind. But most of their force fought on foot like the Slavs and here the *agrarii milites* must have come into their own. Some evidence for the field-service of peasants, close in time to Henry I's wars, comes from a well-known diploma of Otto I for Archbishop Adaldag of Hamburg-Bremen, dated 30 June 937.[3] Here the king strengthened the immunities of four monasteries belonging to the see. Adaldag was to have power over the *liberti* and the *mund-men* of these houses for the purposes of going to the host and to the king's court. He alone could raise and lead them. But once again the diploma does not tell us what they did when they accompanied him. It is worth remembering that Adaldag's see was poor and also that he spent many years with Otto I in Italy. He needed a mounted following and he may have recruited it from the kind of men described in the king's diploma. If he did it is significant that the see of Hamburg-Bremen remained militarily weak compared with others and, in the eleventh century, lay exposed to the rough grasp of the Billung dukes.[4]

1. W. Schlesinger, 'Burgen und Burgbezirke', in his *Mitteldeutsche Beiträge zur deutschen Verfassungsgeschichte* (Göttingen, 1961), p. 161.

2. Widukind, i. 35, p. 50 and i. 36, pp. 51 ff. and esp. p. 53.

3. DO I 11, p. 99: 'Habeat quoque potestatem praedictus Adaldag successoresque eius . . . super libertos et iamundilingos monasteriorum supradictorum in expeditionem sive ad palatium regis.'

4. H.-J. Freytag, *Die Herrschaft der Billunger in Sachsen*, Studien und Vorarbeiten zum Historischen Atlas Niedersachsens, xx (Göttingen, 1951), pp. 17 ff. and references there given.

Another example comes from the country east of the river Saale, the Sorbian March. In 974 Otto II granted the burgal district of Zwenkau to Bishop Giselher and the Church of Merseburg with the provision that no count should coerce the *liberi* attached to the fortress either to build walls or to contribute towards the getting up of expeditions without the bishop's knowledge and his chief advocate's orders. Here we find settlers who had to fortify their burgh but whose services in the *exercitus* seem to have been menial and could consist of a contribution in cash or in kind only.[1] Such payments too are familiar from Frankish custom and we meet them widely on the East-Saxon and Westfalian estates of the monastery of Werden. Tenth-century armies, like their Carolingian predecessors, needed transport, much labour and many servants. Historians have perhaps been too eager to detect ways and means of social ascent for those who performed the chores.

Not very many of the mounted, more heavily armed and better-trained warriors who bore the brunt of the Saxon princes' aggressive and far-ranging wars could have come from the *liberti* and *iamund-lingi* of Archbishop Adaldag, fewer still from the *liberi* of Zwenkau or Widukind's *agrarii milites*. Their burdens were already heavy and varied enough. The horse was an expensive animal in early medieval Saxony. Its theft was punishable by death in the *Lex Saxonum* no less than in other German *leges*, and horse-breeding was on some estates at least a specialized occupation.[2] Even where the holder of a single *mansus* could or had to provide a mount it does not follow that he also possessed the means to equip himself for equestrian service.[3] As war-booty, tribute and presents, horses were much prized and princes who incurred the king's anger or were found guilty before him in judgment often had to pay their forfeitures in horses rather than in silver.[4] In the earliest of his grants to Magdeburg, dated 21 September 937, Otto I stipulated that the congregation should give him a horse, a shield and a lance or two furs every year.[5] It is of course possible that when it came to mounted service Ottonian Saxony knew a quota system just as we encounter it in

1. DO II 89 in *M.G.H. Urk*, II. i. 104: '. . . ut nullus iudex publicus vel comes . . . liberos homines infra eiusdem civitatis terminos et appertinentias positos . . . ad opus muri urbani faciendum aut ad ministrationem expeditionis tribuendam . . . cogere . . . audeat.'

2. *Lex Saxonum*, c. xxix *Leges Saxonum et Lex Thuringorum*, ed. C. v. Schwerin, *M.G.H. Fontes iuris Germanici antiqui* (Hanover and Leipzig, 1918), p. 25. On horse-rearing farms see *infra* p. 25 and nn. 4, 5.

3. On the duty of supplying horses for transport see H. Dannenbauer, 'Paraveredus – Pferd', *Zeitschrift der Savigny-Stiftung für Rechtsgeschichte, Germanistische Abteilung*, lxxi (1954), 55–73 and *Grundlagen*, pp. 257–70.

4. *E.g.* Duke Eberhard in 937. See Widukind, ii. 6, p. 72 and the case of Archbishop Adalbert of Magdeburg in Thietmar of Merseburg's *Chronicon*, ii. c. 28, ed. R. Holtzmann, *S.R.G., Nova Series*, ix (Berlin, 1955), p. 74. For horses as booty see *Annales Fuldenses*, ed. F. Kurze, *S.R.G.* (Hanover, 1891), p. 75 and Widukind, ii. 14, p. 79.

5. DO I 14, p. 102.

Widukind's controversial description of King Henry's fortresses and their upkeep. A capitulary of Charlemagne's had ordered that every five Saxons should equip a sixth for expeditions into Spain and Avar country, every two the third man against Bohemia and that all must go for the defence of the Sorbian March.[1] But there is no evidence that such regulations survived or how they may have worked in the tenth century. When *milites* are next mentioned by Widukind in his *res gestae* they appear unmistakably as the vassalic *comitatus* of the Liudolfing princes and Duke Eberhard fighting out their feuds, with but one exception: the so-called 'Merseburg Legion'. It needs a brief mention.

Very early in Otto I's reign trouble broke out in the south-eastern border region between the Bohemian duke Boleslas and the Saxon and Thuringian marchers. The accession of an untried king threatened established relationships on the frontier and, if Henry had compelled the Bohemians to pay tribute, Boleslas now struck at a petty Slav chieftain who was a client of the Saxons. When this man sought the help of his protectors the army of the Hochseegau between the Saale and the Unstrut and the 'Merseburg Legion' marched.[2] At this point Widukind explained that these men were robbers and thieves whose lives had been spared because they could be useful in a frontier district. Henry I had established them in the march and given them arms and lands to live on a permanent war-footing. Predatory raids on the Slavs whom Widukind usually called barbarians were common even when no host took the field. From his account of the 'legion's' disastrous encounter with the Bohemians in 936 it appears that at least some of its soldiers had horses.[3] Widukind's story of the outlaw-warriors is not quite as improbable as it may sound. There were not only precedents for the deportation of Saxons who had committed death-worthy offences; there were also the measures taken against powerful and irrepressible peace-breakers in Anglo-Saxon England at this very time.[4] In his Exeter laws of 927 King Athelstan, whose sister Henry I secured as a bride for his son Otto, commanded that such men must go with their wives, slaves and movables to an assigned place and never return.[5] The 'legio Mesaburiorum', it has been claimed, formed a military settlement on the Frankish model, and both those who regard the *agrarii milites* as *ministeriales* and those who see in them a class of royal freemen have looked to Widukind's strange story for support.[6] It is too fragile to give any.

1. *M.G.H., Capitularia*, i. 136.   2. Widukind, ii. 3, pp. 68 ff.
3. *Ibid*. p. 69: 'Bolizlav autem videns ... alios in paleis equorum congregandis occupatos.'
4. See the *Capitulare Saxonicum*, c. x of 797, *Capitularia*, i. 72.
5. F. Liebermann, *Gesetze der Angelsachsen* (Halle, 1903), i. 167.
6. G. Baaken, *ubi supra*, pp. 67 ff. and Köpke, *ubi supra*, p. 95.

There was, however, room for more than one kind of soldier to man the huge eastern frontier of the Ottonian empire. The Saxon *exercitus* which shouldered most of the burden in the tenth century still possessed some traces of older territorial and ethnic sub-divisions. The three great stem-areas of Saxony, Westfalia, Engern and Eastfalia were sometimes referred to in charters as *exercitus* or *herescephe* as if they were lands occupied and settled by three armies.[1] The terms 'in exercitu Angariorum' or 'in exercitu Orientalium' may not only have been used to describe locality. Armies made up chiefly of Westfalian or East-Saxon contingents did take the field.[2] The composition of Otto I's Saxon hosts varied with his needs but the pages of Widukind contain enough evidence to show that in them the *miles armatus*, fighting on horseback, formed an ever more important military élite whom one can almost begin to call 'knights'. Unlike the *agrarii milites* they did not sow or harvest themselves but were supported by shares of tribute exacted from the partly-con-quered Slavs or by the produce of land granted to them either *in beneficium* or *in proprietatem*. During the prolonged internal fighting from 937 onwards the war against the Slavs along the Middle Elbe did not go well. The *milites* assigned to Margrave Gero's command suffered losses and could not be supported either by grants of pro-duce from land or gifts of tribute because the Slavs refused to pay.[3] It is important to note the term Widukind employed for the men under Gero's authority: 'milites ad manum Geronis presidis con-scripti'. Whenever he used the term *manus militum* he seems to have thought of a military following, a warband of vassals and com-panions or a specially chosen group of fighters. Henry I himself already had such a force when he was still only duke in Saxony and warred against King Conrad I, and it is set off clearly against the rest of the Saxon *exercitus* in Widukind's stories.[4] Otto I relied on a *manus* of loyal *milites* when he outfaced the conspiracy of the dis-gruntled East-Saxon warriors who in 941 wanted to murder him during the Easter solemnities at Quedlinburg. One of their leaders, Eric, when he saw Otto's *armati* ride up to arrest him, seized his

1. J. Bauermann, '*Herescephe*. Zur Frage der sächsischen Stammesprovinzen', *West-fälische Zeitschrift*, xcvii (1947), 38–68 and A. K. Hömberg, *Westfalen und das sächsische Herzogtum*, Schriften der Historischen Kommission Westfalens, v (Münster, 1963), pp. 1–12 and also J. Prinz, 'Die geschichtliche Entwicklung des oberen Weserraumes im Mittelalter', *Kunst und Kultur im Weserraum 800–1600* (Corvey, 1966), i. 83 ff.

2. *E.g.* the Westfalians in 997. See *Annales Quedlinburgenses*, *M.G.H.*, *SS*. iii. 73 ff. and *cf.* also the 'omnes pene orientalium partium milites' whom Henry, Otto I's brother, won over to his bid for the kingship in 941 (Widukind, ii. 31, p. 92).

3. Widukind, ii. 30, pp. 91 ff.: 'Et cum milites ad manum Geronis presidis con-scripti crebra expeditione attenuarentur et donativis vel tributariis premiis minus adiuvari possent, eo quod tributa passim negarentur, seditioso odio in Geronem ex-acuuntur.' For what follows see c. 31, pp. 92 ff.

4. Widukind, i. 21, p. 30: 'subpeditante illi fortium militum manu, exercitus quoque innumera multitudine.' The *exercitus* here could, of course, also include the warbands of other Saxon lords.

arms and mounted his horse, to fall in the end by the thrust of a lance. The incident, lovingly described by Widukind, is characteristic of the style of warfare that now mattered and also its adepts, the Saxon nobles. Moreover, what the Corvey historian tells us about the maintenance and rewards of Gero's warriors is borne out by record sources, Otto's diplomata for Magdeburg and Meissen. In June 965 he gave the tenth of the silver-dues from five subject Slav tribes to the future metropolis for the upkeep of its lights and the purchase of incense. It was to be paid both from the royal receipts and from those portions which the king's vassals held in fief.[1] A month later the brethren of the foundation, as yet monks, received the tenth part of the honey which the inhabitants of seven Slav *pagi* and a number of burgal districts owed to the king. They were to be given it from his own share and from the quantities which had been granted out in fief to his men.[2] This might in the first place mean counts and commanders of fortresses but they in turn had to reward their *milites* with shares of the proceeds. A grant to the see of Meissen in 971 reveals the sub-allocation of tribute quite clearly. The count distributed honey, furs, silver, slaves, cloth, pigs and wheat out of his share.[3] Money fiefs or something very like them were thus quite common in tenth-century Eastern Saxony and they served above all to support professional mounted soldiers.

Once at least Widukind allows us to know the rewards which outstanding service could earn for a man of this class. At the battle by the river Recknitz in 955, Stojgnev, the king of the Slav Obotrites, was run to ground and killed in single combat by a *vir militaris* called Hosed who then presented Otto I with the head and war-gear of his victim.[4] This feat made Hosed's name and he received a great grant from the king, revenues worth those of a twenty-*mansus* estate.[5] Widukind's wording, 'cum reditu viginti mansuum', seems clumsy if he merely wanted to say that Hosed was given a holding of twenty *mansus*. In stressing the *reditus* he showed what mattered to Hosed and his like: the proceeds of lands worked by subjects,

---

1. DO I 295, p. 412: 'sive nostro iuri aspiciat sive alicui fidelium nostrorum beneficiarium existat.'   2. DO I 303, p. 418.

3. DO I 406, p. 553: '... ut antea quam comes earundem regionum partem sibi a nobis concessam auferat atque distribuat, decimas ... persolvat.'

4. Widukind, iii. 55, pp. 134 ff.

5. *Ibid.* p. 135: 'Merces tam famosi gesti donativum imperiale cum reditu viginti mansuum.' It is probable that the family of the Hoseds were intimately connected with Corvey and this would show handsomely how Widukind used local materials for his *res gestae*. Their name occurs several times in the lists of monks from the later ninth century onwards and also in the *Traditiones Corbeienses* sometime after 965. See *Traditiones Corbeienses*, §11 ed. P. Wigand (Leipzig, 1843), p. 14. A Hosed was abbot from 1001 to 1010. For the list of monks see the *Monumenta Corbeiensia*, ed. P. Jaffé, *Bibliotheca rerum Germanicarum* (Berlin, 1864), i. 68 ff. All this suggests that the Hoseds belonged to the 'vasalli nobiles' of the abbey. A Hosad also occurs as provost of Paderborn in the early eleventh century. See the *Vita Meinwerci episcopi Patherbrunnensis*, cc. lxii, lxiii, ed. F. Tenkhoff, *S.R.G.* (Hanover, 1921), p. 46.

liti and *coloni*, rather than direct cultivation and exploitation. They were primitive rentiers. The number of royal grants to lay nobles extant for the tenth century is not over-large nor is it always possible to assess the standing of the recipient from the size of the gift. Sometimes grants of slaves without land or grants of a few *mansus* with specially-named slaves suggest that the donees would aim at direct development.[1] But many lay nobles in tenth-century Saxony seem to have derived their incomes from food- and livestock-rents owed to them by dependant and scattered *liti*. In the *Traditiones Corbeienses* grants of one or two *familiae* without any mention of demesne are very common, and this meant the transfer of lordship and food-rents. It was not only convenient but necessary to employ this form of exploitation in the Slav marches. It seems that for some decades, at least, dues and revenues exacted from their new subjects offered the best means of support for warriors who spent their time in the *burgwards* and company of their lords. Nor should the more ephemeral opportunities of war, plunder and booty be forgotten when we try to understand the economy of early Ottonian aggression.

The military efficacy of the mounted *milites* continued to make itself felt in the wars against the Slavs. When, early in 955, there were not enough of them available for the defence of Saxony because Otto I had led a large host south to help his brother Henry, Duke Hermann (Billung) did not think it wise to risk a battle against the invading Obotrites. Although his *milites* protested he left a *multitudo*, men and women who had characteristically taken shelter in a fortress, to their fate.[2] They included freemen, 'cives', and were not unarmed but this does not seem to have weighed against the shortage of *milites*. We must now return to Henry I's host and the poetic force of Widukind's story: how the king turned a clumsy army which could not face the Magyars in a head-on clash into one that could. Georg Waitz, Robert Holtzmann and Ferdinand Lot have taken this to mean that until this time the Saxons were not really used to fighting on horseback and had to be massively converted and trained for such service.[3] In the current edition of Gebhardt's *Handbuch der deutschen Geschichte* it is stated briefly that Henry created a mounted army.[4] Saxon warfare in the ninth century must be examined to see whether we cannot go behind Widukind's all too dramatic contrasts.

1. *E.g.* DO I 66, pp. 146 ff. and DO I 71, p. 151.
2. Widukind, iii. 52, pp. 131 ff. Baaken's attempt (*ubi supra*, pp. 20 ff. and n. 44 and p. 64) to identify Duke Hermann's *milites*, including a count of the house of Stade, with the *multitudo* inside the fortress in order to prove that they were 'royal freemen' is hard to reconcile with Widukind's text.
3. Waitz, *Jahrbücher*, p. 101; R. Holtzmann, p. 89; F. Lot, *L'Art Militaire et les Armées au Moyen Age* (Paris, 1946), ii. 143.
4. B. Gebhardt, *Handbuch der deutschen Geschichte* (8th edn., Stuttgart, 1954), i. 169.

When the Frankish kings, Pippin and Charlemagne, defeated their enemies and forced other peoples to accept Frankish over-lordship they expected them in future to obey their commands. The phrase 'imperata facere', favoured by Einhard, summed up a new dependance and almost invariably the orders given included summonses for service with the Frankish hosts to swell their numbers. Saxony was deemed to have become part of the *Reich* and the Saxons counted as *fideles* of the Franks from 785 onwards at the latest.[1] Already in 787 they had to join an East-Frankish *exercitus* to help surround and break Duke Tassilo of Bavaria. Einhard next described them as treacherous auxiliaries in the campaign against the Slav Welatabi in 789.[2] We do not know how they appeared in Charlemagne's armies. Saxon resistance to the Franks, if savage at times, had always been disjointed and it is fairly certain that the Frankish invaders surpassed their opponents not only in political ambition and military purposefulness but also in organization and equipment. Once at least the later version of the Royal Annals reports that a Saxon force was overcome 'equestri proelio'.[3] Were both sides mounted? An early description of a Saxon contingent in the Frankish host comes from Ermoldus Nigellus's pen, his panegyric poem in honour of Louis the Pious, dated between 826 and 828. Banished courtier that he was and anxious to work his way back into favour, Ermold wrote of Louis's successes rather than his problems and devoted much space to a brief but effective campaign against the Bretons in 818. Before describing it he surveyed the contingents which were to take part. The Franks naturally came first, followed by the *gentes subactae*, the peoples who had to send forces to the host. The Saxons were cited after the Alemans and Ermold said that they came with large quivers.[4] Whatever the demands of his poetic craftsmanship, he did not want to be wholly implausible. But to take Ermold at his word and say that the Saxon auxiliaries served as archers would almost certainly be mistaken. In one of Charlemagne's later capitularies it was ordered quite generally that those who had to join the host must have a shield, a lance, a bow with two strings and twelve arrows as a minimum standard of equipment.[5] There is

1. M. Lintzel, 'Die Unterwerfung Sachsens durch Karl den Grossen und der sächsische Adel', *Sachsen und Anhalt*, x (1934), 32 and in his *Ausgewählte Schriften* (Berlin, 1961), i. 96 ff. A joint Franco-Saxon expedition against the Slavs was planned already for the summer of 782. See *Annales regni Francorum*, ed. F. Kurze, *S.R.G.* (Hanover, 1895), pp. 60, 61.

2. *Annales regni Francorum*, p. 78 and *Einhardi vita Karoli Magni*, c. 12, ed. O. Holder-Egger, *S.R.G.* (Hanover and Leipzig, 1911), p. 15.

3. *Annales regni Francorum*, p. 69.

4. Ermold le Noir, *Poème sur Louis le Pieux*, ed. E. Faral, *Les Classiques de l'Histoire de France au Moyen Age*, xiv (Paris, 1964), 116, lines 1510–1516 and esp. line 1516: 'Et Saxona cohors patulis praecincta pharetris.'

5. See the *Capitulare Aquisgranense* (802–3), cc. 9 and 17 in *M.G.H. Capitularia*, i. 171, 172 and J. F. Verbruggen, 'L' armée et la stratégie de Charlemagne', *Karl der Grosse*, ed. H. Beumann (Düsseldorf, 1965), i. 425.

therefore no reason to think that the bow was the Saxons' most characteristic weapon nor does it even follow that they served on foot. Abbot Fulrad of St. Quentin on another occasion was instructed that every one of his *cabalarii* should not only have a shield, a spear, a sword and a short sword but also a bow and more than one quiverful of arrows.[1] The Bretons themselves fought on horseback, but as light skirmishers, engaging and disengaging very quickly. A throwing-spear was their main weapon and it is possible that the Saxons were summoned to what must have been a burdensome and arduous expedition for them because they were thought to be in some way suitable to cope with such tactics.[2]

The next piece of evidence comes from Nithard's account of Louis the German's and Charles the Bald's meetings near Worms in February 842. Nithard paused in his story to describe how they passed the time together in fraternal concord and he dwelt at some length on the warlike games of their followers and war-bands. Saxons, Rhenish Franks, Gascons and Bretons rushed upon one another, wheeled about in feigned flight and then returned to the attack. Eventually the two kings joined in with their military households and there is not the slightest doubt that all this took place on horseback.[3] The conjunction of Saxons with Gascons and Bretons is worth noting, for the last two excelled as lightly-armed horsemen and perhaps the equipment of the Saxon mounted warriors, or their lack of it, distantly resembled theirs.[4] Some more evidence for their style of warfare in the ninth century comes to us from the chronicle of Regino of Prüm, written about the year 908. Under a mistaken date, 860, he described a Breton campaign of Charles the Bald which was to restore the situation in the march. His story of Charles's disastrous and shaming defeat enlarged on events which had happened nine years earlier. A battle against the Bretons was fought on 22 August 851. Charles had brought with him not only his West-Frankish host but also a band of Saxon mercenaries whom he placed in front to break up the attacks of the light Breton horsemen, but at the first rush they were frightened by their javelins and sought shelter in the Frankish *acies*, the line of battle behind them.[5] The

1. *Karoli ad Fulradum abbatem epistola* (806), *Capitularia*, i. 168 and Verbruggen *ubi supra*, p. 423.
2. For the *missilia* of the Bretons see Ermold, lines 1494, 1629 and 1708, pp. 114, 124, 130 and Regino of Prüm who thought that their tactics resembled the Hungarians (*Reginonis Chronicon*, p. 137). Cartloads full of *missilia*, it seems, were stationed behind the Breton horsemen and they turned about after throwing their spears simply in order to pick up new ones (Ermold, line 1494, p. 114).
3. *Nithardi historiarum libri iiii.* iii. c. 6, ed. E. Müller, S.R.G. (Hanover, 1907), p. 38.
4. For the Gascons see the anonymous *Vita Hludowici imperatoris*, c. 4, M.G.H., SS. ii. 609.
5. Regino, p. 79: 'Saxones, qui conducti fuerant, ad excipiendos velocium equorum anfractuosos recursus in prima fronte ponuntur, sed primo impetu spiculis Brittonum territi in acie se recondunt.'

Franks, Regino tells us, were accustomed to fight with swords at close quarters.[1] The failure of the Saxon mercenaries and the Bretons' swift movements and sham flights surprised and confounded them so much that, as he put it, they could neither properly pursue their enemies nor find safety in their own close order.

Regino's narrative is not without its problems. It must be used with caution like so many early medieval descriptions of battles. Its author, writing many years later, was a well-read scholar who knew how to make use of a classical model.[2] But Regino was also a Frankish aristocrat with a deep concern for the behaviour, the failings and the future of his class and there is no need to dismiss his account of the battle of 851 as wholly apocryphal. The Breton mode of fighting, however, can hardly have come as a novelty and surprise to Charles the Bald's West-Frankish warriors and Regino unfortunately does not tell us how the Saxon mercenaries out in front were armed, whether they had to cope on foot or whether they too were mounted and carried spears like their opponents.[3] That they hid amongst the Franks behind them suggests that they were *pedites* but it is not certain and here, for the third time, we encounter Saxons being matched against Breton horsemen. Regino at least makes it clear that their manner of fighting and their weapons differed from those of the Franks *in acie*.

No conclusions can be drawn from a passage in the so-called *Annales Xantenses* which described how some 'Saxones agiles' shadowed a Danish raid along the Lower Rhine in 863 and successfully stopped a landing on the right bank. About their armament or horses we are told nothing. The author in calling them *agiles* had only used their correct epithet which he found in Isidore of Seville's survey of the Germanic peoples in the ninth book of the *Etymologiae*.[4] Uncertainty also surrounds the role of the Saxons at the battle of Andernach in October 876 where Charles the Bald, now emperor, hoped to take advantage of his nephew Louis the Younger's smaller numbers and deprive him of Lotharingia, the Rhineland and perhaps his eyesight. To gain surprise he took the unusual decision

1. Regino, p. 79: 'Franci, qui comminus strictis gladiis pugnare consueverant, attoniti stabant, novitate ante inexperti discriminis perculsi, nec ad insequendeum idonei nec in unum conglobati tuti.'

2. Especially Justinus who served him when he described the methods of the Magyars (Regino, p. 133). Echoes of the passage there borrowed can also be heard in his story of the Breton battle of 851. On Regino in general see H. Löwe, 'Regino von Prüm und das historische Weltbild der Karolingerzeit', *Geschichtsdenken und Geschichtsbild im Mittelalter*, ed. W. Lammers, *Wege der Forschung*, xxi (Darmstadt, 1961), 91–134.

3. E. Dümmler, *Geschichte des ostfränkischen Reiches* (Leipzig, 1887 and reprinted Darmstadt, 1960), i. 351 thought they were *pedites* without question.

4. Cf. *Annales Xantenses*, ed. B. v. Simson, S.R.G. (Hanover, 1909), p. 21: 'At contra Saxones agiles ex altera ripa fluminis agiliter agebant' and *Isidori Hispalensis Episcopi Etymologiarum ... Libri XX*, ed. W. M. Lindsay (Oxford, 1911), IX. ii. 100: 'Saxonum gens ... virtute atque agilitate habilis.' The author of the *Annales Xantenses* may have been a Saxon.

of marching by night. Hincmar, Regino and Meginhard of Fulda have described the encounter, and from what Regino wrote it seems that Charles himself was in the end outwitted and lured into a trap. The Fulda annalist however represented Louis the Younger as the innocent victim of a treacherous attack when negotiations were still in progress and his force had been allowed to disperse to forage for their horses. Once again the Saxons were placed in front and fled after a brief struggle, but the *Franci Orientales* fought well and won a victory which cost the emperor dear in nobles killed and captured, war-gear and treasure lost. From Meginhard's and Hincmar's accounts it appears that Charles's host approached mounted for the attack.[1] Did not heaven itself intervene to show where justice lay by numbing the West-Frankish horses so that they stood still at the critical moment?[2] Given the circumstance that the Saxons were available when Charles's host drew near one might conclude that they had no horses to forage for, but Meginhard wrote that they were frightened only by the sheer size of the emperor's force rather than by any other disparity between them.[3] Being placed in front suggests that once more they had the task of harrassing and disrupting the attackers. In this they may have been successful despite their flight but Meginhard, who above all wanted to point the moral of Charles's defeat, does not tell us. Whatever their role it is very possible that they were mounted like their Franconian companions-in-arms.[4]

Saxons also fought in the battle at the Dyle (891) where Arnolf of Carinthia defeated a Viking army and stormed their camp. The A version of the Anglo-Saxon Chronicle mentions them with the Eastern Franks and the Bavarians and Regino of Prüm's statement that the king collected his troops 'ex orientalibus regnis' helps to confirm their presence.[5] It was an army of horsemen which Arnolf led across the Dyle and then persuaded to dismount because the camp of the Danes could not be approached in any other way.[6] There is no reason to exclude the Saxons from this part of the story.

In 906, during the great feud between the Conradine and Babenberg clans in Franconia, a Saxon warband served Conrad the Elder,

1. *Annales Bertiniani*, ed. G. Waitz, S.R.G. (Hanover, 1883), p. 133 and see n. 2, below.

2. *Annales Fuldenses*, p. 89. Meginhard has the prisoners tell this story to their East-Frankish captors.

3. Their presence does not prove that they had no horses for even if they fought on foot they probably journeyed to Louis the Younger's host, which was summoned in a hurry, on horseback.

4. According to Meginhard (*loc. cit.*) Louis's men were able to pursue their broken enemies and then return to pick up the spoils of the battlefield.

5. C. Plummer, *Two of the Saxon Chronicles Parallel* (Oxford, 1892), i. 82 and Regino, pp. 137 ff. It is hard to see why Dümmler, iii. 350, n. 2 simply dismissed the Anglo-Saxon evidence. Against him see W. Vogel, *Die Normannen und das Fränkische Reich* (Heidelberg, 1906), p. 365 and n. 3.

6. *Annales Fuldenses*, p. 120 and Regino, *loc. cit.*

King Conrad I's father. Most likely they were vassals and dependants of the Conradine house from the other side of the Saxon border. Taken by surprise at Fritzlar, the elder Conrad divided his force into three troops. Two of these, one of *pedites* and one of Saxons, deserted him immediately. Regino is once more our source for this story and since he distinguished the Saxons clearly from the *pedites* it seems as if they were not *pedites* themselves and so escaped the massacre which followed Conrad's defeat and death.[1] But here again certainty is out of the question, and to make up for the ambiguities and sparse hints of the late-Frankish annalists we must turn to a story from a different kind of source, the *Waltharius* epic. Its date remains in dispute. Against the old and strongly-defended view that Ekkehard I of St. Gallen wrote it about the year 930, Strecker in his edition for the *Poetae*-series of the *Monumenta Germaniae Historica* held out for an earlier, Carolingian date.[2] Ekivrid, the Saxon exile who has joined the following of King Gunthar, is the fourth of twelve chosen companions to fight Waltharius for the possession of his treasure. He rides up on a piebald horse and nowhere is it said that he dismounted before throwing his spear.[3] But it is possible, all the same, to notice a difference between him and the other warriors in the poem, friends or foe. He does not seem to have been as well-armoured as they were. For when Walther retaliated and pierced Ekivrid's shield the Saxon had only a simple *tunica* to protect his chest, not a *lorica trilex* or a *tunica aena* like his adversary.[4] As Ekivrid during his brief appearance in the epic is shown up for a backwoodsman of barbarous speech, the detail about his harness cannot have been accidental. It revealed the Saxon at a disadvantage in a way that must have been quite familiar to the poet's contemporaries. They could take the point without difficulty.

So far this survey of Saxon warfare in the ninth century has only listed instances of Saxons taking part in the wars of the Carolingian

---

1. Regino, p. 151.

2. *Waltharius*, ed. K. Strecker, *M.G.H., Poetarum*, VI. i. (Weimar, 1951), p. 2. For a defence of c. 930 as the time of origin see K. Langosch, 'Waltharius', *Verfasserlexikon*, iv. 776–88.   3. *Waltharius*, ed. Strecker, lines 756–80, pp. 54 ff.

4. In lines 263–4, (p. 35), and line 1016 (p. 66), 'tunica' is qualified to show that armour was meant:

> 'Inprimis galeam regis tunicamque, trilicem
> Assero loricam fabrorum insigne ferentem,
> Diripe . . .' and line 1016 (p. 66):

'In framea tunicaque simul confisus aena'. That 'tunica' by itself was only a 'tunic' is shown in lines 1191–4, (pp. 72 ff.):

> 'Aggreditur iuvenis caesos spoliarier armis
> Armorumque habitu, tunicas et cetera linquens:
> Armillas tantum, cum bullis baltea et enses,
> Loricas quoque cum galeis detraxerat ollis.'

Waltharius stripped his victims of their bracelets, buckled belts, swords, hauberks and helmets, as was fair, but not their 'tunicae', their clothes. It is worth noting also that Ekivrid's shield was covered only with ox-hide and lacked the 'umbo', the metal-boss of Waltharius's. (*Cf.* lines. 772 and 776.)

house or in the defence of distant frontiers side by side with Franks
and other peoples of the *Reich*. Yet throughout this period their most
pressing enemies were the Slavs beyond the Elbe and the Danes, and
their largest and most persistent military efforts had to be directed
against them. Neither Widukind nor the earlier writers tell us how it
was done. On the whole the Saxons fought on equal terms against
the Slavs, but even with much Frankish help they fared less well here
than did the Bavarians in the south. When they and the Thuringians
in 872 were ordered to campaign against the Moravians without the
king, and feuds broke up the host, the Fulda Annals recorded a
rumour that their counts on the retreat were dragged off their
horses by the irate women of the country.[1] Against the Danes they
suffered a disastrous defeat in 880 which left long and sombre
memories behind. The nearest source, again Meginhard, recited a
casualty list of two bishops, twelve counts, including the Liudolfing
dux Brun and eighteen royal vassals. Their names are given but many
more had been taken prisoner.[2] If in the following years the Saxons
met new Danish attacks with better results they did not do so single-
handed but with Frisian and East-Frankish help.

Two general conclusions can be drawn. In the first place the
military standing of the Saxons in the ninth century was not particularly high. Einhard, writing after 830 and Ermold a little earlier,
looked down on them as auxiliaries and Meginhard's tale from the
Moravian expedition of 872 is decidedly unflattering. With one
exception, Lothar's war against his brothers in 841, they played a
subordinate role in the armed clashes of the contenders for possession
and power in the Carolingian *Reich*. Charles the Bald hired Saxons as
mercenaries because he could not, like his father, summon them to
his wars. But he employed them as unskilled military labour, not
to say cannon-fodder, and what happened to them was of little
consequence compared to the mishaps of the Franks. At Andernach
Louis the Younger did not treat them any better and counted on his
Rhenish Franks to see him through. Hauberked, well-armed and
well-mounted warriors were usually scarce and it was useful to
make up the numbers of a host with something less excellent and
effective. Louis the Younger and the elder Conrad probably did not
have much choice. This does not detract from the rising importance
of a few Saxon noble families in the East-Frankish kingdom nor
from the new appraisal of the Saxons as a whole by writers such as
Rudolf of Fulda. Widukind, looking back in the seventh decade
of the tenth century, thought that Saxony had once been a servant
and tributary while she was now mistress and free.[3] In military terms

---

1. *Annales Fuldenses*, pp. 75 ff.   2. *Op. cit.* p. 94.
3. Widukind, i. 34, p. 48. Widukind wanted to remind his patrons that they owed this
change to the merits and the cult of St. Vitus at Corvey.

and by standards which the aristocracy of his stemland understood, this rang true.

Our second conclusion must be that the horse mattered in ninth-century Saxon warfare and this not only to convey warriors to the place of action. The evidence from Nithard at least is clear and his mounted Saxons were not merely a few men from Louis the German's permanent entourage. There are enough hints and ambiguities in the other sources to make it difficult to conclude that the Saxons never joined battle on horseback. Yet we have seen that their manner of fighting differed from that of the Franks and did not enjoy the same esteem. Where then did the difference lie? It is of course possible that much of it was not qualitative but quantitative. Saxony, given the large number of her fighting men, mounted as yet relatively few of them. The calamity of Duke Brun in 880, moreover, with its heavy losses of nobles may have destroyed a significant proportion of the well-armed *milites* available and so caused a real setback to Saxon military efficiency which it took a generation to mend.[1] But there may have been a qualitative difference as well, and it is tempting to return to Regino of Prüm's account of the Breton battle of 851 and to Meginhard's description of the early-morning clash at Andernach to discover what it was. In both cases the Saxons were placed in front and not in the main battle and Regino seems to say that the Franks alone fought with swords at close quarters so that normally impact and better weapons would tell. If Saxon horsemen took part in these encounters, as is quite likely, this suggests that they lacked good arms, especially swords, so that it was of no advantage to marshal them in the same *acies* as the Franks. The evidence from *Waltharius* strengthens this impression – it can be no more. Here perhaps lay the shortcomings which gave the Saxons their low military status in the ninth century. Their mounted warriors then may have resembled those 'unarmed' Thuringians whom Henry I had used in 933 to deceive the Hungarians about his new strength.[2] The Frankish style of warfare and the social organization supporting it were of course also changing and, at the same time, often found wanting against the Vikings and Magyars; but Saxony remained too isolated and aloof to follow suit very rapidly.

That this does in fact bring us a little nearer to the problems of the early tenth-century Saxons can be shown both from Widukind and another source, the *Antapodosis* of Liudprand of Cremona. To

1. This was quite possible as other examples show. At the battle of Fiorenzuola (near Piacenza) in 923, as Flodoard cautiously reported, 1,500 men were rumoured to have fallen. Liudprand ended his account of it with the observation that Italy had been very short of knights ever since. He wrote at least 35 years after the event. This is not unlike Regino of Prüm's famous opinion that the battle of Fontenoy in 841 had weakened the Frankish élite for ever. See Flodoard, *Annales*, p. 19; Liudprand, *Antapodosis*, ii. 66, p. 67 and Regino, p. 75.   2. See p.15, n. 5.

the Saxon historian Henry I's *milites* were simply not accustomed to pitched battle.[1] The evidence from the *Antapodosis* is much more explicit but also harder to use. Liudprand joined the Ottonian circle in 956 and began writing his book in 958. What he had to say about Henry I's victory against the Magyars in 933 is confused chronologically and also adorned lavishly by the verse and the fictitious oratory with which he liked to enliven his work. But Liudprand sometimes used his speeches to explain motives and to help his readers to understand the events which followed. Just before the battle at Riade is due to begin, he has Henry I address his men to give them a piece of advice. On approaching the Hungarians nobody, however fast his horse might be, was to outride his fellows. They should help to cover one another with their shields, receive the first volley of the Magyars' much-feared arrows and then ride fast to close with their enemy so that he should not have a chance of shooting a second time.[2] The Saxons, then, in Liudprand's story, formed their *acies* and did as they had been told so that everything happened according to plan. The Hungarians lost their nerve and fled before they could fire a second arrow. Liudprand had opportunities of getting to know the Ottonian house-traditions about the battle of 933. He had seen and even admired the murals which depicted these triumphs in the king's hall at Merseburg and he, like Widukind, makes it apparent that there was little fighting because the enemy fled too soon. His story of what Henry I wanted his *milites* to do need not be taken literally and yet it seems to go to the heart of the matter. It should be compared with Regino of Prüm's mention of the Saxon mercenaries in 851 who did not fight in the *acies* and with the weapons of the Franks. This then is what Henry's *milites* may have learned to do by 933. It is as if their drill-master reminded them not to forget the important lessons just at the moment they were to be put to the test. Widukind's contrast between the 'rudis miles' of 924/926 and the 'miles iam equestri proelio probatus' in 933 now becomes a little clearer.

It does not follow, however, that these changes in the style of Saxon warfare and whatever social consequences they may have had all fell dramatically into the seven or nine years between the conclusion of the armistice with the Hungarians and the battle of 933, as

---

1. Widukind, i. 32, p. 45: '. . . militi . . . bello publico insueto . . . non credebat'.

2. *Antapodosis*, ii. 31, p. 51: 'Cum ad Martis proludium coeperitis properare, nemo sotium velotiori, quamquam habeat, temptet equo praeire. Verum clipeis altrinsecus operti primos super scuta sagittarum ictus recipite; deinde cursu rapido impetuque vehemntissimo super eos irruite, quatinus non prius vobis secundo sagittarum possint ictus emittere, quoad vestrorum sibi armorum sentiant vulnera pervenisse.' J. F. Verbruggen, *De Krijgskunst in West-Europa in de Middeleeuwen*, Verhandelingen van de Koninklijke Vlaamse Academie voor Wetenschappen, Klasse der Letteren, xx (1954), 181 leant perhaps a little too heavily on this passage to prove the importance of tactical order in medieval warfare.

the Corvey historian would have his readers believe. On the contrary, they were slow processes which began much earlier and had by no means been completed then. Henry needed a military following that could compare with the warriors of his rivals in the *Reich* long before he had to buy peace from the Magyars. He needed it for his early conflict with King Conrad I and his armed clash with Conrad's brother Eberhard near the Eresburg in 915 and again to extort some kind of recognition for his kingship from Duke Burkhard of Suabia and Arnulf of Bavaria in 920 and 921. For these 'confrontations', as they would now be called, he had a powerful *comitatus* with him which could at least threaten to fight if necessary. He employed it also to seize lands from the archbishop of Mainz in Thuringia and Saxony at an uncertain date in the course of his struggle with Conrad I.[1] Other Saxon nobles, like Count Thietmar, Henry's military tutor, probably had not only the expensive weapons and horses required for these occasions but also a few mounted and well-armed followers who knew how to use their superior equipment.[2] But more of them were needed and the Hungarian raids into northern Germany, beginning in 906, which found these regions to be particularly defenceless, only made it more urgent to increase the number of *milites* who could ride together and use their swords in close-quarter combat. Their total strength in Saxony was never very large though probably increasing throughout the tenth century. But up to 955 it did not suffice to fight the Slavs, the internal wars and the Hungarians at one and the same time. Otto's long absence in Italy from 966 to 972 was felt to impose a strain not only on loyalties. It is impossible even to suggest a figure for the size of Saxon contingents during the decades when the Ottonians acquired their *imperium*. The number of *milites* that could be assembled for an occasion was always much smaller than the total potential. Military power remained obstinately local. When Widukind spoke of a host of thirty-two 'legions' he merely meant an army that seemed very large to him and the only one that took the field, for Otto's war against Hugh the Great in 946, had been collected from all his 'kingdoms'. It was joined by Louis d'Outremer himself and the count of Flanders, both of whom Otto could not normally hope to see in his company.[3]

It would be well worth knowing how the technical problems, the manufacture of hauberks and swords and the breeding of horses, were solved by the Saxons in the first half of the tenth century, a period of rising demand. Smithies have been discovered in the

1. Widukind, i. 22, p. 33.
2. Widukind, i. 24, p. 36: 'Thiatmarus . . . vir disciplinae militaris peritissmus.'
3. *Ibid.* p. 37 where Count Thietmar pretended to have thirty *legiones* at his beck and call and iii. 2, p. 105: 'magnus valde exercitus, XXX scilicet duarum legionum.' Flodoard, *Annales*, p. 102: 'maximum colligens ex omnibus regnis suis exercitum.'

excavations of royal *palatia* in Saxony and there is some archaeological evidence also for iron-production in the Hanover region at this time.[1] For Eastern Saxony, the Liudolfings' base, we possess at least one text. In 960 Otto I granted to Magdeburg a *villula* in a forest where iron-ore had been dug and he left future operations to the enterprise of the monastery.[2] The raw materials for the manufacture of arms were thus at hand and it is perhaps not irrelevant that from about 900 onwards an improved type of sword suitable both for cut and thrust began to supersede the heavy, pattern-welded makes of Carolingian times.[3] The need for more horses is reflected in a royal diploma of a date which almost supports Widukind's stories of urgent preparations. In 929 Henry I put his house in order and assigned a dower to his wife Mathilda: Quedlinburg, Pöhlde, Nordhausen, Grone and Duderstadt were granted to her for life and she was to possess all their appurtenances, their *familiae*, their equipment and their *equariciae*.[4] The word *equariciae*, 'horseries', does not occur again in Henry I's or later Ottonian diplomata.[5] We cannot assume that stud-farms were never again alienated from the royal demesne when so much else was. That they were mentioned on this occasion is therefore no accident. Otto I's consent to his mother's endowment is duly recorded in the diploma. At a time when horses were especially valuable and in demand Mathilda's interests had to be protected. It was no gratuitous precaution either,

1. P. Grimm, 'Archäologische Beobachtungen an Pfalzen und Reichsburgen östlich und südlich des Harzes', *Deutsche Königspfalzen*, ii. 293 and *Nachtrag*, p. 298. On iron in Lower Saxony see W. Nowothnig, 'Funde zur Eisenforschung in Niedersachsen', *Neue Ausgrabungen und Forschungen in Niedersachsen*, ed. H. Jankuhn (Hildesheim, 1965), ii. 269. Iron-mining and an iron-industry in Westfalia from the early Middle Ages onwards are common ground amongst Westfalian historians; *e.g.* B. Kuske, *Wirtschaftsgeschichte Westfalens*, 2nd edn. (Münster, 1949), pp. 121–4 and H. Rothert, *Westfälische Geschichte* (Gütersloh, 1949–51), i. 139 ff. I am indebted to Professor and Mrs. Hawkes for their advice on this subject.

2. DO I 214 (*Urk.* i. 295 ff.) and *Urkundenbuch des Erzstifts Magdeburg*, i, no. 21, ed. F. Israel and W. Möllenberg (Magdeburg, 1937), pp. 29 ff. The editors thought that the exact location of 'Gramaningorod' where the diggings lay remained unknown but it evidently belonged to the *pagus* of the metropolis.

3. On swords see H. Jankuhn, 'Ein Ulfberht-Schwert aus der Elbe bei Hamburg', *Festschrift für Gustav Schwantes*, ed. K. Kersten (Neumünster, 1951), pp. 212–29, H. R. Ellis Davidson, *The Sword in Anglo-Saxon England* (Oxford, 1962), p. 47 and K. Tackenberg, 'Die Bedeutung der Schwertsignierungen auf dem Abdinghofer Tragaltar', *Westfälische Forschungen*, xiii (1960), 13–20. Jankuhn thought that these Ulfberth swords with a higher carbon-content and their centre of gravity nearer the hilt came perhaps from the middle-rhenish region, not excluding southern Westfalia. Did the new technique find its way eastwards or had the Saxons to import their best swords?

4. DH I 20 of 16 Sept. 929 (*Urk.* i. 56): 'cum omni suppellectili, cum equariciis ibidem inventis potestati illius possidenda perpetualiter praedistinamus.' Already Waitz drew attention to this passage (*Jahrbücher*, p. 99, n. 1 and p. 102).

5. For another example of its use see the *Ius Familiae Lintburgensis*, Conrad II's diploma for his new foundation at Limburg, in which the obligations of the *familia* were set down. See *M.G.H., Constitutiones et Acta Publica*, ed. L. Weiland (Hanover, 1893), i. 88. *Cf.* also the ninth-century St. Gallen *formula* in *M.G.H., Formulae* ed. K. Zeumer (Hanover, 1886), p. 387.

for when the Liudolfings fell out amongst themselves less than two years after Otto's coronation the possession of these six strongholds with their farms became important to the king and his resentful brothers. The dowager queen, according to the later of her two biographers, was expelled by both her warring sons, Otto and Henry.[1] The pointed reference to the *equariciae* of five royal demesne complexes in 929 suggests that something was done to increase the number of mounts available for the *milites*.

Great defensive efforts in early medieval societies, however, have usually left one characteristic common trace behind them: the tradition that they cost the church, especially the monasteries, much of their accumulated landed wealth, a heavy toll of enfeoffments and violent disseisins. Now the military measures of the Saxons in the first half of the tenth century soon ceased to be defensive. New and more lands became available quickly, thanks to their conquests, and Widukind already wrote of Henry I that there was not a man of consequence in Saxony whom he did not advance either by the grant of high office – he meant countships – or fiefs.[2] We know at the same time that while Henry was arming his rivals in southern Germany and the west, Arnulf of Bavaria, Burkhard of Suabia and Giselbert of Lotharingia were doing the same. Here there is plenty of evidence for the transfer of monastic lands to lay nobles. The Hungarian raids hit some Bavarian houses very hard so that their agrarian *familiae* disintegrated and their endowments were easily taken over.[3] In Suabia, St. Gallen and Reichenau suffered losses, and Duke Giselbert of Lotharingia too for some time enfeoffed vassals on the estates of the ancient and venerable foundations under his control.[4] Did Henry I not have to resort to the same means to build up his military following? It has already been mentioned that before 919, as duke in Saxony, he occupied estates of the see of Mainz. We do not know whether he surrendered them all again later. Two Thuringian counts with Frankish connections and blood-ties were, according to Widukind, overwhelmed during these struggles and Henry gave their lands to his own *milites*.[5] The word's double meaning of 'vassal' and 'warrior' here clearly coincided and what Henry did is further evidence that the process of enlarging the Liudolfing *comitatus* had begun long before 924. He can moreover be shown to have encroached on monastic possessions. In 941 Otto I granted to

1. *Vita Mathildis reginae*, c. 11, M.G.H., SS. iv. 290 ff. The author of this life had the brothers act in collusion at an uncertain date.   2. Widukind, i. 39, p. 58.
3. K. Reindel, *Die bayerischen Luitpoldinger 893–989* (Munich, 1953), pp. 80–92.
4. On Burkhard's spoliations see Waitz, *Jahrbücher*, p. 44 and the sources there given. For Giselbert of Lotharingia see the *Miracula S. Maximini*, cc. 11, 12, M.G.H., SS. iv. 231 ff. and E. Hlawitschka, 'Herzog Giselbert von Lothringen und das Kloster Remiremont', *Zeitschrift für die Geschichte des Oberrheins*, cviii (1960), 422–65 and esp. pp. 455 ff.
5. Widukind, i. 22, p. 35: 'Burchardum quoque et Bardonem . . . in tantum afflixit et bellis frequentibus contrivit, ut terra cederent eorumque omnem possessionem suis militibus divideret.'

his godson Siegfried, the son of Margrave Gero, everything that
Gero himself had held of the king as fief in two vills, Egeln and
Westeregeln, both in the Saxon Schwabengau. It was not unusual
for the king to help a father endow his son during his own lifetime
especially if he stood as close to him as the margrave did to Otto.
The grant included a newly-built fortress, slaves and a forest. Only
one part of Gero's fief in the two vills could not be so easily converted
into *proprietas* for his son, the estate of St. Wigbert of Hersfeld
which the king had assigned to the margrave to hold.[1] It is more
likely that Otto had 'inherited' this land from his father than that he
himself had seized Hersfeld temporalities during the early years of
his reign. For the relationships between the Liudolfings and the
abbey were old and troubled. Henry I's father, Duke Otto, had been
her lay abbot and the establishment of his family's lordship and
following in Thuringia had got under way in his time. At least
twelve places of the monastery's possessions there had fallen into
his hands by 899.[2] The struggle for the controlling positions in
Thuringia between the archbishops of Mainz and the Conradines
on one side and the Liudolfings on the other was already two decades old when King Conrad I attempted to extricate Hersfeld from
Henry's grasp after Duke Otto's death in 912. When Henry himself
became king the abbey had to exchange properties with him, probably not to her advantage.

There is better evidence still that Hersfeld lands were seized by
nobles at royal orders or at least with royal encouragement and that
the king responsible for these encroachments was Henry I. It comes
from the *Miracles of St. Wigbert*, Hersfeld's Anglo-Saxon patron
saint, which were written at the monastery early in Otto I's reign,
if not before.[3] As a source for Henry I's fortress-building and the
early history of Quedlinburg the *Miracles* have, thanks to Carl
Erdmann, come into their own, but some portions of the text
remain unpublished.[4] The author divided his subject-matter roughly
into two parts so that the first twelve stories revealed the saint as a
helper and protector of the monks and laymen who sought his
intercession while all but one of the remaining six incidents were
devoted to St. Wigbert as the avenger of his servants' wrongs:
violent attacks on the abbey's property, theft and perjury in aid of

1. DO I 40, *Urk.* i. 126: 'hoc dumtaxat excepto quod de predio sancti Vuicberti ad
abbatiam Heruluesueld nominatam pertinente prestitum ei habuimus.'

2. *Urkundenbuch der Reichsabtei Hersfeld*, ed. H. Weirich (Marburg, 1936), I. i, no. 37,
p. 67. On the early Ottonian advance into Thuringia see H. Patze, *Die Entstehung der
Landesherrschaft in Thüringen*, Mitteldeutsche Forschungen, xxi (Köln-Graz, 1962), i. 68 ff.

3. MS. 76. 14 Aug. 2, fos. 38–40, Herzog August Bibliothek, Wolfenbüttel. For a
description of this manuscript see O. Heinemann, *Die Handschriften der Herzoglichen
Bibliothek zu Wolfenbüttel* (Wolfenbüttel, 1898), vi. 396–9. Excerpts from the *Miracula S.
Wigberhti* were first edited by Waitz in the *M.G.H., SS.* iv. 224–8.

4. C. Erdmann, 'Beiträge zur Geschichte Heinrichs I', *Sachsen und Anhalt*, xvii
(1941, 42, 43), pp. 15–21 and *ubi supra*, pp. 59–67.

these crimes. Quite generally the author asserted that some of the invaders were backed by royal power. One of them, a certain Erlolf, entered a vill of the monks, Hungen in the Wetterau, and established himself there with all his household under the shelter of the king's orders.[1] The intruder was then struck down twice by a languishing disease and when he returned for the third time to occupy the place the saint suddenly deprived him of an eye. The noble whose misdeeds and mishaps were thus held up as an example to frighten off others was an important man with vassals of his own.[2] An Erlolf appears as Hersfeld's *advocatus* in one of Henry's exchanges with the abbey and it is tempting to identify him with the culprit of the *Miracula*.[3] That he should be the king's friend rather than the abbey's need not surprise us. Hersfeld undoubtedly possessed a large estate at Hungen, the vill Erlolf seized with royal backing, from the late eighth century onwards. It is mentioned in a diploma of Charlemagne's in 782 and in the so-called *Breviarium Lulli*, a ninth-century list of the abbey's holdings.[4] Hungen lay near the northern boundary of the *pagus Wetereiba* which stretched in a north-easterly direction from the Taunus range towards Frankish Hessia and the Saxon-Thuringian border. The Conradine family dominated this area and Conrad I's brother Eberhard also commanded a considerable Saxon vassalage on the other side of the frontier. It is all the more important therefore to discover Henry I trying to extend his own following into the Frankish-Hessian border-country and to win adherents inside Conradine territorial preserves and that Hersfeld was to pay the cost in land. The struggle between the Liudolfings and the house of Conrad I had not yet ended and both sides, seemingly, were preparing for another armed clash. Henry thus had special reasons for seeking to add to his military strength at Hersfeld's expense. Whether Saxon churches lost lands to his *milites* early in his reign is not known. Thietmar of Merseburg and Gerhard, the author of the *Life* of St. Udalrich of Augsburg saw in the first Saxon king a sinner who needed much praying for, but his memory never

---

1. *Miracula*, c. 13, M.G.H., SS. iv. 226: 'Quidam quidem regia suffulti potestate . . . res et predia sancto Dei a fidelibus contraditas per vim diripiebant. Quidam itaque talium Erlolf nomine quendam locum fratrum usui pernecessarium Hohunga vocatum, regalis censurae presidio subnixus, cum suis omnibus aggressus est inhabitandum.' An Erlolf occurs amongst the witnesses of a ninth-century *traditio* to Hersfeld (*Urkundenbuch*, no. 28, p. 49).

2. MS. 76. 14 Aug. 2, fo. 39: '. . . collecta suorum manu', and 'Infelix ille noviter exasperatus et obstinatus undique collectis militibus et amicis adhuc tercio locum repedabat eundem.'

3. DH 33 of 932, *Urk*. i. 68: 'Tradidit igitur nobis idem abbas cum consensu fratrum . . . et manu advocati sui Erlolf nuncupati. . . .' No king is mentioned by name in the *Miracula* but in the only other clear reference to a ruler it was Henry I without a doubt. See *Miracula S. Wigberhti*, c. 5, p. 225.

4. *Urkundenbuch . . . Hersfeld*, no. 17, pp. 29 ff. and the *Breviarium S. Lulli, ibid.* no. 38, p. 72: 'In pago Wetreibun: in villa que dicitur Houngun hub(as) xl, mansus xxviii.'

became as clouded and unblessed as that of his contemporary, Duke Arnulf of Bavaria.[1]

The skills acquired by the Saxon *milites* found plenty of use during the Ottonian century. Their sword-play was thought to be formidable and as long as lances were hurled or thrust by hand rather than couched under-arm in the later manner, the last and critical stages of a battle turned on that. As late as 1075, at the battle of Homburg, Lampert of Hersfeld tells us, the Saxon knights excelled with their swords and carried two or three apiece.[2] In the tenth century the equipment and appearance of their forbears could strike even contemporaries as rough and simple. Widukind himself lets us know that in 946 most of Otto's Saxons wore straw hats on their expedition into the West-Frankish kingdom.[3] Helmets were a luxury which only a few magnates could afford. Benedict of St. Andrea of Monte Soratte, who must have seen the northern hosts at Rome in 962 or 964, singled out Otto's Wendish auxiliaries and the crude carts and gear of their Saxon masters as an especially frightening and barbarous sight, but he did so, paradoxically, in a Latin which would have made the Corvey historian, steeped as he was in Sallust, blush.[4]

The Saxon *milites* who were so indispensable in the calculations of their masters, the Ottonian kings and their princes, the margraves of the eastern frontier, rarely occupy the front of the stage in Widukind's *res gestae Saxonicae*. Although he presented the *exercitus* as the most important institution of the early Saxon *Reich*, his use of the word *miles* does not make it possible to construe a coherent social group out of the military followings of his heroes, the Liudolfing rulers, Duke Hermann, Margrave Gero and the younger Wichmann. Their *milites* cannot be compared to the rank and file of a modern army because not only the host as a whole but each great man's following within it had its own hierarchy. Individuals from these bands of mounted warriors only reached Widukind's notice when they committed great crimes like killing the king's half-brother, as one of them did, or when they distinguished themselves as much as Hosed.[5] For the rest they disappear behind their masters, the *prefecti*, usually counts, and the *principes militum*. From them they expected their rewards and their licence to pillage.[6] If the lord they obeyed

1. *Thietmari . . . Chronicon*, i. 24, pp. 30 ff. and *Gerhardi Vita S. Oudalrici*, c. 3, *M.G.H., SS.* iv. 389.
2. *Lamperti . . . Opera*, ed. O. Holder-Egger, *S.R.G.* (Hanover and Leipzig, 1894), p. 219: 'Prima certaminis procella hastas et lanceas consumpsit. Reliquam partem gladiis, qua pugnandi arte plurimum excellit miles Saxonicus, peragunt, precincti singuli duobus vel tribus gladiis.'
3. Widukind, iii. 2, p. 105.
4. *Il Chronicon di Benedetto*, ed. G. Zucchetti, *Fonti per la storia d'Italia* (Rome, 1920), p. 175.
5. Widukind, ii. 11, p. 77. A *miles* called Mainzia, probably one of Henry's (Otto I's brother) killed Thankmar, his half-brother, in 938.
6. Widukind, ii. 11, pp. 74 ff. and iii. 68, p. 143.

fell foul of the Ottonian regime like the younger Wichmann, they suffered penalties with him and for him and Widukind is anxious to let his readers know this.[1] His reserve and exclusiveness are to some extent remedied by his greatest successor among the Saxon historians, Thietmar of Merseburg. In his *Chronicon*, written between 1012 and 1018, individual *milites* have become more important and claim a larger place than they did in Widukind's work. Their deaths, the feuds waged by their lords to avenge them, their attacks on episcopal property and vendettas even against their *seniores* were very much part of Thietmar's historiography. He too employed *miles* in the sense of 'vassal' as well as 'mounted warrior', including men of very high rank indeed.[2] For the vassalage and company of kings, bishops and lay-magnates he also favoured the term 'satellites' as Regino and others had done before him. From his frequent use of epithets like 'egregius', 'inclitus' and 'optimus' it is clear that these men were nobles, nor is it easy to find in Thietmar evidence that they already felt the competition of humbler folk in their lords' military followings.[3] *Clientes* and other forerunners of the *ministeriales* were not unknown. How many of them may have hidden in the lower ranks of a large *comitatus* or formed the warband of a lesser noble can only be guessed but they had not yet displaced, let alone absorbed, their betters in the service of the great.[4]

It would be dangerous to identify only one class in Saxon society with the complex military structure it had to support during the tenth century. But the *milites* of Henry I's and Otto the Great's mounted hosts were for the better part nobles rather than royal freemen or *ministeriales*. Even Widukind does not altogether conceal this. When he mentioned the *commilitones* of Henry, Otto's brother, Thankmar, his half-brother and the Conradine Eberhard in 938 or the *socii* of the younger Count Wichmann, he must have implied nobility. Had it been otherwise he could not have called them the companions-in-arms of great princes. It was this class, some hundreds of nobles, who slowly and obscurely achieved the technical improvements in their style of warfare that made the aggressive policies of Henry I's reign possible. Under the direction of their first native

---

1. *Loc. cit.* and *supra*, p. 39, n. 5.

2. Thietmar, i. 10 (p. 16) called his two great-grandfathers 'milites optimi et genere clarissimi'. *Cf. supra* p. 20.

3. Thietmar, vi. 5 (p. 280), vi. 15 (p. 292), vi. 22 (p. 300), vi. 28 (p. 306), vii. 53 (p. 464). The Wettin Frederick was the *amicus* and *satelles* of Margrave Ricdag of Meissen (iv. 5, p. 136). This is not to say that Thietmar's *satellites* were always of aristocratic birth. The Slavs in the suburb of Meissen to whom he once applied the term certainly were not (v. 9, p. 230). Widukind too occasionally used *satellites* for *milites*, *e.g.* ii. 11, p. 76, line 16.

4. For *clientes* in Thietmar see vii. 4, p. 402. The *milites servi* of Otto III's diploma to Bishop Hildiward of Halberstadt, DO III 104, *Urk.*, II. ii. 516 of 992, are much harder to pinpoint than Stengel, *ubi supra*, pp. 73 ff. suggested. They could have been anything from mounted warriors to half-armed peasants.

king they emerged as the military equals of their rivals in the South and West. Henry had of course the added advantage of being able to use the warlike resources of his stemland better than any Late-Carolingian ruler could before him. In the ninth century Saxons had fought the Obotrites and other Slav tribes, often with Frankish help, and none too successfully. In the tenth the aggressive wars in the East became, at least up to the great Slav rising of 983, almost a Saxon monopoly of which the native nobility reaped the chief rewards. They were also until this date fought with much success. The Saxon nobility of these two centuries was very large. To recall the abbot of Corvey's diploma of May 887, even with his immunity impaired he could retain thirty noble vassals exclusively for his own service. The size of his aristocratic military following at other times must have been larger still.[1] The many grants and long witness-lists of the *Traditiones Corbeienses* in the ninth century reveal hundreds of nobles holding widely-scattered and fragmented landed possessions and revenues.[2] Given the system of *co-hereditas* by which large kins of agnates and cognates had expectations or interests in an estate, even massive accumulations of landed wealth could crumble or shift relatively swiftly within or between family-groups.[3] The *nobilis pauper* was no rarity and even in a rich and important *stirps* there was scarcely room for more than two or three of its members to cut a great figure in the world in any one generation.[4] The rest had to seek service, perhaps with the king, or, more often, with their own better-placed kinsmen in the church or in secular office. The situation of those who belonged to an obscure and less wealthy family was worse, and before the period of the conquests it was worse for the whole Saxon aristocracy. If the social gulf which stretched between the *milites* and their leaders and lords seems very wide to us, it does not necessarily follow that they were only *liberi*, let alone of unfree birth. The relationship of vassalage and service itself created the distance. An Ottonian king was a man to beware of even in his cups and Widukind praised in Henry I the *regalis disciplina* which kept his warriors in their places.[5] Nor should it seem surprising that nobles were horsed out of the resources of his stables and stock-farms rather than their own. A century later, Bishop Meinwerk of Paderborn, who knew how to profit from the

1. As is implied in DK III 158. *Cf. supra*, p.17, n. 2.
2. L. Fiesel, 'Offleben und Kaierde in den *Traditiones Corbeienses*', *Braunschweigisches Jahrbuch*, xliv (1963), 5–41.
3. K. Schmid, 'Zur Problematik von Familie, Sippe und Geschlecht, Haus und Dynastie beim mittelalterlichen Adel', *Zeitschrift für die Geschichte des Oberrheins*, cv (1957), 1–62.
4. *Miracula S. Wigberhti*, c. 3, *M.G.H., SS.* iv. 224 and *Die Urbare der Abtei Werden*, i. 72: 'Uulfric quondam nobilis i solidum. nunc noster litus est.' These were hard cases.
5. Widukind, i. 39, p. 59: 'Et licet in conviviis satis iocundus esset, tamen nichil regalis disciplinae minuebat. Tantum enim favorem pariter et timorem militibus infundebat, ut etiam ludenti non crederent ad aliquam lasciviam se dissolvendum.'

embarrassments and the economic immobility of the *nobiles* in Westfalia, often gave them horses and also arms to sweeten the hard bargains he drove for the possession of their lands.[1] Tenth-century Saxon society could only support a very small élite. The *stirpes* of Widukind's *principes* and *prefecti* had the lion's share of the comital and higher honours and most of the better places in the church as well. The rewards of their *milites* were much more modest but neither the Saxon *Reich* nor the cultural riches, which transcended, if they did not justify its rough and brutal beginnings, could have been created without them.

1. *Vita Meinwerci*, cc. xliii, lv, lxvi, lxviii, lxxii, lxxiv, lxxxv, cix (pp. 39, 44, 47 *bis*, 48, 49, 52, 57), and more.

THE BATTLE AT THE LECH, 955.
A STUDY IN TENTH-CENTURY
WARFARE*

3

955 WAS THE *annus mirabilis* of the nascent German kingdom and all those who had hitched their stars to the fortunes of its Saxon ruler, Otto I. The last embers of a great feud which had divided the royal house and the aristocratic clans in all the duchies were stamped out. The Magyars whose crippling razzias had at one time tested the defences of Saxony and Bavaria to their limits, suffered a defeat in a pitched battle, of such magnitude that it could not be avenged and forced them to live in their new homes between the Middle-Danube and the Carpathians henceforth on the defensive themselves. Lastly the enemies of the Saxons nearer home, the Slavs between the Lower Elbe and the Oder who had used the troubles of the *Reich* and the Hungarian raids to counter-attack Saxon overlordship, were crushed in another pitched battle that was fought under conditions no less critical than those at the Lech on 10 August. This second engagement Otto and his margraves endured and won in Eastern Mecklenburg by the river Recknitz on 16 October, late in the campaigning season. From now onwards Saxon domination inexorably advanced, tribute flowed in from ever-larger regions and the conquerors' religion moved across the frontiers into their strongholds on Slav soil. The way to empire lay wide open.

Of these events the battle at the Lech must be reckoned by far the most important. It was the last act in the great civil war of the previous two years and without it the excessive strain on Saxon military resources which had been acutely felt in the 940s and 950s would have made the conquests in Slavania during the next decade far less likely. On the outcome of the *bellum publicum*, the term by which contemporaries distinguished the battle against a *hostis communis* from their current feuds, the fragile structure of the *Reich* hung. War was the perennial occupation of the German nobles, their *milites* and the Magyars in the tenth century. Both waged it for economic and social as much as for political reasons. To understand the encounter at the Lech and the campaigns that led

* A map of the part of Central Europe including the battlefield is provided. The author wishes to point out that in this period the city of Augsburg was somewhat to the south of the confluence of the Wertach and the Lech.

to it, is worthwhile not only for the devotees of military history or
'Decisive Battles'. We can learn from these events much about the
growing Ottonian empire, about the ways and means of its success.

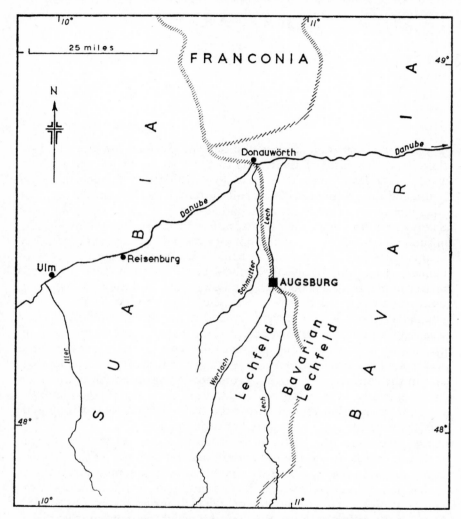

By 955 the Hungarians (or Magyars) had been raiding Western
Europe for sixty years. We must ask why, if we want to know the reasons
for their defeat and its meaning for the regions they had infested. They
were originally not one people but several who in the ninth century
inhabited an area the Byzantines named Lebedia, probably west of the
Don and on the banks of Lake Maeotis.[1] Advancing across Southern

---

[1] Constantine Porphyrogenitus, *De administrando imperio*, c. 38, ed. Gy. Moravcsik (Buda-
pest, 1949), p. 171 and the *Commentary*, ed. R. J. H. Jenkins (London, 1962), p. 147. N. Fettich,
Die Metallkunst der landnehmenden Ungarn, Archaeologia Hungarica, xxi (1937), pp. 162 ff.
For a general survey of early Hungarian history see B. Homan, *Geschichte des Ungarischen*

Russia these tribes of hunters, fishermen, horse-and-cattle nomads had come into contact with richer and better-equipped peoples like the Chazars, the Rus of Kiev and the Byzantines and had acquired some of the products of their civilization. Our main sources for their fortunes in the steppes and along the rivers of this region are the Greek government compilations, Leo VI's *Tactica* and above all Constantine Porphyrogenitus's *De administrando imperio*.[2] In the latter the Hungarians were called Turks but we also learn that dissident elements from the Chazars joined them and formed one of their tribes. The dangers of their situation amidst the Pechenegs pressing from the east, the Byzantine empire, the Bulgars and the Rus forced them into, at any rate, the beginnings of a more ambitious political organization and brought to the fore the dynasty which eventually ruled over all the Hungarian peoples, the Arpads, and a number of other princely clans who also had powers over more than one tribe. The mounted warrior became in the ninth century the backbone of their society and this aristocratic nomadism determined both its means and its ends. The economy to maintain the princes and horse-archers needed a large and continuous supply of precious metals and artefacts and the Magyars of the period of settlement in the late ninth century already owned products of very superior craftsmanship as their magnificent silver sabretache-mountings and wrought ornaments show.[3] The resources to satisfy these demands, slaves, fabrics, gold and silver, came their way through war or commerce with their neighbours in Southern Russia. When in 895 the Pechenegs forced the Magyars out of their camping areas in Atelkuzu, 'the land between the rivers' west of the Dnieper, across the Carpathians and into the Danubian basin, they also dislodged them from the sources of their precious metal supplies and other necessities. The Magyars did not find it difficult to establish themselves in the valleys of the Theiss, the Danube and their tributaries, nor was the country unsuited to them, but the *Landnahme* was a great crisis in their nomadic existence all the same, not least of all an economic crisis. The raids into Western Europe served in the first instance as a substitute for their former contacts with the great Russian trade-routes which were now for the most part barred to them. They opened up new sources of precious metals, artefacts and fine cloths as well as opportunities for capturing slaves and women which they would have needed if Constantine Porphyrogenitus's story of the Pechenegs' attack on their South-Russian camps is to be believed. According to him the families of the Magyars were destroyed while the mass of the warriors had been on an expedition westwards.[4] Among the atrocity tales in East-Frankish annals describing early Hungarian inroads one

---

Mittelalters (Berlin, 1940), i, pp. 32 ff. For a discussion of the raids from a Hungarian viewpoint see T. v. Bogyay, *Lechfeld Ende und Anfang. Ein ungarischer Beitrag zur Tausendjahrfeier des Sieges am Lechfeld, 955* (Munich, 1955).
[2] Cc. 38–40.   [3] N. Fettich, *op. cit.*, pp. 221 ff.
[4] *De administrando imperio*, c. 40, ed. cit., pp. 176–7.

at least lends some colour to the emperor's report. The *Annales Fuldenses*, under the year 894, mentioned one of the first raids into Pannonia, then a vast Bavarian march, and they relate that the Hungarians killed all the men and old women, dragging the young ones away with them.[5]

The pattern of camps developing into settlements which served as bases for long-distance raids and where the raiders stored their loot, treasures and dependants continued after the *Landnahme*, the occupation of the plains on both sides of the Middle-Danube by the Magyars. It would however be a mistake to assume that the fierce razzias against which the military and political organization of the late-Carolingian world failed at first so lamentably, served only economic ends. The Hungarians had to reconnoitre their new frontiers and they soon discovered that their neighbours were firmly settled agriculturists living in conditions very different from those of the steppes or the thinly populated Danubian plain. The Bavarians to the west moreover had a stake in Pannonia, the old Carolingian march between the Raab and the Danube, which they were determined to defend.[6] The devastation of this area and of Moravia to the north of it served a political purpose for it secured the new camping grounds against surprise attacks and created a no-man's-land between them and the East-Frankish kingdom. But the raids were also a way of life. The Magyars arrived in South-Eastern and Central Europe as nomads and their aristocracy knew no other mode of existence. The Slav settlements they found in or near their new areas of occupation could be subdued and exploited and these areas themselves and adjoining territories like Croatia offered room enough for nomadic migrations. Even in the twelfth century, Otto of Freising who had travelled through Hungary on the Second Crusade tells us, the inhabitants still lived summer and autumn in tents.[7] But nomadism at home or 'nomadism in one country' was not enough because it offered no rewards. The raids also helped to preserve a social order that favoured the horse-borne warriors and their leaders and left sedentary functions to the base of the population whether Magyars, their captives or Slavs, though the Hungarian historian Gyula Török, who has recently presented and interpreted new archeological evidence of the *Landnahme*-period, has perhaps overdrawn the distinction between the peaceful

---

[5] *Annales Fuldenses*, ed. F. Kurze, Scriptores Rerum Germanicarum in usum scholarum = S.R.G. (Hanover, 1891), p. 125 and *Annalista Saxo* for the year 906, Monumenta Germaniae Historica Scriptorum Tomus, vi = M.G.H. SS. pp. 591 f. *Cf.* also Liudprand of Cremona's *Antapodosis*, ii. c. 28 in *Die Werke Liudprands von Cremona*, ed. J. Becker (Hanover and Leipzig, 1915), p. 51.

[6] In a famous letter addressed to Pope John IX in 900 and sent in the name of the Bavarian episcopate, clergy and people, Pannonia is described as 'nostra maxima provincia'. For the text see *Codex diplomaticus et epistolaris regni Bohemiae*, ed. G. Friedrich (Prague, 1907), i, p. 32. For the history of the late-Carolingian frontiers see E. Klebel's articles, 'Die Ostgrenze des Karolingischen Reiches' and 'Herzogtümer und Marken', both in *Die Entstehung des Deutschen Reiches*, ed. H. Kämpf, Wege der Forschung, i (Darmstadt, 1956), pp. 1 ff., 42 ff. and pp. 58–9.

[7] *Ottonis et Rahewini Gesta Friderici I. Imperatoris*, i. c. 32, ed. B. von Simson, S.R.G. (Hanover and Leipzig, 1912), p. 50: 'Toto estatis vel autumpni tempore papiliones inhabitant.'

settlers and a belligerent aristocracy, Finno-Ugrian cattle-breeders ready for arable farming, and a Turkish upper crust interested only in war and the spoils of war. His conclusion that the peace-loving agrarian Hungarians of the common people were the main formative and progressive influence in the tenth century remains open to question.[8]

As nomads, however, the raiders did not conquer, let alone settle, more lands than they had already secured. They devastated, sacked and took prisoners. 'Depopulatio' was the usual expression used by the chroniclers to describe the havoc they wrought but this could mean anything from the abduction of hundreds to the temporary flight of rural populations frightened by rumours. At the same time the leaders of the Magyars came to know their West- and South-European enemies, to conclude alliances and mercenary treaties with them, exact tributes and exploit their feuds as a means of maintaining their military ascendancy. Between 898 and 955 Italy, the East-Frankish kingdom, Burgundy, Aquitaine and the West-Frankish regions, suffered some thirty raids, the worst of them during the earlier three decades, although some areas, especially Lower Lotharingia, were not hit until 954. Some of these expeditions differed very markedly from the rest not only as military enterprises but also in the make-up of the Magyar hosts and the enormous distances covered, notably those of 926, 937 and 954. We shall have to return to them.

It is now time to look at the other side. The distribution of the Hungarian attacks in time and place suggests that only for Bavaria and Saxony with Thuringia, the duchies of the eastern frontier, did they present a real threat to their existence. Elsewhere these expeditions only exposed the widespread insecurity and the want of an accepted political order, which were in fact a legacy of late-Carolingian times. The dynasties and adventurers who had seized their thrones when Carolingian blood or prestige failed were not yet taken for granted and could not count on the support of their leading vassals. Conversely, the Carolingians in France in their struggle to survive found themselves at the mercy of princes who wanted to discredit and ruin them, as Hugh the Great and his allies tried to do when they allowed the countryside round Reims to be pillaged by the raiders and Louis d'Outremer had to remain inert at Laon for want of their troops in 937.[9] The monastic and episcopal historians of the late tenth and early eleventh centuries moreover convey a false impression of the terms on which *christianitas* and *barbaries*, the pagan Magyars, met during these decades. The Italian kings, Berengar I, Hugh and Berengar II, established mutually advantageous relations with Hungarian armies and found even the payment of tributes helpful because it enabled them to tax the churches and the poor

---

[8] Gy. Török, *Die Bewohner von Halimba im 10. und 11. Jahrhundert*, Archaeologia Hungarica, xxxix (Budapest, 1962), pp. 112–13, 122–3.

[9] Richer, *Histoire de France*, ed. R. Latouche (Les Classiques de l'Histoire de France au Moyen Age, Paris, 1930), i, p. 138: 'Rex enim, copias non habens, ignominiam pertulit . . utpote a suis desertus.'

for their own purposes, as Liudprand of Cremona complained.[10] The house of Arnulf of Bavaria entered into political connections, perhaps even a marriage alliance, with the marauders which lasted up to the very eve of the battle at the Lech.[11] The behaviour of Christian rulers towards the Magyars thus varied with circumstances and this is true even of the Saxon dynasty. In 924 Henry I made a truce and paid tribute after the lucky capture of a Hungarian prince.

Nor must it be thought that the methods of waging war used by the German frontier peoples and its purposes differed so very much from those of their fast adversaries from the Danubian plain. The Hungarians, as has been said, never attempted the wholesale conquest or occupation of the older settlements in the German stem-duchies; they wanted to strip, plunder and impoverish them by tribute and for a time they came near to success. But the Bavarians and Saxons themselves made war to impose tribute and to have other *gentes* serve them, as Widukind vividly conveys. The Saxons hunted for slaves quite as savagely as the Hungarians did in their wars against the Slavs: they killed those whom they did not want and took back the rest, often to resell.[12] It does not appear that the plunder which successful armies captured from Magyar swarms they intercepted on their way home in Italy, France and Bavaria was returned to the original owners. Nor did either the Germans or the French during these decades avoid all peaceful contacts with the raiders. A bishop was able to redeem a monk of Orbais from them; the captured daughter of a Suabian count was offered for sale by the Hungarians at Worms and bought by an inhabitant of that city.[13]

These incidents and the dealings which individual princes, nobles and even religious houses had to enter into with the Hungarians are evidence of harsh realities. Monastic foundations on the whole suffered most under the attacks but if the marauders singled them out for pillage and destruction it was not because they warred against Christianity as such but because monasteries were usually rich in movables and easy to seize.[14] Later monastic writers often complained that the lay nobility had not defended the monks but had looked only to their own safety.

---

[10] Liudprand, *Antapodosis*, v. c. 33 (p. 151), wrote about Berengar II's tax to buy off the Magyars in 947: 'Fecit autem hoc non ut populi curam haberet, sed ut hac occasione magnam pecuniam congregaret. Quod et fecit.'

[11] K. Reindel, 'Herzog Arnulf und das Regnum Bavariae', *Zeitschrift für bayerische Landesgeschichte*, xvii (1954), pp. 219–21 and in *Die Entstehung des Deutschen Reiches*, Wege der Forschung, i, pp. 249 ff. Reindel however rejects a marriage alliance between Arnulf and a Hungarian princess.

[12] *Die Sachsengeschichte des Widukind von Korvey*, i. c. 35, ed. H. E. Lohmann and P. Hirsch, S.R.G. (Hanover, 1935), p. 50: 'Puberes omnes interfecti, pueri ac puellae captivitati servatæ.' This was the fate of the inhabitants of Jahna, a town of the Daleminzi, later in the March of Meissen.

[13] Flodoardi *Historia Remensis Ecclesiae*, ii. c. 10, M.G.H., SS. xiii, p. 458. For the count's daughter see *Lantberti Vita Sancti Heriberti*, c. 1, M.G.H., SS. iv, p. 741. The story suggests that prisoners bought of the Hungarians *en route* remained slaves. An Italian margrave in 921, according to Liudprand (*Antapodosis*, ii. c. 62, p. 65), with great presence of mind concealed his identity and was ransomed as a mere 'miles' by one of his own vassals.

[14] For an attempt to negotiate and purchase immunity for the monastery of Lobbes in 954 see Folcwin's *Gesta Abbatum Lobiensium*, c. 25, M.G.H., SS. iv, p. 66.

There was no great solidarity in opposing the Magyars or even in regarding them as the common enemy. From 926, however, it is possible to speak of a steadily more successful resistance to the raiders in areas where they had hitherto found the going easy. Henry I's victory at Riade in 933 is here perhaps less important than the fate which a Hungarian attack on Saxony suffered in 938, in the middle of the seething rebellion against Otto I. The new fortifications now proved themselves not so much as places of refuge standing sieges but as centres from which counter-raids could be launched and the Hungarians worn down. They lost heavily in men and horses and part of their force was destroyed in a marsh on the Lower Elbe. After 938 Saxony did not see them again as invaders.[15]

Even more encouraging were the wars fought by the Bavarians from 943, when Duke Arnulf's brother Berthold, a friend of the Ottonian regime, won a victory at Wels in the Traungau (now in Austria) which surpassed anything achieved so far against the Magyars in the judgement of Adalbert of St. Maximin, the continuator of Regino of Prüm's chronicle.[16] Duke Berthold had superseded the sons of Arnulf who in his day had been on good terms with his new eastern neighbours and there may have been domestic reasons for this war with them. It is the site of the battle which must be noted: Wels lies on the Traun, the southern tributary of the Danube nearest to the valley of the Enns which at that time marked the frontier. When Otto's brother Henry received the duchy in 948 the fighting began again and once more seems to have been close to the no-man's-land, if not inside it, rather than in the Bavarian hinterland which the Magyars had penetrated so frequently on their expeditions further west. In 950, moreover, Henry for the first time led a host right into Hungary and broke through to the settlements of his enemies. His methods were not so very different from those the Pechenegs had employed against the Magyars in the steppes of Southern Russia. Hrotsvitha of Gandersheim in her *Gesta Ottonis* exultantly described how Henry seized the spoils they had collected there from all over the world and carried away not only their booty but also the women and offspring of their nobles.[17] The Hungarians no longer commanded the initiative and their situation grew worse because Bohemia had been drawn more closely to the *Reich* by Otto I at the same time. It became critical two years later when Henry received the marches of Verona and Aquilea as his part of the spoils from the German invasion of Italy in 951.[18] The way into Italy had always been open to the Magyars and although her many cities were not entirely suited to their style of warfare they could threaten to pillage and devastate the open country in

---

[15] Widukind, *Res Gestae Saxonicae*, ii. c. 14, p. 79.

[16] *Reginonis Abbatis Prumiensis chronicon Cum Continuatione Treverensi*, ed. F. Kurze, S.R.G. (Hanover, 1890), p. 163 under the year 944.

[17] *Hrotsvithae Opera*, ed. P. Winterfeld, S.R.G. (Berlin, 1902), p. 215, ll. 390-4.

[18] *Continuatio Reginonis, ed. cit.*, p. 166 and R. Köpke and E. Dümmler, *Kaiser Otto der Grosse* (Jahrbücher der Deutschen Geschichte, Leipzig, 1876), p. 208.

order to be bought off with tributes. Besides, Lombardy and Aquilea had usually served them as their route back from expeditions to France, Burgundy and Aquitaine. Key-points on this route in the hands of an enemy could bar it or make it unsafe. The established routines of the razzia, the mode of existence of the militant tribes and their princes, were thus threatened. Something out of the ordinary had to be done to save them.

Mention has already been made of certain Hungarian raids which differed from the rest. That of 937 afflicted at least eight *patriae*, Franconia, Suabia, Lotharingia, *Francia Minor*—the dioceses of Reims and Sens—the Duchy of Burgundy, Aquitaine and Italy.[19] Its purpose is far from clear. On a march which led further and further west and then southwards it was impossible to take slaves because the raiders' movements would eventually have been paralysed by their growing column of captives. It is unlikely that they mounted them, and yet we hear of men and women being seized everywhere in Lotharingia and France. There was much arson and casual murder and people died of maltreatment, exposure and hunger, suffered when they were taken haphazardly and dragged along the roads by the invaders.[20] But Flodoard and other monastic writers also mention escapes and evidently prisoners were often abandoned or so carelessly guarded that they could get away.[21] Nor can it have been easy to move accumulating booty further and further into hostile regions. The great raid of 937 then seems oddly aimless unless its purpose was merely to terrorize and make the most of the insecurity and instability inevitably attending the recent accession of new rulers: Otto I in the East-Frankish kingdom, Louis d'Outremer in the West.

The great raid of 954 can be seen much more clearly as a political enterprise designed to break the chain of setbacks and misfortunes of the last few years and to make the most of the feuds among the Hungarians' most dangerous enemies, the masters of the Saxon *Reich*. There is at least one source, the *History of the Bishops of Cambrai*, which reveals a personality in command of the expedition, the karchas Bulksu.[22] Constantine Porphyrogenitus explains that the office was the third-highest amongst the Hungarian tribes and it appears to have been hereditary.[23] If Bulksu was not a member of the house of Arpad he had, all the same,

---

[19] For the course and direction of the 937 expedition see R. Lüttich, *Ungarnzüge in Europa im 10. Jahrhundert*, Historische Studien, lxxxiv (Berlin, 1910), pp. 88–93 and P. Lauer, *Le Règne de Louis IV d'Outremer*, Bibliothèque de l'École des Hautes Études 127 (Paris, 1900), pp. 20–7. G. Fasoli, *Le Incursioni Ungare in Europa nel Secolo X*, (Florence, 1945), pp. 163–71.

[20] For a general, if highly coloured, description of Hungarian atrocities in 926 and 937 see Adso's *Miracula et Translatio Sancti Basoli Confessoris*, cc. 7, 8 and 9 in Migne, *Patrologiae Latinae*, cxxxvii, 663–64 and v. Flodoard's *Historia Remensis Ecclesiae*, i. c. 25 (M.G.H., SS. xiii, p. 447) for the burning of villages round a monastery in the Rémois.

[21] Escapes are mentioned in the St. Basle miracles as reported by Flodoard (*op. cit.*, ii. c. 3, p. 451) and in his *Annales*, ed. P. Lauer (Collection de textes pour servir à l'étude et à l'enseignement de l'histoire, Paris, 1905), p. 67. *Cf.* also n. 13 *supra* where Flodoard retold the tales of 'captivi reversi'.

[22] *Gesta Episcoporum Cameracensium*, M.G.H., SS. vii, p. 428: 'rex Bulgio'.

[23] *De administrando imperio*, c. 40, pp. 178–9.

more authority than the princely heads of individual tribes. He had been baptized during a visit to Constantinople sometime between 945 and 948. The emperor himself received him, loaded him with gifts and also bestowed on him the rank of *patrikios*. These were high honours for a barbarian prince and the condition attached to them must have been to leave the empire's provinces unharmed in future. At any rate, according to the late eleventh-century Byzantine historian Johannes Skylitzes, Bulksu broke his pact with God by violating Greek territory again.[24] This in itself however shows that his interests ranged from the southern to the north-western frontiers of the Hungarian settlement. He stood for the razzias and the nomadic organization that went with them at a time when they had outlived their usefulness and could not be fitted into the changed military and political environment of the Magyars in Central Europe. The attempt to preserve them ended on the banks of the Lech.

The troubles of the *Reich* which Bulksu sought to exploit had begun in 953, a year before he and his army intervened. Liudolf's rising against his father Otto and his uncle Henry of Bavaria was, like the first great crisis of Otto I's reign, that of 937–40, a disruptive and incoherent affair. The interests of the king's opponents were diverse and conflicting. The feud in the royal house gathered behind it enemies of its recent advance into Bavaria and Lotharingia and these enemies took their places on both sides, that of the rebels and in Otto's camp. The rising grew out of the Italian expedition of 951–2, but it also had certain features which cannot be explained solely by the rancours of the moment: there was, to begin with, the clash between nephew and uncle, Liudolf's resentment against Henry of Bavaria whose position Otto had had to make as nearly regal and equal to his own as possible. Uncle-nephew feuds were common in the Saxon nobility and it was not accidental that the young prince drew two angry nephews of Hermann Billung, Otto's friend and trusted commander on the Lower Elbe, over to his side.[25] His *comitatus* moreover included not only Suabians from his duchy but also the pick of the younger generation of high-born Franks and Saxons. This too, the belligerent following of a king's son, was a Germanic institution older than the tenth century. Finally Liudolf's place in the royal house had become less secure since his father's second marriage in 951, to Adelheid, who brought with her the best available claim to the Italian crown. Duke Conrad of Lotharingia, Otto's son-in-law, had been alienated because his arrangements with Berengar II in Italy were all but disavowed by the king. Henry seems to have been very close to Adelheid in these conflicts and, of course, his own interest in Aquilea and Verona set him against any accommodation with Berengar.[26] Conrad's loss of

---

[24] In *Georgii Cedreni Historiarum Compendium*, ed. I. Bekker (Corpus Scriptorum Historiae Byzantinae, Bonn, 1839), ii, p. 328.

[25] Widukind, *op. cit.*, iii. cc. 19 and 24.

[26] Henry escorted Adelheid to her future husband at Pavia. See Hrotsvitha's *Gesta Ottonis*, *ed. cit.*, p. 223, ll. 653–63, 681–2. For the effect of their alliance on Liudolf, p. 225, ll. 735–40.

face alone would have created a feud between the two men. To be even with Henry, whom they detested, Liudolf and his brother-in-law entered into relations with the Count-Palatine of Bavaria, Arnulf, one of the sons of the great duke Arnulf, who had not forgotten his family's former ascendancy in the duchy. Others of his house joined and so did Archbishop Herold of Salzburg. The biographer of Otto's youngest brother Archbishop Brun of Cologne had good reason to make his hero say to the young Liudolf that he was playing his enemies' game and not his own in heading the rebellion.[27] On the other hand Brun himself, who became Otto's representative in Lotharingia during this crisis, had to find strange allies in the noble clans which had not accepted Conrad's *ducatus* but wanted to restore one of their own, especially Count Reginar III of Hainault and his kin of the house of Duke Giselbert.

The war was fought treacherously and went badly for Otto who refused to abandon his brother. Henry's enemies got their revenge on him when they seized Regensburg and all his treasures in 953 and drove out his wife and children. Both Liudolf and Conrad had been willing to come to terms with the king but he wanted them to hand over their followers for punishment and this they refused to do. Their loyalty to their following engaged the sympathies even of Otto's men and the *Life of Brun* tells us that Liudolf could not be persuaded to accept his father's terms for his companions-in-arms: penalties coupled with vague promises for their eventual restoration.[28]

The Hungarians appeared on the scene of the war in Bavaria late in February or early in March 954. The charge that Liudolf and his friends had called them in seems to have been made at once and led to violent scenes at the assembly at Langenzenn in mid-June when new attempts were made to restore peace and concord. At the time of their arrival the general situation was worse for Henry than for his enemies; he, if anyone, needed new allies. Liudolf claimed that the raiders had been enticed against him so that he was compelled to treat with them for the protection of his people.[29] Only the Luitpoldings, the family of the count-palatine, had ready access to the Magyar princes and perhaps this was their way of fighting for their inheritance. But Bavaria suffered from the large Hungarian army under Bulksu and it is clear that the invaders came on their own account using the feuds in the *Reich* as they advanced.[30] Liudolf and Conrad can be found each busy on his own. Distances were great and this may explain the disjointed character of these internal wars. One of Liudolf's Frankish friends, Count Ernst, had a

[27] *Ruotgeri Vita Brunonis Archiepiscopi Coloniensis*, c. 18, ed. I. Ott, S.R.G. Nova series x (Weimar, 1951), p. 17: 'Causam tuam tractas cum inimicis tuis.'
[28] *Ibid.*: 'Si paulo iratior est seductoribus tuis, cito mitescet.'
[29] Widukind, iii. c. 32, p. 119: 'Conductos adversum me pecunia, fateor, obtinui, ne me mihique subiectos laederent.' He gave them guides into Franconia so that his own duchy, Suabia, was spared. See also *Continuatio Reginonis*, p. 168 and Thietmar of Merseburg, *Chronicon*, ii. c. 7, ed. R. Holtzmann, S.R.G., Nova series ix (Berlin, 1955), p. 46.
[30] Widukind (*loc. cit.*) has Duke Henry say at Langenzenn: 'quia hostes . . . maligne ac pessime conducerentur, quo via eis iterum laedendi aperiretur'.

thousand *familiae* of agrarian dependants taken off his lands.[31] At Worms the Hungarians were able to cross the Rhine as Conrad's allies and were given a regal feast with presents of gold and silver. Conrad undoubtedly wanted to use them against his enemies in Lotharingia, Brun and Reginar, but they do not seem to have allowed themselves to be so employed. At Maastricht they parted from their patron and flung themselves on the monasteries and dioceses of Belgium and Northern France, notably Lobbes and Cambrai, regions where they had never been before, though they did not find themselves unopposed there, especially at Cambrai.

The most important consequence of their raid through Southern Germany was to tilt the balance of advantage against Liudolf and Conrad. Otto's immediate march to Bavaria with an army to fight the *hostis communis* was a regal gesture and the progress of the Magyars through Lotharingia further discredited the rising.[32] It lost its justification as a feud. By April 955 Regensburg, its last stronghold, surrendered. Liudolf had already done so and lost Suabia and his vassals. Conrad had abandoned his cause in June 954 on slightly better terms: he lost his duchy but kept his station, his allods and a powerful *comitatus* of knights and was exiled only for the duration of a campaign against the Slavs of Brandenburg under the command of Margrave Gero.[33]

For the Hungarians their success in 954 had not been altogether reassuring and the costs in casualties and from disease were high. But the German feuds subsided very slowly and this tempted them to try their luck again. Early in July 955 they sent an embassy to Otto I in Saxony to find out what they could about the situation. Their visit 'ob antiquam fidem et gratiam' in Widukind's words was scarcely over when messages arrived from Henry of Bavaria, barely restored to his duchy and ailing, that the enemy had swarmed over the frontier and had decided to fight it out with the king.[34] It seems as if the plan to attack once more was made and set in motion even before the embassy could have reported back and other sources too make it appear that this time the Hungarians came to stand their ground rather than raid, and fight a pitched battle rather than move on.[35] From what is known about them this was against most of their earlier practice, a last attempt to vindicate their power of ranging across Western Europe unhindered. Fighting first and foremost as horse-archers, they usually sought to avoid close-quarter action with German mounted troops. In 933 they fled as soon as they saw the new *miles armatus* of Henry I.[36] On other occasions it was

[31] Widukind, iii. c. 30, p. 118.
[32] It also gave the king an opportunity to lay waste Bavaria and so wear out his brother's enemies.
[33] *Ibid.*, iii. c. 42, p. 122.
[34] *Ibid.*, iii. c. 44, p. 123: 'statuuntque tecum inire certamen'. The Hungarian ambassadors received presents, a sign perhaps that Otto would have been glad of peace at this time.
[35] Cf. n. 48 *infra*.
[36] *Reginonis Chronicon*, p. 133: 'Perpaucos gladio, multa milia sagittis interimunt.' For the 933 campaign see Widukind, i. c. 38, p. 57.

rain hampering their archery which gave to Saxon and Lotharingian warriors their chance.[37] Their military success depended on speed, short combats and on eluding the slower-moving hosts of Western, Central and Southern Europe as they did in 954 when Otto found that they had gone when he reached Bavaria.[38] It is possible that they continued to count on the divisions amongst their enemies and hoped that Otto would not be able to collect an army so soon after the risings or keep it together and command it effectively at the critical moment. This had happened to Berengar I in 899 and to Louis the Child in 910. The very size of the Magyar effort in 955 suggests that the nomad aristocrats wanted to do more than to repeat their exploits of 937 and 954 and to take bigger risks to gain their ends.[39]

The battle at the Lech is mentioned in contemporary and later annals widely but we possess only two sources which tell us much about it in detail: the *Res Gestae Saxonicae* of Widukind of Corvey and the *Life of Bishop Udalrich* of Augsburg.[40] Widukind was not an eyewitness nor did he write close to the scene of the events he described so well, but he may have had a good report from one of Otto's sparse Saxon following who had taken part in the fighting. Gerhard, the author of the *Life of Bishop Udalrich*, belonged to the great bishop's *familia* and became provost of the cathedral church.[41] He was at Augsburg when the Hungarians besieged it in August 955, but he stayed with his lord when they moved away to fight Otto's army. Since Gerhard confined his work to what he saw and experienced in the household and the surroundings of Bishop Udalrich he denies us a detailed account of the battle. Nonetheless Gerhard's topography and his vivid narrative alone make it possible to locate the area where the main encounter took place. Besides Widukind and Gerhard, Ruotger's *Life of Brun*, Thietmar of Merseburg's Chronicle and the St. Gallen Annals only enlarge our knowledge by a few, albeit important, details. Lastly one must not ignore the traditions of Magyar historiography, the works of the Anonymous Notary of King Bela and of Simon of Keza. If their accounts cannot contribute much to the actuality of events in 955 they reveal the literary evolution of the memories left behind by the great catastrophe which ended the heroic age of Hungarian national history.

There has been much controversy about the site of the battle, so much that the question where it happened has almost blotted out the

---

[37] Widukind, ii. c. 14, p. 79: 'Urbani videntes hostes et ex itinere et ex pluvia, quae ingens erat, segniores, audacter erumpunt', in 938. Rain saved the monks of Lobbes in 954. See *Gesta Abbatum Lobiensium* (M.G.H., SS. iv, p. 67): 'Subsequitur post haec pluvia pergrandis, quae gentiliciam illis sagittandi artem cordarum distentione frustravit.' In later Hungarian tradition it rained at the battle of the Lech.

[38] Widukind, iii. c. 30, p. 117: 'Illi autem diverterunt ab eo', contradicting what he had written just before: 'disponerentque publico bello eum temptare'.

[39] So Ruotger thought. See *Vita Brunonis*, c. 35, pp. 35–6: 'Aggravata est ultra modum superbia . . . gentis Ungrorum, seducta, credo, superioris anni successu.'

[40] *Gerhardi Vita Sancti Oudalrici Episcopi*, M.G.H., SS. iv, pp. 377 ff.

[41] On Gerhard see W. Wattenbach, *Deutschlands Geschichtsquellen im Mittelalter*, ed. R. Holtzmann (Tübingen, 1948), i. 257 and M. Manitius, *Geschichte der Lateinischen Literatur des Mittelalters* (Munich, 1923), ii, pp. 203 f.

questions of what happened and how it happened. Some medievalists, driven perhaps rather than supported by the formidable Delbrück, the German military historian, have sought to locate it on the Bavarian, the right, bank of the Lech.[42] Widukind, who strangely interrupted his account of the battle's first phase to tell his readers about the anxieties and set-backs of the Saxons' simultaneous war against the Slavs, wrote: 'While these things were done in Bavaria.' But it seems perverse to prefer the evidence of Widukind, writing in distant Corvey, to that of Gerhard from whose narrative it appears that the two armies must have met somewhere to the north-west of Augsburg on the left bank of the Lech well beyond the place where it is joined by its tributary, the Wertach.[43] More serious evidence for the right bank is to be found in the Salzburg Annals edited by Bresslau. But the bald text which reads: 'A very large Hungarian army was killed in Bavaria by the River Lech' does not purport to be either a close account of events or a precise location.[44] A great many Magyars undoubtedly were killed on Bavarian soil on 10 August and afterwards. The Salzburg annal cannot over-ride the careful narrative of the preliminaries and the aftermath of the main encounter which Gerhard provides and Widukind fills in neatly. Let us follow the story of St. Ulrich's biographer and comment on its problems:[45] the Magyars poured into Bavaria in numbers larger than ever before and crossed the Lech into Suabia where they burnt down the Church of St. Afra, now in, but then just to the south of, Augsburg. They swarmed over the whole country from the Danube up to the southern forests as far as the next western tributary of the Danube, the Iller. This is an important point: they did not move further west but allowed themselves to be found by the royal army. On 8 August they

[42] H. Delbrück, *Geschichte der Kriegskunst* (Berlin, 1907), iii, pp. 113 ff., 684 ff. W. Erben, *Kriegsgeschichte des Mittelalters*, Beiheft 16 der Historischen Zeitschrift (Munich and Berlin, 1929), pp. 70 f., 74 f.

[43] D. Schäfer, 'Die Ungarnschlacht von 955', *Sitzungsberichte der Königlich Preussischen Akademie der Wissenschaften* (philosophisch-historische Classe), xxvii (1905), pp. 552 ff. and Lüttich, *Ungarnzüge*, pp. 153 ff. A battle site to the north-west of Augsburg runs counter to local tradition and to the view held by many historians, notably by H. Bresslau (*Historische Zeitschrift = H.Z.* 97, 1906, pp. 137 ff.) and R. Holtzmann, *Geschichte der Sächsischen Kaiserzeit* (Munich, 1943), p. 163, according to which the battle was fought on the left bank of the Lech but south of Augsburg, on the ground known as the Lechfeld. The evidence for this rests on a vision of St. Udalrich many years before the battle in which St. Afra took the bishop to the Lechfeld and later showed him the 'loca belli', the places where the Hungarians would be fought (*Vita Sancti Oudalrici*, c. 3, p. 389). It is by no means a necessary conclusion from the text that these must be on the Lechfeld. The difficulty is that Otto and his relief-army would then have had to arrive from the west and manœuvre well to the south of Augsburg to be able to approach from that direction, a time-wasting movement which makes his concentration even harder to explain. Had he then been defeated his communications with Franconia and Saxony would have been cut and his only refuge an Alpine redoubt of the kind Hitler may have contemplated in 1945. This was no plan for a Saxon king in the tenth century. B. Eberl, 'Die Ungarnschlacht auf dem Lechfeld (Gunzenlê) im Jahre 955', *Schriftenreihe des Stadtarchivs Augsburg* 7 (Augsburg, Basle, 1955), pp. 38 and 69, attempted to have the best of both sides of the Lech by arguing that the decisive encounter took place on 11 August on the Bavarian Lechfeld and that the action on the 10th was only a beginning. His view, however, works the sources much harder than they can bear. Many details, e.g. the site of the Hungarian camp, must remain uncertain.

[44] *Annales ex annalibus Iuvavensibus antiquis excerpti*, M.G.H., SS. xxx, ii, p. 743: 'Ungarorum maximus exercitus occisus est in Baiowaria iuxta flumen Lemannum.'

[45] *Vita S. Oudalrici*, c. 12, M.G.H., SS. iv, pp. 401 f.

laid siege to Augsburg. The city, the area round the cathedral, the bishop's seat and one or two other foundations, possessed walls which Udalrich himself had caused to be built many years ago against earlier Hungarian attacks in Suabia.[46] But it must be remembered that the last of these had passed through the duchy in 937 so that in this emergency the fortifications looked poor. There was an enclosure of stone, essential for protection against the raiders, but it lacked height and, above all, towers. Bishop Udalrich rose to the situation. His knights had coped with the first Hungarian assault outside the eastern gate (St. James) facing the Lech where the enemy thought they could rush the fortifications. All night the besieged were working to patch up the ramparts and to build block-houses on them at places which the bishop had chosen himself. It must have been a sombre and moving scene inside the enclosure, for while the men were working the women in the city at Ulrich's orders held processions and prayed for its delivery.[47] The crisis came next day when the bishop's knights, commanded by his brother Count Dietpold, had to sustain the assault from all sides. The Hungarians, according to Gerhard, approached with siege-engines, a sign that they were trying to learn from their enemies. Stone walls had hitherto for the most part defeated them and were regarded as the only safe refuge since the raiders lacked both the skill and the staying-power for prolonged sieges. Their assault on 9 August began cautiously: they fought shy of closing with the defences and had to be driven forward by the lash. Battle had not yet been joined however when the Hungarians learned that Otto with his army was approaching. Their informant was Berthold the son of the same Bavarian Count-Palatine Arnulf who had fought in vain and lost his life for the recovery of his family's position in the previous year. Berthold came from a castle on the southern bank of the Danube, the Reisensburg, some twelve miles downstream from Ulm. He is thus a crown-witness for Otto's approach from the northwest and a battle site in that direction from Augsburg. His action is evidence also that the Hungarians could still count on allies in the stem-duchy when the existence of a great family was at stake. On receiving the news, the Magyar leader at once called off the attack, held an assembly and moved his whole army away to meet Otto in the field. Gerhard has the besiegers' reason that if they won the pitched battle not only Augsburg but the whole *Reich* would be at their disposal.[48]

Otto had left Saxony at an uncertain date in July with only a small following of Saxon warriors. More could not be spared from the threatened Slav frontiers.[49] He had little time to concentrate an army against an enemy already in the field and Ruotger may be trusted when

---

[46] *Op. cit.*, c. 3, p. 390 and E. Herzog, *Die Ottonische Stadt*, Frankfurter Forschungen zur Architekturgeschichte, ii, ed. H. Keller (Berlin, 1964), pp. 186–90.

[47] *Vita S. Oudalrici*, p. 401. Gerhard speaks of 'religiosae mulieres in civitate congregatae' rather than 'sanctimoniales'. The city at that time did not yet possess a nunnery.

[48] Gerhard, *Vita* (p. 402): 'et in occursum gloriosi regis ire coepit, ea ratione, ut illo cum suis superato, victor rediens civitatem et totum regnum libere habere potuisset'.

[49] Widukind, iii. c. 44, pp. 123 f.

he reports that this was the king's greatest anxiety.[50] A date had been fixed for a Lotharingian contingent to join him which Archbishop Brun of Cologne was unable to meet.[51] From Widukind's narrative it is almost impossible to reconstruct the times and places of Otto's concentration. As he drew nearer Augsburg and pitched camp, perhaps still on the northern banks of the Danube, Frankish and Bavarian contingents joined him, the latter most likely sent by his brother from Regensburg where Henry lay ill, slowly dying.[52] The best arrival of all was Conrad's —Widukind still calls him *dux*—with a strong force of mounted men. How high military skills ranked in tenth-century East-Frankish society can be seen from the Corvey historian's brave words that at his coming the knights did not wish to postpone battle any longer in the hope of further reinforcements. But by this time a Bohemian contingent had joined and also the Suabians under their new duke, Burchard, Henry's son-in-law.[53] Only Liudolf was missing, looked after and detained regally at Bonn by his uncle who may have rendered a by no means unimportant service in this way.[54] But Brun's biographer found it necessary to put forward yet another explanation for the absence of the Lotharingians at the Lech: the Hungarians might after all give Otto the slip and plunge westwards as they had done before.[55] It was no more than a hopeful apology belied by the situation and meant that the forces available for the battle were not very large, smaller than the Magyars'. This impression is strengthened by an important detail related by Gerhard. When night fell on 9 August, Count Dietpold with the knights of the see of Augsburg left the city and joined Otto's host.[56] The Hungarians too had moved off but it left the place undefended and its clerical inhabitants had to wait anxiously on their walls for the outcome of events they could not see. Marauding troops from both armies had made contact so that both knew that battle was imminent.

At this point it is necessary to ask how strong the forces engaged actually were. For the Hungarians this is an almost impossible question to answer. They had, in the opinion not only of Gerhard but also of other authorities, brought exceptionally large numbers and one writer, Adalbert of St. Maximin, imputed to them the boast that unless the earth swallowed them or heaven collapsed they could not be beaten.[57] But Hungarian armies always seemed much more numerous than they were because of their habit of swarming over large areas in small

---

[50] *Vita Brunonis*, c. 35, p. 36: 'Imperatoris quidem spiritus agitabatur in ipso, quia non erat ei tempus exercitum congregandi.'

[51] *Ibid.*, c. 36, p. 37: 'Cum videret se ad prestitutum diem seniori et fratri suo . . . cum auxiliaribus copiis non posse occurrere.'

[52] Schäfer, *op. cit.* (p. 561), thought that Otto's army gathered close to Blenheim.

[53] Widukind, iii. c. 44, p. 125.

[54] Ruotger, c. 36, p. 37. In 936, at the time of Otto I's coronation, his brother was similarly detained in Saxony and kept out of the way. *Cf.* Widukind, ii. c. 2, p. 67.

[55] Ruotger, *loc. cit.*

[56] Gerhard, *Vita S. Oudalrici*, p. 402.

[57] *Continuatio Reginonis*, p. 168. and *cf.* Flodoard, *Annales*, p. 141: 'Hungari cum inmensis copiis et ingenti multitudine. . . .' The St. Gallen annalist spoke of 100,000 (M.G.H., SS. i, p. 79).

groups when there was no enemy in the field against them. They could afford to do this also because they knew how to re-concentrate very quickly with the help of smoke signals.[58] During the years of their greatest successes they may often have been less strong in numbers than the armies that sought to oppose them. We know that Berengar I at the Brenta in 899 outnumbered them so heavily that they were willing to surrender their booty, remounts and prisoners to be allowed to go home.[59] It was otherwise in 955. The victory of few, trusting in God's miraculous powers, over many was common ground between Ruotger and Gerhard as writers of bishops' Lives and the battle at the Lech a shining example.[60] In Widukind it was *virtus* and, as shall be seen, better weapons which overcame superior numbers.[61] We may be fairly certain that the Hungarians had an advantage though we do not know how great the disparity was. Their enemies had motives for making it seem large.

Is there any chance of calculating Otto's strength at the Lech? To begin with, even small numbers of well-equipped, mounted warriors trained to fight *in acie* mattered and represented an important military investment in the tenth century. At the battle of Lenzen in 929 fifty horsemen were decisive.[62] The loss of fifty under Margrave Dietrich in a mishap during the Slav war of 955 caused alarm and fears throughout Saxony while the king was in the south.[63] At Birten in 939 only a hundred of Otto's knights fought and won against his brother Henry and Duke Giselbert of Lotharingia whose host was said to be 'magnus satis'.[64] We owe these details to Widukind but they should warn us to treat his figures for the battle at the Lech with caution. He divided the Ottonian army of 955 into *legiones* and by *legio* in general the Saxon historian meant a force of *milites* capable of independent action in the field. He cited the strength of the Bohemian *legio* as a round one thousand,[65] a suspect figure, and Otto's own following, he informs us, was the largest formation of all for he picked a select band from all the tribal contingents as well as keeping his own Saxons about him. But

[58] Widukind, i. c. 38, p. 57: 'more suo igne fumoque ingenti agmina diffusa collegerunt' (933) and *Ekkeharti (IV.) Casus Sancti Galli*, ed. G. Meyer von Knonau, Mitteilungen zur Vaterländischen Geschichte xv, xvi (St. Gallen, 1877), p. 199: 'Nam hostes non simul ibant; sed turmatim, quia nemo restiterat. . . . Silvis quoque centeni vel minus interdum latentes eruperant' (926).

[59] Liudprand, *Antapodosis*, ii. c. 13, p. 43.

[60] Ruotger, *Vita Brunonis*, c. 35, p. 36: 'Fiduciam habuit (Otto) per Christum ad Deum, qui potens est salvare in paucis, sicut in multis.' Gerhard, *Vita S. Oudalrici*, c. 12, p. 402: 'Rex igitur cum tantum exercitum Ungrorum perspexisset, aestimavit, non posse ab hominibus superari, ni Deus omnipotens eos occidere dignaretur.'

[61] Widukind, iii. c. 46, p. 127: 'Superamur, scio, multitudine, sed non virtute, sed non armis.'

[62] *Ibid.*, i. c. 36, p. 53 and W. Brüske, *Untersuchungen zur Geschichte des Lutizenbundes*, Mitteldeutsche Forschungen, 3 (Münster, Cologne, 1955), pp. 17 f.

[63] *Ibid.*, iii. cc. 45, 46, pp. 126–7.

[64] *Ibid.*, ii. c. 17, p. 82. They were only part of Otto's force divided from the rest by the Rhine. We do not know how large a part, but could they have defeated an enemy much more than three or four times as strong?

[65] *Ibid.*, iii. c. 44, p. 125: 'electi milites mille' suggesting well-armed horsemen exclusive of servants.

these contingents themselves Widukind also called *milia* so that *legiones*
and *milia* were used to denote the same thing: the units of a host.[66]
With two *legiones* of Suabians, one of Franconians, three of Bavarians
and the two already mentioned there would thus have been an army of
over eight thousand mounted men available for the battle and this
leaves attendants and perhaps further Slav auxiliaries to be counted.[67]
It is the synonymous use of *legiones* and *milia* which makes it difficult to
accept one thousand literally as the strength of these contingents. *Legio*
was a literary importation and whether the *milia* were derived from
ancient divisions of Germanic peoples or the Old Testament they too
furnished Widukind with the imagery to fashion and give stature to his
story. Set against his and also Thietmar of Merseburg's sober figures
elsewhere, a thousand men for a *legio* is far too many. Duke Boleslas of
Poland's best gift to Otto III after their meeting at Gnesen in the year
1000 was a force of three hundred *loricati* for his Roman expedition [68]
Would these not have been a *legio*? The strength of the legions we meet
in the works of the two greatest Saxon historians of the Ottonian period
remains uncertain; it varied, but must be counted in hundreds which
rarely, if ever, reached the one thousand mark. It is therefore hazardous
to assume a figure greater than three to four thousand for the entire
Ottonian host at the Lech. Comparisons are more useful than guesses
and there is at least some rough-and-ready evidence to show that the
German and Slav forces at the Lech were much smaller than the army
Otto I had led into France in 946.[69]

The 10th had been fixed for the battle and on the 9th the troops
were ordered to fast and prepare themselves. Next morning they rose
at dawn and swore peace and mutual help to one another.[70] This was
not unusual nor an idle ceremony, for the king's host included the bitter
enemies of last year: Conrad and Duke Henry's men, the Augsburg

[66] *Ibid.*, pp. 124 f.: 'In quinta, quae erat maxima, . . . ipse princeps vallatus lectis ex omnibus militum milibus alacrique iuventute.' The figurative use of 'milia' as an equivalent for
'legiones' occurs also in Thietmar's *Chronicon* (vi. c. 58, p. 346) and in the Magdeburg Annals
where Thietmar's thirty legions of Slavs (*Chron.* iii. c. 19, p. 120) are turned into thirty
'milia' (M.G.H., SS. xvi, p. 157).

[67] W. von Giesebrecht, *Geschichte der deutschen Kaiserzeit* (5th ed., Leipzig, 1881), i, p. 831
construed a figure of at least eight thousand on this basis and Köpke-Dümmler, *Otto der
Grosse*, p. 256n. 1, wanted the legions to be even larger. R. Holtzmann, *Geschichte der Sächsischen
Kaiserzeit*, p. 163, reckoned with legions of a thousand men each. D. Schäfer, *Die Ungarnschlacht
von 955*, p. 563 n. 2, calculated a total of at least 6500. Delbrück counted between seven and
eight thousand expert mounted warriors (*Gesch. der Kriegskunst*, iii, p. 113) but more recently B.
Eberl, *Die Ungarnschlacht auf dem Lechfeld*, p. 35 and n. 56, thought that his figures and Schäfer's
were too low. The only Ottonian host for which we possess precise details in the tenth century
numbered 2100 'loricati'. Whether it was raised to enable Otto II to fight the Saracens in 982
or to avenge his defeat a year later, it would be rash to assume that the German troops already
with the emperor amounted to more or even as many. See *M.G.H. Constitutiones et Acta
Publica*, ed. L. Weiland (Hanover, 1893), i, pp. 632 f. and M. Uhlirz, 'Der Fürstentag zu Mainz
im Februar-März 983', *Mitteilungen des Instituts für Österreichische Geschichtsforschung*, lviii (1950),
p. 283.

[68] Thietmar, *Chron.* iv. c. 46, p. 184.

[69] The strength of the army in 946 Widukind gave as thirty-two legions as against only
eight at the Lech (*Res Gestae Saxonicae*, iii. c. 2, p. 105). Thietmar thought Otto's host in 955
small for the occasion. See *Chron.* ii. c. 9, p. 48: 'Collegit undiquessecus octo tantum legiones.'

[70] See Widukind, i. c. 36, p. 52 for a similar oath before the battle at Lenzen against the
Slavs in 929.

knights and former followers of Liudolf. Treachery in action against the Hungarians or the Slavs was not unknown in the tenth century.[71] The advance towards Augsburg from the north-west, under banners erect, was deliberately routed through difficult and rough country so that the Magyars should not be able to break it up by their archery, their chief weapon.[72] The Lech lay within sight not very far on the left; closer still a small stream, the Schmutter, parallel to it, does not seem to have been more than a minor obstacle.[73]

Widukind's use and adaptation of Roman military terms must not lead one to the conclusion that Otto's forces moved in well-drilled formations. The Bavarians forming three *legiones* came first—their stemland having been over-run it was their right to be in the van. The Franks, placed under Conrad, followed them. The fifth group was Otto's own and like his father in 933 he had an *angelus*, a St. Michael's standard carried in front of him, a reassurance of past victory.[74] The sixth and seventh units were made up by the Suabians; the last, where all the baggage and transport had been placed as well, was the Bohemians' under their duke Boleslas. In modern military parlance all this would be called an advance to contact before deployment. The Hungarians saw to it that it was otherwise. They crossed the Lech to the right bank—a detachment may have been stationed there from the start— and then recrossed it further downstream and, moving round the rear of the last *legio*, began to break it up by their arrow-fire before finally launching an attack with their well-known cries.[75] The Bohemians were worsted at once with heavy casualties in dead and prisoners and lost the baggage of the entire host. Their rout soon involved the Suabians as well; they too were overcome, badly mauled and scattered. It was the crisis of the battle, more or less at its very beginning, which brought near-disaster and probably eliminated a good part of the three groups hit from the frontal collision to come. Now there must have been a good deal of space between the various *legiones* or Otto would not have been free to decide what he did. 'Seeing', so Widukind wrote, 'that there had been a misfortune and his rearward troops were in great danger' the king ordered the fourth *legio* under Conrad to turn about and cope with the enemy's surprise attack.[76] If the Hungarians' encircling move-

---

[71] E.g. at the Brenta in 899. Liudprand wrote (*Antapodosis*, ii. c. 15, pp. 44 f.): 'Nonnulli plane Hungariis non solum pugnam non inferebant, sed, ut proximi caderent, anhelabant.'
[72] Widukind, iii. c. 44, p. 124: 'erectis signis procedunt castris'. It meant being ready for imminent action. When his brother Henry and the Lotharingians approached Otto in 939 'erectis signis' before Birten it was a provocation which left the king with no doubts about their intentions.
[73] For the axis of advance see Schäfer, *op. cit.*, pp. 566–7.
[74] Widukind, *loc. cit.*, p. 125: 'coramque eo angelus penes quem victoria' and C. Erdmann, *Die Enstehung des Kreuzzugsgedankens* (Stuttgart, 1955), pp. 17 f., 38 f. See also his article 'Kaiserliche und Päpstliche Fahnen im Hohen Mittelalter', *Quellen und Forschungen aus Italienischen Archiven*, xxv (1933–4), pp. 20–1.
[75] Widukind, *loc. cit.*
[76] Ibid.: 'Rex autem cum intellexisset bellum ex adverso esse.' I have followed W. Bulst (*Historische Vierteljahrschrift* 28, 1934, pp. 187 ff.) and H. Beumann, *Widukind von Korvei* (Weimar, 1950), pp. 83 f. for the translation of 'ex adverso'.

ment brought about the crisis, the Salian's intervention restored the situation for he not only flung them back again but also freed the prisoners they had taken, regained what had been looted and returned to his overlord in time for the frontal battle. The feat was helped to some extent by the circumstance that the Magyars had started to plunder rather than press their advantage and pursue the fugitives; but even so Conrad's deed astonished contemporary connoisseurs of warfare by its daring and success.[77]

When battle came to be joined in front everything favoured the Germans. Otto himself led in his forward *legiones* carrying the Holy Lance. We do not know how he deployed them but to be effective they must have been formed into a line, an *acies*, however irregular. In close-quarter fighting with spears and especially swords the great majority of the Hungarians had no chance against the heavier arms and the much better protective equipment of their opponents. Widukind allows us to see where the balance of advantage lay in Otto's address before the decisive attack: 'We know that they are for the most part destitute of all arms.'[78] Not only offensive but also defensive weapons must be included here, shields, iron helmets and above all hauberks which could resist the heavier swords of the assailants. It is clear that only a few Hungarians, the leaders, had the equipment to fight with Otto's host hand to hand on anything like equal terms.[79]

Widukind's description of the battle almost ends with Otto himself riding into the attack at the head of his troops. There was little more to be said. The bolder Hungarians at first resisted but were dumbfounded when they saw their fellows turn tail and flee. The braver warriors thus found themselves isolated and surrounded by Otto's *armati* and so perished in the midst of their enemies.[80] These are the last details relating to the battle proper which Widukind told his readers. The remainder of his recital is devoted to the pursuit, the casualties and the execution of the Hungarian princes. The very brevity of his account of what was after all the main combat, the frontal encounter, is perhaps significant.[81] It has already been noted that the Magyars did not usually seek or, if they could help it, accept action at close quarters with their western enemies. From Widukind's bald sentence about the end of the fighting it appears that even the battle of 10 August 955 was, tactically speaking, no exception. Many fled as soon as the frontal

---

[77] That they looted either reveals a slackening of their much-praised discipline or, more likely, their inability to fight a long-drawn-out engagement to the end.

[78] iii. c. 46, p. 127: 'Maxima enim ex parte nudos illos armis omnibus penitus cognovimus.'

[79] This situation still held good in the middle of the twelfth century. According to Otto of Freising the Hungarian country knights were in the process of adopting the heavier fighting equipment of the Germans then and learning how to use it from the foreign mercenaries of the king's household and immigrés. See *Gesta Friderici*, i. c. 32, p. 51.

[80] Widukind, *loc. cit.*, p. 128: 'Hostium audaciores primum resistere, deinde, ut socioviderunt terga vertere, obstupefacti nostrisque intermixti extinguuntur.'

[81] Widukind's descriptions of battles are usually generous and, Saxon noble that he was, his interest in them did not stem only from readings in Sallust. The account of events at the Lech in 955 is one of his best battle-pieces, the least likely to have been bungled, and it makes sense.

attack of Otto's *legiones* came in and those who stayed to receive it had not got a chance. One must ask how they ever expected to win when they decided to stay their ground outside Augsburg and risk a pitched battle. Evidently they pinned their hopes on the turning movement which they executed so skilfully at the very beginning and they counted on achieving a decision by the confusion and disorder that would follow. This agrees with what is known about their methods elsewhere and the experiences recorded in the Byzantine handbook, Leo's *Tactica*.[82] When the ruse miscarried they had played their trump-card and lost. The development of the battle itself thus seems to confirm the impression that the whole Hungarian enterprise in 955 strained the resources and capacities of the invaders beyond their limits.

Defeat alone however would not have annihilated the Magyar army or altogether discouraged it from returning and continuing as far as possible the expeditions into Western and Southern Europe. The raiders had suffered setbacks before and this even during the early and most successful decades of their attacks. What turned the defeat at the Lech into an irreparable disaster was the relentless pursuit of the vanquished by Otto's host and the Bavarians, alerted and stationed along the many rivers which had to be crossed on the retreat to Pannonia. For the inhabitants of Augsburg the sight of the Hungarians returning was at first not reassuring but they rode past the city and crossed the Lech abandoning both their camp and their captives. Gerhard is here once again an eyewitness and he tells us that Otto's forces came hard upon the heels of their opponents and were able to close with some of them thus causing further casualties.[83] The Hungarians must have mounted at day-break, like the Germans and Bohemians, and it is not surprising to learn that their horses were tired out by the early afternoon when their army began to disintegrate. Many took refuge in the nearest villages for a brief rest and were surrounded by the *armati* of Otto's host who simply set fire to the buildings and burnt their enemies inside them.[84] It was therefore not only the Magyars who caused damage, destruction and food-shortages on the estates of the see of Augsburg at this moment.[85] The flight across the Lech claimed more victims because having to make for the eastern banks at random men and horses were drowned when

---

[82] *Annales Alamannici* (M.G.H., SS. i, p. 54) for 910: 'Ungari ... bello insperato multos occiderunt.' Regino of Prüm, borrowing from Justinus, gave one of the best western descriptions of the Hungarians' style of warfare (*Chron.*, pp. 132 f.) in which surprise, turning movements and simulated flights played a great part. Leo's *Tactica*, xviii, 55–7 in A. F. Gombos, *Catalogus Fontium Historiae Hungaricae* (Budapest, 1937), ii, pp. 1420, 1438 (Latin translation).

[83] *Vita S. Oudalrici*, p. 402.

[84] Widukind, iii. c. 46, p. 128.

[85] Gerhard, *Vita*, c. 13 (pp. 402–3) described the shortages, devastation and fire-damage on Bishop Udalrich's and his clerks' lands. The tenth-century warrior did not have to be far from home before he behaved as if he were on enemy territory. Another duchy was almost as much in the East-Frankish kingdom. Widukind's phrase: 'ab utriusque exercitus latrocinantibus agminibus' (iii. c. 44, p. 124 and *cf. supra*, p. 57.) shows that Otto's army too plundered the country-side as it drew nearer Augsburg in 955. For a later example of a Saxon army's behaviour on the estates of one of their own margraves see Thietmar, *Chron.* vi. c. 56, p. 344. They took everything except the slaves and there was arson.

they could not gain a footing. By about four o'clock Otto himself reached Augsburg where he spent the night with Bishop Udalrich before setting off into Bavaria on 11 August. Orders had been given, perhaps already the previous evening, for all ferries and fords of the rivers further east to be guarded. To many of the Hungarians they became death-traps. Lastly the fortified places of the duchy, just as those of Saxony in 938, did their best service as bases for counter-attacks and from them the destruction of the fleeing Magyars was completed.[86]

All these details can be pieced together from Widukind and Gerhard. A St. Gallen annal adds to them the news of another action fought by the Bohemians, perhaps during the pursuit, when a Hungarian prince, Lel, fell into their hands.[87] The honours of capturing him and another leader and of taking a share of the rich jewellery and accoutrements by which they were distinguished from the rank and file were claimed also for the knights of the Count of Ebersberg.[88] However, the most important prisoner picked up in the rout was Bulksu himself who may be regarded as the heart and soul of the 955 expedition. He and his fellow-princes were taken to Regensburg and together with many others executed by hanging. Widukind's account suggests that the deed was Duke Henry's, the other contemporary or near-contemporary sources only mention the bare events: capture and the gallows. Later traditions held Otto responsible and it is doubtful whether Henry who, it is true, had suffered most by the invasion of 955 and was savage in his revenges, acted without his brother's orders or consent. The murder of the Hungarian leaders must be seen through the eyes of tenth-century commentators, especially again Widukind's.[89] They suffered an evil death, a fate that was shameful and terrible for a warrior, let alone for a prince. But the Saxon monk thought they deserved nothing better and from the silence of the others it seems that few would have disagreed with him. Yet it was one of the earliest executions, if not trials, of war-criminals in Europe and Bulksu at least nominally a Christian and Byzantine dignitary. Later generations were not so sure about the justice of the treatment meted out to them. The twelfth-century Bamberg author of the *Vita Heinrici II, Imperatoris* who mentioned the executions was anxious to legalize them and spread the responsibility, asserting that Otto caused this to be done by the judgement of his princes.[90] The Hungarian heroes

[86] Gerhard, c. 12, p. 402 and Widukind, *loc. cit.*
[87] *Annales Sangallenses Maiores*, M.G.H., SS. i, p. 79.
[88] *Chronicon Eberspergense*, M.G.H., SS. xx, p. 12. The detailed description of their golden bells and necklaces and the silver cruciform shield-bosses out of which Count Eberhard had a chalice and other church ornaments made lends some colour to the story of the eleventh-century Ebersberg chronicler who wrote the history of the comital house and its monastic foundation. According to him the Hungarian princes were brought to the castle before being sent to Regensburg.
[89] Widukind, iii. c. 48, p. 128. According to Simon of Keza the Hungarians massacred all their German prisoners as a reprisal when they heard of their princes' death. Though greatly exaggerated this may contain a vestige of truth. See Gombos, *Catalogus*, iii, p. 2144.
[90] *Adalberti Vita Heinrici II, Imperatoris*, i. c. 3, M.G.H., SS. iv, p. 792: 'et reges eorum . . . Ratisponae, principibus hoc fieri adiudicantibus, in patibulo suspendit.' The judgement of the 'principes' may also have been introduced to reconcile the deed with the constitutional

and victims of 955 had become the ancestors of Christian kings and neighbours.

Why were they killed? If the slaughter of prisoners was not unusual in the tenth-century wars between the Saxons and the Slavs, the hanging of the Hungarian princes must be set against the Liudolfing dynasty's, indeed Otto's, own earlier dealings with these enemies. In 924, as has been mentioned already, the capture of a Hungarian chieftain enabled Henry I to negotiate a peace-treaty with his people. In 938 Otto I himself accepted a ransom for one of their leaders and if treasure was especially useful to him at this moment when he had to fight for his survival on the throne, it counted for much with a German king at all times.[91] Otto was a hard and ruthless man but not insensate; his severities were calculated. The reason for this grim aftermath of the battle must be looked for once again in the make-up of Hungarian tribal nomad society. Their leaders alone gave cohesion to the mounted hosts on the raids. The Magyars were extremely sensitive about their fate and not only, as has been seen, offered ransoms to redeem them from captivity but even for the recovery of their mutilated bodies. On the expedition of 954 a noble, possibly a kinsman of Bulksu's, was killed outside Cambrai and his head displayed on the walls by the defenders.[92] Unable to avenge the injury the Hungarians in the end offered to restore all the booty and prisoners they had taken in the district as well as peace in return for the head. During the first day of the siege of Augsburg in 955 they abandoned the assault on the eastern gate when one of their leaders fell and, having recovered his body, they retreated to their camp in dismay.[93] Otto I must have known these characteristics of the Magyars and in killing off their princes he probably hoped to paralyse and disrupt them for many years to come, particularly those forces in their midst which lived for and by the razzia. Gerhard in his *Life of St. Ulrich* seems to support this interpretation when he made the hangings take place 'in ignominiam gentis eorum'.[94] Nor was Otto disappointed in his expectations. There is no evidence for any Hungarian activity on the Bavarian marches between 955 and 973; on the contrary, part of the lost no-man's-land was slowly reoccupied from the west in this period. In 956 the Hungarians were anxious to establish friendlier relations with Byzantium while the victors, significantly, received a Greek embassy with rare presents and congratulations from the *basileus*, a sign of their rising prestige.[95] Seven years later Pope John XII, now hostile

---

proprieties of the twelfth-century empire where princes could not be condemned in so summary a fashion or suffer such penalties.

[91] Widukind, ii. c. 14, p. 79: 'pretio magno redimitur'. Only seven weeks before the executions the king had treated Hungarian ambassadors with the customary diplomatic decencies. V. *supra*, n. 34.

[92] *Gesta Episcoporum Cameracensium*, M.G.H., SS. vii, p. 428.

[93] Gerhard, *Vita*, c. 12, p. 401: 'Caeteri denique, cum eum terra tenus mortuum cadere viderunt, magno timore et lamentatione eum rapientes, ad castra reversi sunt.'

[94] *Ibid.*, p. 402.

[95] Widukind, iii. c. 56, p. 135 and Cedrenus, *loc. cit.*

to the man he had crowned emperor, sought to stir up new raids against the *Reich* but to no avail.[96] Amongst the many embassies that elbowed their way at Otto's last Easter-court, held at Quedlinburg in 973, there was an especially large one from Hungary with the gifts of honour due to a powerful neighbour. The diplomacy of conversion and official encouragement for Bavarian missionaries was under way.[97]

The Ottonian victory had neither been easy nor uncostly.[98] Here too the casualties amongst the nobility counted foremost: Dietpold, the brother of Bishop Udalrich and Reginbald his nephew, an ancestor of Hermann of Reichenau the historian and scholar, amongst the Suabians, and above all Conrad, the ancestor of the Salians, whose bravura had turned the scales. His contribution to the victory and his death expiating his alliance with the Hungarians a year before the battle were widely recorded in the chronicles.[99] Widukind's account of it poignantly underlines the importance of the superior defensive armour on the winning side. The 10th of August was a hot day and Conrad, to rest for a moment and recover his breath, loosened the straps of his helmet when an arrow hit him in the throat.[100] Possibly the helmet was joined to his hauberk by a curtain of mail similar to that worn by some knights on the Bayeux Tapestry.[101] The quality and efficiency of armour amongst the victors varied too with the standing of their owner. At the battle of Birten in 939 Henry, Otto's brother, was struck on the arm and badly bruised but his *triplex lorica* protected him against worse injury.[102] What weighed in the eastern and Hungarian wars of the Ottonian armies were the mailshirts, better weapons and appropriate skills of the rank-and-file *milites*, the *miles armatus* of Widukind's stories. Their ascendancy over superior numbers can be traced as late as 990 when the Bohemian duke, Boleslas II, was advised not to fight a Saxon host under Archbishop Giselher of Magdeburg and seven Saxon counts because though small it was of superb quality and all iron-clad.[103] Not for nothing did the pagan Slavs in one of their chief sanctuaries, the Rethra, dress the effigies of their gods in helmets and hauberks.[104]

Only the secular history of the battle at the Lech has been told here. It had a religious, liturgical and ideological import in shaping the Ottonian empire and determining its coming links with Rome. Most

[96] Liudprand, *Historia Ottonis*, c. 6, p. 163.

[97] For these developments see R. Holtzmann, *Geschichte der Sächsischen Kaiserzeit*, p. 224.

[98] This is reflected in the chronicles. E.g. *Annales Hildesheimenses*, S.R.G. (Hanover, 1878), p. 21: 'Otto rex Ungarios cum magno periculo sui suorumque magna et cruenta cede prostravit.'

[99] For references see Köpke-Dümmler, *Kaiser Otto der Grosse*, pp. 259–60. His jewellery and accoutrements were recovered years later from the Slavs in the March of Merseburg.

[100] Widukind, iii. c. 47, p. 128.

[101] Sir James Mann, 'Arms and Armour', in *The Bayeux Tapestry*, ed. Sir Frank Stenton (London, 1957), pp. 58 ff.

[102] Liudprand, *Antapodosis*, iv. c. 24, p. 118.

[103] Thietmar, *Chronicon*, iv. c. 12, p. 144: 'Exercitus hic quantitate parvus, qualitate sua optimus et omnis est ferreus.'

[104] *Ibid.*, vi. c. 23, p. 302: 'interius autem dii stant . . . galeis atque loricis terribiliter vestiti'.

recent work on the victory of 955 has been concerned with these problems, the shape of ideas rather than the conditions which gave rise to them, so that historians in asking new questions of the sources are in some danger of neglecting their older, primary uses.[105] The patron saint of 10 August was St. Lawrence and to him Otto I had vowed the foundation of a bishopric at Merseburg if by his intervention Christ would deign to give him victory and life.[106] It was as the defender of churches and the grateful recipient of God's favour in the most critical hours of his reign that Otto I appeared at his coronation, not as the *imperator* proclaimed by his troops of Widukind's wish and suggestion.[107] We do not know exactly how the victors celebrated their triumph and honoured their commander on the morrow of the battle, but the aristocratic Saxon historian was not alone in regarding these festivities as an imperial coronation preferable to the Roman one.[108] Officially, however, the victory at the Lech was remembered and extolled in the papal privilege sanctioning the archbishopric of Magdeburg and her suffragan sees, in the veneration of St. Maurice who came to be associated with the Holy Lance Otto had carried into the battle and in the special honours paid to St. Lawrence on 10 August when the archbishops of the *Reich* wore their *pallia*.[109] Otto, therefore, although he accepted his new dignity at the hands of the pope gave it manifestations which reconciled it with the sentiments of his aristocratic warriors. It is clear that he himself wanted the feast of St. Lawrence kept so solemnly to express the causal link between the battle and the *Reich* he was trying to build. It furnished a justification for it and a standard of values which the German nobles of the tenth century understood and more or less accepted. The quality of Otto's generalship has been much disputed but there can be no doubt that the military and political uses he made of his victory did not fall short of the visions of a Clausewitz.

A period of great disturbance and uncertainty in Central, Western and Southern Europe was brought to an end in 955. It is safe to date the economic rise and development of many regions from the middle of the tenth century although it is far less certain how much the Hun-

[105] The thousandth anniversary of the battle at the Lech and of Otto I's imperial coronation brought forth a spate of studies, largely, though not exclusively ideological. For a bibliography see *Deutsches Archiv*, 12 (1956), pp. 595 f. and H. Beumann's valuable article 'Das Kaisertum Ottos des Grossen', *H.Z.*, 195 (1962), p. 530 and H. Büttner's 'Der Weg Ottos des Grossen zum Kaisertum', *Archiv für mittelrheinische Kirchengeschichte*, 14 (1962), p. 44, n. 1. Both these also in 'Das Kaisertum Ottos des Grossen', *Konstanzer Arbeitskreis für mittelalterliche Geschichte* (Konstanz, 1963). It is possible that the reaction against 'positivistic' history amongst German scholars has gone too far.

[106] Thietmar, *Chronicon*, ii. c. 10, p. 48.

[107] See the much-commented passage in Widukind, iii. c. 49, p. 128: 'Triumpho celebri rex factus gloriosus ab exercitu pater patriae imperatorque appelatus est.'

[108] Another monument to this kind of imperial tradition is the 'Modus Ottinc' a generation behind Widukind. See *Carmina Cantabrigiensia*, no. 11, ed. K. Strecker, S.R.G. (Berlin, 1955), p. 33 and the important articles of K. Hauck in *Liber Floridus, Mittellateinische Studien Paul Lehmann . . . gewidmet* (St. Ottilien, 1950), pp. 230 ff. and in *Geschichtsdenken und Geschichtsbild im Mittelalter*, ed. W. Lammers, Wege der Forschung, xxi (Darmstadt, 1961), pp. 181 f.

[109] Beumann, 'Das Kaisertum Ottos des Grossen', *H.Z.* 195 (1962), pp. 552 ff. and separate edition pp. 30 ff.

garians alone can be blamed for economic stagnation and losses at its beginning. The battle ending the razzias helped to create the conditions in which a renewal of literary, artistic and religious life east of the Rhine and in Lotharingia became possible and it gave birth to a new order among the contestants for the Carolingian inheritance, the 'neophyte kings' as Cardinal Humbert later called them, by exalting the standing of the Saxon dynasty and its warriors in Western and Southern Europe and even in Byzantium.[110] For the destruction of the Magyar army in 955 was felt to be an event of European significance noted by chroniclers well beyond the frontiers of the *Reich*.[111] The well-wishers of the Ottonian house were not the only ones to sing its praises for having freed Europe from a calamity. Over a century later Bonizo of Sutri, Gregory VII's apologist, said nothing less.[112] There may have been little solidarity or sense of common interest amongst the feud-ridden aristocracies of late- and post-Carolingian Europe as their dealings with the Magyars some- times show. But the battle at the Lech and its historiography helped to create such sentiments, and too much scepticism about their existence or relevance can no more help the historian than too little.

[110] *Humberti Cardinalis libri tres adversus simoniacos*, ed. F. Thaner, M.G.H., Libelli de lite imperatorum et pontificum i, p. 211.
[111] The references are collected in J. F. Böhmer, *Regesta Imperii ii, Die Regesten des Kaiser-reichs unter den Herrschern aus dem sächsischen Hause 919–1024*, ed. E. von Ottenthal, Erste Lieferung (Innsbruck, 1893), pp. 121–2.
[112] *Bonizonis episcopi Sutrini Liber ad amicum*, ed. E. Dümmler, M.G.H., Libelli i, p. 581.

Note

For a critical survey of the sources see L. Weinrich, 'Tradition und Individualität in den Quellen zur Lechfeldschlacht 955', *DA*, 27 (1971), pp. 291-313.

4

Ottonian government

A BOUT the purposes and ends of kingship in the tenth century we are well-informed. A glance at a coronation *ordo* will sum them up. Let us look at that redacted in the monastery of St Alban at Mainz around the year 960 which seems to stand especially close to the Ottonians. Here one of the bishops prayed: 'Let him (the king) be of singular equity in judgements' and 'may he please God in all things and always walk in the path of righteousness'. The aims of government are set out again in language of great solemnity in the orations after the anointing of head, chest and shoulders: 'May he defend and exalt your holy church and rule the people committed to him by You with justice.' He is to use his sword to destroy betrayers of faith, enemies of christianity and to help widows and orphans. With his sceptre of virtue and equity he should 'please the pious and frighten wicked men.'[1] When we turn to the Ottonian historians of the tenth and early eleventh centuries, their tone was no less elevated and daunting about the ends of royal rule. Often they consciously echoed the liturgical prose of the *ordines*. Widukind of Corvey had an account of Otto I's coronation at Aachen in 936 and made full use of it. Here too the delivery of the sword was accompanied by an injunction to expel all enemies of Christ, barbarians (pagans) and bad christians. These two phrases were often used together in the ninth and tenth centuries reminding us that christians sometimes helped the Vikings, collaborated with Magyar raiders and treated the possessions of the church no better than pagans did. The sceptre and staff were delivered with the words: 'Exhorted by these insignia may you correct your subjects with paternal chastisement' but this was coupled with the admonition never to be wanting in *miseratio*, pity. When we turn now to Widukind's account of Otto I's death on 7 May 973 and the lament of his following, we read: 'His men (*populus*) recalled that he had ruled his subjects with paternal piety, freed them from their enemies, overcome the proud adversaries, Hungarians, Saracens, Danes and Slavs, destroyed the heathen sanctuaries . . . and set up churches with bodies of clerks and monks'. These phrases respond to the admonitions of the archbishop of Mainz at Otto's sacring in 936. Here is a king who in Widukind's mind had fulfilled his coronation vows. We must above

1. Cited from P. E. Schramm's text of the *Mainz Ordo* in his *Kaiser Könige und Päpste*, iii (Stuttgart, 1969), pp. 96–100.

all note the *paterna pietas*. The expression conjures up Max Weber's category of a patrimonially, as against a bureaucratically governed society.[1]

In the festive and almost processional prose of the Quedlinburg Annalist who began his work around the year 1008, the liturgical echo from the *ordines* is even clearer. In 1021 the Emperor Henry II spent Palm Sunday at Walbeck and Easter at Merseburg where envoys from all over Europe hurried to pay their respects to him. For Whitsun he went to Magdeburg to stay with Archbishop Gero and then on to Allstedt, a royal estate and residence, where he held court 'with senate and people' as the Annalist liked to express it, 'pleasing the pious with mildness and terrifying the wicked with strict judgement'.[2] These few passages could be enhanced by many more, from Thietmar of Merseburg, Ruotger's *Life of Archbishop Brun of Cologne*, the two biographies of Queen Mathilda, Liudprand of Cremona, Hrotsvitha of Gandersheim and Brun of Querfurt. All these authors made forceful, if not unanimous statements about the purposes of government against which the Ottonians were measured, praised or blamed. About its means and methods they kept almost total silence. They were not interested in administration and the *munera sordida*.

If we ask ourselves how the historiographers of the tenth century valued administrative activity, we must first of all remember their milieu. For the most part they addressed a small circle, a predominantly aristocratic, ecclesiastical upper echelon to which as often as not they themselves belonged: bishops, abbots, the clerical *familia* of cathedral and monastic communities. A number of highly placed administrators always belonged to this upper layer: provosts, *vicedomini*, episcopal *camerarii* and *capellani* and in, say Thietmar's *Chronicon*, they were mentioned quite frequently, occasionally also the household officers of a ruler and even a margrave or the subordinate commanders of fortresses enter his narrative. Rarely is anything said however about the lower agents of administrative tasks, especially from the laity, the *judices*, *vicarii* and *exactores* who were enumerated behind counts in the immunity clauses of diplomata, following Carolingian models. In the narrative sources we look for them almost in vain. Thietmar mentioned *villici* three times. Once he spoke of an imperial reeve into whose house the chronicler's mortally wounded cousin, Werner, was carried by his following after the abduction of an heiress. As the official at once reported his unexpected guest to the emperor, he became in Thietmar's text the *villicus iniquitatis* of St

---

1. *Widukindi Monachi Corbeiensis Rerum Gestarum Saxonicarum Libri Tres*, ii. 1, 36 and iii. 75, 5th ed. by P. Hirsch and H. E. Lohmann, *Scriptores Rerum Germanicarum in usum scholarum ex Monumentis Germaniae Historicis separatim editi*, henceforth cited *SRG* (Hanover, 1935), pp. 66, 96, 153.

2. *Annales Quedlinburgenses, Monumenta Germaniae Historica Scriptorum Tomus III*, p. 86, henceforth cited *MGH. SS*.

Luke's Gospel (xvi. 8). In another passage the chronicler related how the reeve of Bishop Suitger of Münster was killed by a young noble before his master's eyes but what mattered to Thietmar was the dishonour inflicted on the victim's lord.[1] Otto I, it is true, once granted a *hoba* of land to one of his reeves and employed the full solemnity of a diploma to do so.[2]

The humbler chores of administration remained on the whole beneath the notice and interest of the higher clerical and lay aristocracy. Here the story of Gunther the hermit is instructive. He came from a powerful and wealthy Thuringian family and was converted to the monastic life by St Godehard at Hersfeld in 1006 making over much of his patrimony to the abbey. It seemed to him inappropriate that he should serve in the ranks of the choir-monks for very long and at his own stipulation he was, without much experience, placed in charge of a cell he had endowed. The pettifogging cares of its management proved too much for him and his life in religion almost broke down.[3] Even in the circles of monastic reform at Gorze where the aim was to rebuild orderly estate management with the help of *censiers* in the Carolingian tradition, the attitude towards administrative skills wavered. The biographer of John of Gorze defended the tough business methods of his hero with a certain unease.[4] The temptations and dangers of administrative tasks were and remained important moralistic commonplaces. Nonetheless it is possible to detect a mounting esteem for administrative skills and more interest in details in some of the episcopal *Vitae* of the late eleventh and twelfth centuries. The biographer of Meinwerk of Paderborn (1009–36) writing *c.* 1155, had much to say about the bishop's journeys of inspection to supervise the *villici* of his estates and these *villici*, it must be noted, also witnessed some of his charters.[5] Administrative talent was decisive in the ascent and career of Bishop Benno II of Osnabrück (1068–88). At one time King Henry IV, Bishop Hezilo of Hildesheim and Archbishop Anno of Cologne competed

1. *Thietmari Merseburgensis Episcopi Chronicon*, vii. 5, viii. 24, ed. R. Holtzmann, *SRG, N[ova] S[eries]*, ix (Berlin, 1955), pp. 404, 522. For the third mention of a reeve see iv. 34, p. 171.

2. MGH, *Diplomatum Regum et Imperatorum Germaniae Tomus I. Conradi I. Heinrici I. et Ottonis I. Diplomata*, ed. Th. Sickel (Hanover, 1879–84), no. 87, p. 169 f., henceforth cited *DO I*, followed by the number.

3. *Wolfherii Vita Godehardi Episcopi, Vita Posterior*, c. 8, MGH, *SS*, xi. 201 f. On Count Gunther's conversion see H. Grundmann, 'Adelsbekehrungen im Hochmittelalter: Conversi und nutriti im Kloster', in *Adel und Kirche, Gerd Tellenbach . . . dargebracht von Freunden und Schülern*, ed. J. Fleckenstein and K. Schmid (Freiburg, Basle, Vienna, 1968), pp. 332–4.

4. *Vita Iohannis Gorziensis*, cc. 87–89, MGH, *SS*, iv. 361 f. The author was John of St Arnulf, Metz.

5. *Vita Meinwerci Episcopi Patherbrunnensis*, cc. 146–51, ed. F. Tenckhoff, *SRG* (Hanover, 1921), pp. 77–80 and H. Bannasch, *Das Bistum Paderborn unter den Bischöfen Rethar und Meinwerk (983–1036)* (Paderborn, 1972), pp. 289–306. For *villici* as the bishop's helpers in pleas and as *adstantes* in charters see *Vita*, cc. 111, 195, pp. 58 and 113.

for his services as his *Vita* and a letter in Meinhard of Bamberg's correspondence testify.[1] Administrative skills were almost the sole qualifications of Hermann of Bamberg for the episcopate and they played also a notable part in the rise of Wazo of Liège as described by his biographer Anselm.[2] It is legitimate to conclude from these sources that the search for such abilities became more intensive and their importance rose at least from the middle of the eleventh century onwards. In the biographical writings of the Ottonian age the stress marks had been different and these themes did not stand to the fore so much.

The silences of the tenth-century chroniclers and annalists about the ways and means of government were not accidental. Even Widukind of Corvey's famous account of Henry I's defensive measures, the castle-building and the creation of a *militia equestris*, had a typological ring. It exemplified the king's *prudentia* and it has proved hitherto very difficult indeed to fit the story of these passages into the archaeological evidence for fortress building in ninth- and tenth-century Saxony and to identify Henry I's exact place in it.[3] Let us therefore turn to the documentary evidence, the royal diplomata. They are of course better sources for the acts of government because they themselves emanated from the most important specializing institution of the Ottonian rulers, their chancery. Yet it would be mistaken to contrast them too sharply with the narrative sources and to hope that they will invariably disclose means and methods where Widukind thought only of ends or of deeds nobly accomplished. The diplomata too proclaimed the ritual and homiletic functions of kingship if only to lend the greatest possible weight and force to the legal and fiscal changes enjoined in their dispositive clauses. To give an example: Otto I's grant of *banni* and rights to his most favoured foundation, St Maurice Magdeburg in 965, including castle-work, is one of several which tell us something more specific about the building and maintenance of fortresses in Saxony than did Widukind.[4] It also has an elaborate and solemn *arenga* beginning thus: 'Because it is known to be the office of the royal and imperial dignity that it should vigilantly guard the venerable places intended for the worship of God against the onrush of annoyances so that the servants of Christ labouring for the hope of the heavenly kingdom and supplicating the Lord for the sins and offences of the people in the aforesaid places may be the freer to do so and because it is also believed

---

1. *Vita Bennonis II. Episcopi Osnabrugensis*, cc. 6–10, ed. H. Bresslau, *SRG* (Hanover, Leipzig, 1902), pp. 6–12 and *MGH, Die Briefe der Deutschen Kaiserzeit*, *V*, *Briefsammlungen der Zeit Heinrichs IV*, ed. C. Erdmann and N. Fickermann (Weimar, 1950), p. 177 f.

2. Anselm of Liège, *Gesta Episcoporum Leodiensium*, cc. 39–48, *MGH, SS*, vii. 210–18.

3. Widukind, i. 35, p. 48 f.

4. *DO I*, 300 of 9 July.

that the secure establishment of the service of God constitutes the prosperity and the good estate of the earthly kingdom and empire, therefore we . . . for the remedy of our soul . . . and also for the well-being and safety of our kingdom and empire' and then the dispositive clauses begin. In this text the *arenga*'s theme was picked up in the promulgation and disposition and so underlined solemnly the higher ends to which the considerable transfers of rights and powers to St Maurice were being made. Walter Ullmann has rightly observed that the *arenga* 'constituted the crux of the charter from an ideological point of view'.[1] It also gave to the diploma something of the sacral aura that attended its source, the king. It was an object to be treated with reverence and this applied also to the many diplomata which lacked *arengae*.

Of all the institutions which the Ottonians developed from East-Frankish, Carolingian precedents, their chapel and chancery were the most impressive. Their products, the diplomata, became technically accomplished and beautiful by any standard. Chapel and chancery were staffed for the most part by a clerical elite which combined ability with high birth although there were among the notaries less prominent men who did not rise into the ranks of the capellanate and whose origins have remained obscure. The *capellani* of the emperors and their careers, their close connections with cathedrals where they had been educated, served and still held benefices, have been studied magnificently by two generations of scholars, beginning with S. Görlitz and H.-W. Klewitz and culminating in J. Fleckenstein's magisterial work on the court chapel, first of the Carolingian and then the Ottonian and Salian emperors.[2] He was able to show that these men not only followed the court as their masters' clerical *comitatus* but could also be employed on important missions outside it. A royal chaplain bore Otto I's demand for the excommunication of Duke Hugh the Great to a synod of West-Frankish and Lotharingian prelates held at Trier in 948. Then he escorted the papal legate, Marinus of Bomarzo, who had been there, to meet Otto in Saxony.[3] Imperial *capellani* collected relics in Italy and distributed them in the Saxon north, they attended and even presided over Italian *placita* and

1. W. Ullmann, *Law and Politics in the Middle Ages* (London, 1975), pp. 210 ff.
2. That the chapel and the royal *iter* have been the central preoccupations of scholarship is no accident. For the chapel see S. Görlitz, *Beiträge zur Geschichte der Hofkapelle im Zeitalter der Ottonen und Salier bis zum Beginn des Investiturstreits, Historisch-diplomatische Forschungen*, i, ed. L. Santifaller (Weimar, 1936), H.-W. Klewitz, 'Cancellaria. Ein Beitrag zur Geschichte des geistlichen Hofdienstes', *Deutsches Archiv für Erforschung des Mittelalters* (henceforth cited *DA*), i (1937) and 'Königtum, Hofkapelle und Domkapitel im 10. und 11. Jahrhundert', *Archiv für Urkunden-forschung*, xvi (1939), pp. 102–56 and separately, *Wissenschaftliche Buchgesellschaft* (Darmstadt, 1960). J. Fleckenstein, *Die Hofkapelle der deutschen Könige, ii, Die Hofkapelle im Rahmen der Ottonisch-Salischen Reichskirche, Schriften der MGH*, 16/II (Stuttgart, 1966).
3. *Les Annales de Flodoard*, ed. P. Lauer, *Collection de Textes pour servir à l'Étude et à l'Enseignement de l'Histoire* (Paris, 1905), p. 119 f.

went on diplomatic missions. Court clergy acted as intermediaries in quarrels between, for instance, Thietmar of Merseburg and the young Ekkehard, later Margrave of Meissen, even though the chancellor Gunther was Ekkehard's brother.[1] In local assemblies they held, as the emperor's emissaries, the foremost place. A *capellanus* of Henry III headed the list of witnesses on a Hersfeld charter of 1047–50 recording an important landgrant made by the hermit Gunther many years before.[2] Once Henry II employed his chaplain Helmiger to reconnoitre and secure a difficult route across the Carinthian Alps in a military emergency when he found that the one he wanted to use on his Italian expedition of 1004 was blocked by the enemy.[3]

The number of *capellani* rose markedly, especially under Otto III who attracted and held a brilliant *comitatus* round his person. Henry II in turn kept up his clerical following, recruiting it assiduously and promoting his chaplains to bishoprics with forethought and deliberation. He, if anyone, was the conscious architect of a *Reichskirche*. At a given time in Otto III's and Henry II's reigns there might be about fifteen imperial *capellani* in service but they would not necessarily be available all together but instead relieve one another for tours of duty while enjoying frequent leaves of absence.[4] The number of *capellani* who could be employed on tasks outside the chapel or chancery at any one moment cannot have been much more than a handful. Above all a surplus of chaplains did not necessarily mean administrative growth. The aristocratic following of a king, including his *clerici*, was there because it was there. Often it had no other purpose than companionship and prestige.

This did not mean that *capellani* were uninfluential. They sponsored royal grants and advised. Yet neither then nor later did the chapel develop wider administrative functions, especially more continuous, systematic and routine links with the local powers, the counts and the sealed communities over which they presided. Nor must the chancery's capacities as a writing office be overpressed. When Henry II in 1005 summoned a host for his Polish war under the royal ban from within his palace and all his *comitatus*, as Thietmar reported, there is no evidence to suggest that it was done with the help of written messages.[5] By this time, moreover, vassallic contingents dominated the Ottonian armies and if counties still mattered for the mobilization of *milites* it can only have been because counts and margraves stood to the fore among the lay vassals. Later, ecclesiastical princes did receive sum-

1. Thietmar, viii. 21, 22, p. 518 f.
2. H. Weirich, *Urkundenbuch der Reichsabtei Hersfeld*, I, i (Marburg, 1936), p. 176: 'Engelpreht capellanus imperatoris.'
3. *Adalboldi Vita Heinrici II. Imperatoris*, cc. 33, 34, *MGH*, *SS*, iv, p. 691 f.
4. This figure has been arrived at by a careful perusal of J. Fleckenstein's surveys in his *Hofkapelle*, ii. The totals for Otto III's and Henry II's reigns were, according to him, about 35. This allows some insight into the rates of turn-over.
5. Thietmar, vi. 19, p. 296 f.

monses in writing and it is at least possible that the practice went back to the tenth century. At any rate in Italy the post-Carolingian kings, Berengar I and Hugh of Arles, had gathered armies not only by oral messages but also 'per libros', as Liudprand of Cremona informs us. Once Rather of Verona mentioned an imperial *preceptum* of Otto I's ordering him and other bishops to besiege Garda and this meant a mandate in writing.[1]

The clerical followers of the Ottonians were nothing if not *litterati*. They included writers, poets, *savants* and saints, for instance Liudprand, Adalbert of St Maximin, Leo of Vercelli, Burchard of Worms, Heribert of Cologne, Bernward of Hildesheim, Wipo and for a time also Gerbert and Brun of Querfurt. There were besides scribes and illuminators of distinction. Most of them served their kings well and enjoyed the rulers' *familiaritas* of which more will be said later. That they made no attempt to enhance their sphere of action outside the court, had good reasons. Their primary duty was the service of the travelling royal chapel (with the chancery) and whatever the pull of their kin and patrimonies, their chief interests outside the *curia regis* lay in the ecclesiastical immunities, the cathedral closes and royal collegiate churches where they were beneficed. The propagandists of the papal reform movement were in the habit of denouncing the confusion of spheres in the lay and clerical orders but the historian of the later Ottonian and Salian Church must observe how strictly and deeply they were already separated. The *capellani* did not feel prompted to suggest to their royal masters even a return to Carolingian practices like the issue of capitularies for the instruction of *missi* or the despatch of such *missi* north of the Alps, the formation of administrative records and the keeping of archives. We find royal *missi* in this period mainly in Italy and here royal clerks came into their own. In Germany there were occasional *nuncii* to bear the king's will to the feuding monastic and cathedral *familiae* of Lorsch and Worms in 1023.[2] We do not know who was sent. For certain public functions, as we shall see, especially those which called for a measure of literary skills, the Ottonians borrowed the Church wholesale. Yet for this very reason it was less closely enmeshed with the cadres of lay power

---

1. Liudprand of Cremona, *Antapodosis*, ii, 9 and iii, 41 in *Liudprandi Opera*, 3rd ed. J. Becker, *SRG* (Hanover, Leipzig, 1915), pp. 42, 93. *Die Briefe des Bischofs Rather von Verona*, ed. F. Weigle, *MGH, Die Briefe der Deutschen Kaiserzeit*, i (Weimar, 1949), no. 16, p. 82. The extent to which Charlemagne and Louis the Pious could send out mobilization orders in writing should not be exaggerated. For the eleventh century Cosmas of Prague, writing *c*.1119, has Henry III summon his forces for the invasion of Bohemia in 1040 by letters. See *Cosmae Pragensis Chronica Boemorum*, ii. 9, ed. B. Bretholz, *SRG*, N.S., ii (Berlin, 1955, reprint), p. 95.

2. *MGH, Constitutiones et Acta Publica*, I, no. 35, ed. L. Weiland (Hanover, 1893), pp. 78–80 and also *MGH, Diplomatum ... Tomus III. Heinrici II. et Arduini Diplomata*, ed. H. Bresslau (Hanover, 1900–3), no. 501, henceforth cited *DH II*, followed by the number.

than in tenth-century Wessex. The companionship which the use of the written vernacular fostered, is missing.

Throughout the tenth century the amount of written government in Germany remained relatively inconspicuous apart from the diplomata, of which we possess more than 1300. There are some royal letters and mandates but not many and some correspondence addressed to rulers but it cannot compare in volume with the huge Carolingian collections. Great was the astonishment of John of Gorze, Otto I's envoy at Cordoba from 953 to 956, when he discovered that all requests and petitions to the Caliph Abder-rhaman III had to be redacted in writing and that a large secretariat existed for this purpose and to draft written replies.[1] The sole Ottonian administrative document we possess to-day is the *Indiculus Loricatorum* of 981. This set down very succinctly the contingents of hauberked and mounted warriors which a number of Lotharingian, Rhine-Frankish, Suabian and Bavarian bishops, abbots and lay princes had to lead in person or send to Otto II in Italy 'ad supplementum' (Thietmar, iii. 20), *i.e.* to reinforce his army for the disastrous campaign against the Sicilian emir which culminated in the defeat at Capo Colonne on 15 July, 982. The *Indiculus* with its much abbreviated entries appears as a single leaf in a patristic manuscript given by Henry II to Bamberg. It is a copy of something that was really used at court to obtain the 2090 *loricati* listed and it records decisions as to who must lead his men and who could stay behind.[2] If there were similar texts, for instance for Otto II's great reprisal expedition against the West-Frankish kingdom in 978, they have not come down to us nor were there any obvious sequels.

It has been shown moreover that the sizes of contingents for Italy as they appear in the *Indiculus*, in some cases at least constituted real *servitia debita* which were regarded as fixed and certain until the later twelfth century when, for instance, the archbishop of Cologne and the bishop of Augsburg still owed 100 *milites* as they had done in 981. The *Indiculus* thus recorded permanent quotas of the great churches for the Italian expeditions and it has been pointed out that the need for such a list must go back to Otto I who periodically called for reinforcements or reliefs during his long stay in Italy from 966 to 972.

---

1. *Vita Iohannis Gorziensis*, cc. 120, 128, MGH, SS, iv, pp. 371, 374.
2. *MGH, Constitutiones et Acta Publica*, i, no. 436, p. 632 f. and see K. F. Werner, 'Heeresorganisation und Kriegführung im Deutschen Königreich des 10. und 11. Jahrhunderts', *Ordinamenti Militari in Occidente nell'alto medioevo, Settimane di studio del Centro italiano di studi sull'alto medioevo*, xv (Spoleto, 1968), pp. 805–13, 823–40 and L. Auer, 'Der Kriegsdienst des Klerus unter den sächsischen Kaisern', i and ii, *Mitteilungen des Instituts für Österreichische Geschichtsforschung*, lxxix (1971) and lxxx (1972), henceforth cited *MIÖG*. From a notice in the mid-twelfth-century *Annalista Saxo* (*MGH, SS*, vi. 622) about the daily consumption of Otto I's court it appears that there were *scripta* bearing on this topic but we cannot be sure whether the *Annalista* had a tenth-century administrative record before him.

Yet there is no evidence of any force as large as Otto II's *supplementum* setting off then.

The Ottonian *Reich* north of the Alps knew nothing like the great spate of Witan ordinances in the vernacular so characteristic of tenth-century Wessex. The synods of the German churches continued to promulgate important *capitula* as they had done in the ninth century and often their councils were held together with great royal court assemblies to which the princes and their followings came in large numbers from all the stem regions. For the *placitum* and *conventus synodalis* at Augsburg in 952 we possess a synodal protocol which has survived in two transmissions, both Weingarten manuscripts. It met at Otto I's behest since he wanted, so we learn from the preamble, to deal no less with the *negotium spirituale* as with the state of the *imperium christianum*.[1] The venerable Carolingian concept re-appears here as if to say that Otto I too saw himself as a *rector populi christiani* despite his recent setback in Italy when the *princeps* Alberich would not have him come to Rome. The protocol has a full list of the bishops taking part and also an account of the solemn procedure: the humble *postulatio* for Otto's presence and his promise to be the helper and defender of the bishops' measures, very reminiscent of King Arnulf's role at the Synod of Tribur in 895. Among the *capitula* which follow, one deserves special attention. It decreed that women living furtively with clerks should be punished ruthlessly by the bishop or his emissary but if the lay power forbade it, let the woman be coerced to suffer the penalty, flogging and shearing, by the royal power. Such recourse to the king to override local secular authority was rare.[2] Characteristically the clash of jurisdiction appears only in the synod's protocol. For the assembly of the lay princes at Augsburg we have no texts to match although we know it to have been a very important one where a Byzantine embassy watched King Berengar II of Italy and his son Adalbert do homage to Otto I and become his vassals 'before all the host'. Only the historians, Widukind, Adalbert of St Maximin and Liudprand in his *Legatio*, record these events and their setting.[3]

Bishops naturally stood to the fore in dealing with difficult topics which lay astride the boundaries of church and lay juristic spheres, such as the status of the offspring of beneficed, albeit unfree priests who contracted marriages with women of free birth. In Lent 1019 the Emperor Henry II and at least eight Saxon bishops met in a church on the south side of the new royal residence at Goslar to debate the question. Bishop Bernward of Hildesheim had raised it and we know of it only thanks to a Hildesheim notice of 1025. Did the lay princes

1. MS Stuttgart HB VI, 114, fos. 142–3ʳ and MS HB VI, 112, fos. 122ᵛ–4 and *MGH, Constitutiones et Acta Publica*, i, no. 9, pp. 18–20.

2. c. 4, *op. cit.* p. 19.

3. Widukind, iii. 11, p. 110, *Reginonis Abbatis Prumiensis Chronicon cum Continuatione Treverensi*, ed. F. Kurze, *SRG* (Hanover, 1890), p. 166; Liudprand, *Legatio*, c. 5, *ed. cit.* p. 178 f.

present, including Duke Godfrey II of Lower Lotharingia, Duke Bernhard Billung II and Count Siegfried (perhaps of the Northeim comital family) take part in these deliberations? The Hildesheim notice suggests that the discussions of the leading men (*proceres*) – and this cannot mean only bishops – moved to and fro for a long time before they backed the judgment that the priests and their offspring remained serfs.[1]

For the whole Ottonian period we have only one capitulary for the German *regna*, dated Frankfurt, 951. It dealt with the coercion and kidnapping of widows and virgins and here, for once, the capitularies of Otto I's Carolingian predecessors as well as canonistic authorities were brought forward and cited in support before an assembly of bishops and counts. Abductions and forcible marriages were not uncommon and here the abettors and perpetrators of these offences were threatened with ecclesiastical penalties, clerks with degradation, laymen with anathema. We hear nothing of secular punishments.[2] Before Otto at Frankfurt also a sentence or *Weistum* was found that abbeys which enjoyed the right to elect their heads could not be given away in *proprium* to any one. A *Weistum* was not a capitulary or law but a general rule derived from a pending case, a clarification which settled a dubious issue and was therefore normative once it had been declared. Yet between 919 and 1025 the leading German legal historian of the Middle Ages has found only three *Weistümer*, the Frankfurt sentence, the Goslar verdict on the married priests which was recorded, as we saw, as a synodal decision, and lastly a diploma of Otto II which restored an Italian count to his wife's lands which should not have been infiscated for his offence under Otto I.[3]

In as far as diplomata repeated the same *formulae* and applied similar immunity clauses from institution to institution, in as far as the liberties of Gandersheim, Quedlinburg and other privileged houses were granted to new foundations, the principle of the *Weistum*, the sentence found before the king, might be seen to work through any of these august documents. In this way they could be, and often were, normative and acted as substitutes for more general statements of precepts and their public propagation.[4] The great Carolingian family settlements, like the *divisio regnorum* of 806, the *ordinatio imperii* of 817, the *descriptiones* of 842–3, had no echo among the Ottonians who in any case were unable to divide their *regna*. Instead we find Henry I ordering his house in 929 and part of his settlement was characteristically set out in a diploma which granted a number of important East Saxon *palatia* and royal *curtes*, their lands, fortresses and appurtenances

1. *Constitutiones et Acta Publica*, i, no. 31, p. 62 f. and H. Krause, 'Königtum und Rechtsordnung in der Zeit der sächsischen und salischen Herrscher', *Zeitschrift der Savigny-Stiftung für Rechtsgeschichte, Germanistische Abteilung*, lxxxii (1965), p. 36.
2. *Constitutiones et Acta Publica*, i, no. 8, p. 17.
3. Krause, 'Königtum und Rechtsordnung', pp. 35 ff.
4. Krause, pp. 16–29.

to Queen Mathilda. The *exordium* of the text has a distinctly legislative tone: 'It has pleased us to dispose our house *ordinaliter* with God's help.' The arrangements which follow are described as a *legalis moderatio* and they acquired this character because the king's pleasure was matched by the solemn consent of his eldest son Otto and the request of bishops, leading men (*proceres*) and counts.[1]

The paucity and modesty of central legislative, administrative and fiscal institutions in the Ottonian *Reich* remain puzzling. Their seeming reluctance to develop in a period of reconstruction, success and rising prosperity confronts the historian with some difficult questions. What held these vast stem-regions – in the tenth century called *regna* – and their *primores* together under the Ottonians and why did their *Reich* prove so much more enduring without the more sophisticated and above all so avidly and consciously self-educative apparatus and court of the earlier Carolingians? An older generation of German constitutional historians, beginning with Georg Waitz, was aware of a discrepancy, an anomaly almost, which the entourage of the tenth-century rulers and the writers until and including at least Thietmar of Merseburg's generation, did not feel. The Burgundian Wipo, the *capellanus* of Conrad II and mentor of Henry III, was the first to voice anxiety about the want of an educated lay nobility and the need for men schooled in law.[2] The abbot and historian of a Bavarian aristocratic family monastery, Williram of Ebersberg, echoed these sentiments in the third quarter of the eleventh century.[3] Let us return to Waitz. In volume vi of his *Deutsche Verfassungsgeschichte* he expressed his astonishment about the fewness of institutions and persons to cope with the ever-enlarging tasks of the emperors when it might have been expected that they needed a growing number of helpers for the exercise of royal power in justice and in the host and 'for the affairs of the state and of the Church'.[4] In volume viii of his, to this day, awe-inspiring work, when he came to discuss finance, he noted acutely the rising importance of money from the mid-ninth to the mid-twelfth century but once again he observed: 'There was a total want of higher supervision over financial affairs, of income and expenditure in the *Reich*.'[5] Waitz's successors looked beyond the everyday of administrative practice, of organization and methods, or the lack of them. They dealt above all in definitions, the nature, roots and character of the early medieval 'German state'. They were haunted by the problem of public as against private power which they derived from the legal thought of their own world, by the question whether the medieval *Reich* and its developing territories were truly states or

1. *DH* I, 20 of 16 Sept., Quedlinburg.
2. *Wiponis Opera*, 3rd. ed. H. Bresslau, *SRG* (Hanover and Leipzig, 1915), p. 81 f.
3. *Chronicon Eberspergense*, MGH, SS, xx, p. 14.
4. G. Waitz, *Deutsche Verfassungsgeschichte*, vi. 2nd ed. G. Seeliger (Berlin, 1896), p. 323 f.
5. G. Waitz, *op. cit.* viii (Kiel, 1878), pp. 216–18.

hybrids derived from the sphere of private law. If Keutgen, von Below and Waas answered this question in the affirmative they differed in what they regarded as the essence of the Frankish and early medieval German polity.[1] Was it kingship or dualism, that is to say: were hierarchical or horizontal bonds the more important? Was it founded on Germanic or late Roman pre-suppositions? Waas saw its core in the royal ban and mund while others, like Meister and Heinrich Mitteis were inclined to assign to the Frankish kingdom the character of a state with genuine officials and subjects bound by oaths, as *fideles*, to their kings.[2] Its erosion was to Meister the work of feudalism, whereas Mitteis, thanks to his comparative analysis, was more cautious and would only allow that the developing feudal custom of later twelfth-century Germany helped to bring about the emasculation of the *Reichsgewalt*, the central power, in its train, not because there was too much of it but rather because there was too little.[3]

What characterized all these studies was their schematic, generalized, root-and-branch method, their preference for monocausal changes and explanations, their tendency to force the infinite variety of local developments in Germany into single and very hard moulds.[4] In more recent years these attempts, including attempts to understand Carolingian, Ottonian and Salian Germany in this fashion, have given way to quite a different approach to the *péripéties* of the *potestas publica* in the *Reich*. The older school assumed – with some exceptions – the state and a volume of government without asking very precise questions of how it worked from day to day. It was in its abstractions a shadow-history of institutions that did not really exist. In the orientation of much German scholarship during the past twenty years all these generic assumptions have disappeared. Prosopography has taken the place of legal axioms. Early medieval political society in East Francia became simply large family groups, closely inter-related and contesting for places and honours close to their kings or their own more powerful kinsmen in the church. The Carolingian rulers maintained their *Reich* by their links with a small number of noble clans whom they had established in all parts of their huge empire. These leading men and their followers in turn penetrated the provincial aristocracies by intermarriage or by royal favour, replacing

1. F. Keutgen, *Der deutsche Staat des Mittelalters* (Jena, 1918); G. von Below, *Der deutsche Staat des Mittelalters*, i, 2nd ed. (Leipzig, 1925); A. Waas, *Herrschaft und Staat im deutschen Frühmittelalter, Historische Studien*, 335 (Berlin, 1938) and reprint (Darmstadt, 1965).

2. A. Meister, *Deutsche Verfassungsgeschichte von den Anfängen bis ins 15. Jahrhundert*, 3rd ed. (Berlin, 1922); H. Mitteis, *Lehnrecht und Staatsgewalt* (Weimar, 1933) and reprint (Darmstadt, 1958).

3. Meister, *op. cit.* pp. 90 f., 112, Mitteis, *op. cit.* p. 448.

4. See W. Schlesinger, 'Verfassungsgeschichte und Landesgeschichte' in his *Beiträge zur deutschen Verfassungsgeschichte des Mittelalters, ii: Städte und Territorien* (Göttingen, 1963), pp. 9–41 and *Anhang*, pp. 254–61 for a discussion of some of these problems.

the defeated after risings and forfeitures.[1] The Ottonian Reich too could be explained in terms of the Liudolfing marriages and the network of kinship, affinity and so inheritance which gave to the Ottonian rulers the entry into Suabia, Bavaria and Lotharingia and also those parts of *Francia* which they did not acquire by the successful outcome of the conflicts in Otto I's early years. Familial relationships, always fluctuating, traceable in the *Libri Memoriales*, imposed their pattern on rule and lordship. Its themes became fewer and even the institutions that did exist, disappear behind the personal links between people. The *capella regis* too has its prosopography. It must however be observed that one explanation of Ottonian Government and its development, familiar to H. Mitteis and R. Holtzmann, has not been shaken or altered, namely the view that after the second great crisis of Otto I's reign, the rising of his son Liudolf and his son-in-law, the Salian Conrad, with their ill-assorted friends and allies (953/4), the church was deliberately and purposefully enhanced in rights, riches and powers and made to occupy the place in government which the fluctuating loyalties of dukes and counts, including members of the *stirps regia*, could not be trusted to fill reliably.[2] Yet this shift too was much slower and much less deliberate than is sometimes assumed.

Kinship and *amicitia* lead us back to the patrimonial society, to the extension of the king's rule from his household, his *palatium* over his *familiares* to others, less closely tied to him and less physically near to him. They too were his *fideles* and had obligations but they were claimed less frequently and consistently. Here we have a specific condition of Ottonian government, its uneven intensity in the various regions of the *Reich*: its greater weight and import in Saxony compared with *Francia*, the Rhineland, Lower Lotharingia and, in descending order, Suabia, Bavaria and Carinthia. The most telling evidence for this is the survey of the royal itinerary from 919 to 1024, the number and duration of stays in Saxony set against those else-

1. Of fundamental importance here is G. Tellenbach, *Studien und Vorarbeiten zur Geschichte des grossfränkischen und frühdeutschen Adels* (Freiburg, 1957) with contributions by J. Fleckenstein, F. Vollmer, K. Schmid and J. Wollasch. See also K. F. Werner, 'Bedeutende Adelsfamilien im Reich Karls des Grossen', in *Karl der Grosse, Lebenswerk und Nachleben*, i, ed. H. Beumann (Düsseldorf, 1965). English translation with an ample bibliography by T. Reuter, *The Medieval Nobility* (Amsterdam, New York, Oxford, 1979). See also K. Leyser, 'The German Aristocracy from the ninth to the early twelfth Century A Historical and Cultural Sketch', *Past and Present*, xli (1968). Here pp. 161 ff.

2. R. Holtzmann, *Geschichte der Sächsischen Kaiserzeit (900–1024)*, (Munich, 1943), pp. 180–4 and *cf.* for instance J. Fleckenstein, *Grundlagen und Beginn der deutschen Geschichte* (Göttingen, 1974), pp. 145 ff. English translation by B. S. Smith, *Early Medieval Germany* (Amsterdam, N.Y., Oxford, 1978), pp. 122 ff. Institutional history quite apart from the royal chapel and the royal *iter* has held its own with W. Kienast, *Der Herzogstitel in Frankreich und Deutschland* (Munich, Vienna, 1968) and see *ante*, lxxxviii (1973), pp. 584 ff., the chapters devoted to constitutional problems in W. Störmer, *Früher Adel* (see *infra*, p. 96, n. 3) and the splendid recent study by H. Maurer, *Der Herzog von Schwaben* (Sigmaringen, 1978). For further recent work on duchies see *DA*, xxxv (1979), pp. 288–90.

where, even places much frequented by the Ottonians like Aachen (Otto III), Cologne, Ingelheim and Frankfurt. In the tenth century the number of stays in Saxony surpassed those in all the other duchies added together and those in Bavaria in the ratio of eighteen to one. Under Henry II, the Bavarian Liudolfing, the preponderance of Saxony compared with Bavaria, formerly the least visited duchy, lessened a little but it was still ten to one. In respect of the other duchies the lead of Saxony remained almost constant, only Suabia saw a little more of Henry than it had seen of his predecessors.[1]

The large patrimony of the Liudolfings, much enhanced by Carolingian fisc in the later ninth century and Henry I's marriages, lay mostly in East Saxony and Thuringia. An area roughly from the north of Magdeburg to Merseburg on the Saale, including the Harz as royal *forestis* and much of the upper Leine valley, served as the base for further expansion beginning with Henry I: the massive assault on the Slav tribes beyond the Elbe and Saale rivers. It reached its greatest momentum during the years after the Battle at the Recknitz on 16 October 955. Most of the Saxon high nobility who achieved permanent commands and positions along that frontier owed their ascent as individuals and as ancestors of ducal, margravial and comital clans with a large future, to these wars: the Stade counts, the Billungs at Lüneburg, the margraves of the Northern March, known as the Haldensleben, the nephew of Margrave Gero, called Thietmar, the Wettins at the Eilenburg and the Ekkehardine margraves of Meissen. The whole Ottonian family, not only the kings, had stakes in these frontiers, Otto I's brother Henry, his half-brother Thangmar and his son Liudolf.[2] The denser network of institutions which we look for in vain elsewhere, can be found here. The margraviates and countships of these East-Saxon and Thuringian marches remained much more regal than the *comitatus* of the hinterland further west in Engern and Westfalia, not to mention other stem areas. Here Otto III and Henry II could tamper with appointments and the leading men were accountable for their doings, liable to suffer disgrace in a way almost reminiscent of Anglo-Norman England during the first two generations after the conquest. There developed a network of burgwards and *burgbanns* which bound both Saxon and Slav populations to castlework, dues and watch services. About all these we are relatively well-informed. The diplomata of Otto I for Corvey and Magdeburg,

---

1. C. Brühl, *Fodrum, Gistum Servitium Regis* (Cologne, Graz, 1968), i, pp. 116 ff. and for the figures cited here see H. J. Rieckenberg, 'Königstrasse und Königsgut in Liudolfingischer und Frühsalischer Zeit (919–1056)', *Archiv für Urkundenforschung*, xvii (1941), pp. 68, 89 and separately (Darmstadt, 1965), pp. 37, 58. The number of stays are but a rough guide. For their duration under Otto I see now E. Müller-Mertens, *Die Reichsstruktur im Spiegel der Herrschaftspraxis Ottos des Grossen*, pp. 79 ff., *Forschungen zur Mittelalterlichen Geschichte*, xxv (Berlin, 1980).

2. K. Leyser, *Rule and Conflict in an Early Medieval Society Ottonian Saxony* (London, 1979), p. 19.

later ones for Gandersheim and Merseburg tell us how the fortifica-
tion system worked, or was meant to work, in their respective areas.[1]
The grant to Corvey of 940 is the earliest text of its kind. Under the
terms of Otto I's diploma Abbot Folcmar and the monks serving
God, St Stephen and St Vitus, were to have the *bannus*, *i.e.* powers of
enforcement, over the men who had to take refuge in the fortress
that had been built in the monastery's ambit. There also they must
work on the upkeep of the defences and, if the case of Magdeburg is
a parallel, pay a due. The populations affected by this grant lived in
three *pagi* and in the jurisdiction of four counts who were forbidden
to enforce any other *burgbann* (*i.e.* castlework) over them. The abbot
or his nominee, an *advocatus*, had the sole right of wielding these
powers.[2] Here then a profitable sanction, which cut across the ordinary
competence of counts, was entrusted to the monastery which held of
course lands ubiquitously in the area. It is evident that the shift of
right and power to Corvey was newer than the obligation of fortress-
building as such. It enhanced the immunity and adapted it to new
conditions. We know from the example of Hersfeld that new fortresses
where the monks and their *familia* could shelter, were built at Henry
I's orders and also that they had to be of a higher standard than had
hitherto sufficed so that they could withstand the Magyars. We must
note moreover that Corvey, one of the most privileged Carolingian
monastic sanctuaries in ninth-century Saxony, was a centre for other
important experiments and advances in Government, not least of all
the first minting operations east of the Rhine, outside Frisia.[3]

Otto I's grant to Magdeburg in 965 transferred to his most favoured
foundation the royal ban and the castle-work labour services due to
the 'imperial right'. They were owed by the inhabitants of the surrounding countryside and the diploma did not give a geographical
specification as the Corvey one had done. Many of the vills were
grouped together and subject to the monastery already as they had
been to the royal *curtis* before it was given to St Maurice. We can
however catch a glimpse of the magnitude and extent of the *burgbann*
here from an earlier gift of Otto's to Magdeburg, the grant of secular
tenths, payable by the Slavs to the burgh. To this was added the
tenth due from all the Slavs who had to take refuge and therefore work
at the fortresses of Frohse, Barby and Kalbe.[4] All these burgwards
then could exact extensive labour services as well as taxes from the

1. *DO I* 27 for Corvey, 19 Apr. 940, *DO I* 300 of 9 July 965 for Magdeburg,
MGH, *Diplomatum Regum et Imperatorum Germaniae Tomi II. Pars Prior. Ottonis II.
Diplomata* (Hanover, 1888), 214 (henceforth cited *DO II*) for Gandersheim, *DO II*,
89 of 30 Aug. 974 for Merseburg, granting the burgward Zwenkau. See K. Leyser,
'Henry I and the beginnings of the Saxon empire', *supra*, p. 19, n. 3.

2. *DO I*, 27.

3. See P. Berghaus, 'Das Münzwesen', in *Kunst und Kultar im Weserraum 800–1600*,
i (Corvey, 1966), p. 214 f.

4. *DO I*, 222a, 222b of 23 Apr. 961.

subject Slavs and, according to another version of Otto I's gift, the Germans too. A systematic and contiguous network of fortifications, of labour services and an organization to maintain them, appear to be vouchsafed by these diplomata and so lend some substance to Widukind's sweeping passages.

Besides these burdens on the rural population there grew up a system of castle-guard binding the East-Saxon counts and bishops to garrison dangerously exposed fortresses in person and hold them for the king for a fixed number of weeks with their *milites*. The two best-documented examples are the Arneburg, north of Magdeburg, and Meissen but there were others. The Arneburg was occupied in 997 by Archbishop Giselher of Magdeburg who had to keep it for four weeks. He fell into a Slav ambush but regained the fortress and guarded it for his term. Then he marched out, apparently without waiting for his relief, Margrave Lothar of the Northern March, Thietmar of Merseburg's uncle. The Slavs used the interval to set the burgh on fire. Lothar could not extinguish the blaze and abandoned the open gate. Accused later before Otto III, he cleared himself with an oath.[1]

Thietmar himself had to serve in the key stronghold of Meissen with the *milites* of his see and more than once mentioned the arrival and departure of reliefs in passing.[2] There were permanent *custodes* (keepers) under the margrave and also Slavs settled in the suburb who had to perform guard duties. We find royal *satellites* in occupation in 1003 but the main burden of defence lay upon the counts and bishops of the hinterland who came and went regularly by turns.[3] The Meissen garrison duty went back to Henry I's reign. Thietmar, unfortunately, has not told us in any detail how the castle-guards were arranged but it seems that each tour of duty lasted for four weeks just as in the case of the Arneburg. Henry II kept a careful eye on the fortress and its security. In 1009 he committed it for the time being to Count Frederick of Eilenburg. Shortly afterwards his *nuntius* introduced the new permanent margrave, Hermann.[4] In 1015 he hurriedly sent him from his field army to the defence of the threatened stronghold. When he heard how critical the situation was, he directed additional forces, bishops, including the archbishop of Magdeburg, and counts, to carry out urgent repairs outside their normal turns. Whatever routines governed the reliefs, there is no doubt that the emperor was in charge.[5]

Saxony, above all again East Saxony and the marches, furnish evidence for a fiscal system. Admittedly it is fragmentary like all

1. Thietmar, iv. 38, pp. 174–7.
2. Thietmar, vi. 55, p. 342; vi. 79, p. 368; vii. 23, p. 426; vii. 25, p. 428; vii. 53, p. 464.
3. Thietmar, iv. 5, p. 136; v. 9, p. 230. For the Slav settlers see *ibid.* and vi. 55, p. 342, vii. 23, p. 424. For the royal *satellites* whose presence made it impossible for Margrave Gunzelin to hand over Meissen to Boleslas Chrobry in 1003 see v. 36, p. 260.
4. Thietmar, vi. 54, 55, p. 342.
5. Thietmar, vii. 23, p. 424 f.

other evidence for administrative and governmental procedures and this because of the very nature of the diploma. We hear of *census*, tribute, *mal*, *malhure* and *osterstuofa* only when they have been or are on the point of being granted away though, fortunately, the contexts sometimes also tell us what the kings kept. What levies and dues then could the Ottonian rulers command besides the produce and yields of their patrimonies and the royal demesne of which however tenths and *nonae* were often given to favoured churches and apart from the episcopal and abbatial *servitia*? It is by no means easy or indeed always possible to distinguish 'seignorial' from 'public' dues. In most of their *regna* north of the Alps the Liudolfings seem to have possessed vested rights over widely scattered exactions going back to the Carolingian fisc. In East *Francia* the bishops of Würzburg in 923 and 992 sought confirmations for the grant of a tenth out of the tribute which a number of *pagi* and Slav populations used to pay to the *fiscus dominicus*. Whether they still did is another question. The relevant diplomata, including that of King Arnulf of 889, all employed the past tense. Honey and coats had made up this tax, called *stiora* or *osterstuofa*. That the bishops wanted their rights to be confirmed by Henry I and Otto III suggests that vestiges of these royal *tributa* may have survived but tenths from the produce of a large number of royal vills were also at stake. Bishops clung to the privileges of their sees whatever the odds.[1]

In Suabia it was the abbot of Reichenau who presented Otto I and his grandson with ancient Carolingian grants of tribute for confirmation. Under these the monastery had a share of the dues payable to the king from certain Suabian *pagi*, notably the Breisgau, as well as the ninth part from the royal fisc at Sasbach.[2] Here too demesne- and other types of revenue appear side by side. The agents of the abbey, it was laid down, should take away its portion before the bulk of the *census* and tribute was divided between the king and his counts. Counts thus had their share, probably the lion's share, of these exactions. It was part of their *beneficium* and in this way the kings added something vital to their position which in so many areas seems to subsist and grow of its own accord. Sometimes, indeed, the language of the diplomata unequivocally presses home the regal character of comital revenues. When in 951 Otto I, after ostentatiously consulting his son, Duke Liudolf, gave to Bishop Hartbert of Chur the entire

---

1. *DH I*, 6 of 923, MGH, *Diplomatum . . . Tomi II. Pars Posterior. Ottonis III. Diplomata* (Hanover, 1893), 110 of 992 (henceforth cited *DO III*), MGH, *Diplomata Regum Germaniae ex stirpe Karolinorum*, III *Arnolfi Diplomata*, ed. P. Kehr (Berlin, 1940), 69 of 889 and K. Bosl, *Franken um 800* (Munich, 1959), pp. 25 f., 32. On *osterstuofa* see M. Gockel, *Karolingische Königshöfe am Mittelrhein*, *Veröffentlichungen des Max-Planck-Instituts für Geschichte*, xxxi (Göttingen, 1970), pp. 96–98, 102.

2. *DO I*, 277 of 21 Feb. 965, tampered with but accepted as a precept by Otto III's chancery in 990. See *DO III*, 61. T. L. Zotz, *Der Breisgau und das alemannische Herzogtum*, *Vorträge und Forschungen Sonderband*, 15. Herausgegeben vom Konstanzer Arbeitskreis für mittelalterliche Geschichte (Sigmaringen, 1974), p. 146 f.

proceeds of the *comitatus* of Chur, the context stated that they had hitherto belonged to the royal chamber and power.[1] We do not know the reality behind such assertions of principle. In tenth-century Suabia dukes not only deputized for the king but also enjoyed many of his rights.[2] The real loser may have been Liudolf.

In Saxony we find rather more *census* and exactions of all kinds than elsewhere. It is possible to account for this not only as a function of the permanent state of war along the eastern frontiers and the brisk trade in slaves and booty which it nourished. Under the terms which the Saxon nobles were deemed to have gained from the Franks after three decades of fighting, they had to become christians, pay tithes but not tribute.[3] So at least their historical traditions and consciousness explained to them their place in the Frankish *Reich*. Yet for those who were not noble, the *liberi, frilingi* and *liti*, the introduction of the comital constitution had inevitably imposed new burdens and they lay behind much of the social tension in ninth-century Saxony, culminating in a peasants revolt, the Stellinga rising of 841/42. As native kings the Ottonians were more aware of and stood more closely behind these burdens in their stemland than elsewhere. There is not much evidence that they lessened them though their rule brought other compensations.[4] Quite early in Otto I's reign Quedlinburg was endowed with a tenth of garments payable in two royal fortresses.[5] Above all we encounter *census*, sometimes called *mal* or *malhure* owed by free men or *malman*, not only in kind but also in money. Their incidence lay widely scattered across Saxony: at Schieder (near Detmold), Enger (near Herford), Geseke (diocese of Paderborn), Möllenbeck (diocese of Minden), Medenheim (near Northeim), Rinchhurst and Buxtehude (near Hamburg).[6] Some of these payments were modest, an ox or two every year, and others very substantial, for instance the five hundred rams which the free men of the Ambergau had to render annually at the royal *curtis* of Dahlum.

1. *DO I*, 139, 15 Oct. and H. Maurer, *Der Herzog von Schwaben*, p. 156 f.
2. *op. cit.* pp. 136 ff., 302 ff.
3. K. Leyser, *Rule and Conflict*, pp. 5–7.
4. Henry II, at his first coming in 1002, released the Thuringians from an ancient *census* of pigs. See Thietmar, v. 14, p. 236.
5. *DO I*, 18 of 20 Dec. 937.
6. For Schieder and Enger see *DO III*, 245 of 997, *DH II*, 100 of 1005 and *DH II*, 210 of 1009 (unexecuted). For Geseke see *DO I*, 196 of 958 (*malhure*) and *DO I*, 113 (*tributum et hurie*) at a place not far from the nummery. For Möllenbeck see *DO II*, 189 of 979 and *DH II*, 42 of 1003, for Medenheim, *DO II*, 274 of 982. For Rinchhurst and Buxtehude see *DO I*, 205 of 959: 'censum quod Saxonice mal vocatur.' For *malman* and their status the diplomata granted to the see of Minden, *DO I*, 227 of 961, *DH II*, 189 of 1009, *MGH, Conradi II. Diplomata*, ed. H. Bresslau (Hanover, Leipzig, 1909), no. 165 of 1031 (henceforth cited *DK II*) and *Heinrici III. Diplomata*, ed. H. Bresslau and P. Kehr (Berlin, 1926 and 1931), no. 2 of 1039 (henceforth cited *DH III*) must be compered with Conrad II's diploma for Abdinghof of 1032 (*DK II*, 176) and its paraphrase in the *Vita Meinwerci*, c. 214, p. 126 where they are called 'liberi homines'. See also *DH III*, 269 of 1051. Some of the literature is cited and discussed briefly by H. Bannasch, *Das Bistum Paderborn*, p. 27, n. 94.

It had been granted by Otto III to Bishop Bernward of Hildesheim in 1001 but was taken away from him again by Henry II, perhaps because Bernward had honoured and favoured Henry's Saxon rival for the kingship, Margrave Ekkehard of Meissen. In 1009 Gandersheim received Dahlum and the five hundred rams as part of an exchange transaction.[1]

The chance survivals of these *census* grants make it difficult to answer the question whether they still were, if they had ever been, part of a coherent whole, a system.[2] We do not know how dues of this kind were collected and used by the Ottonian kings, how local agents, *exactores*, arranged matters with the travelling court. Most likely the rams helped to swell the servitia needed for the maintenance of a huge royal following. According to a twelfth-century source Otto I had for his table a thousand pigs and sheep every day.[3] The itinerant king could pick up payments in money and in kind on his way at one of his many Saxon *palatia* but some of the regions where we find *census* were rarely, if ever, visited. There the counts probably enjoyed the bulk of such revenues unless they were replaced by a favoured churchman.

More important than scattered *census* must have been the tolls. Here again alienations and exemptions were frequent and lavish but quittances had their limits. Even privileged grantees, like the merchants of Magdeburg, had to pay duties at certain places: Mainz, Cologne, Bardowick and, not least of all, Tiel on the Waal, the exit and entry port for the journey to England.[4] Of these the tolls of Mainz and Cologne had come into the possession of their respective archbishops although the diplomatic evidence for this is surprisingly meagre.[5] Bardowick and Tiel, however were royal toll stations. At Bardowick, lying so close to the centres of Billung lordship, it is likely that the dukes were allowed a share of the profits but Otto I disposed over them and the mint as his grant to St Michael, Lüneburg,

---

1. *DO III*, 390, *DH II*, 206.
2. A formidable body of scholarly opinion associated the payment of *census* with Frankish state-colonisation and the dues owed by 'royal liberi', royal freemen (*Königsfreie*), *e.g.* H. Dannenbauer, 'Freigrafschaften und Freigerichte', in his *Grundlagen der Mittelalterlichen Welt* (Stuttgart, 1958), pp. 318 ff. For a critical discussion see H. K. Schulze, 'Rodungsfreiheit und Königsfreiheit. Zur Genesis und Kritik neuerer verfassungsgeschichtlicher Theorien', *Historische Zeitschrift*, ccxix (1974).
3. *Annalista Saxo*, MGH, SS, vi, p. 622. The author had a written source: 'sicut scriptum invenitur', *cf. supra*, p.76, n. 2.
4. *DO II*, 112 of 975 and *DO II*, 140 of 976. The Magdeburg merchants and their servants staying at Tiel were subject to 'iudiciaria severitas' there. See also Conrad II's diploma of 1025, *DK II*, 18. For the important royal mint at Tiel see G. Hatz, 'Tieler Denare des 11. Jahrhunderts in den schwedischen Münzfunden', *Commentationes de nummis saeculorum IX–XI in Suecia repertis*, ii (1968), pp. 97–190.
5. *DO II*, 95 of 975 for Mainz. For Cologne see F. W. Oediger, *Die Regesten der Erzbischöfe von Köln im Mittelalter, I 313–1099, Publikationen der Gesellschaft für Rheinische Geschichtskunde*, xxi (Bonn, 1954–61), nos. 527 (of 979), 827 (a papal privilege of 1052).

in 965 shows.[1] At Tiel there was a royal *curtis* which belonged to the Empress Theophanu's dower. Twice at least the emperors themselves, Otto II in 977 and Henry II in 1005, can be shown to have stayed at the place, a sure sign of its importance.[2] Sizeable revenues must have flowed into the coffers of the Ottonians from this source nor can it have been unduly difficult to transport the yields. Some of the more lucrative customs dues in and about Magdeburg and along the Elbe to the south of it helped to endow the future archbishopric and the see of Meissen but what remained in Ottonian hands was substantial. Very little is known about the management of royal toll stations. We no longer hear of *missi* in charge of them as in Charlemagne's Thionville Capitulary of 806.[3]

More valuable still and crucial for Ottonian military society in East Saxony were the tenths and tributes paid by the Slavonic peoples of the East-Elbian and Sorbian *pagi*. We know of them thanks to a group of much less isolated diplomata which record the enormous annual flow of revenues in silver and in kind wrung from the Slav tribes. Thietmar looking back in the early eleventh century, described in a memorably terse phrase how Henry I, having built Meissen, used it to subject the Milzeni on the eastern bank of the Elbe and forced them to pay *census*.[4] Widukind spoke of the *tributa* which during the crisis of 940 were being withheld thus threatening the vital nerve of the Saxon military establishment.[5] Grants of tenths on sales in newly gained Slav regions, like the country of the Hevelli, begin with the very foundation of St Maurice, Magdeburg.[6] In 961, three months after the gift of the *decimae* due from the Slavs and Germans in various frontier burgwards – we have already cited it – Otto gave to his favourite monastery a secular tenth from all *census* and sales taxes levied in Lusatia, Selpoli and another Slav region whether they were held by the king, the counts or anyone else under royal sanction.[7] Lusatia can only have been lightly occupied at this time for in 963 Margrave Gero had to wage a savage campaign to overpower it and reduce it 'to the last degree of servitude' as Widukind wrote.[8] These secular tenths were often used to endow new foundations and must not be confused with tithes which the same diploma conferred

1. *DO I*, 309.
2. It did not lie on the usual itinerary. See *DO II*, 146 of 977 and *Annales Hildesheimenses*, 1005, ed. G. Waitz, *SRG* (Hanover, 1878 and reprint, 1947) p. 29 for Henry II's stay over Lent. For Theophanu's dower see *DO II*, 21 of 972. Otto III granted the *curtis* to St Mary's, Aachen. See *DO III*, 258 of 997 and *DO III*, 347 of 1000.
3. *MGH, Capitularia Regum Francorum*, ed. A. Boretius and V. Krause (Hanover, 1883–97), i, p. 123.
4. Thietmar, i. 16, p. 22.
5. Widukind, ii. 30, p. 91 f. and Leyser, *Rule and Conflict*, p. 32.
6. *DO I*, 14 of 937.
7. Cf. *supra*, p. 83, n. 4 and *DO I*, 231 of 961, 29 July.
8. Widukind, iii. 67, p. 141 f. and R. Köpke and E. Dümmler, *Kaiser Otto der Grosse, Jahrbücher der Deutschen Geschichte* (Leipzig, 1876), p. 384 f.

lavishly in seven *pagi* with named fortresses 'from all the fruits and profits (*utilitates*) on which Christians give tithes and they shall pay when by the grace of God they have become Christians'.[1] In 965 Magdeburg received the whole *census* of honey which the Slavs of the *pagus* Neletici had to pay and the 'entire tenth' of honey due from six further Slav *pagi* and seven named fortresses regardless of whether the king was holding in demesne or had granted the honey to someone in *beneficium*.[2] A little earlier Otto I, in another diploma, gave to St Maurice an even more valuable gift, namely the tenth part of the *census* in silver 'which is paid by the Slav nations subject to us into the public fisc of our majesty'. The Slav tribes were duly named: the Ucri, Riezani, Riedere, Tolensane and Circipani and the gift was to be used for lights and incense.[3] Margrave Gero had crushed the Ucri in 954.[4] Once again the tenth was to be paid out of whatever the emperor held himself and what he had granted *in beneficium* to his *fideles*.

Another such grant which throws a little more light on the incidence and handling of tribute, was made by Otto I to Bishop Folcold of Meissen in 971 while the emperor stayed in Ravenna. Otto II and the Empress Adelheid were mentioned as sponsors. Here the tenth part of the tribute from five provinces (large *pagi*), Dalaminze, Nisane, Diedesa, the Milzener Land and Lusatia, was given to the bishopric. The count must pay it before he took away and distributed the share 'which we have allowed him'. The tribute of these Sorbian and trans-Elbian peoples consisted of honey, furs, silver, slaves, garments, pigs, wheat and sales taxes. Their whole economy was being ransacked. Otto II's consent to this valuable gift appears in an unusual, clumsy clause in which he speaks in the first person.[5]

The Ottonians employed these huge flows of rents, chattels, slaves and food in the first place not to endow churches but to maintain their troops on a war footing in the burgwards of the newly gained lands beyond the Elbe–Saale line. In all the diplomata we have discussed there are references to portions of *census* being held in

1. Cited by G. Constable, *Monastic Tithes from their Origins to the Twelfth Century*, (Cambridge, 1964), p. 71.

2. *DO I*, 303 of 965, 28 July. The wording suggests that the entire *census* was granted and holders of portions *in beneficium* either lost their shares or had to hold them of St Maurice in future. The gift was confirmed by Otto II, less than a month after Otto I's death. See *DO II*, 30 of 973, 5 June.

3. *DO I*, 295 of 965, 27 June. This gift was confirmed twice by Otto II, a clear sign of its importance. See *DO II*, 31 of 973 and *DO II*, 118 of 975. The tribes were settled in Mecklenburg and Northern Brandenburg.

4. Widukind, iii. 42, 54, pp. 122, 134.

5. *DO I*, 406 of 971 and see W. Schlesinger, *Kirchengeschichte Sachsens im Mittelalter*, i, p. 41, *Mitteldeutsche Forschungen*, 27/I (Cologne, Graz, 1962). He took the view that the diploma was completed only in Otto II's reign. The grant could not take effect in all the areas named. See also W. Schlesinger and H. Beumann, 'Urkundenstudien zur deutschen Ostpolitik unter Otto III', in W. Schlesinger, *Mitteldeutsche Beiträge zur deutschen Verfassungsgeschichte des Mittelalters* (Göttingen, 1961), pp. 309 ff.

beneficium by counts and others who in turn divided and sub-allocated shares to the men under their command. The amounts were large enough to feed and reward warriors and so keep them in garrisons for years on end rather than allow them to disperse into landed holdings. For the early decades of the Saxon invasions and occupation of Slav territory this was essential and here, just as in Anglo-Norman England, the *beneficium* in land for *milites* was of much slower growth. Only in this way could the burgwards be secured permanently and Saxon lordship driven home. Hundreds of warriors were thus established and depended on royal *census* and *adquisitio*. Here lay a reservoir of power for the Ottonian rulers which they could and did control closely.

This does not exhaust the tide of tribute for besides the conquered peoples there were the new clients of the Saxon kings, the dukes of Bohemia and for a time also those of Poland, at any rate Miesco I (†992) who punctually paid for the lands he held beyond the river Warthe. In 991 Archbishop Giselher of Magdeburg secured a gift to himself and to his church from Otto III, still under age and more likely therefore his mother, the Empress Theophanu. Giselher was to have a third of the *census* 'which should be paid to our royal fisc from the whole of Bohemia every year in whatever form it may be, in gold, in silver, in cattle or other things, great and small'. As two thirds were gathered on the king's behalf so the archbishop and his successors should receive his third in all these commodities.[1] Tribute from Bohemia seems to have been paid to the Ottonians ever since 929 though scarcely without some interruptions.[2] Cosmas of Prague's figure for the annual render, 120 head of cattle and 500 mark is not out of keeping with the terms of Otto III's grant. Unfortunately his diploma does not tell us how it was transported and stored, whether it came by river or by land. Magdeburg, Meissen and Merseburg were obvious centres for delivery yet we know that other royal *palatia* in Saxony also contained treasures.[3]

With the collapse of the Saxon bastions in the great North-West Slavonic rising of 983 when the Wilzi, the Hevelli and the Obotrites, to name only the principals, burnt and destroyed most of the Ottonian strongholds east and north-east of Magdeburg, many of the tribal tributes came to an end. Boleslas Chrobry's devastating campaigns and conquests round Meissen had the same result in Henry II's reign. Yet there were massive compensations for these losses, for in the

---

1. *DO III*, 71. See W. Wegener, *Böhmen, Mähren und das Reich im Hochmittelalter* (Cologne, Graz, 1959), pp. 49 ff. For Miesco see Leyser, *Rule and Conflict*, pp. 25, 44.
2. Widukind, i. 35, p. 50 f. Between 936 and 950 Duke Boleslas I defied Otto I. There were breaks also during Otto II's and early in Henry II's reign.
3. *Chronica Boemorum*, ii. 8, p. 94. For treasures in other royal residences see the *Annales Altahenses Maiores*, ed. E. L. B. v. Oefele, *SRG* (Hanover, 1891), p. 11 and *Annales Hildesheimenses*, p. 23. In 971 Dornburg went up in flames 'cum omni regali thesauro'.

meantime even more valuable assets had been discovered and developed in the Old-Saxon regions, the silver deposits in the Harz Mountains by Goslar.[1] Exploitation which had begun under Otto I, seems to have grown in volume rapidly towards the end of the tenth century as the huge numbers of surviving coins, especially the Otto and Adelheid pennies, testify.[2] With so much silver available in the Liudolfing *patria* it is not surprising that the Ottonians issued a considerable number of minting privileges in Saxony usually coupled with new market rights as well. Otto I granted six of them: at Meppen (for Corvey), Wiedenbrück (Osnabrück), Magdeburg, Bremen, Gittelde and Odenhausen (Herford).[3] Before this, in Carolingian Saxony, only the sees of Osnabrück and Bremen and the abbeys of Corvey and Herford had enjoyed minting rights. Now Corvey, Osnabrück and Bremen received a second mint each and Magdeburg too, the second one being at Gittelde. We possess three new Saxon minting grants for Otto II's reign and – this is significant for the swift development of the mines – no less than eight for Otto III's.[4] The greater number of these, it is true, fell into the period of his minority when such favours may have been more easily come by for those with the right connections but these privileges all the same reflect a widely felt need for more minting facilities. There were also confirmations of existing rights which may have been lucrative for the king, his entourage and chancery.

Once again we know very little about the operation of the mines and the organization of the royal mints.[5] Yet two conclusions stand out. The Ottonians had come a long way from their financial beginnings when their treasure was a hoard which they treated as kings had done time out of mind before them, as a means to govern. When Henry I died he divided his lands and riches among his sons of whom Otto, and Otto alone, had already been chosen for the kingship. When he in turn set up his son Liudolf in Suabia and his son-in-law Conrad in Lotharingia as dukes in 949 and 945, he gave them treasures of gold and silver so that they could use them as a political capital to reward their men and increase them for the sake of future largesse and as a visible sign of success. We know this from the bitter com-

1. W. Hillebrand, 'Von den Anfängen des Erzbergbaus am Rammelsberg bei Goslar', *Niedersächsisches Jahrbuch für Landesgeschichte*, xxxix (1967), pp. 103–14.

2. G. Hatz, *Handel und Verkehr zwischen dem Deutschen Reich und Schweden in der späten Wikingerzeit. Die deutschen Münzen des 10. und 11. Jahrhunderts in Schweden* (Lund, 1974), pp. 38 ff., 41–47.

3. V. Jammer, *Die Anfänge der Münzprägung im Herzogtum Sachsen. (10. und 11. Jahrhundert)*, *Numismatische Studien*, 3/4, ed. W. Hävernick (Hamburg, 1952), p. 28. at Odenhausen (*DO I*, 430 of 973) a Carolingian grant was revived.

4. Jammer, *op. cit*, but she overlooked *DO III*, 142 of 994 for Memleben which must be added to Otto III's new grants.

5. E. Kraume, 'Münzprägung und Silbererz-Bergbau in Mitteleuropa um die Jahrtausendwende (950–1050) unter besonderer Berücksichtigung des Herzogtums Sachsen', *Der Anschnitt*, 13, 4 (1961) was not available to me.

plaints Widukind had Otto voice at the assembly of Langenzenn in June 954 when a further attempt was made to restore peace between the warring members of the Liudolfing house. Otto accused his son and Conrad of having given part of these treasures to the Magyars so that they, the enemies of Christ, went home loaded with them. The charges seem to have been true and the Hungarians had also been given *servitia* as a host at Worms just as the king was on his journeys round the *Reich*.[1]

It can also be said that the enormous wealth of the Ottonians gave their regime staying power regardless of the adventures and setbacks of the younger generation, Otto II and Otto III. Neither was ever short of an imposing Saxon and wider following. Their lavishness, especially Otto II's, was notorious.[2] The young emperor, the last one ever to be crowned by a pope in his father's lifetime, had never known the difficult and often desperately critical times which his forbears had to survive. There is no evidence of any kind of central accountancy in the later tenth century. Treasures were the business of *camerarii* and so it is perhaps significant that we hear a little more about these officials in the entourages of Otto III and Henry II than we do before. Five of Otto III's chamberlains are known to us by name. One of them, Count Tammo, was the brother of Bishop Bernward of Hildesheim and accompanied the emperor on his secret journey to Venice in April 1001. He also appears as *discoforus* (steward) and later in the year guarded the castle of Paterno for the emperor.[3] Of the others at least three seem to have been Saxons too, for they were rewarded with lands lying east of Magdeburg across the Elbe, in eastern Thuringia near Naumburg and near the Eilenburg by the river Mulde.[4] Chamberlains collected the annual *census* owed by Venice to the *Reich* of which Otto remitted a part but kept fifty pounds.[5] More striking still is the very high position which the *camerarius* Frederick held under Henry II. His *obit* in the Quedlinburg Annals is unfortunately mutilated. Of high birth, we are told, he stood foremost among the *primates*

---

1. Widukind, iii. 32, p. 119: 'Auro meo et argento, quibus filium generumque ditavi, hostes Christi sedes suas remeunt referti'. For the Hungarians at Worms see iii. 30, p. 118.

2. Thietmar, viii. 20, p. 516: 'Secundi Ottonis larga benignitas cunctis pleniter arridens' and *Gesta Archiepiscoporum Magdeburgensium*, c. 12, *MGH, SS*, xiv, p. 385: 'Sublevabat modo nobilium modo ignobilium inopias, extollebat tam prediis quam honoribus circumquaque Christi ecclesias.'

3. *Iohannis Diaconi Chronicon Venetum et Gradense*, *MGH, SS*, vii, p. 33: 'Rainardus, Tamo, camerarii' and also *DO III*, 393 of 1001, 18 March, *DO III*, 403 of 1001, 12 May. on Tammo at Paterno see *Vita Bernwardi*, c. 35, *MGH, SS*, iv, p. 774.

4. *DO III*, 113 of 993 for Ermenold. On him see also Thietmar, v. 6, p. 226. *DO III*, 172 of 995 for Tiezo and *DO III*, 346 of 1000 for Reginher. The Rainardus (*cf. supra* n. 3) may be identical with him. For Otto III's 'imperialis minister et sibi dilectus cubicularius', Wolpharius, see Iohannis Canaparius, *Vita S. Adalberti Episcopi*, c. 23, *MGH, SS*, iv, p. 592. On royal household offices in general see P. Schubert, 'Die Reichshofämter und ihre Inhaber bis um die Wende des 12. Jahrhunderts', *MIÖG*, xxxiv (1913), pp. 427–501.

5. *DO III*, 397 of 1001.

familiares and this is to some extent borne out by his sign on Henry II's *pactum* for Pope Benedict VIII (1020). It appears behind those of the prelates and lay princes but before those of the other household officers and lay nobles. In 1018 Frederick conducted the peace negotiations with Boleslas Chrobry on Henry's behalf at Bautzen. When he died in 1023 the emperor spent much for the salvation of his soul. Frederick may have nursed a design to disinherit the sons of clerks for the benefit of the fisc.[1] There are other indications, albeit faint ones, that Henry II, brought up as he was in a cathedral close, entertained more ambitious administrative plans. For a time at least all the royal lands in Saxony were placed under Archbishop Giselher of Magdeburg, perhaps to survey them. When Giselher died in 1004, Henry came to Giebichenstein, the Magdeburg castle, and inspected his accumulated treasures as if he had it in mind to appropriate them as *spolia*.[2]

The Giebichenstein is of interest for another reason. It served Henry II and later also Conrad II and Henry III as a state prison. Already Otto II had carried off the garrisons of his enemies, Reginar of Hainault and Lantbert, to Saxony in 974. In 1004 Count Henry of Schweinfurt, a defeated rebel, was detained at the Giebichenstein during the king's pleasure.[3] In 1014 one of four Italian enemies from the Este family was brought there and held for several years. Duke Ernst of Suabia paid for his rebellion with detention at the archbishop's castle in 1027. Guarding important prisoners became yet another of the many forms which the *servitium regis* of prelates might take.[4]

After all this we must not be surprised that the Liudolfings' itinerary pivoted so heavily on Saxony and it may be suggested that this was so not only because of the surpluses which their lands yielded there, the rich ecclesiastical *servitia* and choice of palaces at their disposal but even more the enormous revenues, the patronage and more extensive and far-reaching royal rights that they could wield there.

1. On Frederick see the *Annales Quedlinburgenses*, 1023, *MGH, SS*, iii, p. 88 f., Thietmar, viii. 1, p. 492 and *DH II*, 427 of 1020. For Frederick's plans against clerks and their offspring see *Die Ältere Wormser Briefsammlung*, ed. W. Bulst, *MGH, Die Briefe der Deutschen Kaiserzeit*, iii (Weimar, 1949), no. 58 but Bulst's identification of 'Fridericus quidam Vultdensis' with Henry II's chamberlain must remain somewhat doubtful and if Frederick was indeed prominent among the king's *familiares* the writers of the letter would have been singularly inept. On another chamberlain of Henry II's see *DH II*, 232 of 1011.
2. Thietmar, v. 44, p. 270: 'Inde rex . . . ad castellum . . . nomine Givikansten pergens, omnia quae ibidem ab Gisilero antistite collecta sunt, singulariter perspicit et haec esse superflua testatur.' On the royal lands committed to Giselher's supervision see Thietmar, v. 39, p. 264 f.
3. Leyser, *Rule and Conflict*, p. 95.
4. Thietmar, vii. 1, p. 398, viii. 1, p. 492. For Duke Ernst see H. Bresslau, *Jahrbücher des Deutschen Reichs unter Konrad II* (Berlin, 1879 and reprint, 1967), i, p. 219 and n. 4. In 1009 Bishop Arnulf of Halberstadt became the jailer of the deposed Margrave Gunzelin. Thietmar, vi, 54, p. 342.

Not for nothing did Henry II call Saxony the hall of paradise, a haven of safety and all abundance.[1] The Salians too, after all, did not resist this magnetic field. The great Saxon aristocratic rising of 1073 in the last resort only wanted to reduce the massive and very down-to-earth exercise of royal power, stepped up still further by Henry III and Henry IV, to the measure of what was normal elsewhere, *i.e.* the level of ordinary itinerant kingship. The East-Saxon aristocracy wished to be governed as much or as little as were the rest of their kind in *Francia*, Bavaria, Suabia and Lotharingia. This is the meaning of the demand voiced again and again by the Saxon lords that Henry should not reside in Saxony so long and so often.

This takes us to the most essential and carefully administered institution of the Ottonian and Salian *Reich*: the royal *iter*, the kings' migrations round their *regna*. It was the primary and most characteristic feature of their Government and so it was felt to be by contemporaries. Thietmar of Merseburg once remarked how could he remember all the movements of the Emperor Otto III through his bishoprics and *comitatus*? Itinerant kingship is a type of rule which must be contrasted with domination based on a fixed residence, a staff of officials, correspondence and regular supervision of subordinate provincial powers. When the Ottonians entered into diplomatic relations with Byzantium and Cordoba, they could begin to learn something about this antithesis to their own governance: *i.e.* power exercised from a great palace standing in and sustained by a capital city, a rich and money-based economy. The purest embodiment of a palace-centred autocracy with a huge establishment of slave guards, servants, eunuchs, fiscal officials, secretaries and spies was the Caliphate of Cordoba. We have already mentioned John of Gorze's mission there described in the *Vita Iohannis*. Here Abder-rhaman III appears as an unapproachable ruler surrounded by secrecy and intimate servants, his khassa, but between him and his nobles there was none of the *familiaritas*, the close bonds of a king and his following which in the *Reich* counted almost as an institution. The Ottonians had no wish to imitate the court of Cordoba and, with the shortlived exception of Otto III, their reception of byzantine court culture was limited. It lay largely in the spheres of representation, of imagery and styles in the visual arts.[2]

To understand the Ottos' and Henry II's itinerant kingship we must first of all realize that they had a near-monopoly of long distance communications, they, their empresses and other members of the royal kin, for instance the great dowagers, like Queen Mathilda and the Empress Adelheid, Otto III's grandmother. From her we have a

---

1. Thietmar, vi. 10, p. 286.
2. O. Demus, *Byzantine Art and the West* (London, 1970), pp. 79 ff. and K. Leyser, 'The Tenth Century in Byzantine–Western Relationships', *Relations between East and West in the Middle Ages*, ed. D. Baker (Edinburgh, 1973), pp. 42 ff. Here, *infra*, pp. 116 ff.

letter to show how these journeys were arranged. It was sent from Augsburg to a Würzburg clerk, perhaps the *vicedominus* in 994 or 995 announcing her arrival on 13 August, expecting quarters and sustenance for herself, her company, her horses and her waggoners.[1] The Ottonians and they alone and whoever belonged to their following, could move freely from *palatium* to *palatium*, royal *curtis* to royal *curtis*, bishop's city to bishop's city, also episcopal manors and be reasonably sure that at the end of a hard day's ride anywhere from Magdeburg to Rome, they would have a place to lay their heads and something to eat for men and horses. Their servants, emissaries and countless messengers also had these facilities and could exact hospitality. Dukes, margraves, counts, bishops and abbots had no means of moving freely, that is without heavy expense beyond the areas of their competence. There was now no *cursus publicus*. The monopoly the Ottonians enjoyed and the facilities they might grant as a favour are well illustrated by an incident in the *Life of St Ulrich* of Augsburg. After a last pilgrimage to Rome the aged bishop visited Otto I and Adelheid at Ravenna on his way home in 971. When they parted the emperor gave him many pounds of gold, Italian treasure, and also thoughtfully arranged his lodgings and the necessary *servitia* for him with his *fideles* and this at least throughout the Romagna.[2] Exactly the same was done for Bishop Bernward of Hildesheim when he took leave of the young Otto III for the last time near Rome on 20 February 1001. The emperor sent some of his men with the bishop and his train. They were to conduct him northwards and this ensured splendid receptions and hospitality for him in Lombardy on the way home. It did not prevent Bernward returning to Saxony with a gastric affliction of the kind travellers bring back occasionally from the south even now.[3] Conversely it is worth remembering Gregory VII's predicament in 1077 when he wanted to travel to Germany and the princes who had invited him and on whom he relied, were in no position to secure his *susceptio* and *servitium* in Lombardy to which they had no rights themselves. Only Henry IV could make these available and he did not want to. The fiasco at Canossa was the pope's if looked at from that point of view. Henry by appearing outside the castle as a penitent thus got him off the hook.

Given their monopoly, the kings themselves were therefore the principal binding agents and communications between the various *gentes* and *regna* under their lordship. By their journeys they gave to the *Reich* the best cohesion possible. Their sacrality was displayed in

1. *Die Tegernseer Briefsammlung (Froumund)*, ed. K. Strecker, *MGH, Epistolae Selectae*, iii (Berlin, 1925, reprint 1964), p. 16. The collection is described by H. Glaser in *Handbuch der bayerischen Geschichte*, i, ed. M. Spindler (Munich, 1968), pp. 451 ff.
2. *Vita S. Oudalrici*, c. 21, *MGH, SS*, iv, p. 407.
3. *Vita Bernwardi*, c. 27, *op. cit.* p. 770 f. and *cf.* c. 19, p. 767. While Bernward stayed at Rome Otto III would not let him spend any of his own but had everything needful lavishly furnished to the bishop and his following and this for six weeks.

ever-repeated solemn entries, festival coronations and crown-wearings and it had thus an indispensable role to play. It was a substitute for the bureaucracy Waitz found so painfully wanting. We would be wrong to regard all this as archaic, primitive and even backward. Ottonian itinerant kingship in the tenth century was no stagnating institution. On the contrary it developed and greatly enhanced its functions. The settings of the emperors' stays were quite consciously built up so that the representation of the royal office could become more complex and magnificent. There had risen by the end of the tenth century a cluster of fine *palatia* and cathedral churches, with halls, lodgings and workshops which have in many cases been probed archaeologically with impressive results, especially at Magdeburg. Here Otto I not only built his *Dom* but also a palace with quite exceptional and imposing features.[1] Huge complexes of demesne, labour services and the flow of tribute, including silver, which we have already discussed, lay behind these ambitious elevations just as Charlemagne's great palace and minster at Aachen are unthinkable without the reserves of royal land, the labour services and the Avar treasure.

The material base of the royal *iter*, the *servitia* of the Ottonian lands and fiscs and then, increasingly under Henry II, the bishoprics and, less often, royal abbeys enabled the Ottonians to move along a network of routes, radiating from Saxony with their large following of at least some hundreds which could easily swell into an army to turn peaceful into belligerent itineration. In order to rule the kings had to appear in person, gather the princes of the *patriae* about them, dispense justice, make peace between enemies, reward and punish. Writers like Bishop Adalbold of Utrecht, before his promotion a chaplain of Henry II and also his biographer, and Constantine of St Symphorion to whom we owe a *Life of Bishop Adalbero II of Metz*, dwelt on the elementary necessity of royal visits to the various *regna* which made up the *Reich*. If they did not happen from time to time, then even nobles could not protect themselves against robbery and devastations.[2] At Benedictbeuren in Bavaria two counts, 'false defenders', seized what was left of the monastery's estates after the confiscations of Duke Arnulf and gave it to their vassals 'because the emperor (Otto I) was absent and entangled in expeditions'.[3] We are listening to an eleventh-century tradition but its message echoed a not uncommon experience.

All the same the royal *iter* is not the whole story of Ottonian government, even outside Saxony. A travelling king meant that those who

1. *Rule and Conflict*, p. 90, n. 41.
2. *op. cit.* p. 103.
3. *Chronicon Benedictoburanum*, *MGH*, *SS*, ix, pp. 218, 233 and see also W. Störmer, *Früher Adel Studien zur Politischen Führungsschicht im Fränkisch-Deutschen Reich vom 8. bis 11. Jahrhundert*, *Monographien zur Geschichte des Mittelalters*, 6, ii, ed. K. Bosl (Stuttgart, 1973), p. 452.

had business to transact or favours to seek must first find him and follow his *iter*. For our theme the many journeys which petitioners, men seeking some favour or planning an intrigue, had to make to a distant court, are as important as the royal migrations and so are their messengers and letters. The *Vitae* of bishops and the histories of their sees and of abbeys are full of this traffic. It was extensive and grew. *Legati* sped between a bishopric or a monastery and the court during vacancies, often all the way to Italy.[1] Moreover the visit of the king and his intervention had to be prepared and this held good also for lay lords. The Ottonians seem to have been well-informed about lands which local courts, comital pleas, adjudged to them, that is to say the possessions of malefactors and rebels. When they re-granted such estates, their diplomata recorded the judicial forfeiture in order to strengthen the title of the donee. Messages were also carried swiftly to inform the ruler of trouble in a region of the *Reich* far away from where he happened to be staying. The news of the murder of Count Wichmann by his rival Balderich and his wife Adela of Elten on the Lower Rhine in 1016, reached Henry II in Burgundy.[2] Less startling events were reported too, for instance the expulsion of the monk Wido from Gorze when he had already been selected for the embassy to Cordoba in 953.[3]

These transmissions were not always verbal. In the not so rich letter collections of the tenth century we find chance survivals of news, complaints, requests for favours and for help though they contain nothing quite so striking as the original dispatch of Margrave Aribo of the Eastern March to King Arnulf in 891 giving him a bulletin from the Morawian frontier.[4] The tenth- and early eleventh-century pieces which concern us here, come from the collections of Rather of Verona, Gerbert and the monastery of Tegernsee. Here, for once, we find some evidence for royal commands sent to counts in writing. There is a mandate of Otto III, addressed to the Bavarian count Thiemo, threatening him with the loss of the emperor's grace if he continued to harass the abbey's lands and possessions.[5] Under Henry II the monks more than once sought the royal *jussus* against

1. *E.g.* the election of Gero to the archbishopric of Cologne in 969 had to be reported to Otto I at Pavia. See Thietmar, ii. 24, p. 68 and *cf.* the promotion of Hildiward to the see of Halberstadt, *Rule and Conflict*, p. 33. For the Magdeburg clerks and vassals sent to Otto II near Rome after the death of Archbishop Adalbert in 981, see Thietmar, iii. 13, p. 112. For the mission of a group of Alsatian hermits to Quedlinburg, see *DO I*, 199 of 959.

2. Alpert of Metz, *De Diversitate Temporum*, ii. 13, *MGH, SS*, iv, p. 715 f.

3. *Vita Iohannis Gorziensis*, c. 116, *op. cit.* p. 370.

4. H. Schwarzmaier, 'Ein Brief des Markgrafen Aribo an König Arnulf über die Verhältnisse in Mähren', *Frühmittelalterliche Studien*, vi, ed. K. Hauck (Berlin, New York, 1972), pp. 55 ff.

5. *Epistolae Selectae*, iii, no. 94, p. 99, perhaps of the year 1000. See also M. Uhlirz, *Die Regesten des Kaiserreiches unter Otto III. 980 (983)–1002*, J. F. Böhmer, *Regesta Imperii*, ii, 3 (Graz, Cologne, 1957), nos. 1342, 1343. The latter, addressed to a Count Otto, ordered the restitution of some vineyards.

their enemies and corrupt judges who might deprive the monastery of an estate by a false verdict. Their case, so the monks pleaded, should be reserved for judgment in the king's presence.[1] The letter extolls the greatness of royal power and the irresistible force of its commands. Against Count Thiemo however, who was troubling them again, the monks now wrote to invoke the help of the Duke of Bavaria, Henry V.[2] We can conclude that there were far more of these communications than have survived. The pieces in the collections made for literary purposes cannot have been exceptional and there are references enough to letters also in chronicles, Thietmar's for instance.[3]

Nonetheless the personal visit to court was a safer means to anticipate or circumvent a rival or to transact any business. The Tegernsee correspondence merely confirms this. Letters had to do when for some reason or another the writer could not travel.[4] There is a remarkable story in the *Life of St Ulrich* of Augsburg which demonstrates how dangerous it was not to seek out the emperor, however far away he might be.[5] St Ulrich, at the end of his long pontificate had at first sought to promote his own nephew to be his successor and this, as far as possible, in his own lifetime. This was the business he had called on Otto I to discuss. The scheme however miscarried and the nephew, Adalbert, died. Ulrich himself ended his days on 6 July 973. Some of the Augsburg clerks and the advocate then set off for the emperor's court bearing the late bishop's staff. When they came to Worms where Otto II had been as recently as 28 June, they found Duke Burkhard II of Suabia (954-73) and his wife, the daughter of Otto I's brother, Henry of Bavaria. Naturally the clerks revealed to the duke what their business was and so fell into a trap. For he told them that the emperor these days was far away in the remotest corner

1. *Epistolae Selectae*, iii. no. 68, p. 74 f: 'O quam magna regalis potentia! Dicit tantum: "Fiat!" et perpetratum est', and see no. 83, p. 90. For another example of invoking royal intervention to postpone a case in a comital plea see *Udalrici Codex*, no. 29 of 1065. *Monumenta Bambergensia, Bibliotheca Rerum Germanicarum*, V, ed. P. Jaffé (Berlin, 1869), p. 56 f.

2. *Epistolae Selectae*, iii. no. 76, p. 85: 'ductori'.

3. A letter secretly brought to Otto I is thought to have induced him not to promote Abbot Richar of Magdeburg to the new archbishopric. See Thietmar, ii. 22, p. 64. The emperor manifested his indignation and anger to Archbishop Adalbert, for the all too solemn reception of Hermann Billung in Magdeburg 'per epistolam' (Thietmar, ii. 28, p. 74). Adalbert sought to excuse himself 'per legatos' (*loc. cit.*). An *epistola deprecatoria* was given to Otto III by Bishop Franco of Worms on behalf of his brother Burkhard. The emperor kept it in his bag as a reminder. See *Vita Burchardi Episcopi*, c. 3, *MGH, SS*, iv, p. 834. The legate Frederick in 1001 carried papal and imperial letters addressed to the bishops and 'other princes' in Germany about the Gandersheim dispute. See *Vita Bernwardi*, c. 28, *op. cit.* p. 771.

4. *Epistolae Selectae*, iii. no. 61, p. 69 to Duke Henry, later King Henry II, and no. 88, p. 93 f. to the Luxemburg Duke Henry V: 'et modo regem non possumus adire'.

5. For what follows see Gerhard's *Vita S. Oudalrici Episcopi*, c. 28, *MGH, SS*, iv, p. 415 f. Gerhard in his narrative may have wanted to palliate the Augsburg clerks' blunder. I have translated part of the passage freely.

of his kingdom and that on the road by which they had to travel, they would find everything very dear and all the grass under defense (*i.e.* no pasture from road verges) so that they would be hard put to it to feed themselves and their horses. 'Our emperor will come quite soon and hold a royal colloquy at Erstein (in Alsace). You can reach that easily. I suggest you go home now and as soon as my reliable messenger announces to you the date of this colloquy don't hesitate to come. You'll find me there as your firm helper and I will agree to your election unequivocally.' Their candidate was a certain Werner. They believed him and returned to Augsburg. Shortly afterwards the duke's *nuntius* duly came and told them that the meeting at Erstein would be held as indicated. In the meantime however Burkhard had worked with all his push on behalf of a cousin, Henry, and it appears that Otto II knew nothing of his dealings with the Augsburg clerks. The canons were made to believe that the emperor had already decided and so driven to elect Henry as if he had been the imperial nominee. Many an episcopal election in the tenth and early eleventh century followed this pattern. In the end Otto II learned what had happened but accepted Henry, though with some reserve. He too had after all been over-reached. If you ask where he had been 'in the remotest corner of his kingdom', he was no further away than Aachen and the Lower Rhine.

Government in the tenth century was thus about communications. Horses and messengers were the most important *dramatis personae* in this struggle for communications. All these visits to court however, the *nuntii* and their messages, verbal and written, were *ad hoc*. Men visited their itinerant kings when they had to, not as a matter of routine. This only happened at *Hoftage*, the solemn *curiae* which the great men of the region attended and sometimes also those much further away or even the *primores* from the whole *Reich*. This brings us to the institution of the king's *familiaritas*, already mentioned twice.[1] Since the migrant ruler was the government and communications between him and the regions, the *patriae*, were often uncertain, slow and expensive, to have friends who were near him and had his ear, was all-important. The *familiaritas* of an emperor was a gift of God. It imposed great responsibility on those who possessed it as Abbot Bern of Reichenau reminded Archbishop Gero of Magdeburg: 'You must use the talent of the king's *familiaritas*' – the biblical expression is significant – 'on behalf of the afflicted and downcast'.[2] The king here was Henry II. Thietmar of Merseburg, in a brief biographical sketch of the Wettin count Dedi, an enemy of his own

---

1. See *supra*, pp. 75, 94.
2. F.-J. Schmale, *Die Briefe des Abtes Bern von Reichenau, Veröffentlichungen der Kommission für geschichtliche Landeskunde in Baden-Württemberg*, Reihe A Quellen, 6 (Stuttgart, 1961), no. 3, p. 21 f. and see Mathew, 25, 14 ff. The letter is dated between 1012 and 1014.

family whom Thietmar's cousin Werner killed, recorded glumly how Dedi advanced in Otto III's favour after being reconciled to him and in a short time earned his grace and *familiaritas*. He became in fact the *patricius*, known better as Ziazo and was a very dangerous opponent to have.[1]

We must now draw our conclusions. Ottonian government grew out of or subsisted on the débris of Carolingian and this, we must not forget, in the least developed portion of the Frankish Empire. It explains the fragmentary character of all the manifestations we have surveyed. One of the underlying reasons for the decline of the written word and its failure to regain ground swiftly, was the serious literary and cultural situation of post-Frankish Europe, especially Germany's in the first quarter of the tenth century. Continuity was not broken but at risk. We must distinguish clearly between the growth of a military and fiscal system in East-Saxony and the marches, the outcome of a state of permanent war, and the less intensive royal governance elsewhere. The sacral aura that attended the Saxon rulers after they had won their victories and acquired their *triumphi*, in part made up for the want of more sophisticated administrative procedures. Much government remained ceremonial and ritual. The kings themselves, by their *iter* and sacrality gave to the *Reich* its cohesion and impetus. Their very success made it unnecessary to resort to more written communications, more elaborate methods of linking the moving centre and the localities. Usually *fidelitas* sufficed. It also meant that institutions like the burgwards in the *Altland* and the Sorbian marches could be allowed to fade away again or used to reward nobles and churches. The beginnings of a more close-meshed administration existed in East-Saxony and Thuringia but they later fell into the hands of the rising territorial powers. Administrative skills were not overpraised, even by the writers of monastic reform with their flair for *censiers*, surveys and careful reckoning. In the earlier Middle Ages, however and even in the twelfth century the most ingenious and inventive regimes were by no means always the stablest.

The sheer wealth of the Ottonians whether it was the spoils of aggressive war in Sclavania and Italy or the more lasting silver mines and their lavish output from about 990 onwards, enabled them to dominate their surroundings whatever the style and complexion of their policies: the spendthrift expeditions of Otto II, the width and ardour of Otto III's conceptions and the hard-faced grasp of Henry II. They could afford their mistakes and still command an imposing following. The solidity and endurance of their *Reich* owed something to this steady flow of treasure from the Harz mines. It was like a second wind. The Carolingians had not been so fortunate. Once they had distributed their booty, once the Avar riches had come into

---

1. Thietmar, vi. 50, p. 336 f.

the hands of nobles and churches, they had no such continuing and substantial source of movable wealth produced in the very heartlands of their rule.

Note (p. 94)

There was one bastion of their lordship where the Ottonians could wield power from a palace situated in a considerable city, the capital of their Italian kingdom. At Pavia they came to possess important money revenues, services and controls administered by a *magister camerae* which made it a more than merely convenient place to stay. The institutions of the Italian kings, their predecessors, which they took over, invited use. We know that Otto I resided at Pavia frequently and sometimes for longer stretches of time than he did at most other royal *palatia*, not excluding Saxon ones. He stayed there from September 962 until Easter 963 (April 19) and again from December 969 until Spring 970. As Otto was an exceptionally restless, migrant ruler, the length of his sojourns at Pavia is remarkable. The sheer scope and the amenities of lordship available through the *instituta regalia*, as recorded in a nostalgic text of the eleventh century (c. 1027), may explain his interest and attraction. Nonetheless the services and revenues administered from the palace in Pavia depended on a local hierarchy entrenched in its offices which did not fit easily into the Ottonians chosen entourage. Their attempt to blend the two milieus or impose their own at Pavia only led to the erosion and dispersal of the resources at their disposal. For the text of the *Instituta Regalia et Ministeria Regum Longobardorum et Honorantiae Civitatis Papiae*, see ed. A. Hofmeister, *MGH. SS.* xxx, pp. 1444-1460.

5

THE TENTH CENTURY IN
BYZANTINE-WESTERN RELATIONSHIPS

Let us first of all look at the physical conditions of Byzantine links
with western Europe and especially the continental core of it,
north of the Alps. The land-route was blocked. The Magyars who
poured into the Danubian Basin and Pannonia during the last years
of the ninth century, had seen to that.[1] It was not to open again
until the first quarter of the eleventh as Rodulf Glaber described in
a famous passage of his *History*. 'At that time', when the Hungarians under their king Stephen had turned to conversion, 'nearly all
those from Italy and Gaul who wanted to visit the Lord's sepulchre
in Jerusalem abandoned the usual sea journey and travelled through
this king's country.'[2] He suggests that even the Italians preferred
the new route by land. The embassies which the emperor Basil I
had sent to the East-Frankish king, Louis the German, in 871 and
873 always met him at Regensburg and they could well have
travelled overland.[3] It was the time of the great missions to Moravia and Bulgaria and of almost uninterrupted peace between the
empire and its northern neighbours. For much of the ninth century
moreover the far-flung south-eastern marches of the East-Frankish
Carolingians and their Slav client lordships bordered upon the
Byzantine spheres of influence in Dalmatia and Serbia.[4] The arrival
of the nomad warriors and the destruction of the great Moravian
principality which was their first deed in Central Europe thus
created for Venice that near-monopoly of communications between Constantinople, Lombardy and the Rhineland which she
seems to have enjoyed throughout the tenth century. This in itself
gives the period a certain claim to be considered as a distinct
moment in east-western relationships. If the Venetians were well-
prepared for the opportunities which events in the Danubian
plain presented to them early in the century, the chrysobull they
gained from the emperors Basil II and Constantine in 992 makes it
clear that they had used them to the full. By this time they had become agents and carriers on behalf of third parties and picked up
much business on their way to Constantinople.[5]

Venice not only controlled the passenger-traffic between north-
alpine Europe and Byzantium, she also handled the post. There is
an important ducal *decretum* of 960 which enjoined that no Venetian

was to carry letters from Lombardy, Bavaria or Saxony or any other places to Constantinople either to the emperor or to any other Greek. Only the customary correspondence from the doge's palace was to pass as usual. For it had happened that letters from the Italian kingdom, Bavaria and Saxony addressed to the emperor had given great offence and that the displeasure they caused was visited also on the carriers, the Venetians.[6] The *decretum* spoke of all this as a recent evil and it is worth remembering that Otto I's envoy, Liudprand, was in 960 detained by the Byzantine authorities at Paxos and unable to reach Constantinople.[7] It is by no means clear why Romanus II and Otto were on bad terms at this moment. Could the Byzantine government have got wind of the Saxon king's missionary plans, the consecration of a Latin bishop who was to be sent to Kiev?[8] It is even less certain why the Italian kings, Berengar II and his son Adalbert, should have sent offensive letters to the emperors Constantine VII and Romanus II as the *decretum* complained and as Liudprand later asserted in one of his acrimonious conversations with Nikephoros Phokas.[9] Though their relations with the Macedonian dynasty had been bad they needed allies now against the coming invasion from the north.

The *decretum* about the posts between Venice and Byzantium carried a large number of *signa* headed by the doge's and besides the patriarch of Grado and his bishops, sixty-five laymen gave it solemnity and force. Its tenor suggests that there could be correspondence between the princely courts of the West and the emperor's without the trouble and expense of embassies, or even messengers. Berengar and Adalbert, who, if Liudprand is to be believed, had a reputation for meanness, may have sent their letters to Constantinople by private Venetian channels rather than their own envoys. In 968 the bishop of Cremona, on the mission made famous by his polemic, expected to be able to communicate with the Ottonian court from Constantinople either by letter or by courier.[10] Venice sometimes also transmitted news from the East to the distant centres of the Franco-Saxon kingdom. It was one of her doges, Petrus Candidus II, *imperialis consul et senator*, who in 932 addressed a letter to King Henry I and Archbishop Hildibert of Mainz with the news of some strange and miraculous events in Jerusalem which were to lead to the conversion of the Jews. Petrus Candidus's call for their baptism or expulsion came as from an imperial dignitary and a synod at Erfurt in 932 duly took notice of it.[11] In distant Ottonian Saxony the place of Venice in all dealings with the East is sometimes casually reflected in the chronicles. Under the year 1017 Thietmar of Merseburg entered into his *Chronicon* with his own hand a note that four great Venetian ships, loaded with spices and dye-stuffs, had been lost at sea.[12]

This by no means exhausts Venice's role as the successful broker and agent of Byzantium's relationships with the West in the tenth century. Once at least, in 967, Otto I used a Venetian, Dominicus, perhaps the *presbyter et cancellarius* of the 960 *decretum*, as his envoy to Nikephoros Phokas, who later told Liudprand of Cremona that the ambassador's promises had caused him to abandon a planned expedition against the Ottonian invaders of Byzantine territories in southern Italy. He was already marching through Macedonia. Liudprand reveals that Dominicus had exceeded his instructions and given away too much so that the Saxon emperor repudiated his engagements.[13] Such tactics would not have been uncharacteristic of Otto who had employed them before. If Nikephoras really meant what he said about his campaign-objective in 967, Dominicus would have done Otto I a signal service in deflecting the basileus with promises. For as the Byzantine conquests advanced in the tenth century the distances between the Asiatic and the European theatres of war grew larger. More than ever campaigns had to be planned far in advance and once abandoned could not be easily resumed. How much the services and goodwill of the Venetian ducal palace were in demand both amongst the Ottonians and the Macedonian emperors can be seen from the pages of John the Deacon's chronicle, especially his account of Peter II Orseolo's reign. Otto III belatedly became the *compater* of the doge's son Peter who at his confirmation in Verona in 996 took the name Otto and when the emperor visited Venice secretly in 1001 he stood godfather to one of his daughters.[14] To counter this invasion of his sphere of authority Basil II in 1005 insisted that Peter Orseolo's most important son John, who had in 1004 become his father's colleague, should marry a Byzantine princess, an Argyros, at Constantinople and reside there for a season. He himself, a kinsman of the bride, furnished the wedding feast.[15] Now the spiritual relationship of *compaternitas* created bonds not only between godchild and godfather but also between the latter and the child's parent. After 996 Peter Orseolo appears as Otto III's *compater* in the diplomata which the Saxon emperor gave to the doge, and John the Deacon, the adroit manager of their connections, made much of this relationship in his chronicle.[16] In 1004 moreover, Henry II, Otto's successor, took care to renew it when he sponsored the confirmation of another ducal son who then became his namesake.[17] This happened at Verona and the parallel with the act of 996 is very striking. The great Byzantine marriage of the Orseoli in 1006 therefore must be seen as a challenge to all this Ottonian *compaternitas*. Basil II did more still. Whereas in the past the sons and successors of doges on their visits to Constantinople had only been given the court rank of *protospatharios*, the young John Orseolo was made a *patricius*. At the same time the emperor was ostentatiously less generous to his younger brother, the godchild of Otto III.[18] There was already something strained in the links which tied Venice to Byzantium and John the Deacon wrote that this festive journey and the marriage took place only after many entreaties from the emperor so that in the end the Orseoli had to accept the invitation.[19]

Travellers of whatever kind then between western Europe and Byzantium in the tenth century went by sea for a good part, if not the whole of the way. The only time when a doge's son – it was in 913 – tried to return overland from the customary visit to the imperial palace was not an encouraging experience. As he was about to enter Croatian territory, Michael, the ruler of the Zachlumi, captured him, seized all the rich presents which stood for both his importance and his clientage in Byzantine eyes and, worst of all, handed him over to Symeon of Bulgaria.[20] He could be recovered at a price. Yet the sea-journey too was not to be chanced lightly or for pleasure. It took at least twenty-four days, the recorded best time in this period (Liudprand's in 949) and at worst, Liudprand's return in 968/9, well over three months. Leo, the *synkellos* and later metropolitan of Synada, in the second letter he wrote from his embassy to Rome and Otto III's court in 997, mentioned that he had suffered ship-wreck in mid-sea and Bishop Bernward of Würzburg, Otto III's envoy to Basil II in 995, according to one source succumbed to an epidemic on board ship on his way to Constantinople. By other accounts he and a large number of his companions died on Euboea.[21] Liudprand of Cremona had to endure contrary winds at Lepanto but suffered far worse delays at the hands of imperial officials and agents along his route in 968. Their chicanery and ill-will wrung from him many a tear and curse and, if we can accept his story, greatly aggravated the dangers and increased the expenses of his way home to the Ottonian court and his see.[22] Yet this too must be counted as one of the risks of the journey. Whether the route led through Thessaly or hugged the coasts and islands, the Byzantine authorities controlled travellers and meted out facilities according to the quality of their papers and recommendations. When the doge Peter Orseolo's sons and the Argyros bride returned home they received help and attentions all along so that they must have had an exceptionally well-favoured and easy journey.[23]

For aristocratic and exalted churchmen like Archbishops Gero of Cologne, Arnulf of Milan and Bishop Werner of Strassburg to be sent to Constantinople by the Ottonian and Salian emperors was perhaps an honour, certainly an opportunity to acquire new relics for their sees but also a possible sentence of death. Liudprand himself may have died on the mission which was to bring Theophano, John Tsimiskes's niece, to Italy for her wedding with Otto II.[24] In 1027 Bishop Werner of Strassburg set off for Constantinople as Conrad II's ambassador in search of another marriage alliance. The land-route through Hungary was by this time open but not for him and his large train of attendants and livestock which he had collected for the journey. Refused entry by King Stephen he had to cross the Alps and attempt the uncongenial sea journey from Venice after a long delay in the march of Verona. He had a wretched passage down the Adriatic and died in Constantinople in October 1028 without having visited Jerusalem as he had hoped to do with the *basileus*'s help. With Constantine VIII's death shortly afterwards the embassy finally lost its purpose for the Salians and the letter with the golden bull which Bishop Werner's colleague, Count Manegold, brought home with him was thus dearly bought.[25]

So far we have looked mainly at the agents and means and it is time now to look at the heart and substance of Byzantine-western relationships in the tenth century. The Greeks had seen Charlemagne's empire come and go. It had made a profound impression on them, much deeper than Theophanes's ironical and caricaturing description of Charles's coronation and anointment at Rome in 800 would suggest. 'Rome', so he dismissed the distasteful business, 'is now in the power of the Franks', and this meant barbarians.[26] More than three centuries later John Cinnamus with greater bitterness and anger echoed and enlarged on this theme. Yet the *basileus* of the Franks', as Theophanes called Charlemagne once and once only, left a legacy that could not be ignored. Barbarians though the Franks were, they and their heirs differed, ever since the creation of the Carolingian *Reich* and its church, from the barbarians of the steppes and the German peoples of the migrations that had once been, and were still, so to say, on the books of the empire, Leo VI's *Tactica* for instance. For although Charlemagne's Italian and East-Frankish successors were by now far less dangerous than the Bulgars, their place amongst the *ethne*, the peoples surrounding Byzantium, remained a problem to the Byzantine authorities. In the *Kletorologion* of Philotheos of 899, for instance, it appears at first sight that Frankish envoys ranked below Bulgarian ones at the imperial court but the *atriklines*, the official responsible for protocol at state banquets, had to distinguish carefully between Franks holding appointments (*cheirotonias*), in the first place bishops, and those who did not (*paganoi*). The former were to be called and seated as befitted their rank.[27] In a scheme of gradations otherwise so clear, here was a trace of vagueness.

The Franks' special relationship with the papacy, of which the

basileis owned themselves to be the spiritual sons, was founded on
new ideas and uses of late-Roman antiquity that were wholly irreconcilable with the divine mission and universality of the one
Roman Empire the Byzantines knew to be theirs and theirs alone.[28]
Much of Byzantine policy towards the West in the ninth and tenth
centuries was concerned not so much with territorial interests and
frontiers or alliances against the Arabs in the central Mediterranean
as with finding some acceptable theory or formula, some idiom
from a vast arsenal of diplomatic devices by which the ideological
challenge could be fitted into the traditional but vigorous political
philosophy of the Christian Roman Empire of Constantine's heirs.
Frontiers were negotiable and legal fictions for letting barbarians
keep possession of them always at hand, provided the intruders
conformed in other and more important ways to the scheme of
things and values in the Byzantine world. Most of the *ethne* accepted the conventions of an ideal order of relationships between the
emperor and themselves which the Greeks had fashioned; only the
Franks, encouraged by the papacy, had begun to dissent.[29] There is
some irony in the Franco-Byzantine settlement of 812 when it was
Charlemagne who made territorial concessions: he abandoned
Venice which he could not have held in any case but insisted on
addressing his hard-pressed Byzantine opponent as 'brother' and
on receiving from Michael I Rangabe's ambassadors an endorse-
ment of the *nomen imperatoris* and the *laudes* which belonged to it.[30]
The scars of this great breach struck into the wall of Byzantine
self-consciousness can be traced in the tenth-century compilations of the emperor Constantine Porphyrogenitus. The heirs of
the Carolingians, now once more local kings but still with larger
horizons and sense of opportunities, the 'king of Saxony', the
'king of Bavaria' or of 'Gaul' and 'Germany', all these were still
addressed as spiritual brothers and letters to them began with a
solemn invocation. Against this the *basileus Bulgarias* remained a
spiritual son.[31] To the Byzantines the latter meant a warmer relationship and closer dependence on the Roman Empire, to the
Franks their spiritual brotherhood spelt an ascent towards equal-
ity.[32]

German scholarship has devoted much ingenuity to interpret
all these forms of address collected in Book II, ch. 48 of the *Book of
Ceremonies* and to identify the situations and embassies when they
may have been employed.[33] By the early tenth century their term
rex had come to denote for the Greeks in the main one of the
Christian rulers of the Frankish kingdoms as against the *archontes*
of, say, the Magyars or (before 927) the Christian Bulgars, but
was it applied also to the dukes who were gaining kingly powers in
some regions of the former Carolingian *Reich*? For the history of

the new political order in the West and its ties with Byzantium this is of some importance. What then are we to make of the 'king of Bavaria', seemingly the most incongruous and unaccountable *inscriptio* in the list of addresses? It could not well have been the emperor Arnolf (887–99) for he was more than a local *rex* in a fraction of the Frankish *Reich*.[34] For a time at least he became once more something like a king over 'Great Francia', as the Byzantines called it, who forced his way into Italy and Rome to be crowned by Pope Formosus. The embassies sent to him in 894 and 896 speak for his importance in Leo VI's calculations.[35] Possibly the *rex Baioure* was the Liutpolding Duke Arnulf (907–37), Henry I's rival. In 935 he invaded northern Italy, called by the count and bishop of Verona in search of a new king. Although Hugh of Arles drove him out he threatened to come back and this alone might have persuaded the emperor to take notice of him.[36] Most likely however the 'king of Bavaria' in the *Book of Ceremonies* was none other than Otto I's own brother, Henry, to whom he gave the Bavarian *ducatus* in 947. By 952 Henry had acquired a large stake in Italy, the marches of Aquilea and Verona. Above all his daughter Hadwig was meant to become the second western bride of the young emperor Romanus II, Constantine's son. Henry's regal ambitions were not only made manifest in two great risings against his brother but they received also a kind of recognition in Ottonian house historiography and even from Otto I himself. When the duke of Bohemia was forced to submit in 950 he was placed under Henry's lordship.[37] Otto, so Widukind wrote, 'made peace and concord' with his brother (947) and he has them both rule together harmoniously, advancing the *res publica* and fighting enemies. They shared a *paterna potestas* over their *cives*.[38] Bavaria was and remained a *regnum* in the usage of Ottonian writers. Some of this must have been known in Constantinople and the Byzantine embassies sent to the *Reich* in 949 and 952 may well have brought letters to Henry, the possible father-in-law of a Macedonian emperor, addressing him as king. Was he not said to have been 'formidable even to the Greeks' in Ruotger's *Life of Brun*? It seems as if Ruotger in this very phrase alluded to some special honours which the Byzantine envoys paid to Otto's brother.[39] The Greeks preferred many *reges* in *Francia* to a single, all-powerful one. However those historians who have made the indivisibility of kingship the foundation-stone of a new *regnum Teutonicorum* rising under the Saxon rulers, may find some comfort in a famous passage of the *De Administrando Imperio* (30/73) where the White Croats were described as subject to Otto, 'the great king of *Francia* and Saxony.' Yet to the Byzantines a *megas rex* like a *megas basileus* might have kings of lesser rank under him.[40]

Too much weight should perhaps not be placed on every expression the learned emperor used. When he enlarged on the family history of his son's first wife, Bertha-Eudocia and of her father King Hugh, he mentioned that Berengar I had enjoyed a *basilea* in Italy (though he shared it with Rudolf of Burgundy) and that the elder Bertha, Hugh's mother, had ruled 'imperially' for ten years after the death of her husband, Margrave Adalbert of Tuscany.[41] These were ambiguous terms. The fragmentation of Carolingian kingship, the murderous wars between the kins and affinities of its representatives from 875 onwards and more still after the death of Arnolf in 899, seemed to restore Byzantium to her former place in the West of their own momentum. At least they offered her great opportunities to re-unite western Rome and perhaps the whole Italian kingdom with Constantinople. It is characteristic for the empire's orientation in the tenth century that it never made any exceptional or all-out effort to seize these openings. There were several good reasons for this. At first the shattering aggressive power of the Bulgarians under Symeon confronted it with greater necessities nearer home and then the progressive decline of the caliphate of Baghdad with far greater chances and hopes in Asia. What was happening along the empire's frontiers in Asia Minor and Armenia did not altogether differ in kind from the splintering of lordship and the diminution in the size of armies typical of the late- and post-Carolingian West, especially Italy. In the East too the Empire's enemies tended to become less formidable. Local dynasties, like the Buyids and the Hamdanids, took over positions at the centre which they could not fully hold so that authority and government broke into smaller and less resilient shares for untrustworthy subordinates and military adventurers. The empire only needed a few determined and active rulers, such as it found in Romanus I Lecapenus, Nikephoros Phokas and John Tsimiskes, to seize the territorial spoils. By comparison the situation in Italy was far less tempting. For despite the emperor Basil's gains in Apulia and Calabria between 876 and 886, Byzantium's South-Italian stake had been much reduced by the loss of nearly all Sicily and the unending attacks of the Arabs against the coasts of the mainland, especially Calabria.[42] The Greeks were fighting on more than one front here. Their Italian subjects suffered much and many coastal settlements had to be abandoned for the safer hill-tops. Sometimes even the capital of the Calabrian theme, Reggio, where the Fatimite general and emir of Sicily, Hasan, in 952 enforced the building of a mosque, had to be evacuated. The population did not love its Byzantine governors and their soldiery. The satellite principalities to the north, especially Capua-Benevento and Salerno, were unreliable although their cultural and social bonds with

Constantinople remained close.[43] Their rulers received court ranks and mandates (*keleuseis*) rather than letters (*grammata*) from the *basileus* but the empire's standing with these princes rested on its successes and failures against the Arabs and here much depended on naval supremacy. To Otto I's ambassador Nikephoros Phokas could indeed boast that he alone possessed maritime power and skills, but in the fighting round Calabria and Sicily the units of the Byzantine fleet often came to grief, not least of all his own in the Straits of Messina in 964.[44] His attempt to save the last Greek stronghold in Sicily, Rametta, ended in disaster. It was in this direction that his great successor, Basil II, near the end of his life wanted to lead an expedition in person, not against the Lombard principalities and the outposts of the Ottonian *Reich*.[45]

Yet even if none of the tenth-century masters of Constantinople wanted to fight Justinian's wars over again, they never ignored or wholly neglected the corrupt and seedy, but at the same time sophisticated, struggles for possession, both in the *regnum Italicum* and at Rome. The resources they employed were modest, but they could always count on a large clientage on the spot. Until the Ottonians and their mixed armies of Saxons, Slavs, Lotharingians, Suabians and Bavarians arrived, Byzantine influence and management were paramount however much a Berengar of Friuli, Hugh of Arles and the Roman *princeps* Alberich sought to be masters in their own houses. For it must be said that if the Greeks had not forgotten Charlemagne nor had these hardfaced and unscrupulous contenders for the Italian kingdom and for Rome, their margraves and counts, all recruited from the Carolingian immigration aristocracy.[46] Berengar I's panegyrist, writing shortly after 915, lost no time in presenting his hero as Charlemagne's descendant and he had the last emperor Charles (*ob* 888) on his deathbed point to Berengar as his true successor in Italy and Rome to whom the great would submit. At his Roman coronation he and Pope John X could be likened to Constantine and Sylvester, only the times had changed for the worse.[47] Hugh of Arles did everything in his power to gain imperial coronation and effective control over the city which Berengar never had, first by marrying the foremost of the Theophylacts, the *senatrix* Marozia, and when this failed, by ceaseless military pressure. Even Charlemagne's embassies and exchanges with the Abbasid caliphate found a strange echo in this small circle of Carolingian descendants and their affinity. Early in the tenth century Hugh of Arles's mother, the elder Bertha, of whom Constantine Porphyrogenitus wrote with so much respect, sent a letter by a Moslem captive to the caliph al-Muqtafi (902–8) with overtures for an alliance against Byzantium. In it the margravine of Tuscany spoke of Rome as part of her lordship and claimed that her forces were stronger than those of the empire. Bertha's envoy conveyed the secret substance of her message by word of mouth, as was customary. She received a gratified, if guarded reply.[48]

Judicious deployment of their naval squadrons in the Tyrrhenian and above all diplomacy were the means by which the emperors secured their influence during the first half of the tenth century and maintained a footing in Rome even during the second. King Hugh's match with Marozia in 932 crossed a plan to ally her daughter to one of Romanus Lecapenus's sons.[49] This might almost have restored Byzantine authority in Rome had not both schemes been thwarted by the revolt of Marozia's son Alberich. He in turn however sought a Greek marriage. To impress his future bride and her escort and perhaps also to have hostages from the insurgent Roman aristocracy he seems to have conscripted a number of noble girls from Rome and the Sabina to serve in his household.[50] When Alberich's son and heir to his regime in Rome, Pope John xii, wanted to shake off Otto i's protection, he turned to Constantinople.[51] In 997 Basil ii's envoy, the *synkellos* Leo, writing to friends and dignitaries in Constantinople, claimed that the elevation of Johannes Philagathos as anti-pope had been his work.[52] Johannes, a Greek from Rossano, was a protégé of the Ottonian court-circle for many years and owed the abbey of Nonantula and the see of Piacenza to its favour but the expelled pope, the Salian Gregory v, was Otto iii's kinsman, his own choice for the Holy See and his *coronator*. The *synkellos*'s letters do not reveal either his doings or his designs very clearly but in one of them, addressed to the patriarch of Constantinople, he boasted that Rome was now in the hands of the great sublime emperor [Basil ii] and that God had moved the heart of the Crescentius who was responsible for Gregory v's expulsion.[53] Johannes Philagathos had become the instrument of the Roman ruling family which had already in 974 and again in 984 seized control of the papacy through a clerical henchman and ruffian, the deacon Franco. The Crescentii, like their predecessors, seem to have maintained useful and close connections with Byzantium. When Franco as Pope Boniface vii found the Holy See untenable in 974 he fled to southern Italy and after another abortive coup in 980, to Constantinople. With Byzantine money he was able to make a further attempt in 984, after Otto ii's death and this time he held the papacy for over a year.[54] The popes whom he and the Crescentii captured, imprisoned and killed were sanctioned or chosen by the Ottonians. That Philagathos and Crescentius ii Nomentanus had been the agents of Byzantine designs in 997 was the view of Arnulf of Milan and Benzo of Alba in the eleventh century.[55] The Greeks were thus able to create difficulties for the new masters of Rome at all times and the Saxon emperors' hold there remained precarious. It might be argued that neither side could harm the other very much at the furthest distance and limit of power from its native centre. Yet Rome was for both more than a frontier city in central Italy.

Let us return to the less devious and more public dealings of Byzantine diplomacy with the Rome of the West. In the collections of the *Book of Ceremonies* the reception of embassies sent by the Roman patriarch and the *princeps* Alberich to Constantinople, holds an important place. It heads the chapter dealing with the arrival of envoys. At the presentation audience the *princeps* of Old Rome had to be referred to as *endoxotatos* by the logothete.[56] In Philotheos's *Kletorologion* this epithet belonged to the order of the *magistroi* which was listed immediately before the dignities reserved to the imperial family.[57] When the greetings on behalf of the reigning pope, his bishops and clerks had been spoken by the envoys, the Roman *princeps* and his *archontes*, the allied nobles who shared offices and power under him had their 'most faithful services' (δούλωσιν) presented to the emperor. Nothing could express the purposes and suit the proprieties of Byzantine state ceremonial and the ideas behind it better. Underneath these formalities it is clear that from time to time Roman aristocratic society in the tenth century still looked to the court of Constantinople for favours and help. Its new autonomy was not wholly irreconcilable with a distant membership of the empire.[57a]

The same impression is conjured up by another text in the *Book of Ceremonies*, the *état* of the fleets and military missions which were despatched by Romanus Lecapenus in 934 and 935 to overawe the rebellious princes of Salerno and Benevento and the disloyal subjects of the theme Langobardia and also to secure King Hugh's alliance and help.[58] The *patrikios* Kosmas came with a mixed squadron of ships, including seven Russian transports and his force consisted of small detachments from every kind of unit in the imperial army. There were horsemen from the themes Thrakesion and Macedonia as well as guards and almost all the *gentes* in the empire's service for pay contributed a few score men: Pharganoi, Chazars, African Moslems and Sicilians, Magyars and some Armenian volunteers. There were also a few engineers.[59] This glittering variety of armament, dress and tongues served a purpose. Together they displayed the universality and cosmocratic horizons of imperial rule. The grandiose spectacle which normally awaited foreign envoys in Constantinople was here exported from the palace to show the local Italian rulers where they belonged. The account of the *protospatharios* Epiphanios's mission to Hugh of Italy in 935 listed the presents intended for the king and then those

which were to be given to the margrave of Spoleto, seven counts
and six bishops.[60] Hugh's entourage and his treacherous vassals
received as much attention as their master and again there is a
strong suggestion of clientage in the munificence and also in the
make-up of the gifts which included items of Byzantine court
dress.[61] Epiphanios carried with him an additional store of presents
which he could employ on his expedition, perhaps to gratify important insurgents when they made their submission. He accoun-
ted for what he had spent and returned the rest.[62] These tactics of
diplomacy and bribery, combined with a demonstration of force,
seem to have been successful: the disaffected princes were pacified,
the provincials of the theme subdued. In 938 Epiphanios, the
patrikios Kosmas and the *strategos* of Langobardia can be found at
Benevento making a grant to its bishop.[63]

It has been thought that only those occidental rulers who had
interests or aspirations in Italy and Rome were flattered by these
imposing Byzantine diplomatic missions which later the Ottonians
and Salians had to repay in kind if they wished to be seen as equals
of the *basileis*. Their ambassadors could not appear in any less
splendour and lavishness.[64] Now it is true that between 899, the
year of the emperor Arnolf's death, and 945 we hear nothing of
Greek embassies to the East-Frankish kingdom with but one
possible exception. In Widukind of Corvey's *res gestae Saxonicae*
there is a stray note about one of the abbots of his house, Bovo II
(900–16): he earned fame because he was able to read and trans-
late a Greek letter for King Conrad I.[65] W. Ohnsorge believed that
it was brought to the East-Frankish court by envoys of Leo VI in
912.[66] It is not easy to see however what the ageing and ailing emperor can have wanted from the successor of Louis the Child who,
at the very beginning of his reign, faced desertions and a diminution of his kingship. He could not have done much to help Leo's
Carolingian protégés and kinsmen by marriage, Louis the Blind
and his son, Karl Constantine.[67] We have seen that Venetians
sometimes carried correspondence from the East-Frankish kingdom to Byzantium and, no doubt, also in the reverse direction.
Could it not be therefore that Conrad received an imperial letter
brought by a returning traveller, a merchant perhaps, rather than
an emissary of rank from the court of Constantinople?[68] The Byzantine chancery's *grammata* to foreign rulers were often documents of great solemnity and splendour but it is questionable
whether this one was more than a fleeting incident in the troubled
reign of Conrad I which but for Widukind's interest in abbot
Bovo's scholarship stirred no memories.[69] Although one or two
Greek monks and guests can be found at Reichenau *c.* 920, Byzantine links with Francia were at this time tenuous. Henry I received

no embassies from the empire nor do we know how the doge's letter was presented to him. Perhaps his acquisition of the Holy Lance in 935 and his planned journey to Rome were to prepare his entry into this larger world of cultural riches and superior political skills, presided over by Byzantium. When the first Greek envoys did arrive at the Ottonian court, on October 31 945, they aroused much interest. They came *cum muneribus*, as ambassadors should.[70] Otto I had for some time given shelter to a dangerous enemy of King Hugh of Italy, margrave Berengar of Ivrea and Hugh's daughter was now the wife of Constantine's son. More likely however the embassy wanted to make known the Porphyrogenitus's sole rule after the removal of the Lecapenoi and to treat with the Saxon king about the Magyars who were raiding the lands of the empire. Other envoys, as we have seen, followed in 949 and 952 and again in 956 when Widukind of Corvey, in the best Carolingian tradition, recited their gifts, not to make Otto appear as the client of the Greeks but to proclaim the fame of his victories and the *dilatatio* of his empire.[71] Perhaps the more fulsome of the two protocols for letters addressed to Frankish kings in the *Book of Ceremonies* was revived to greet Otto on this occasion. In the *intitulatio* it enlarged on the supremacy of the Roman emperors but in the rich flow of honorific predicates for the addressee it recognised the new possessor of Charlemagne's or at least Arnolf's inheritance.[72] As the husband of Adelaide, the widow of King Hugh's son Lothar, Otto was the incoming master of Italy and already in 951 the deprived bishop of Verona, Rather, saw in his invasion a hallowed purpose with an imperial undertone: Otto had aspired to the Italian kingdom only to end injustices (like Rather's expulsion) and to bring back the *rectitudo Christianae legis* and this by imperial *potestas*.[73]

Yet it would be mistaken to confine Byzantine interests and spheres of influence in the West to the horizons of Italy. The forms and style of imperial diplomacy, the all-important flow of precious commodities, works of art and relics which was so much part of them, directly or indirectly, reached the whole of occidental Europe. In the course of the tenth century the ruling families there, new and old, came to accept this style as the norm, the only correct idiom of kingly converse. There is as yet no evidence of any Byzantine embassies visiting either the conquering successors of Alfred or the later Carolingian kings of France fighting for survival.[74] The first known initiative to forge new links between the West-Frankish kingdom and Byzantium came from Hugh Capet. Early in 988 Gerbert drafted a letter for him addressed to the emperors Basil and Constantine. In it Hugh asked for a Byzantine princess, a *filia sancti imperii* which he duly called the Roman

Empire for his son Robert. Neither Gaul nor German – and he meant by them Otto III's men – would harass the empire's frontiers if the alliance came about. This was to be Hugh's main service in return for the bride, besides the expressions of respect and awe the *basileis* always liked to hear from a Frankish king.[75] Here lay indeed new possibilities for the older empire to pare down the claims of the Ottonians, yet no serious negotiations followed this overture. Robert almost immediately afterwards married nearer home.[76] Later his relations with Byzantium seem to have been momentary: a Jerusalem pilgrimage of Bishop Odalric of Orléans gave him the opportunity to exchange amicable messages and presents with the emperor Constantine VIII.[77]

Long before this time however both the Capetians and the kings of Wessex had shared and imitated the usages of Byzantine diplomacy in their dealings with one another. William of Malmesbury in the *Gesta Regum* has described amongst the glories of Athelstan's reign the eagerness with which foreign princes sought the hands of his sisters in marriage. His account, as he himself made clear, closely followed a tenth-century panegyric poem which he both quoted and paraphrased. The suitor of Athelstan's sister Eadhild was Hugh the Great whom William mistakenly called *rex Francorum*.[78] There follows a full list of the presents offered to the king of Wessex by Hugh's princely envoys at Abingdon in 926: perfumes hitherto unknown in England, precious stones, an onyx vase with carved scenes, the sword of Constantine with a nail relic, a banner of St Maurice and a lance, once Charlemagne's which had always brought him victory and was rumoured to have been that of Longinus. There was also a jewelled crown. The relics and their distribution amongst English sanctuaries have left a greater imprint on monastic traditions and histories than the secular gifts.[79] They suggested that the divine favour and the *virtus* that had once been Charlemagne's had now been transferred to Athelstan. Very sacred relics, like particles of the cross, were also amongst the gifts which the emperors sent to western rulers but they were never unaccompanied by articles of secular luxury and display of Byzantine manufacture.[80] Here Duke Hugh's presents to Athelstan clearly reflected the all-pervasive fashions of Byzantine diplomacy. It is likely that his onyx vase was a classical piece which had once belonged to a Carolingian treasure, but an onyx cup was also one of the gifts entrusted to the *protospatharios* Epiphanios for the king of Italy in 935. A remarkable number of onyx chalices of the tenth and eleventh centuries in the treasury of St Mark's, Venice testify to the Greeks' superb craftsmanship and near monopoly in this medium.[81] William of Malmesbury's list of exotic presents had other features in common with Widukind of Corvey's and the *état* in the *Book of Ceremonies*.[82] Ambitious western rulers now had to be seen to possess and to be able to exchange such gifts if their *amicitia* was to be worth courting. Athelstan was said by William of Malmesbury to have sent back to Duke Hugh offerings of almost equal value and renown together with the bride.

How well aristocratic society in the West had come to know and like the gold and the luxurious artefacts of Byzantium appears also from the mid-eleventh-century epic poem, *Ruodlieb*, written at Tegernsee. The author, however, may have been a *monachus palatinus* of Henry III's clerical entourage for he described the courts of kings and what passed in them in a manner far from hackneyed and commonplace. When the hero of the poem after many signal services takes leave of his lord, the *rex maior*, he received rich gifts including minutely and accurately described Byzantine gold coins and a piece of jewellery closely resembling the so-called necklace of the empress Gisela found at Mainz.[83] Boekler and others have distinguished between the classical, the Carolingian and the Byzantine sources of Ottonian art, and the Mainz treasure has been categorically assigned to Byzantine models.[84] It had the shape of a *loros*, a pendant sash worn by the *basileis* and their empresses which appears in more than one place and form on Ottonian full-page illuminations and ivories. The later Saxon emperors and their Salian successors seem to have adopted it and made it their own just as occasionally they liked to be shown crowned by Christ in their gospel books and sacramentaries.[85]

The precious objects which Greek ambassadors brought with them to gratify and overawe the acquisitive kings of the post-Carolingian West could nurse new styles and artistic experiments. The arrival of a Byzantine princess to marry one of them could do this even better and more besides. Most of the matrimonial projects mooted and endlessly negotiated between the court of Constantinople and Carolingian, Ottonian and Salian rulers came to nothing and this makes the marriage between Otto I's son and *co-imperator*, Otto II and Theophanu in 972 all the more important. The bride, it is true, was not a *porphyrogenita* and there were men who advised the old emperor not to receive her into his family.[86] She came with a large following and treasure and their presence gave to the Ottonian court a much closer view of its great rival in the East than it had ever possessed before.[87] It did not change the character of relations already well established through diplomacy but it enlarged them. It opened new avenues for Byzantine influence in the small and select circle of the Liudolfing house, their affinity, their favoured prelates and monasteries. The evidence is ubiquitous: the ivories, enamels, jewellery, goldsmith work, illuminated manuscripts and seals of the later Ottonians could not have been commissioned and created without Byzantine models, nor are they belittled by the direct uses, imitations and adaptations of Greek exemplars.[88] For it is equally characteristic of the late tenth-century *Reich* that it had already experienced and absorbed Byzantine teachings in many spheres, not least of all the visual representation of emperorship.[89] These lessons had now become part of its own make-up and so paradoxically strengthened it in its dealings with Basil II and his successors. The Byzantine influence did not lessen but it encountered increasingly self-conscious and self-reliant native traditions. Yet it could still happen in the middle of the eleventh century when many German *scriptoria* and work-shops had two or three generations' experience behind them that a gold and purple letter which the emperor Constantine IX Mono-machos sent to Henry III was simply used to decorate an altar in the Salian ruler's new foundation, St Simon and Jude, at Goslar.[90]

With Otto III the emulation of Byzantine imperial thinking en-tered a new phase, but it was short-lived. Otto, following the *basileis* and traces of the Roman past, conferred offices and titles of rank on Saxon, Italian and unreliable Roman nobles.[91] Amongst the traditions which gathered round his meeting with Boleslas Chrobry at Gnesen in 1000 are some which suggest that he too wanted to found an *oikoumene* and a family of rulers tied to him by brotherhood or *amicitia*.[92] When his cousin Brun whom he had so recently imposed on the Roman Church crowned him in 996, Otto had at least temporarily taken something away from the con-stitutive powers of the papacy in the making of a western emperor. In his palace at Rome he could be seen from time to time dining alone at an elevated semi-circular table.[93] But it was difficult to turn a Saxon king's clerical and lay *comitatus* into a hierarchy of office-holders. In between the solemn crown-wearings and other occas-ions when they wished to stand for the majesty of Christ, the Ottonians had to be very approachable and live informally, not to say gregariously, with those who enjoyed their *familiaritas*. When Thietmar of Merseburg described Otto III's march to Gnesen only a few years after the event he wrote: 'there came with him Ziazo who was then *patricius*.'[94] We know Ziazo as an East-Saxon noble, most probably a forbear of the Wettins. Otto's titles sat lightly on those who received them and were soon forgotten.

To discover the Byzantine heritage of Theophanu's son we must perhaps look in another direction. The empress's Greeks may have had a share in his early upbringing though it is hard to prove. Certainly Otto possessed something more than a mere spark of that Greek diligence and finesse which in a famous letter he invited Gerbert to rouse and cherish.[95] In the Byzantine world it was very common for a powerful and highly placed layman, even emperors, to have a monk as a spiritual counsellor and friend, a guide with whom to communicate. The charisma of the gifted ascetic who had the vision of God would ensure that he gave the right advice to a troubled penitent.[96] In western monasticism this relationship which often by-passed *ex officio* authority was rare. Here rulers, founders and benefactors wanted to be associated with a monastic community, its prayers and its saints. Most of the monastic reform movements of the tenth and eleventh centuries moreover sought to strengthen the rule, the common life of the institution and to reduce the individuality of its members. The only man in the West who caught something of the spirit of these intimate bonds between Greek monks and great men of the world was Otto III. His short life is full of encounters and close personal associations with monastic saints and spiritual mentors: Ramwold of St Emmeran, Adalbert of Prague, Brun of Querfurt, St Nilus and St Romuald.[97] In the *Lives* of these men, or in the case of Brun his own writings, Otto was an important figure and severally they wanted to claim him as their own and draw him away from his more mercurial clerical friends and counsellors. The emperor sought and followed the rigours of their penitential advice and it is perhaps significant that his relations with abbot Odilo of Cluny, who often visited his court, were friendly but not as close.[98] Here no less than in other respects Otto III was half a Byzantine to whom it had fallen to rule the Saxon *Reich*.

These personal traits and the general enhancement of Byzantine influence in the Ottonian environment were not admired and welcomed by everyone. They aroused both resentments and controversies. Men looked upon Otto III's doings at Rome with mixed feelings as Thietmar dryly observed.[99] Already Widukind of Corvey had held up Greek deceit and trickery when he wanted to explain one of Otto I's military setbacks in Apulia.[100] The infant Otto III's Byzantine descent could be used as a justification to desert his cause in 984 and to accept his cousin, Duke Henry II of Bavaria, as king instead.[101] The empress Theophanu had enemies in the Ottonian family circle, notably her mother-in-law Adelaide and Bishop Dietrich of Metz who seems to have suspected her loyalty when Otto II invaded Byzantine Calabria in 982 and fought disastrously against the Sicilian emir.[102] It was a catastrophe that called for culprits. Liudprand of Cremona was not alone when he attacked the cultural pre-eminence of the Greeks in his *Legatio* by a mixture of grotesque caricature and belittlement. Otloh's *Liber Visionum* and one of the codices containing the *Life of Bernward of Hildesheim* record the vision of a nun to whom Theophanu had appeared and lamented her torments in hell. They were her punishment for introducing noxious Greek luxury, jewellery and fashions

into the *Reich* where they had hitherto been unknown. She had led
other women into sin because they now desired such things and
here lay the burden of her offence. Against this however the
emperor Henry III wanted to link his descent with Theophanu's
name and for this very reason imitate Byzantine manners and
styles.[103]

The princess and her following were not, of course the only
Greek immigrés north of the Alps in the tenth century. There is
scattered evidence of Greek monks and sometimes refugee bishops
not only at Reichenau but also in Lotharingian monasteries and
sees, at Dijon and at Cologne.[104] The court of Edgar, whose kingship had imperial overtones, attracted foreigners as that of a ruler
over many peoples should. Not only Flemings, Danes and continental Saxons but also a Greek bishop whom the Ely tradition
branded as a clerical go-getter, can be found in his entourage.[105]
For the most part, however, knowledge of and contact with Byzantium were in the tenth century the privilege of only a few in the
West and they prided themselves not a little, as did Liudprand of
Cremona, on their expertise.[106] The relationships of the East-
Roman and Ottonian courts which had so markedly shaped the
tastes and the ambitions of the later Ottos, Henry II and their
circle, were exclusive. Diplomacy was the main channel of communication, if not the only one. With the opening of the land route
through Hungary in the first decades of the eleventh century all
this changed. For it made possible and encouraged the movement
of many more pilgrims to the Holy Sepulchre than the sea-journey
had attracted in the tenth and all these overland travellers to Palestine had to pass through Constantinople and the imperial provinces
on their way. Many of them stayed in the capital to refresh themselves and see the sights. The easier route alone may not explain the
rising cult of the Jerusalem pilgrimage as an act of penance and
sanctification but its appeal could not have spread without it.[107]
The old-established relations between the imperial courts, the
solemn embassies, as we have seen, did not come to an end but
they were overshadowed now by a far more continuous and extensive traffic of pilgrims from regions, especially France, which
had hitherto possessed very little first-hand knowledge of the
Greek world. If men had once visited Byzantium in scores, they
now did so in their thousands and this created a new atmosphere.[108]
An age of diplomacy and highly privileged trade gave way to an
age of mass contacts. Gregory VII's famous plan to come to the
rescue of Constantinople and the Christian brethren in the East
becomes more understandable when it is remembered that his call
to arms in 1074 was addressed to princes and nobles quite a few of
whom had been there and visited the sanctuaries and relics of the

capital.[109] Rodulf Glaber who sang the praises of the new route also saw the new urge to visit the Holy Places as a movement, something unheard of in the past.[110] Moreover it seemed to him that it had begun with the humble, the *ordo inferioris plebis* and spread upwards towards higher ranks of society before reaching the princes and, lastly, women.[111] Rodulf's impressions were faulty in detail but right in the round. A few aristocratic ladies had now and again ventured to Jerusalem in the tenth century but perhaps many more did so in the eleventh.[112] There is some evidence of poor men like the wandering priest Haimerad, of obscure Suabian origin, making the journey at his own prompting.[113]

A few of the more literate pilgrims, especially if they came from Lotharingia or Bavaria, could have read what Liudprand of Cremona had written about the eastern Empire in his *Antapodosis* and *Legatio*. His works spread across the Alps and enjoyed literary success notably in Lotharingia and however much his feelings towards the Greeks changed they became an important source of knowledge about Byzantium.[114] Modern historians here only follow in the footsteps of a Sigebert of Gembloux and other eleventh-century scholars. Yet paradoxically Liudprand's angry polemic, the *Legatio*, belonged to a single moment of the empire's relations with the Roman Church and the Ottonians, a moment that was soon past even for him.[115] It set out to create tensions where there had been little before and it contained also an element of personal vindication. For in the *Legatio* Liudprand has been shown to have joined Pope John XIII's side in the debate about the meaning and purpose of Otto I's imperial coronation.[116] He addressed the Ottonians, father and son, as *imperatores Romanorum* who had toiled for the restoration and exaltation of the Roman Church while the pretended Roman emperor, the *basileus*, slept. Their past services to St Peter had earned him, Liudprand, his safe return home from the dangerous embassy and he called upon them to do more still: Nikephoros Phokas and his patriarch were to be summoned and judged by a papal synod. Otto I and Otto II, both now crowned emperors, should carry out the sentence.[117] Did Liudprand wish to make some amends for his own conspicuous role in the depositions of John XII and Benedict V?

The target of the bishop of Cremona's venom and abuse was Nikephoros Phokas first and foremost and certainly not the Macedonians, the young emperors Basil and Constantine, then under the military ruler's tutelage. In more than one place Otto I's ambassador appears almost as a camp-follower of the legitimist interest.[118] For Liudprand in 968 had friends and contacts in Constantinople from his earlier embassy in 949 and some of the gifts he had to distribute were intended for them. Nikephoros Phokas

paid Otto's ambassador much attention but he also sought to
isolate him and have him watched by his police. It is possible that
the covert purpose of the bishop's mission was to befriend discon-
tented circles, enemies of Nikephoros Phokas's regime in Constantinople, under the guise of conducting official negotiations which
at this moment he and Otto I knew could not succeed.[119] Otto's
policies and campaign in southern Italy had reached an impasse
and here lay a possible way out. Lastly the *Legatio* was written also
to court the interest and loyalty of Italian nobles and clergy who
were accustomed to Byzantine influence, gifts and patronage as the
Liudprand of the *Antapodosis* had been himself. If Nikephoros
Phokas appears as a bad paymaster who despised and mistrusted
his Italian allies, led by the dispossessed Adalbert of Ivrea, it was
because Liudprand hoped to persuade the remaining adherents of
the king that the Greek alliance could no longer be counted on.[120]
The very vehemence of the *Legatio* reveals how delicate and fragile
the beginnings of Ottonian rule in Italy really were.

Against Liudprand's freshness and novelty it is striking that
much of the contemporary Byzantine information about the *gentes*
in the West, the Franks and the Lombards we meet in the emperor
Leo's *Tactica* and in Constantine Porphyrogenitus's *De administrando imperio*, was old and somewhat out of date. It is doubtful
whether Nikephoros Phokas knew or cared about the enhanced
fighting skills of Otto I's mounted warriors as he knew and cared
about the military capabilities of the empire's northern and Muslim
neighbours. All policy is self-regarding, but Byzantium's relationships with the West were inward-looking in a very special way.
Rather than come to terms with changing situations they were
often more concerned with preserving and insulating the exalted,
ideal status of the empire against contamination. This attitude was
quite logical, given that the *basileus* had been entrusted by God
with the direction of the *oikoumene* in earthly life. It belongs not
only to later centuries of economic failure and political powerless-
ness when emperors and their courtiers clutched tenaciously at
the straws of ceremonial and form to safeguard the substance of
the imperial idea. It held good also in the century of Byzantium's
greatest aggressiveness and material gains. In the West it was increasingly resented and here Liudprand may have been influential.
His anger about slights and supposed slights had even been anticipated by Notker of St Gallen in the late ninth century who, like
Liudprand, presented the treatment of Charlemagne's envoys in
Constantinople as inhospitable and humiliating.[121] The literature
of the eleventh-century pilgrimage to Jerusalem liked to dwell on
the sufferings and hardships that had to be endured and overcome
on the way. The German bishops and lay nobles who took part

n the great overland journey to Palestine of 1065 seem to have
:ounted Greek *imperialis arrogantia* as one of these hardships.[122]

NOTES

While being prepared for publication this paper has put on a
certain amount of weight. I am indebted to Mr Peter Brown
of All Souls College, Mr James Howard-Johnstone of Corpus
Christi College, Oxford, Dr Jonathan Alexander of Manchester University and Mr James Campbell of Worcester
College for their kind interest, advice and suggestions over
points of detail.

1   Constantine Porphyrogenitus, *De Administrando Imperio cc.*
    40/31–4 and 42/15–18, ed. Gy. Moravcsik and translated by
    R. J. H. Jenkins (Budapest 1949) pp. 176 and 182 and vol. II,
    Commentary ed. R. J. H. Jenkins (London 1962) pp. 153ff.
    For the route from Thessalonica to Belgrade mentioned by
    the emperor see C. J. Jirecek, *Die Heerstrasse von Belgrad nach
    Constantinopel und die Balkanpässe* (Prague 1877) pp. 75ff.

2   Rodulf Glaber, *Historiarum Libri Quinque,* III, I, 2 ed.
    M. Prou, *Collection de Textes pour servir à l'étude et à l'enseigne-
    ment de l'histoire* (Paris 1886) p. 52 : 'Tunc temporis ceperunt
    pene universi, qui de Italia et Galliis ad sepulchrum Domini
    Iherosolimis ire cupiebant, consuetum iter quod erat per
    fretum maris omittere, atque per huius regis patriam
    transitum habere'.

3   *Annales Fuldenses,* ed. F. Kurze, *MGH, SRG* (Hanover 1891)
    pp. 75 and 81 and [F.] Dölger, *Regesten [der Kaiserurkunden
    des oströmischen Reiches von 565 bis 1453],* I, *Regesten von 565–
    1025* (Munich/Berlin 1924) nos. 489, 491.
    This was also the time of the greatest insecurity along the
    Dalmatian coastal tracts when Muslim and Slav piracy made
    the sea-journey especially hazardous. The sea route, how-
    ever, appears to have carried most of the diplomatic traffic
    between Charlemagne and Louis the Pious and the Byzantine
    court. Cf. Charlemagne's letter to the emperor Michael
    Rangabe in 813, *MGH, Epistolae Karolini Aevi,* II, ed. E.
    Dümmler (Berlin 1895) p. 556 : 'cum primum oportunum
    navigandi tempus adveniret, legatos nostros ad tuae dilectae
    fraternitatis gloriosam praesentiam mitteremus'. The embassy
    sent in 838 to Venice proceeded to Louis the Pious at
    Ingelheim in 839.

4   See E. Klebel, 'Die Ostgrenze des Karolingischen Reiches'
    in *Die Entstehung des deutschen Reiches,* Wege der Forschung,
    I (Darmstadt 1956) pp. 1–41 and esp. p. 21.

5   [*Urkunden zur älteren Handels- und Staatsgeschichte der Republik
    Venedig,* I. Theil (814–1205)] ed. [G. L.] Tafel and [G.M.]
    Thomas, *Fontes rerum Austriacarum, Diplomataria et Acta,*
    XII (Vienna 1856) no. XVII, pp. 36ff. The text has survived
    in an atrocious Latin translation. It is noteworthy that in the
    preamble the Venetians are classified as *extranei.* In general,
    see [W.] Heyd, [*Histoire du commerce du Levant au Moyen-Âge*],
    I (repr. Leipzig 1923) pp. 114ff and [A.] Schaube,

[*Handelsgeschichte der Romanischen Völker des Mittel-meergebiets bis zum Ende der Kreuzzüge*] (Munich/ Berlin 1906) pp. 17ff. W. Heinemeyer, 'Die Verträge zwischen dem Oströmischen Reiche und den italienischen Städten Genua, Pisa und Venedig vom 10. bis 12. Jahrhundert', *Archiv für Diplomatik* . . . 111 (1957) pp. 79ff, and F. Dölger and J. Karayannopulos, *Byzantinische Urkundenlehre, Byzantinisches Handbuch im Rahmen des Handbuchs für Altertumswissenschaft,* 111.i.1 (Munich 1968) pp. 94ff.

6   Tafel und Thomas, no. XIII, pp. 17ff. The *decretum* also legislated against the slave-trade but here it only enlarged on an older ordinance of duke Orso's (864–81). For its contents and purpose see also Heyd, p. 112ff, Schaube, p. 16, and R. Cessi, *Venezia Ducale,* (Venice 1940) I, pp. 343ff who suggested that the decree's aims were to thwart anti-Venetian propaganda and the intrigues of exiles no less than postal traffic between the two empires (strictly speaking there was as yet no empire in the West). G. Luzzatto, *An Economic History of Italy,* trans. P. Jones (London 1961) p. 52, thought that only private letters were banned by the decree but that official ones from Lombardy, Bavaria and Saxony could be carried. The text does not encourage this distinction, rather the ducal government wanted to check the enterprise of its subjects who conveyed 'foreign' correspondence to Constantinople, if only for the time being and as a gesture to appease the imperial court.

7   Liudprand, *Antapodosis,* 111, 1, in *Die Werke Liudprands von Cremona,* ed. J. Becker, *MGH, SRG* (Hanover/ Leipzig 1915) p. 74, and [R.] Hiestand, [*Byzanz und das Regnum Italicum im 1r. Jahrhundert, Geist und Werk der Zeiten*], Heft 9 (Zürich 1964) pp. 211ff, who cannot quite account for the envoy's detention. W. Ohnsorge, 'Otto I und Byzanz', *Mitteilungen des Instituts für österreichische Geschichtsforschung,* Ergänzungsband XX, i. p. 115 and in two papers, collected in his *Abendland und Byzanz* (Darmstadt 1958) pp. 36 and 272, thought that Liudprand's mission in 960 was to secure Otto I's recognition as *imperator Francorum* from Romanus 11 and that it succeeded. This view, however, wholly ignores the evidence for friction between the two courts, both in the *Antapodosis* (loc. cit.) and in the Venetian *decretum.*

8   This seems to me to be the most likely explanation of the rift. For the consecration of Libutius at Otto 1's Christmas court held in Frankfurt in 959 see the continuator of Regino of Prüm, Adalbert of St Maximin, in *Reginonis abbatis Prumiensis Chronicon cum continuatione Treverensi,* ed. F. Kurze, *MGH, SRG* (Hanover 1890) p. 170 *sub anno* 960. Libutius, a monk of St Alban in Mainz, died in 961 before setting out to Kiev. He was replaced by Adalbert of St Maximin himself.

9   Liudprand, *Legatio,* c. 5, p. 178 where Adalbert alone is referred to. Berengar 11 had died as Otto 1's prisoner in 966 while Adalbert hoped to regain Italy and his kingship with byzantine money and ships. Cf. *Legatio,* c. 29, p. 191 and *infra,* p. 48

10   Liudprand, *Legatio,* c. 1, p. 175 and c. 53, p. 203.

11   *MGH, Constitutiones et Acta Publica*, I, no. 4, pp. 6ff, and cf. no. 3, where however it is made to appear that the news came via Rome.

12   *Thietmari Merseburgensis episcopi Chronicon*, VII, c. 76 ed. R. Holtzmann, *MGH, SRG*, nova series IX (Berlin 1955) p. 492. Thietmar also prided himself a little on being able to tell his readers something about Greek ships, notably what a *chelandia* was and how it was manned. See *Chronicon*, III, c. 23, p. 126.

13   See the continuator of Regino of Prüm, p. 178 *sub anno* 967 and Liudprand, *Legatio*, cc. 25 and 31, pp. 188ff, 192, B. A. Mystakidis, *Byzantinisch-Deutsche Beziehungen zur Zeit der Ottonen* (Stuttgart 1891) p. 23, and P. E. Schramm, 'Kaiser, Basileus und Papst in der Zeit der Ottonen', in his collected works, *Kaiser Könige und Päpste, Gesammelte Aufsätze zur Geschichte des Mittelalters*, III (Stuttgart 1969) pp. 204ff. This supersedes the article as first published in the *Historische Zeitschrift*, CXXIX (1924) pp. 424ff. For Dominicus cf. Tafel und Thomas, p. 25 : 'Ego Dominicus, Presbiter et Cancellarius, ex mandato domini Petri Ducis, Senioris nostri, complevi et roboravi'. It is possible that Nikephoros was bluffing and had marched into Macedonia only in order to threaten the Bulgarians while his ally Sviatoslav attacked them from the East. For the chronology of his Bulgarian campaigns see [S.] Runciman, [*The First Bulgarian Empire*] (London 1930) p. 305.

14   John the Deacon, [*La Cronaca Veneziana*] in *Cronache Veneziane*, I, ed. G. Monticolo, *Fonti per la Storia d'Italia* (Rome 1890) pp. 151ff and 163. See also J. F. Böhmer, *Regesta Imperii*, II, 3, [*Die*] *Regesten* [*des Kaiserreiches unter Otto III, 980 (983)–1002*, M.] Uhlirz (Graz-Cologne 1956) nos 1164d and 1407e.

15   John the Deacon, pp. 167ff, and Georgius Cedrenus, *Historiarum Compendium*, ed. I. Bekker (Bonn 1839) II, p. 452 : 'τὸ ἔθνος οὕτως ὑποποιούμενος' was the purpose of the marriage. This should be set against the motif of Otto III's godfathership in 1001 : 'ad perfecte . . . fidei vinculum confirmandum'. (John the Deacon, p. 163). For the marriage see also G. Schlumberger, *L'Épopée byzantine à la fin du dixième Siècle* (Paris 1900) II, p. 323. Maria Argyros and Basil II were related through the daughters of Romanus Lecapenus, one of whom, Helena, had been married to Basil's grandfather, Constantine VII, while another, Agatha, became the wife of an Argyros. John the Deacon was right when (p. 168) he described the bride as *imperiali editam stirpe* but wrong when, a little later, he made her Basil II's niece (p. 169). The only child of the shortlived couple was however duly named Basil (ibid.).

16   See *MGH, Die Urkunden der deutschen Könige und Kaiser*, II, 2, *Die Urkunden Ottos des III* (Hanover 1893) no. 307 of 999 and no. 397 of 1001. No. 165 of 995 has been doubtfully reconstructed out of no. 307. See also John the Deacon, pp. 154, 161 and 163. On the bond of *compaternitas* between the Carolingians and the popes of the eighth century, see E. Caspar, *Pippin und die Römische Kirche* (Berlin 1914) pp. 39ff.

17 John the Deacon, pp. 167 and 171 and S. Hirsch, *Jahrbücher des deutschen Reiches unter Heinrich II* (Berlin 1862) I, p. 305.

18 John the Deacon, (p. 168): 'Ottonem suum puerulum, qui aderat, fratrem muneribus tantum honoravit.' In the event it was Otto who succeeded Peter II as doge.

19 op. cit., pp. 167ff: 'sedula petitione a Vassylio et Constantino imperatoribus coactus.'

20 op. cit., p. 132. On Michael, prince of the Zachlumi, see *De Administrando Imperio*, c. 33/16 and *Commentary*, p. 137 and Runciman, p. 162.

21 For Leo's journey see [P. E.] Schramm, 'Zwölf Briefe [des byzantinischen Gesandten Leon von seiner Reise zu Otto III. aus den Jahren 997–998'], in *Kaiser Könige und Päpste*, III, pp. 257ff and also 262ff with German translations pp. 269, 273. Schramm's edition of the letters follows that of J. Darrouzès, *Épistoliers byzantins du Xe siècle*, *Archives de L'Orient Chrétien*, VI (Paris 1960), no. 10, pp. 171ff. For Bishop Bernward's embassy in 995 see Uhlirz, *Regesten*, no. 1146a.

22 Liudprand, *Legatio*, cc. 58–65 (pp. 207–12). For Liudprand's itinerary on the return journey see V. Menzel, *Deutsches Gesandtschaftswesen im Mittelalter* (Hanover 1892) p. 214. According to Menzel Liudprand went by ship to an eastern Greek port and then overland to Naupacte where (cf. *Legatio*, cc. 58, 59, p. 207) he was made to embark on two boats which which were too small for his party.

23 John the Deacon (p. 168): 'cui Grecorum seu aliarum gentium incole ubique usque ad patriam non denegabant impertiri obsequia'.

24 *MGH, SS*, III, p. 267, n. 23.

25 Wipo, *Gesta Chuonradi II. imperatoris*, c. 22 in *Wiponis Opera*, ed. H. Bresslau, *MGH, SRG* (Hanover/Leipzig 1915) pp. 41ff: 'tandem cum maximo labore per Venetiam mare Adriaticum ingressus navigio calamitoso Constantinopolim pervenit'. For Bishop Werner and Count Manegold's embassy see H. Bresslau, *Jahrbücher des Deutschen Reichs unter Konrad II.* (Leipzig 1879) I, pp. 234–6 and 271–5, H. Appelt, *Regesten des Kaiserreiches unter Konrad II. 1014–1039*, (Graz 1951) nos 116b and 140a and Dölger, *Regesten*, no. 830. The bishop and the count had set out in the autumn of 1027 and the count returned early in 1029.

26 *Theophanis Chronographia*, ed. C. de Boor (Leipzig 1883) I, pp. 472ff.

27 For the text see [J. B.] Bury, [*The Imperial Administrative System in the Ninth Century*], British Academy Supplemental Papers I (1911) and reprint (New York, no date) p. 156, lines 17–19. Hiestand's translation and interpretation of Philotheos's remarks on the precedence of Frankish ambassadors (*Byzanz und das Regnum Italicum*, pp. 99ff) cannot stand. He takes χειροτονίαι to mean 'letters of credence' and *paganos* 'heathen'. For the correct interpretation of the latter see Bury, pp. 21ff and R. Guilland, *Recherches sur les institutions byzantines* (Berlin 1967) I, pp. 154ff. What Philotheos had to say about the seating of Frankish bishops is, on the whole, borne out by Liudprand of Cremona. In *Legatio*, c. 11 (p.

181) he complained about his own *placement* at the emperor
Nikephoros's table and that his companions had not even
been allowed to dine in the same house. But they were
paganoi, men who held no office or dignity. See also *Legatio*,
c. 19 (p. 186) where his relegation to a place below the
Bulgarian envoy was explained to him : the Bulgarian,
though dirty and wearing a brass chain, was a *patricius* and
ever since the *basileus* of the Bulgars, Peter, had married
Maria Lecapena (927), Bulgarian ambassadors took precedence over those of all other *gentes*. This was not yet the
practice when Philotheos wrote. The Franks mentioned
by him in Bk iv (p. 160, l. 29) appear to have been in the
Empire's service together with other *ethne*. See H. Ahrweiler,
Byzance et la mer (Paris 1966) p. 206, n. 3.

28   For these problems see F. Dölger, 'Die Kaiserurkunde der
Byzantiner als Ausdruck ihrer politischen Anschauungen',
and 'Europas Gestaltung im Spiegel der fränkisch-byzanti-
nischen Auseinandersetzung des 9. Jahrhunderts', in both his
Byzanz und die europäische Staatenwelt (Ettal 1953, and his Wissenschaftliche Buchgesellschaft, Darmstadt 1964) pp. 9ff and
282ff, W. Ohnsorge, *Das Zweikaiserproblem im früheren Mittelalter* (Hildesheim 1947) and his paper 'Byzanz und das
Abendland im 9. und 10. Jahrhundert. Zur Entwicklung
des Kaiserbegriffes und der Staatsideologie', in *Abendland
und Byzanz*, pp. 1ff. O. Treitinger, *Die oströmische Kaiser-
und Reichsidee* (2nd ed. Darmstadt 1956).

29   On this hierarchy and its history see G. A. Ostrogorsky, 'Die
byzantinische Staatenhierarchie', *Seminarium Kondakovianum*,
VIII (Prague 1936) pp. 41ff.

30   Einhard, *Vita Karoli Magni*, c. 28, ed. O. Holder-Egger,
MGH, SRG (Hanover / Leipzig 1911) p. 33, and Charlemagne's letters to the emperors Nikephoras I and Michael I
in *MGH, Epistolae Karolini Aevi*, II, ed. E. Dümmler (Berlin
1895) pp. 546ff and 555ff. For the *laudes* see the *Annales
regni Francorum* for 812, ed. F. Kurze, *MGH, SRG* (Hanover
1895) p. 136. The best recent survey of Charlemagne's and
Pope Leo III's conflict and peace with Byzantium is P. Classen's *Karl der Grosse, das Papsttum und Byzanz* (Düsseldorf
1968).

31   *De Cerimoniis Aulae Byzantinae*, II, c. 48, ed. I. I. Reiske (Bonn
1829) pp. 689ff and p. 691, and cf. the *salutationes*, c. 47, pp.
681ff.

32   F. Dölger, 'Die "Familie der Könige" im Mittelalter', *Byzanz
und die europäische Staatenwelt*, pp. 39ff and also 'Die mittelalterliche "Familie der Fürsten und Völker" und der Bul-
garenherrscher', op. cit., pp. 167ff. The Bulgar ruler Symeon
at times repudiated the spiritual fatherhood of the emperor,
cf. art. cit., pp. 177ff.

33   See O. Meyer, 'Εἰς τὸν ῥῆγα Σαξωνίας', *Festschrift Albert
Brackmann*, ed. L. Santifaller (Weimar 1931) pp. 123–36 and
the review by Dölger, *BZ*, XXXI (1931) pp. 439–42 and
especially [W.] Ohnsorge, 'Drei Deperdita [der byzantinischen Kaiserkanzlei und die Frankenadressen im Zere-
monienbuch des Konstantiños Porphyrogennetos'] *Abendland und Byzanz*, pp. 227ff.

34 This against Ohnsorge (op. cit., p. 247) who would identify the 'ῥήξ Βαιούρη' with Arnolf.

35 *Annales Fuldenses*, pp. 125, 130.

36 Duke Arnulf seized hostages at Verona and took them back with him to Bavaria. Cf. Liudprand, *Antapodosis*, III, cc. 49–52 (pp. 100ff) and K. Reindel, *Die bayerischen Liutpoldinger, Quellen und Erörterungen zur bayerischen Geschichte*, Neue Folge, XI (Munich 1953) pp. 63ff. It could also be argued that if the Emperor Alexander, Leo VI's brother, in 912 sent a letter announcing his accession to Conrad I, the reputed *rex Germanias*, he may also have addressed one to Arnulf. Cf. *infra*, p. 114 and n. 67.

37 Thietmar of Merseburg, *Chronicon*, II, c. 2 (p. 40): 'fratri suimet Heinrico, Bawariorum duci, ad serviendum traditus est.'

38 Widukind of Corvey, *Res Gestae Saxonicae*, II, c. 36, ed. P. Hirsch and H.-E. Lohmann, *MGH, SRG* (Hanover 1935) p. 95 : 'dum unanimes res publicas augent, hostes debellant, civibus paterna potestate presunt.'

39 Ruotger, *Vita Brunonis*, c. 17, ed. I. Ott, *MGH, SRG*, new series (Weimar 1951) p. 16 : 'ipsis etiam Grecis formidabilem.' The editor connected this with Henry's successful offensive against the Magyars in 950.

40 *De Administrando Imperio*, p. 142 and *Commentary*, pp. 97 ff, *megas* here means 'great' or 'superior' rather than 'the elder'. For 'megas rex' see Dölger, 'Europas Gestaltung', op. cit., p. 286, n. 7 and Hiestand, p. 208 and n. 77 where however Otto's designation as a *megas rex* in the *De Administrando Imperio*, c. 30/73 is made to do duty for a style not found in the *Book of Ceremonies*. W. Ohnsorge, 'Drei Deperdita' (pp. 234ff), categorically rejected a royal *inscriptio* for Henry in 952. 'In diesem fränkischen Machtbereich Ottos war für ein Königtum Bayern nicht Platz' (pp. 236ff). Yet the regal character of the Liudolfing *ducatus* in Bavaria was still remembered in the *eleventh* century. Wolfhere, St Godehard's biographer (c. 1035), wrote of the Emperor Henry II's father, Duke Henry II, 'qui eandem provinciam acsi regali sibi dominatione vendicabat'. See the *Vita Godehardi Episcopi Hildeneshaimensis prior*, c. 1, *MGH, SS*, XI, p. 170.

41 *De Administrando Imperio*, cc. 26/37 (p. 110) and 26/71 (p. 112) and Hiestand, pp. 110 and 132. That βασιλεύω was an ambiguous term is suggested by Dölger, loc. cit.

42 J. Gay, *L'Italie méridionale et l'Empire Byzantin* (Paris 1904) pp. 210ff. For the military and political situation on the two fronts in the last years of Constantine VII's reign see A. A. Vasiliev, *Byzance et les Arabes*, II, *Les Relations politiques de Byzance et les Arabes à l'époque de la dynastie Macédonienne*, I, trans. and ed. M. Canard (Brussels 1968) pp. 378ff. For a detailed but perhaps sometimes too dramatic account of the Byzantine-Fatimite wars in southern Italy during the tenth century see E. Eickhoff, *Seekrieg und Seepolitik zwischen Islam und Abendland (650–1040)* (Berlin 1966) pp. 296ff.

43 [V. von] Falkenhausen [*Untersuchungen über die byzantinische Herrschaft in Süditalien vom 9. bis ins 11. Jahrhundert*] (Wies-

baden 1967) p. 34. For the distinction between foreign rulers who received letters and satellite princes who were sent mandates from the imperial palace see Ostrogorsky, 'Die byzantinische Staatenhierarchie', p. 49.

44 Liudprand, *Legatio*, c. 11 (p. 182) : 'Navigantium fortitudo mihi soli inest'.

45 See Eickhoff, op. cit., pp. 345–51 and pp. 382ff for Basil 11's plans in 1025.

46 For this aristocracy and its continuing connections north of the Alps see E. Hlawitschka, *Franken, Alemannen, Bayern und Burgunder in Oberitalien (774–962), Forschungen zur oberrheinischen Landesgeschichte*, VIII (Freiburg 1960).

47 *Gesta Berengarii Imperatoris*, IV, ll. 151–5, ed. P. Winterfeld, *MGH, Poetae*, IV, i, p. 400.

48 For an excellent account of these exchanges see Hiestand, pp. 110ff with German translations of the Arabic texts (pp. 225–9) and also Wattenbach-Levison, *Deutschlands Geschichtsquellen im Mittelalter Vorzeit und Karolinger*, IV, rev. H. Löwe (Weimar 1963) p. 424 and n. 161.

49 G. Fasoli, *I re d'Italia (888–962)* (Florence 1949) pp. 120ff, Runciman, *Romanus Lecapenus*, pp. 192 and 195 where however events are misdated. From the tenor of the emperor's letter it seems probable that it was sent when the news of Alberich's coup had not yet reached Constantinople. Falkenhausen, p. 43, however, agrees with Runciman that Romanus treated the proffered marriage alliance coolly. Cf. also Hiestand, pp. 162–9, Dölger, *Regesten*, no. 625 and H. Zimmermann, *Papstregesten 911–1024, Regesta Imperii*, 11, *Sächsische Zeit* (Vienna, Cologne, Graz 1969) nos 111, 113. For a general appraisal of imperial diplomacy based on the empire's dealings with the peoples of the northern frontier see D. Obolensky, 'The Principles and Methods of Byzantine Diplomacy', *Actes du XIIe Congrès International d'Études Byzantines* (Beograd 1963) I, pp. 45ff.

50 *Benedicti S. Andreae Chronicon*, ed. G. Zucchetti, *Fonti per la storia d'Italia* (Rome 1920) p. 172.

51 Liudprand, *Historia Ottonis*, c. 6, ed. cit., p. 163 and H. Zimmermann, *Papstabsetzungen des Mittelalters* (Graz, Vienna, Cologne 1968) pp. 81ff, also *Papstregesten*, no. 315. For Adalbert, Berenger 11's son, seeking Greek aid see *supra* p. 104 n. 9 and *infra* p. 122.

52 Schramm, 'Zwölf Briefe', nos 1, 2 and 3, *Kaiser Könige und Päpste*, 111, pp. 256–60 and 'Kaiser, Basileus und Papst', op. cit., pp. 220–8. For Philagathos's movements before his elevation see M. Uhlirz, *Jahrbücher des deutschen Reiches unter Otto II und Otto III*, 11, *Otto III 983–1002* (Berlin, 1954) pp. 511–517. On the whole episode see especially Zimmermann, *Papstabsetzungen*, pp. 105ff. For Johannes's earlier career in the royal chapel see J. Fleckenstein, *Die Hofkapelle der deutschen Könige*, 11, *Die Hofkapelle im Rahmen der Ottonisch-Salischen Reichskirche, Schriften der MGH*, 16/ii (Stuttgart 1966) pp. 73ff. For further references see Zimmermann, *Papstregesten*, nos 784, 801.

53 Schramm, 'Zwölf Briefe', no. 1, pp. 256ff.

54 On the Byzantine connections of the Crescentii see also G.
    Bossi, *I Crescenzi*, Atti della Pontificia Accademia d'Archeo-
    logia, XII (1915) p.36. For Boniface VII see Zimmermann,
    Papstabsetzungen, pp.99–103 and *Papstregesten*, nos 524–6,
    575, 582 and 630 with ample references.

55 *Arnulfi gesta archiepiscoporum Mediolanensium*, 1, c.11, *MGH*,
    SS, VIII, pp.9ff: '. . . De quo [Philagathos] dictum est quod
    Romani decus imperii astute in Graecos transferre temp-
    tasset. Siquidem consultu et ope quorumdam civium Roma-
    norum, praecipue Crescentii praedivitis apostolicam sedem
    iam violenter invaserat.' *Benzonis episcopi Albensis ad Heinri-
    cum IV imperatorem libri VII*, 1, c.13, *MGH*, *SS*, XI, p.604:
    'Tercius denique Otto decollavit Crescentium, et cecavit
    papam Sergium [instead of John], eo quod cum Grecis fre-
    quentabant inlicitum commercium.' Cf. also V.Grumel, 'Les
    Préliminaires du schisme de Michel Cérulaire ou la Question
    Romaine avant 1054', *Revue des Études Byzantines*, X (1952)
    pp.5ff.

56 See *De Cerimoniis*, II, c.47 (p.680) for the *chairetismoi*
    (formulae of salutation) spoken by the envoys from Rome
    at their first audience and the *interrogatio* by the logothete.
    For the reception of ambassadors in general see Treitinger,
    op. cit., pp.197ff.

57 Bury, p.135 (text) and pp.29ff.

57a In Constantine Porphyrogenitus *De Thematibus*, ed. A.
    Pertusi, *Studi e Testi*, CLX (Rome 1952) p.94, written in the
    time of Romanus Lecapenus, papal 'self-rule' in Rome was
    still called an innovation. The historical perspectives of the
    emperor were avowedly lofty.

58 *De Cerimoniis*, II, c.44, pp.660–2. For the dispatch of these
    small, part naval, part military and part 'diplomatic' task
    forces and the history of Byzantine relations with Capua,
    Benevento, Salerno, Naples, Amalfi and Gaeta see Gay, pp.
    210ff, Runciman, *Romanus Lecapenus*, pp.177ff and Falken-
    hausen, pp.120ff.

59 *De Cerimoniis*, loc. cit. For the Pharganoi see Ahrweiler,
    Byzance et la mer, pp.110 and 397, n.3. For the transports,
    (*karabia*), op. cit., pp.114 and 409. On the *patrikios* Kosmas
    see R. Guilland, 'Les Patrices byzantins sous le règne de
    Constantine VII Porphyrogénète (913–959)', *Silloge
    Bizantina in onore di Silvio Giuseppe Mercati, Studi Bizantini
    e Neoellenici*, IX (1957) p.197.

60 *De Cerimoniis*, loc. cit., pp.661ff. Hiestand (p.171) has Kos-
    mas command a large army and suffer an 'annihilating defeat'
    at the hands of Margrave Theobald of Spoleto with far-
    reaching consequences, a 'renversement' of Byzantine alli-
    ances in Italy c.935, which he regards as the purpose of Epi-
    phanios's mission. The only source for such a military catas-
    trophe is Liudprand's *Antapodosis*, IV, c.9 (p.108) but the
    frontier warfare he described there stretched over several
    years and his very brief account of it only set the scene for
    one of his more macabre anecdotes (c.10). If Theobald
    really mutilated a large number of captured Greeks, as Liud-
    prand narrated, it is unlikely that Romanus would have
    honoured him with presents only a year later. The story of

the meeting between Kosmas and the defiant Landulf of
Benevento preserved in Cedrenus, II, 355ff does not bear out
the hypothesis of a crushing Byzantine defeat. There is no
mention of any battle and we are very ill-informed indeed
about the course of these hostilities. In general and for his
comment on this passage see P.Lamma, 'Il problema dei due
imperi e dell'Italia meridionale nel giudizio delle fonti lette-
rarie dei secoli ix e x', *Atti del 3° Congresso internazionale di
Studi sull'Alto Medioevo*, Centro Italiano di Studi sull'Alto
Medioevo (Spoleto 1959) pp.155ff and esp. pp.226–9.

61 *De Cerimoniis*, loc. cit., for example the *scaramaggia*, given to
high military and civil dignitaries every year before Palm
Sunday and mentioned frequently also in Philotheos's *Kletorologion* as obligatory dress for various official occasions.
For the annual gifts see Liudprand, *Antapodosis*, VI, c.10
(p.158) who was invited to watch the ceremony in 950 on
one of his embassies.

62 Op. cit., p.662.

63 Falkenhausen, pp.78ff and no.10 (pp.164ff) in her *regestae* of
charters issued by the *strategoi* of Langobardia.

64 When Archbishop Arnulf of Milan entered Constantinople
in 1001 to conclude the negotiations for Otto III's marriage
to a *porphyrogenita* his horse was said to have been shod
with golden shoes. Bishop Werner of Strassburg in 927 then
had to imitate this feat. See Schramm, 'Kaiser, Basileus und
Papst', p.237, n.98 and Treitinger, p.200, n.179. According
to a less legendary source, Archbishop Arnulf 'satis episco-
paliter conversatus est in urbe regia', *Arnulfi gesta archiepiscoporum Mediolanensium*, I, c.13, *MGH, SS*, VIII, p.10.

65 Widukind, III, c.2, p.106.

66 Ohnsorge, 'Drei Deperdita', pp.227ff, and 232ff, 'Byzanz und
das Abendland', pp.34ff, and n.128, also *Konstantinopel und
der Okzident* (Darmstadt 1966) pp.212ff.

67 Leo's illegitimate daughter – not a *porphyrogenita* – was the
first Byzantine princess to marry a Frankish king and future
emperor, Louis III of Provence, who was blinded in 905.
Karl Constantine, count of Vienne (*c.*901–62), was their son.
On this marriage see Ohnsorge, 'Drei Deperdita', pp.229ff,
and Hiestand, pp.90ff, who (p.125, n.57) advanced good
reasons for thinking that the letter sent to Conrad I came
from Leo's brother Alexander.

68 It is difficult to mark the boundary between long-distance
trade and diplomatic missions in the first half of the tenth
century. The immediate successors of the Carolingians in
Italy and Germany could not afford their expensive eastern
embassies. (Cf. *supra*, p.104.) Otto I's earliest ambassador to
Constantinople in 949 was a rich Mainz merchant, and an
experienced slave-trader from Verdun took charge of the
presents on John of Gorze's mission to Córdoba in 953. Cf.
Liudprand, *Antapodosis*, VI, c.4, p.154, the *Vita Iohannis
Gorziensis*, cc.116, 117, *MGH, SS*, IV, p.370 and the pun-
gent remarks on Liudprand of Cremona's own orientation
in G.Arnaldi's 'Liutprando e la storiografia contemporanea
nell'Italia centro-settentrionale', *La Storiografia Alto-
medievale*, Settimane di Studio del Centro Italiano di Studi

sull'Alto Medioevo, XVII (Spoleto 1970) 11, pp. 515ff.

69 Neither the indivisibility of the East-Frankish kingdom in
936 nor the claims of Otto I's brother, Henry *quia natus esset
in aula regali* (*Vita Mathildis Reginae*, c.9, *MGH, SS*, IV, p.
289) need be connected with the arrival of this letter as
Ohnsorge, op. cit., p.233, n.30 and Dölger, 'Die Ottonen-
kaiser und Byzanz', *Karolingische und Ottonische Kunst,
Werden, Wesen, Wirkung, Forschungen zur Kunstgeschichte und
christlichen Archäologie*, III (Wiesbaden 1957) p.53 suggested.
They have perhaps occasionally claimed too much for Byzantine influence, if only to educate the many historians of the
Ottonian period who, before their fine discoveries, neglected
and ignored it. Hiestand (p.170) thought it significant that
shortly after receiving the Greek letter Conrad was called
invictus in the protocol of one of his diplomata (*MGH,
Urkunden*, I, p.17) but although it is singular in his reign the
epithet was at home in the East-Frankish chancery of the
ninth century.

70 *Annales Hildesheimenses*, ed. G.Waitz, *MGH, SRG* (Hanover
1878) p.20 and 'cum muneribus maximis' in the *Annales
Altahenses maiores*, ed. E.Oefele (Hanover 1891) p.8 and
Mystakidis, p.17 where however the embassy is dated 944.

71 For the mission of 949 cf. *supra* p.35 and E. von Ottenthal,
*Die Regesten des Kaiserreichs unter Heinrich I. und Otto I. 919–
973* (Innsbruck 1893, Hildesheim 1967) no.174a. For 952
see Liudprand, *Legatio*, c.5, pp.178ff. For 956 see Widukind
of Corvey, III, c.36, p.135.

72 *De Cerimoniis*, II, c.48, p.691, ll. 13–20 and cf. p.689, ll.4–12.
On the differences between the two protocols see Ostrogorsky, 'Staatenhierarchie', p.50. The more elaborate and
solemn *formula* also mentioned a golden bull whereas the
simpler one for the *rex Saxonias* etc. omitted it but this may
be due to careless compilation.

73 *Die Briefe des Bischofs Rather von Verona*, ed. F.Weigle, *MGH,
Die Briefe der deutschen Kaiserzeit*, I (Weimar 1949) no.7,
p.41, Hiestand, p.206 and H.Keller, 'Das Kaisertum Ottos
des Grossen im Verständnis seiner Zeit', *Deutsches Archiv
für Erforschung des Mittelalters*, XX (1964) p.339.

74 On Byzantine relations with Anglo-Saxon England see R.S.
Lopez, 'Le Problème des relations anglo-byzantines du
septième au dixième siècle', *Byz.*, XVIII (1948) pp.139ff. On
tenth-century English works of art that owed something to
Byzantine prototypes see D.Talbot Rice, 'Britain and the
Byzantine World in the Middle Ages' in *Byzantine Art – An
European Art, Lectures given on the occasion of the 9th Exhibition
of the Council of Europe* (Athens 1966) pp.33ff.

75 *Die Briefsammlung Gerberts von Reims*, ed. F.Weigle, *MGH,
Die Briefe der deutschen Kaiserzeit*, II (Berlin, Zürich, Dublin
1966) no.111, pp.139ff, and A.Vasiliev, 'Hugh Capet of France
and Byzantium', *DOP*, VI (1951) pp.229ff whose genealogies however do not convince. Cf. Dölger, *BZ*, XLV (1952),
pp.467ff.

76 For Robert's marriage to Rozala-Susanna, the daughter of
Berengar II of Italy and Willa, see R.Köpke and E.Dümm-
ler, *Kaiser Otto der Grosse* (Leipzig 1876) p.380 and n.2, and

[Ch.] Pfister, [*Études sur le règne de Robert le Pieux (996–1031)*], B[*ibliothèque de l'*]É[*cole des*] H[*autes*] É[*tudes*], LXIV (Paris 1885) pp. 43ff.

77 On Bishop Odalric's pilgrimage (between 1025–8) see Rodulf Glaber, *Historiarum Libri Quinque*, IV, c.6, ed. cit., pp. 107ff, and Pfister, pp. 349, 353.

78 *Willelmi Malmesbiriensis Monachi de gestis regum Anglorum*, II, 135, ed. W. Stubbs, RS (1887) I, pp. 149ff. For Hugh the Great's marriage see P. Lauer, *Robert Ier et Raoul de Bourgogne (923–936)*, BÉHÉ, CLXXXVIII (Paris 1910) p. 45 and C. N. L. Brooke, *The Saxon and Norman Kings* (London 1963), pp. 135ff, where however Baldwin count of Flanders (*ob.* 918) is wrongly named as Hugh's ambassador instead of his son Adelolf. For the poem see [L. H.] Loomis, ['The Holy Relics of Charlemagne and King Athelstan: The Lances of Longinus and St. Mauricius'], *Speculum*, XXV (1950) pp. 437ff.

79 On the relics and their dispersal see Loomis, and 'The Athelstan gift story and its influence on English Chronicles and Carolingian Romances', *Publications of the Modern Languages Association*, LXVII (1952) pp. 521ff. For a commentary on Hugh the Great's presents and on royal treasures in the early Middle Ages see especially P. E. Schramm and F. Mütherich, *Denkmale der deutschen Könige und Kaiser* (Munich 1962) pp. 26ff, 55, 57, 69, 95ff.

80 Bishop Odalric of Orléans received a large particle of the cross and many cloths of silk for King Robert from the emperor Constantine VIII (*supra* n. 77). Henry II had a relic of St Andrew from Basil II. See Ohnsorge, 'Die Legation des Kaisers Basileios II. an Heinrich II.', *Abendland und Byzanz*, p. 301.

81 G. Henderson, *Early Medieval Style and Civilization* (ed. London 1972) pp. 115 ff. In a late twelfth-century Abingdon notice William of Malmesbury's *vas quoddam ex onichino* (*Gesta Regum*, p. 150) has become an *antiquum vas quoddam ex onichino*, *Chronicon Monasterii de Abingdon*, ed. J. Stevenson, RS (1858) II, p. 276, n. 7. For the onyx cup sent to King Hugh of Italy see *De Cerimoniis*, II, c. 44, p. 661. The 32 onyx chalices in the treasury of St Marks, Venice, are listed, described and illustrated in A. Pasini, *Il Tesoro di San Marco* (Venice 1886) pp. 54ff.

82 Glass-ware and perfumes figure on Epiphanios's list of gifts for King Hugh and on Widukind's (cf. *supra* p. 114and n. 61 and Widukind, III, c. 56, p. 135) though it must be remembered that the Saxon writer lumped together presents from Byzantium, Córdoba and Rome. The theme of exotic animals *Saxonibus antea invisa* (loc. cit.) or perfumes *qualia nunquam antea in Anglia visa fuerant* (William of Malmesbury, loc. cit.) presented by envoys from afar, was common ground for writers who wanted to proclaim the rising renown and authority of their rulers.

83 *Ruodlieb*, v, l. 314 and esp. ll. 321ff, ed. K. Langosch, *Waltharius. Ruodlieb. Märchenepen*, 3 ed., Wissenschaftliche Buchgesellschaft (Darmstadt 1967) pp. 132ff. The jewellery is described in v, ll. 351ff, and on p. 373, no. 144 and pp. 168ff in Schramm-Mütherich, op. cit.

84 A. Boeckler, 'Ottonische Kunst in Deutschland', *I problemi comuni dell'Europa post-Carolinga*, Settimane di Studio del Centro Italiano di Studi sull'Alto Medioevo, 11 (Spoleto 1955) p. 351.

85 That the *loros* (latin *trabea*) became part of Ottonian imperial dress is shown convincingly by J. Déer, 'Byzanz und die Herrschaftszeichen des Abendlandes', *BZ*, L (1957) pp. 405ff. A fine example is the Cluny ivory showing Otto 11 and Theophanu crowned by Christ (Schramm-Mütherich, no. 73 and cf. no. 74), another the great image of Otto 111 in the Reichenau Gospels at Munich (op. cit., no. 108). Whether the golden stole Henry 11 is shown wearing in the Gospels he gave to Monte Cassino (MS Vat. Ottob. lat. 74) belongs to this genre, is less certain (Schramm-Mütherich, no. 141) but the circumscription '. . . caesar et augustus trabeali munere dignus', suggests that it was some kind of *loros*. Monte Cassino lay in a contested sphere of influence between the two empires and here above all the western emperor wanted to be seen as the *basileus's* peer who saw to it that justice was done. For a different view see K. Hoffmann, *Taufsymbolik im mittelalterlichen Herrscherbild, Bonner Beiträge zur Kunstwissenschaft*, IX (Düsseldorf 1968) pp. 77ff who thought that the emperor is shown wearing a deacon's stole as *rex et sacerdos*. See also H. Bloch, 'Monte Cassino, Byzantium and the West in the earlier Middle Ages', *DOP*, III (1946) pp. 166ff. For a full-page illumination of an emperor, again Henry 11, crowned by Christ see H. Jantzen, *Ottonische Kunst* (Munich 1947) p. 103 and pl. 89, the sacramentary he gave to Bamberg.

86 Thietmar of Merseburg, *Chronicon*, 11, c. 15, p. 56. The debate about Theophanu's origins and parentage has not yet ended. It is difficult to discredit Thietmar's statement that she was John Tsimiskes's niece and not the bride the Ottonians really wanted. It is corroborated by her dower diploma (*MGH, Urkunden*, 11, 1, no. 21, p. 29) and Thietmar whose father served the empress had no reason to belittle her. For him she was all the same *immensa nobilitate* (IV, c. 14, p. 148).

87 H. Wentzel, 'Das byzantinische Erbe der ottonischen Kaiser. Hypotesen über den Brautschatz der Theophano', *Aachener Kunstblätter*, XL (1971) pp. 15ff would lead the whole complex of Byzantine objects and works of art associated with Henry 11 back to Theophanu's bridal treasure. I owe this reference to Dr J. O. Alexander.

88 For brief general surveys see Boeckler, op. cit. (n. 84 *supra*), W. Messerer, 'Zur byzantinischen Frage in der ottonischen Kunst', *BZ*, LII (1959) pp. 32ff, K. Weitzmann, 'Various Aspects of Byzantine Influence on the Latin Countries from the sixth to the twelfth Century', *DOP*, XX (1966) pp. 14–19, O. Demus, 'The Role of Byzantine Art in Europe', *Byzantine Art – An European Art*, pp. 89ff.

89 For example the full-face seals of Otto I after 962 (Messerer, op. cit., pp. 41ff) and Liudprand of Cremona's clandestine efforts to buy purple *pallia* for Otto at Constantinople in 968 (*Legatio*, cc. 53, 54, p. 204). Some of the lessons were older. However much the East-Frankish kings, Louis the German,

his sons and their historian Meginhard frowned on Charles the Bald's emperorship they had taken careful note of his new Greek ways as did Hincmar. See *Annales Fuldenses*, 876 ed. F. Kurze, *MGH, SRG* (Hanover 1891) p. 86 and *Annales Bertiniani*, ed. G. Waitz, *MGH, SRG* (Hanover 1883) pp. 130ff. Regensburg, the workshop of Henry II's sacramentary, in the tenth century possessed the *Codex Aureus* of *c*. 870 with its full-page picture of the enthroned Charles, one of the most splendid creations of his court school. Of the two representations of Henry in the sacramentary, one followed this model (Schramm-Mütherich, cf. nos 52 and 111). If Dr J. M. Wallace-Hadrill is right and Charles's 'interest in Late Antiquity was markedly stronger than his alleged interest in Byzantium', *Early Germanic Kingship in England and on the Continent* (Oxford 1971) p. 132, this source too could strengthen the hand of an Ottonian emperor against his Byzantine peers.

90   W. Ohnsorge, 'Das nach Goslar gelangte Auslandsschreiben des Konstantinos IX. Monomachos für Kaiser Heinrich III von 1049', *Abendland und Byzanz*, pp. 319ff.

91   For a survey of these titles and offices in Otto III's entourage see Schramm's article in *Kaiser, Könige und Päpste*, III, pp. 277ff and C. Erdmann, *Forschungen zur politischen Ideenwelt des Frühmittelalters* (Berlin 1951) pp. 105ff. Both wanted to diminish their Byzantine echoes. In the case of Otto III's *logothetes* Fleckenstein, *Hofkapelle*, pp. 107ff has shown that the young emperor borrowed more than a mere word.

92   The sources are quoted and discussed in M. Uhlirz, *Jahrbücher des Deutschen Reiches unter Otto II. und Otto III*, II, pp. 549ff.

93   Thietmar of Merseburg, IV, c. 47, p. 184 and Schramm, *Kaiser, Rom und Renovatio*, pp. 110ff.

94   Thietmar, IV, c. 44, p. 182 : '. . . comitantibus secum Ziazone tunc patricio et Roberto oblacionario.' On his identity which has been much disputed I hope to say something in another place.

95   Preserved amongst Gerbert's letters. See *Briefsammlung*, no. 186, p. 222.

96   K. Holl, *Enthusiasmus und Bussgewalt beim griechischen Mönchtum* (Leipzig 1898). I owe this reference to Mr P. Brown.

97   Perhaps the Calabrian monk Gregory, abbot of Burtscheid, should be added to this list but see A. Hofmeister's critique of Gregory's two *vitae* in 'Studien zu Theophano', *Festschrift Edmund E. Stengel* (Münster/Cologne 1952) pp. 238ff.

98   Otto III's quest for spiritual advice and his penances are described in, for example, Peter Damian's *Vita Beati Romualdi*, c. 25, ed. G. Tabacco, *Fonti per la storia d'Italia* (Rome 1957) pp. 53ff, in the *Vita* of bishop Burchard of Worms, c. 3 (*MGH, SS*, IV, p. 833) and in that of St Nilus, cc. 91, 92, 93, excerpted in op. cit., pp. 617ff. See also Brun of Querfurt's *Vita Quinque Fratrum*, c. 7, *MGH, SS*, XV, II, p. 724 : 'vigiliae tamen, saccus et ieiunium, quibus pollebat'. Some of Otto's friends shared these experiences. For his relations with Odilo of Cluny see E. Sackur, *Die Cluniazenser* (Halle 1892) I, pp. 334ff. That they lacked warmth may be inferred

from a passage in Jotsaldus's *Epitaphium* of the abbot, Bk i,
c.6 : '. . . Principibus et potestatibus christianis . . . ita amica-
bilem et officiosum se reddidit, ut tamquam alter Ioseph ab
omnibus mirabiliter amaretur . . . Concurrat in hunc amorem
Rotbertus rex Francorum; accedat Adheleida mater Ottonum;
veniat etiam Heinricus imperator Romanorum . . .' Otto III
is missing. (*MGH, SS*, xv, p.813.)

99   Otto's ascetic pursuits were reproved in Brun, op. cit., c.7,
p.724. Thietmar wrote : 'multa faciebat, quae diversi diverse
sentiebant' (IV, c.47, p.184).

100 Widukind, III, c.71, p.148 and cf. p.103.

101 *Die Briefsammlung Gerberts von Reims*, no. 26, p.49.

102 Alpertus, *De Episcopis Mettensibus Libellus*, c.1, *MGH, SS*,
IV, p.698.

103 Otloh, *Liber Visionum*, 17, *MGH, SS*, xi, p.385 and the
same story in a codex once belonging to St Michael's,
Hildesheim, *MGH, SS*, IV, p.888. Whether the passage in
Adam of Bremen's *Gesta Hammaburgensis Ecclesiae Pontificum*,
III, c.32, ed. B.Schmeidler, *MGH, SRG* (Hanover/Leipzig
1917) p.174 : 'Ideoque nec mirum esse, si Grecos diligeret,
quos vellet etiam habitu et moribus imitari; quod et fecit'
really refers to Henry III rather than to Archbishop Adalbert
must remain a little uncertain.

104 A South-Italian Greek bishop, Leo, who was expelled for
abetting Otto II's invasion in 982, found a refuge in Liège.
See Rupert's *Chronicon Sancti Laurentii Leodiensis*, c.10, *MGH,
SS*, VIII, p.266. In general see J.M.McNulty and B.Hamil-
ton, 'Orientale Lumen et Magistra Latinitas : Greek influences on Western Monasticism (900–1100)', *Le Millénaire
du Mont Athos, 963–1963, Études et Mélanges* (Chevetogne
1963) I, pp.181ff. For want of concrete evidence the authors
are forced to conclude that these influences were 'imponder-
able' (p.215). B.Bischoff's indispensable paper 'Das grie-
chische Element in der abendländischen Bildung des Mittelalters,' now in *Mittelalterliche Studien* (Stuttgart 1967) II,
pp.246ff prompts caution.

105 William of Malmesbury, *Gesta Regum*, II, 148, ed. cit., I, p.
165. For the Greek bishop see the *Liber Eliensis*, ed. E.O.
Blake, Camden Society, 3rd series, XCII (London 1962)
p.73. I am indebted to Mr James Campbell for this reference.

106 Archbishop Brun's Greek *eloquentia* was praised not only by
his biographer Routger but also in the *Vita Iohannis Gorziensis*, c.116, *MGH, SS*, IV, p.370.

107 On the spirit of the eleventh-century pilgrimage to Jerusalem : R.W.Southern, *The Making of the Middle Ages*
(London 1953) pp.51ff. Also E.R.Labande, 'Recherches sur
les pèlerins dans l'Europe des xie et xiie siècles', *Cahiers de
Civilisation Médiévale*, I (1958) pp.159ff, 339ff.

108 There are some useful pages on French pilgrimages in the
eleventh century in R.Pfister, op. cit., pp.344ff. Cf. also J.
Ebersolt, *Orient et Occident, Recherches sur les influences byzantines et orientales en France avant les Croisades* (Paris/Bruxelles
1928) pp.71ff and H.Dauphin, *Le Bienheureux Richard Abbé
de Saint-Vanne de Verdun, Bibliothèque de la Revue d'Histoire
Ecclésiastique*, XXIV (Paris/Louvain 1946) pp.278ff. Abbot

Richard was said to have headed 700 pilgrims. Duke Robert of Normandy went : 'ingenti multitudine.' Rodulf Glaber, IV, c. 7, p. 108.

109 *Das Register Gregors VII*, 1, 46; 49; 11, 37, ed. E. Caspar, *MGH, Epistolae Selectae* (2 ed. Berlin 1955) 1, pp. 69ff, 75ff, 172ff.

110 Cf. *supra* 103 and Rodulf Glaber, IV, c. 6, p. 106: 'Per idem tempus ex universo orbe tam innumerabilis multitudo cepit confluere ad Sepulchrum Salvatoris Iherosolimis quantam nullus hominum prius sperare poterat.'

111 Ibid.

112 Among the pilgrims from Germany it is easier to find women making the journey in the tenth century than in the eleventh. Cf. R. Röhricht, *Die Deutschen im Heiligen Lande* (Innsbruck 1894).

113 *Ekkeberti Vita Sancti Haimeradi Presbiteri*, c. 4, *MGH, SS,* x, p. 600.

114 See J. Becker's introduction to ed. cit., pp. xxxii ff.

115 He may have gone to Byzantium again on a more festive mission only three years later in 971. Cf. n. 24 *supra*.

116 Ohnsorge, 'Die Anerkennung des Kaisertums Ottos I. durch Byzanz', *Konstantinopel und der Okzident*, pp. 189ff.

117 Liudprand, *Legatio*, p. 175 for the *inscriptio*, c. 5, p. 178; c. 41, p. 197; c. 52, p. 203; cc. 60–2, pp. 208–10.

118 Op. cit., c. 3, p. 177; c. 10, p. 181; c. 41, pp. 197ff; c. 52, p. 203.

119 Op. cit., c. 46, p. 200, l. 11; and c. 55, p. 205, l. 25 and c. 65, p. 212, ll. 6ff. Once Liudprand eluded his guards in a church and received messages from his clandestine connections. In Saxon historiography Nikephoras's downfall in December 969 was linked with his failure against Otto I.

120 Op. cit., cc. 29, 30, pp. 190ff. Cf. also c. 37, p. 194.

121 *Notkeri Balbuli Gesta Karoli Magni Imperatoris*, 11, cc. 5, 6, ed. H. F. Haefele, *MGH, SRG*, new series, XII (Berlin 1959) pp. 52ff.

122 *Annales Altahenses Maiores*, ed. E. L. B. von Oefele, *MGH, SRG* (Hanover 1891) p. 67. Bishop Gunther of Bamberg wrote home : 'Experti enim sumus Ungros sine fide famulantes, Vulgarios occulte rapientes, fugimus Uzos aperte debachantes, Constantinopolitanos vidimus graece et imperialiter arrogantes.'

Note

Bibliographical addendum: *Occident et Orient au Xe siècle*. Actes du IXe congrès de la Société des Historiens médiévistes de l'Enseignement Supérieur Public (Dijon, 2-4 juin 1978), *Publications de l'Université de Dijon*, 57 (Paris, 1979, Société "Les Belles Lettres").

6

THE POLEMICS OF THE PAPAL REVOLUTION

THE habits of political thought and ideological conflict were born in Western Europe during the second half of the eleventh century. The spontaneous fight for their convictions by men who felt passionately that there was something wrong in the established order and working of the *ecclesia* and by those who sought to shield that order against their attacks brought to life a vast literature of controversy. If nothing else, the aspirations which found their common centre at Rome under papal leadership brought in their wake new dimensions and means of establishing truths. As the defenders of the status quo were never tired of pointing out, in vain of course, peace, concord and respect for rank were swept away by forms of agitation which were novel to anyone who had grown up in the cloisters and cathedral schools of early Salian times. Let us listen to one of them, Sigebert of Gembloux. His *Apology against those who challenge the masses of married priests* was written some time after Gregory VII's lenten synod in 1075 where the pope had ordered that the people should no longer accept the offices of incontinent clerks. 'Who does not grieve', Sigebert exclaimed, 'at so great an upheaval in the Church. Which Christian does not, if he has any compassion, feel full of sorrow on seeing Christianity trampled underfoot. What else', he lamented, 'is talked about even in the women's spinning-rooms and the artisans' workshops than the confusion of all human laws . . . sudden unrest amongst the populace, new treacheries of servants against their masters and masters' mistrust of their servants, abject breaches of faith among friends and equals, conspiracies against the power ordained by God ? . . . and all this', he ended his complaint, 'backed by authority, by those who are called the leaders of Christendom.'[1]

Here is, to say the least, the feeling of something new in the ways important issues are debated and brought home to an

audience much larger than that of a few learned men residing at
the better schools, *scriptoria* and courts. It is not as if the urge to
maintain a point of view or justify a policy had not been felt
before. In tenth-century Germany, at the very beginning of the
development which the leaders of reform attacked in the eleventh,
there had been debate about the tasks and functions of the clerical
élite in society, but it was restrained and anxious to avoid offence.
A Ruotger or a Widukind of Corvey can be found defending, the
one in his *Life of Archbishop Brun*, the other in his *Res Gestae
Saxonicae*, the regime in which, as one of its critics remarked: 'duke
and count did the work of bishops and the bishop claimed for
himself the work of duke and count'.[2] Against this sharp hint at
Archbishop Brun's dual role, half political and half religious, his
disciple and biographer pleaded the harmony of his hero's deeds,
combining priestly sanctity with royal strength.[3] The protection
of his church itself demanded of Brun that he should be busy at
home and in the field.[4] It called for a royal priesthood, a *regale
sacerdotium* which in the end was nothing other than the Ottonian
Reichskirche with its manifold tasks, religious, political and economic, and its bishops in the service of the king. Their functions
outside their churches helped to secure the peace of the Church
at large over which they had to mount guard, and the example
of the Old Testament's judges and priests, especially Samuel,
served to explain their role in the Ottonian Empire.[5] It is to them
that Sigebert of Gembloux looked back with nostalgia when he
wrote the life of one of Brun's aristocratic recruits, Bishop Theo-
deric of Metz, for their's was to him a vanished golden age. He
wrote: 'I rightly call the times of Otto (the Great) fortunate when
the *res publica* was reformed by renowned prelates and wise men
restored peace to the churches and integrity to religion. One
could then see and, indeed, experience the truth of the philosopher's saying: "Happy the state whose rulers are philosophers and
whose philosophers rule!" '[6]

On the other side the voices of critics could also be heard, even
in the tenth century. Atto of Vercelli (*c.* 924–960) and more still
Rather of Verona (*c.* 890–974) have been called forerunners of
reform by Augustin Fliche.[7] Abbo of Fleury was perhaps more
successful in public than either the obscure stylist Atto had been
or the eccentric and moody Rather. His writings may have been

one of Cardinal Humbert's sources and there are in his letters and in his *Apologeticus* already traces of the view that a church was an indivisible whole which could not be shared between a bishop and another lord, the altar belonging to the one and the building to the other.[8] Abbo addressed royal patrons and councils but the atmosphere in which he wrote was on the whole enclosed, and despite the rising influence of Cluny, not so very different from that of Carolingian times. It wholly lacked the edge, the fury and volume of the later eleventh century, which respected neither persons nor institutions.

The German scholar Carl Mirbt began his study of the controversial literature in the age of Gregory VII, published in 1894, with a statistical survey.[9] In the period from about 1050 to 1111 he counted a total of 115 polemical works of which he assigned 48 to Italy, 55 to Germany, 11 to France, and one to Spain. He seems to have omitted the Anglo-Norman writers altogether. The tracts of the author, now called the Norman Anonymous, had not yet been included in the Libelli-series of the Monumenta Germaniae Historica nor did Gilbert Crispin's treatise on the validity of simoniacs' sacraments enter into Mirbt's survey.[10] His terminal date 1111 was of necessity an arbitrary choice: Honorius Augustodunensis and others equally belonged, and it should also be mentioned that the Lotharingian cardinal Humbert's book *Against the Simoniacs* is counted as a product of Italy. This formidable bulk of polemical literature was certainly meant for and reached a wide and not only clerical public. Manegold von Lautenbach in the dedicatory letter of his most important political work, the *Liber ad Gebehardum*, related how a pamphlet from the adversary's camp was hawked about everywhere, broadcast in the streets and more secluded places, and treated like a canonical text.[11] The author of this *libellus* was Wenrich, the master of the cathedral-school at Trier.[12] Both he and Manegold wrote perhaps less to make converts than to strengthen their own party and to disseminate the reasons behind its actions, but there can be no doubt about their sense of duty and vocation, especially in Manegold's case. Gregory VII more than once exhorted his followers that they must not only themselves obey St. Peter and his representative but also induce others to do so.[13] Many of his literary partisans received their inspiration to defend or to attack directly from him or from his letters. Initiative and success were on their side. They wrote more and what they wrote lasted better and reached a larger audience.[14] Some of their opponents' works have survived in only one manuscript or none; this warns us not to over-value ideas for their interest to modern critics and historians that meant little to the contemporaries of their begetters and even less to the next generation of writers and possibly never reached them at all.

Distinguished German scholars have had nothing but praise for a work written at Hersfeld in 1092–93, the *Liber de unitate Ecclesiae conservanda*.[15] It was one of the few utterances on the emperor's side which succeeded in reaching fundamentals. Its largest theme is unity within the Church based on St. Cyprian's words: 'He who keeps not . . . unity, holds not the law of God, nor the belief of the Father and the Son, nor the faith by which he should be saved.'[16] The author, whoever he may have been, stood in old ways, when the king had been the vicar of Christ unquestionably and this had determined his place in the Church whose *rector* and defender he was by rights. But he also knew that the repetition of past beliefs was of no avail against the force of the currents which threatened to tear them away. When he wrote, civil war had been waged in Germany for some seventeen years, and his strongest arguments lay against the consequences of the Gregorian upheaval rather than its texts. These he refuted as best he could, but the justice of Henry IV's kingship depended in the last resort on the disasters which the destructive violence of zealots had wrought. Their calls to arms were against the divine order and the nature of the Church's constitution. From the very beginning of the agitation, simoniacs and those who favoured them, the lay-givers of altars and churches, had been branded as heretics. In the *Liber* the weapon is reversed and resistance to rightful authority is branded as heresy: 'It is a great heresy to resist God's order who alone has power to grant empire.'[17] God gave rule, he cited St. Augustine, to Marius, Caesar, Augustus, Nero and Vespasian, some good and some horrible emperors, Constantine the Christian; and Julian the Apostate.[18] To go against his ordinance, as some fifteen named bishops fighting against Henry IV had done, meant that human and divine laws had ceased to count 'amongst them and against them'.[19]   To have

raised the conflict into a matter of faith and to advocate violence
were in his eyes crimes which soiled the causes for the sake of
which they had been committed. Peace and concord he regarded
as the higher values and it is as partisans and agitators that the
Hildebrandines are denounced by him with the help of St.
Cyprian and St. Augustine. Yet it is just in using the authority
of the *De civitate Dei* that the author disappoints, for he did not
quite know what to do with the classical definitions of justice and
the nature of a true *res publica* which he found there:[20] 'The
commonwealth is the affair of the people, but the people is not
any assemblage of men, gathered together in any fashion, but a
gathering of the multitude united together under a common law
and in the enjoyment of a common well-being.'[21] The author of
the *Liber* cited these definitions which St. Augustine had taken
from Cicero and the Roman tradition, but there were few conclusions he could base upon them. The refrain of his argument
that peace was good and that established rulers should be obeyed
rings through again, but nothing more. He made better headway
with his charge that Gregory VII and his bishops were usurping
the functions of both powers, that of kings and that of priests,
reducing the former to a mere nothing.[22] He sought to show this
from the events of the day about which he was well informed, and
it is his historical judgement rather than his stock of political ideas
that lend force to his case.[23] The *Liber de unitate Ecclesiae conservanda*
contains in its bulky pages a war-weary strain akin to the views of
the *Politiques* in the French Wars of Religion: the continuity of a
certain order of things must be defended against the heat and
fury of fanatics. Unfortunately, the German Henry IV was not
the man to attract and hold such sentiments round him: the three
books of the *Liber* drew no immediate echoes nor answers. We
possess them only because Ulrich von Hutten in 1519 found a
manuscript, since lost, in the library of Fulda and liked its contents so well that he printed it a year later. Launched by so
dangerous a firebrand, the *Liber* was at once prohibited by the
authorities. The date is no accident. The anti-papal sentiments
of German humanists at the beginning of the Reformation were
fanned by their historical discoveries. Later not only some of
Sigebert of Gembloux's writings but also the *Vita Heinrici Quarti*,

a moving and yet highly contrived dirge on the memory of a much-execrated man, were placed on the Index.[24]

Let us return to Sigebert's opening sentences in the *Apologia*: they may serve to describe the characteristics of the polemics as a whole and the atmosphere in which they changed hands. First of all the tone is harsh and uncompromising and yet Sigebert is regarded as a man of moderation, at least by German scholars.[25] To a greater or lesser extent this aggressiveness was a common trait of the writers on both sides. They did not intend to discuss issues in a spirit of liberalism. Scripture, canon, patristic authority or history interpreted, these were their weapons and they used them to hammer home their points past all rejoinders. They approached their task asking questions of detail: Could the ordinations given by a simoniac bishop be valid? Were the sacraments of priests so ordained of use or not to those who received them? Could a king be excommunicated or—in Gregory VII's values the lesser evil—could he be deposed? Could his vassals be released from their oaths of fidelity? Yet sooner or later they stumbled over larger, more fundamental and timeless questions and stated them in their own terms, terms unfamiliar to us but all the same distinctly recognizable. Let us follow one of them, Manegold von Lautenbach, as he approaches his most famous utterance, that in which he is thought to have put forward a doctrine of popular sovereignty. In his *Liber ad Gebehardum* he pursued the question whether a king—always Henry IV—could be rightly excommunicated and set aside. The letter on this subject which Gregory VII sent to the Germans in 1076 is cited in full and Manegold offered to demonstrate to his readers that the pope's commands contained only what his office and the application of the Church's teaching required.[26] In his letter Gregory had stood by the justice of his sentence against Henry's person; he did not yet speak about the place of kings in the Christian world as he saw it and the diabolical character of secular governments pursuing only their own ends. Manegold, to bear out his source, then plunged into an account of kings murdered, deposed, censured, excommunicated and humbled. Secular rebellions here stood cheek by jowl with ecclesiastical sanctions.[27] He simply argued that Henry IV's sins and crimes were more enormous than those of a Maurice, Childeric, Louis the Pious or

Lothar II, the stock examples. Manegold dwelt on his vices, catalogued them and named even some of his mistresses, which gives perhaps a hint at the kind of public he aimed at. It was not interested in erudite, academic argument only.[28] The misfortunes of worthless kings are then continued and brought down to some very recent history, the royal blood-feuds of eleventh-century Hungary. It was not a very good example, but the 'tyrants' who came to grief in this case all happened to be protégés and kinsmen by marriage of the Salian dynasty. Manegold's list is indiscriminate and he seems to have thought that the deposed rulers were always in the wrong and their enemies right simply because they succeeded in deposing them. But it is important to note that in his tirade the fallen kings had both private misdeeds and public acts of injustice to answer for. He wanted to show that the word 'king' did not carry with it immanent powers and merits and that kingship was an office, a rank which could be forfeited for misconduct. A strict analogy with the grades in the Church was to apply.[29] From abuse and obscenity our author suddenly turned to attack the widely held and, until then, rarely challenged belief in the inviolate and charismatic sacredness of the crown and its wearer. The office and its holder could be separated.

At this point Manegold reached the heart of the conflict. Seen in political terms, and of course no writer in the eleventh and early twelfth centuries saw it in what historians or sociologists would now call political terms, the struggle was about rights and powers, their origins and status and how the visible representatives of authority in the Church stood towards one another. Manegold wrote:[30] 'As the royal rank and power excel all other earthly powers so, to wield it, one must not appoint someone criminal or infamous but someone who surpasses others not only in place and rank but also in wisdom, justice and piety. For it is necessary that he who has the care of all and must govern all should also excel all by the superior grace of his virtues. Let him wield the power given to him with the greatest fairness; the people do not exalt him to give him leave to tyrannize but so that he should defend them against the tyranny and wickedness of others.' If the king, who was chosen to coerce evil men and shield the good, himself turned into a cruel despot, 'is it not obvious that he should deservedly fall from the rank granted to him and the people be freed from his lordship and their submission since he himself first broke the covenant for the sake of which he was set up?' This meant that kingship existed to perform certain tasks agreed on in a 'pact'. If the ruler failed to perform these, all obligations to him lapsed. Manegold then used an analogy that can hardly have been flattering for the people to be governed and reveals him as the uncouth controversialist he was, compared with some of his no less zealous partisans, for instance Bernold of Constance. For, he said by way of common-sense reasoning, if someone committed a herd of swine to a keeper for a wage and the swine-herd then did not look after, but stole, slaughtered and destroyed his charges,[31] one would surely not in the end pay him his wages but chase him away. The people, however, who elected, obeyed and deposed kings in this case were first and foremost the German princes and their noble vassals. It is not surprising that in later and quieter times Manegold was thought to have been un-mannerly: his polemic, although it pleased some of Gregory VII's German adherents, was rumoured not to have won papal approval.[32]

None the less, he had stated the essentials of a contract of government. By this the office of a king was not to be at the mercy of human failings which had to be borne with patient resignation. Manegold thought of deposition for unworthiness as a discipline which had been observed by the ancient Romans when they expelled Tarquin. The responsibility of the great, he argued, was greater even in venial transgressions than that of humble people; that of kings was greatest of all and so he led his readers back to Henry IV's vices and sins. [33] In a later chapter of his work, the *Liber ad Gebehardum,* he returned to the theme of rationalized kingship. At this point he wanted to remonstrate against those who sought to prove that papal absolutions from oaths of fealty were wrong as well as disastrous. Human nature, Manegold wrote, excelled that of all other animate creatures in that being capable of reason, it does not rush into action haphazardly, but finds out the causes of things with the aid of rational judgement. It cares not only for what is done but also how it is done. Nobody can make himself emperor or king. The sole purpose for which the people set a ruler over themselves is to govern them justly, give everybody his own, help the good, destroy the wicked and do justice to all. If he fails them he thereby absolves the people from their due subjection. The oath of obedience is governed by reason and nobody is obliged to obey and follow wherever a raging and insensate man might want to lead.[34] Right reason then and a common-sense, self-evident standard of justice were to govern the relationships between ruler and ruled, the German king and his princes. Manegold here argued those questions of authority and obligation which troubled his contemporaries most of all, and he did not broach them solely from the point of view of the Church. He had in fact spelt out a rational justification for the secular aspects of the great revolt against the Salian king. His *pactum* is something more than the traditional bonds between the king and the nobles who did him homage and swore him fealty.[35]

Manegold did not know Aristotle's *Politics* nor could he have laced a coherent doctrine of natural law into his image of the kingly office and its controls. He was not troubled by the question how the people could make a contract of government without a preceding social contract because he took the existence of the community for granted. It seems that in his heat and hurry to pursue more immediate ends he was scarcely conscious of having said something of great moment; he certainly did not give his remarks on the contract of government precedence over those massive sections of his book which merely repeated rather vehemently what was common ground amongst Gregory VII's literary supporters. When he first mentioned the *pactum* it was a covenant which stood above the king and his electors, binding them both. The ruler was set up for the sake of the covenant and those who swore fidelity joined him in observing it. They bound themselves, man for man, to be his helpers and companions in upholding peace and justice. But when Manegold returned to the theme he spoke of the contract as the constitutive act itself by which the king had been raised to his office, a *pactum quo*, not a *pactum pro quo*.[36] This may have been no more than a slip, since the purpose of the contract in his argument and the consequences of its breach by the king remained the same. It shows, however, that Manegold was more anxious to press his conclusions than to work out the premises on which they were based. He could do this because he believed the pope's authority in absolving Christians from their oaths of fealty to be sufficient in any case. To justify this authority the contract-theory was not needed.

On the other side it was argued that oaths were inviolate and had always and amongst all people been held sacred. Kingship, too, was as old as the beginning of the world, older than Christianity. It was fortified by God after it had already existed for some time in its own right. Wenrich of Trier, in his treatise, seems to put forward a historical justification for the secular power, now forced to fight for its age-old status.[37] But it was no more than a hint, nor can it be said that Petrus Crassus' *Defence of Henry IV* succeeded in summoning the resources of Roman law to the king's rescue. Peter, the only layman amongst the polemicists, came from Ravenna, where some instruction in the elements of Roman legal science was available and working lawyers could bring principles of Roman private law to bear on their daily practice.[38] He thought that Henry IV's kingship was inviolate not only because it had been given to him by God but also because it belonged to him by the same right as any heir enjoyed. He cited ample material from the *Institutes* and the *Codex Justinianus* to prove the sacrosanctity of private inheritance. Could anyone be so unreasonable as to believe that one could do against a king what the law forbade in the case of a private individual, namely, deprive him of his just possession?[39] These words, addressed to the insurgent Saxons, ignored the heart of their case since they claimed to defend their hereditary rights and liberties against a king turned tyrant.[40] To be able to reason as he did Peter had to show, first of all, that the authority of Roman civil law was continuous and universal, and it was here rather than in his strained appeal to the rights of private inheritance that the *Defensio Heinrici* gained new ground. All peoples were subject to these sacred laws in the sense that some could learn by studying them directly while to others they were brought home in the guise of custom and long use. Whether men were conscious of them or not, these laws held sway. To make this plausible Crassus had to equate the legislation of Ancient Rome with medieval custom where they agreed, as they did in the matter of inheritance. The Roman emperors had not excluded themselves from the benefit of this rule nor their successors or later kings. Long possession of the realm could not be challenged lawfully and rebellion was a poor substitute for laws. Without them man lived not much better than brutes that knew neither authority nor property.[41] All this was said, however, only to denounce and demand judgement against Gregory VII who had broken with all laws. Crassus' call to those who were to judge him belonged to a tradition of ferocious proceedings against popes in ninth- and tenth-century Rome with their grotesque publicity and afflictive penalties. He used, albeit clumsily, scriptural authority, papal decretals, St. Augustine, and St. Ambrose side by side with the *Institutes* without a sense of incongruity, let alone conflict.

Crassus' awkwardness as a polemicist betrays his lack of schooling or rather his peculiar schooling which placed him at a disadvantage against the monastic and clerical writers. The strong idiosyncracies and temperamental methods of so many of the eleventh-century controversialists were conditioned by the fact that they did not possess an adequate apparatus of political concepts between them. Their writings performed the important service of revealing the need for such an apparatus. Phrases like the *ius gentium, ius civile, civilitas* and *res publica* belonged to the political vocabulary of this prolonged crisis without forming the base of a coherent secular political theory. Peter Crassus' *Defensio*, too, has survived only in one manuscript, and like other pamphlets on the king's side, his was stillborn. Here again the theorists of change and the right order in the world, as Tellenbach called it, had the better of the argument for the moment.[42] Cardinal Deusdedit in his *Libellus contra Invasores*, completed in 1097, knew that Roman law and the canons could conflict. When they did, he made it clear, the former must be rejected because sacerdotal authority, instituted by God, surpassed royal power.[43] Their offices were separate, but secular wealth and might must minister to the Church's requirements. The dominant school of political theologians and canonists who in the twelfth century succeeded in finding agreed terms of reference and in building an imposing edifice of papal theory upon them, owed much to Deusdedit.

Gregory VII himself was the sternest and most unrelenting exponent of the ideas which his measures sought to impose. He taught what he did, and teaching was not the least important means to make his actions effective. His letters to Bishop Hermann of Metz, for instance, especially that of 1081, not only seem to sum up his cause, but became the lapidary texts which his opponents sought to break and his literary supporters interpreted, enlarged and so helped to propagate yet further. Read in isolation, however, they cannot wholly do justice to the convictions which drove him, especially in the matter of earthly, secular rule. Gregory VII has not suffered at the hands of the devoted bands of scholars who have set out and elucidated his ideology but he has, much more than most decisive figures, come to be understood in many different and conflicting ways. No historical metaphysician or marxist could see in him only the spokesman of forces latent in eleventh-century society or the Church; too much of the impulse in the war for the *libertas ecclesiae*, to take only the most obvious expression of what he wanted, came from him alone. His sense of mission was overpowering. Even if it could be shown that all his ideas were found in older traditions and already widespread in the reform-movement before his pontificate, there would remain the frightening severity and heroic persistence with which he pressed them, regardless of the consequences to himself or to others. He had, to say the least, the temper of a revolutionary.

The early middle ages knew more than one meaning for the word *libertas*. There was what has been called subjective liberty, belonging to an individual by virtue of his birth and standing, which really defined his relations to those above and below him.[44] There were also the *libertates* which performed similar functions for privileged churches and later privileged towns. The term could equally be applied to a kingdom to describe its freedom from feudal dependence on another. Here *libertas* really meant almost the same as *potestas* and *honor*. The writers of the Ottonian period, now and again, also had an objective sense for the word 'liberty' when it stood for a universally recognizable and everywhere applicable contrast to servitude and enslavement.[45] There could be many ambiguities about the status of a free man; there was none about that of a slave. In general, however, *libertas* and honour increased as its subject had obligations towards a higher rather than a lower overlord and the highest liberty was to depend on God alone. In this way Gregory VII could argue that the kingdom of Hungary was freer as a vassal of St. Peter and his successors than as a satellite of the empire.[46] For the same reason, however, the question of the origin of secular government and its place in the hierarchy of legitimate powers came to be and remained at the centre of the conflict. The defenders of kingship and its rights and standing in the Church, writers like Hugh of Fleury and the Norman Anonymous, began and ended their case by setting out once more its direct divine ordination and dignity, regardless of the individual qualities of a king.[47]

The possession of much subjective freedom, independence from the wills of others, in the early middle ages thus necessarily belonged to those who also possessed power, the rulers of Western Europe and their great nobles. Highly prized as it was, it could not be, even for this privileged minority, wholly an end in itself but had to serve, both in theory and in practice, positive purposes. It was in his authoritative claim to decide what these purposes were to be that Gregory VII came into conflict with the emperor and, sporadically, rulers like Philip I of France. By divine justice the Church must be freed from lay-domination: kings and nobles, no less than bishops and priests, should honour, help and defend her with a new humility and this for their own good as much as the advancement of reform.[48] To understand Gregory's programme and what he regarded as the right relations between the successors of St. Peter and the successors of Constantine or Charlemagne, his idea of justice is even more important than that of *libertas*. It demanded that service to God, the Church, its earthly head and their needs should take precedence over the bread-and-butter politics of 'who whom', of feuding and princely land-hunger.[49] For in the eleventh century service to God and dependence on his will could not be an experience only of the inner man, it had to manifest itself in loyalty and unquestioning obedience to the pope as the successor of St. Peter to whom the Church had been entrusted. Obedience to him became in the course of the battle against simony, clerical marriage and lay-control the touchstone of whether a man served in the camp of Christ or in that of Satan. Just as Cardinal Humbert had passionately turned against those who would distinguish between the spiritual and the secular attributes of a benefice, and insisted that not only the altar but also the lands and other possessions of a Church were sanctified, so Gregory VII demanded a new unity of belief and action. Men, especially rulers, must seek to make St. Peter their debtor and merit their rank or good fortune by placing themselves at his disposal as soldiers, tributaries and pressure-groups.[50] Those who followed these precepts would be rewarded by the prince of the apostles not only in the next life but also in this with victory and more honour. Those who disobeyed were the sons of pride whose actions followed only their own will, pursuing temporary instead of lasting ends. In this scheme of things the place of the powers that were depended on their willingness to accept a role of useful service: there is plenty of evidence that the pope viewed the ordinary ambitions and activities of the princely ruling class with, at best, misgivings and, more often, with intense dislike.[51]

In Gregory VII's attitude towards secular government one should perhaps distinguish between his dealings with the fringe, the homilies he addressed to the nascent kingdoms and societies on the frontiers of Europe, and his collision with old and established powers like the Salian *Reich* and Capetian France. To the former, Norway, Denmark, Poland, Bohemia, Hungary and the kingdoms of Spain he wanted to impart the rudiments of Christian behaviour or higher standards of justice and the sum of all his messages was that power entailed responsibilities.[52] To their leaders closer relations with Rome were generally advantageous and meant a step up in the world of western states, an increase of honour and *libertas* which did not conflict with *iustitia*. But it was different with the older thrones where justice demanded that their freedoms should be reduced and that they must be subordinated to the higher judgement of the papacy. Their honour and customs were not to stand in the way of the Church's freedom which belonged to her as the bride of Christ.[53] Gregory's second letter to Bishop Hermann of Metz was written at the height of the crisis that arose when he staked everything on Henry IV's renewed excommunication and deposition. It once again gave a lead to those who felt uneasy about the attack on established traditions and the turmoil, including full-scale wars, it entailed. Were kings, he wrote, exempted from the power to bind and to loose, which Christ entrusted to St. Peter? Who could be exempted from this universal grant except the wretch who did not want to bear God's yoke and so bowed to the devil, refusing to be one of the sheep of Christ? This miserable liberty, however, is of no profit to him because the more he refused to bear the yoke out of pride the more he shall wear it at the last judgement.[54] Here then justice, as Gregory VII felt it, clashed with the freedom of secular powers to pursue their own ends in their own way. This freedom was not only wretched but also illusory since it led to eternal damnation. True freedom was to be found only in the kingdom of heaven.[55] It is characteristic that one of Gregory VII's commentators, the able Bernold of Constance in his *Apologeticae Rationes* toned down the stridency of his exemplar. Here the Lord's yoke is gentle and to bear it is to reign; to reject it meant to submit to the devil's tyranny without thereby escaping from the Church's power.[56]

Rarely have the forces of heaven been summoned so directly and confidently to influence the minds and the behaviour of men as they were by Gregory VII. He had his own favourite examples to proclaim the nothingness of mere earthly authority, its duties to a higher order of things and its perils if it failed or lapsed in them. The best known is a sentence suggesting not only the human but even the diabolical origin of secular government. At the height of the passion which runs through the whole of his letter to Hermann of Metz, he exclaimed: 'Who does not know that kings and dukes began with those who did not know God and in their blind greed and intolerable presumption wanted to rule over equals, i.e. other men, with pride, pillage, murder and in the end all the crimes in the world at the devil's instigation?'[57] This passage has been much brooded over because elsewhere in his letters the origin of principality and the source of royal power are not called evil; on the contrary, they were given to their holders by God. His homilies to the Spanish kings insisted on this and his letter to William the Conqueror written in 1080 began: 'We believe your prudence must know that God distributed the apostolic and royal dignities, both higher than any other in the world, so that they shall govern it.' The king's office was to be under the care and guidance of the Holy See.[58] To Countess Adelheid of Turin he wrote: 'Honour and power were granted to you by God so that they shall be applied to his service and that of his people , in this case the monks of Fruttuaria.[59] The divine commission, therefore, bound those who received it to accomplish more for the Church, to be humbler and juster and to receive papal directions gladly. Scholars have sought to find a consistent theory of the state in Gregory's letters despite these conflicting groups of utterances or to show that they contain no contradictions. It is not easy to do this. Recently a German historian, Nitschke, held that what Gregory VII wrote of the diabolical origin of kingship only referred to its beginnings in pagan times.[60] Pagans who did not know God could not be ruled by his dictates and their governments must therefore have been evil. In a Christian setting, however, a prince who belonged to the following of the Church and showed due devotion was part of a divine order. Those who offended and disobeyed must be followers of the devil. There could be no separate sphere for the state. But this interpretation, if anything, enlarges the ambiguities and uncertainties in Gregory's thought and introduces an element of permanent dualism into his world. According to Augustin Fliche royal power was of divine origin for Gregory VII in the same sense as Gregory the Great in his *Moralia* expounded that the devil's power too had been granted to him by God and is just in its origins but unjust in its will.[61] This seems very forced. Is it not possible that Hildebrand as pope never reached a rounded theory of secular government and that his views remained rugged and dissonant, drawing a distinction between good and evil rulers rather than the nature of the authority common to them both? He came to know the men he had to deal with and found most of them wanting. Here too his followers and literary partisans toned down and polished the tenor of his ideas. Cardinal Deusdedit said of kingship that it was a human invention which had been allowed but not willed by God. Hence its power was at first *de facto*, whereas the priestly authority had from its Old Testament beginnings divine legitimation.[62]

The examination of all government, secular and ecclesiastical, was to become the *ex-officio* province of the papacy. In an ascending scale of responsibility Christian kings would have to answer for their subjects before God, like priests and bishops, but the supreme pontiff would have to render account for them.[63] In this way they remained organs of the Church, albeit subordinate ones. It followed also that they were responsible for the slaughter of men whom they led into battle for the sake of conquest and power. Thousands were killed and for this princes might occasionally say 'mea culpa' without meaning it or wishing that they had not led their fellow-men to perdition.[64]   A condemnation of all purely secular warfare lies behind these sombre sentences.   There was no room for it in Gregory VII's convictions and this must be set against his own calls to war in the cause of St. Peter and the Church.[65]   The need to use arms was accepted by him and that they were used furnished his opponents with their bitterest and most repeated charges.   Here lay a *confusio ordinis*, an offence against the way the roles had been distributed.   Had Henry IV accepted the place now meant for him, it could be argued, all wars under the authority of St. Peter would have been crusades.

To the idea that secular government must be supervised by the *sacerdotium*, which Gregory VII handed on to the political theologians of the twelfth century, notably Hugh of St. Victor, must be added another.   The last paragraph of his letter to Hermann of Metz began: 'Let those therefore whom the Church calls to a governance or an *imperium* . . . obey humbly.'[66]   Twice events drove him to stake his claims in the election of a German anti-king.   Suitability, usefulness and devotion to Rome were to be the criteria of the German princes' choice.[67]   Further, the pope must confirm it and approve of the elected king.   In the last sentences of the letter hereditary succession to the throne is condemned almost as if the Church called men to rule principalities as it called them to be bishops and abbots under the new dispensation. Manegold von Lautenbach's virulent views on the appointment and deposition of rulers developed a theme of which the main chord had already been struck.

Is it permissible, then, to speak of 'the political ideas of the papal revolution'?   Gregory VII and his circle often insisted that they were not innovating but only returning to the wise, right and just precepts of the Fathers.   It is worth examining these claims, sometimes echoed by modern scholars, for a moment. They were, of course, in the eleventh century fiercely anachronistic, since the Gregorians challenged custom, tradition and established practices with their own vision of the past and the argument of lasting truth.   It was not admitted that this truth had itself at one time been historically conditioned and been part of the way in which the Church was organized and had lived in the later Roman empire.   A minatory clause in a privilege of Gregory the Great's, to cite only one example, could thus become one of the justifications for Henry IV's excommunication and deposition.[68] Gregory VII's own and his followers' attitude to history was ambivalent. They cited historical precedents when these seemed to favour their programme, but they rejected them in favour of ultimate principles when the past seemed to stand in their way or stood condemned in the light of their values. Their opponents could claim with some justice that many examples which showed rulers under the duress of ecclesiastical sanctions could not remotely justify the actions now taken by the curia. The Gregorians could not claim a monopoly of support from early decretals and the Fathers. The uses they made of their texts, St. Cyprian, St. Augustine, St. Ambrose, Gelasius and Gregory the Great were not always better than their opponents' and did not unequivocally give them the better case. The same authority counted for both parties and was appealed to by both; this in itself shows that the claim, that there was nothing new in the aims of the movement led by Gregory VII, must not be taken literally.

The second and better reason for the view that we are dealing with sweeping changes and a revolutionary upheaval lies elsewhere. Much has been written by German scholars, Hauck, Erdmann and Haller about the ways in which Gregory VII's urgency over reform in the Church and his ideas of the right relations between Rome and the ruling secular strata of catholic Europe, emperor, kings and princes, were translated into action.[69] The pope never denied, but on the contrary expressly asserted, that new counsels and expedients could be used to enforce divine justice and come to the rescue of neglected canons.[70] These counsels included the boycott, agitation, subversion, and the utmost publicity for the papal programme and its justification. The polemical literature belonged to the new arsenal of weapons which the Gregorians created for themselves. It was revolutionary almost in the marxist sense that it is not enough to discover the truth but that one must make it one's business to transform what exists in order to make it prevail. The leaders and writers of the papal reform movement were ready to do this, and in this cause volcanic figures like Humbert and Gregory VII and lesser ones, Anselm of Lucca and Deusdedit, the Germans Manegold von Lautenbach and Gebhard von Salzburg spent their lives, suffered and refused to compromise. To bring about the rule of divine justice, as they saw it, on earth they were ready not only to persuade but also to force the recalcitrant against their will, knowing what was good for them in the timeless manner of revolutionary idealists.

It has already been said that political ideas in the classical sense only appear in the polemics of the eleventh and early twelfth centuries incoherently, in flashes. But the spate of appeals to opinion in the new genre, developed during and as part of the investiture conflict, did not end when the struggle was over. It is with us still as long as it remains meaningful to argue about questions of right, authority and the use of powers. The successors of Manegold and his generation in the Church wrote with greater precision and commanded a vaster armoury of organized knowledge, above all a new legal science, to fight over the dangerous and brooding legacy which the first collision between *regnum* and *sacerdotium* left behind. The ideologies of early medieval Europe had been challenged and in part destroyed. Given the Church universal, empire and kingdoms had always been regarded as the most exalted powers within it. The idea of frontiers between them or areas where they did not overlap was unknown. But as secular governments refused to accept in full the new curbs on their *libertas* and despite all papal teaching regarded them as affronts to their *honor* and *potestas*, such frontiers became inevitable. An almost Hobbesian note is sounded in an anecdote told of Henry IV's son Henry. When urged not to hang a count under the walls of his defiant castle for fear of divine censure, he is reported to have said: 'The heavens are the Lord's heavens, but the earth he has given to the sons of men' (Ps. cxiii, 16).[71]   There had been no theory of the secular state as such, but as a result of the great crisis it was all ready to be born. The very compromises over lay investitures found in the West, in England and France in the early twelfth century, helped to divide what had hitherto been one. The distinction between *spiritualia* and *temporalia* could be enlarged. Following on the development of more secular government and better administration in many parts of Europe, it was.

Lastly, the ascendancy of the new hierarchy of ideas and values which had been so necessary for the Church's self-realization, its new orders and improving organization, helped to create another kind of new frontier. To describe it, it is worth while recalling

Rousseau's idea of the relations which should exist between the sovereign General Will and government and his warning that governments had a general will of their own and could have interests of their own.[72] Some development of this kind began to trouble the Church in the twelfth century. The idea of a Christian society encompassed by the *ecclesia* in a religious and social sense and directed by the papacy grew apace in a way which made the writers of the eleventh century look like poor cousins, but there was now an ever more self-protective *ecclesia* with a formidable apparatus of government which had to justify itself to stronger secular powers.[73] The struggle for the Church's freedom turned into a struggle for clerical privileges. The ideal and the privileged institution confronted one another. The widening distance between them did not escape the ever more self-confident critics of the medieval Church.

[1] *Monumenta Germaniae Historica* (henceforth cited *M.G.H.*), *Libelli de Lite Imperatorum et Pontificum* ii, 438 (henceforth cited *Libelli*).

[2] Archbishop William of Mainz in a letter to Pope Agapitus II, dated 955 in *Monumenta Moguntina*, ed. P. Jaffé (Bibliotheca Rerum Germanicarum III, Berlin, 1866), p. 348: 'Dux comesque episcopi, episcopus ducis comitisque sibi operam vindicat.'

[3] *Ruotgeri Vita Brunonis* ed. I. Ott, *M.G.H. Scriptores Rerum Germanicarum* (henceforth cited *S.R.G.*) Nova Series (Weimar, 1951), c. 20, p. 19. For Ruotger's interpretation of Brun's more than ducal powers in Lotharingia cf. F. Lotter, Die *Vita Brunonis* des Ruotger, *Bonner Historische Forschungen* 9 (Bonn, 1958), pp. 115 ff.

[4] Ruotger, *op. cit.* c. 25, p. 26.

[5] *Die Sachsengeschichte des Widukind von Korvei*, ed. P. Hirsch and H. E. Lohmann, *S.R.G.* (Hanover, 1935), p. 44: 'Ac ne quis eum (Brun) culpabilem super hoc dixerit, cum Samuelem sanctum et alios plures sacerdotes pariter legamus et iudices.' Cf. also Ruotger, *op. cit.*, c. 23, p. 24.

[6] *Vita Deoderici Episcopi Mettensis*, c. 7, *M.G.H. Scriptorum Tomus* iv, 467.

[7] A. Fliche, *La Réforme Grégorienne* I (Louvain, 1924), p. 60 ff.

[8] *op. cit.*, p. 51 and 'Apologeticus ad Hugonem et Rodbertum Reges Francorum' in Migne, *P.L.* 139, coll. 465, 466. Abbo censured above all simoniacal transactions between prelates and clerks.

[9] C. Mirbt, *Die Publizistik im Zeitalter Gregors VII* (Leipzig, 1894), p. 86. Two of his polemics, however, Guido of Arezzo's *Letter* and the *De Ordinando Pontifice* of French origin are prior to 1050.

[10] J. Armitage Robinson, *Gilbert Crispin Abbot of Westminster* (Cambridge, 1911), pp. 67–70 and 111–24, and also W. Holtzmann, 'Zur Geschichte des Investiturstreites', *Neues Archiv* 50 (1935), pp. 246 ff.

[11] *Manegoldi ad Gebehardum Liber*, *M.G.H.*, *Libelli* I, 311, l. 13 f.

[12] *Wenrici Scolastici Trevirensis Epistola*, ib. p. 284 ff.

[13] *Gregorii VII Registrum*, ed. E. Caspar in *M.G.H.*, *Epistolae Selectae* ii (Berlin, 1955), i, 71, p. 103 (henceforth cited *Reg.*); ii, 49, p. 190; vii, 23, p. 500 f.

[14] K. Erdmann, 'Die Anfänge der staatlichen Propaganda im Investiturstreit', *Historische Zeitschrift* 154 (1936), p. 491 ff. and esp. pp. 511–12.

¹⁵ R. Holtzmann in W. Wattenbach, *Deutschlands Geschichtsquellen im Mittelalter*, ed. R. Holtzmann (Tübingen, 1948), i, 3, p. 406 called it the most valuable and important of all the *libelli*. Cf. also C. Erdmann, *Die Entstehung des Kreuzzugsgedankens* (Stuttgart, 1935 and 1955), p. 241 and A. Hauck, *Kirchengeschichte Deutschlands* (3rd ed., Leipzig, 1906), iii, 856.

¹⁶ *Liber de Unitate Ecclesiae Conservanda*, Bk. I, i *Libelli* ii, 185 and *Thasci Caecili Cypriani de Catholicae Ecclesiae Unitate* ed. G. Hartel, in *Corpus Scriptorum Ecclesiasticorum Latinorum* iii (Vienna, 1868), I, 215. The translation is by John Fell, *Of the Unity of the Church by Cyprian* (Oxford, 1681), p. 10.

¹⁷ 'Magna quidem heresis est Dei resistere ordinationi, cuius solius est potestas dandi imperii.' *Liber de Unitate* II, c. 20, *Libelli* ii, 237.

¹⁸ *loc. cit.* and *De Civitate Dei* V, c. 21 Corpus Christianorum Series Latina xlvii, xlviii (Tunshout, 1955), p. 157.

¹⁹ *Libelli* ii, 237, l. 13–14.

²⁰ *Liber de Unitate* I, c. 17, p. 210 f. and *De Civitate Dei* II, c. 21, p. 53 f., XIX, c. 21, p. 687 f.

²¹ From R. W. and A. J. Carlyle, *A History of Medieval Political Theory in the West* (Edinburgh, 1903), i, 4.

²² *Liber de Unitate* II, c. 15, pp. 230–31. The author's argument was here firmly based on Gelasius I's definitions. Cf. Carlyle, *op. cit.* i, 190–92.

²³ E.g. his case against a historical example frequently used in papal literature, the deposition of Childeric, the last Merowingian king by the Franks in 751. *Liber de Unitate* II, cc. 2 and 3, pp. 186, 189.

²⁴ Mirbt, *op. cit.*, p. 102.

²⁵ '. . . der nichts weniger als ein Heisssporn war', R. Holtzmann in *Deutschlands Geschichtsquellen im Mittelalter* i, 3, p. 399 and cf. M. Manitius, *Geschichte der Lateinischen Literatur des Mittelalters* (Munich, 1931), iii, 334.

²⁶ *Manegoldi ad Gebehardum Liber*, c. 28 *Libelli* i, 361 l. 29 ff. The letter also in *Gregorii VII Epistolae Collectae*, Monumenta Gregoriana ed. P. Jaffé (Berlin, 1865), p. 535 ff. On Manegold see G. Koch, 'Manegold von Lautenbach und die Lehre von der Volkssouveränität unter Heinrich IV', *Historische Studien* xxxiv (Berlin, 1902).

²⁷ Manegold, *op. cit.*, c. 29, pp. 361–4.

²⁸ Manegold's boorishness and plebeian excesses gave offence and later caused his admirers some embarrassment. See Gerhoch von Reichersberg's *Epistola ad Innocentem Papam*, Libelli iii, 232 f.

²⁹ Manegold, *op. cit.*, p. 365, ll. 1–3.

³⁰ *op. cit.*, c. 30, p. 365.

³¹ *loc. cit.* However coarse the comparison it echoed a phrase in the treatise of Wenrich of Trier against whom Manegold had taken up the cudgels. Wenrich had written that it was new and unheard of to change kings, the Lord's anointed, as if they were village-reeves. (*Libelli* i, 289, l. 34.) Manegold thought it was neither new nor, in the manner, mistaken.

³² Gerhoch von Reichersberg, *op. cit.*, *loc. cit.*

³³ Manegold, *loc. cit.*, l.44 f.

³⁴ Manegold, *op. cit.*, c. 47, p. 391 f.

³⁵ On these reciprocal relations see F. Kern, *Kingship and Law*, translated by S. B. Chrimes (Oxford, 1948), pp. 75–9.

³⁶ Manegold, *op. cit.*, c. 30, p. 365: '. . . cum pactum, pro quo constitutus est, constet illum prius irrupisse.' c. 47, p. 391: 'At vero si quando pactum, quo eligitur, infringit. . . .'

³⁷ *Wenrici Scolastici Trevirensis Epistola* c. 4, Libelli i, 289, l. 30 f.

³⁸ K. Jordan, 'Der Kaisergedanke in Ravenna zur Zeit Heinrichs IV', *Deutsches Archiv für Geschichte des Mittelalters* ii (1938), p. 85 ff.

³⁹ *Petri Crassi Defensio Heinrici IV. Regis* c. 6, Libelli i, 443 ff.

⁴⁰ See *Brunos Buch vom Sachsenkrieg* c. 25, ed. H. Lohmann, Kritische Studientexte des Reichsinstituts für ältere deutsche Geschichtskunde ii (Leipzig, 1937), p. 29: Igitur

expergiscimini et hereditatem vobis a parentibus vestris relictam liberis vestris relinquite; nec . . . vos et liberos vestros . . . servos fieri permittite. The Saxons justified their revolt against Henry IV with the same arguments that Peter damned it.

[41] Petrus Crassus *op. cit.*, p. 445, l. 7.

[42] G. Tellenbach, *Church, State and Christian Society*, translated by R. F. Bennett (Oxford, 1940) p.1.

[43] *Deusdedit Presbyteri Cardinalis Libellus contra Invasores et Symoniacos* . . , Prologus and c.3, Libelli ii, 300 and pp. 352-53. The *auctoritas-potestas* antithesis was taken from Pope Gelasius I.

[44] Tellenbach, *op. cit.*, p. 15 ff. and esp. p. 21. See also H. Grundmann, 'Freiheit als religiöses, politisches und persönliches Postulat im Mittelalter', *Historische Zeitschrift* 183 (1957), p. 23 ff.

[45] Widukind von Korvei, *op. cit.*, p. 84. Widukind adopted this sense of *libertas* from his literary model, Sallust.

[46] Reg. II, 63, p. 218.

[47] *Hugonis Monachi Floriacensis Tractatus de Regia Potestate et Sacerdotali Dignitate* c. 1, Libelli ii, 467. After quoting Gregory VII's sentence on the vicious and even satanic origins of royal government from the second letter to Hermann of Metz (cf. infra, n. 57) he rejects it as frivolous because the Apostle had said: *Non est potestas nisi a Deo.* (Rom. XIII, 1.) 'Constat igitur hac sententia, quia non ab hominibus, sed a Deo potestas regia in terris est ordinata sive disposita.' In Bk. II, cc. 6 and 7, p. 493 f. Hugh advanced a doctrine of non-resistance. For the Norman Anonymous see *Tractatus Eboracenses* IV, Libelli iii, pp. 663, 679.

[48] Reg. I, 75, p. 106 f. to Philip I of France; *ibid.* VII, 21, p. 498 to King Haakon of Denmark: 'Inter ceteras ergo virtutes . . . ecclesiarum defensionem in mente tua volumus eminere.' *Ibid.* VII, 23, p. 500, l. 26 f. to William the Conqueror.

[49] Reg. III, 10, p. 267, l. 5 ff. Reg. VII, 11, p. 473 ff.

[50] A. Nitschke, 'Die Wirksamkeit Gottes in der Welt Gregors VII', *Studi Gregoriani* v, ed. Borino (Rome, 1956), p. 158 with many examples. In 1074 Duke William VI of Aquitaine was asked to frighten his overlord, King Philip I, into a more respectful frame of mind with the help of other French magnates. Reg. II, 18, pp. 150–51.

[51] E.g. Reg. II, 5, p. 130; Reg. IV, 2, p. 295, l. 10, the first letter to Bishop Hermann of Metz (1076). Reg. IX, 37, p. 630: '. . . sed secularem cautelam et rationem divine legi preponens . . .' was written to William the Conqueror because he had imprisoned Bishop Odo of Bayeux, his half-brother.

[52] Reg. VI, 13, p. 415 to the King of Norway; Reg. II, 51, p. 192; VII, 5, p. 464; VII, 21, p. 497 to the kings of Denmark; Reg. II, 73, p. 233 to Duke Boleslav II of Poland; Reg. VII, 11, p. 473 to Duke Wratislav of Bohemia; Reg. II, 63, p. 218 to Duke Geisa of Hungary; Reg. IV, 28, p. 343 to the rulers and princes of Spain; VII, 6, p. 465 and IX, 2, p. 569 to Alphonso VI of Castile.

[53] Gregory's best-known utterance on this is in Reg. IV, 3 of 1076. About Henry IV he wrote: 'Non inflatus spiritu elationis consuetudines superbie contra libertatem sancte ecclesie inventas defendat.'

[54] Reg. VIII, 21, p. 548.

[55] *ibid.*, p. 562, l. 24.

[56] Libelli ii, 97. Elsewhere, however, in Gregory's letters, alienation from God was servitude to demons. Cf. Reg. VIII, 21, p. 555, l. 13 f. and also IX, 3, p. 575.

[57] Reg. VIII, 21, p. 552, l. 13.

[58] Reg. VII, 25, p. 505 with the sun and moon analogy.

[59] Reg. I, 37, p. 59, l. 8.

[60] Nitschke, *op. cit.*, p. 190 f. His is one of the most arresting interpretations of Gregory's mind and thought to which I should like to acknowledge my debt.

[61] A. Fliche, *La Réforme Grégorienne* (Louvain, Paris, 1926), ii, 403 ff. E. Voosen, *Papauté et Pouvoir Civil à l'époque de Grégoire VII* (Gembloux, 1927), p. 162, held that there is no contradiction. One must distinguish between the divine source and the historical origin of royal government in Gregory's thought. But it is not clear that Gregory, in his letters, drew this distinction. W. Ullmann, *The Growth of Papal*

Government in the Middle Ages (London, 1955), p. 271 n. 1, takes the view that there is no problem.

⁶² Deusdedit, *op. cit.*, Libelli ii, 353, l. 27: '. . . eo quidem permittente, non tamen volente.'

⁶³ Reg. VIII, 21, p. 559: 'De tot enim hominibus Deo reddituri sunt rationem, quot sue dominationi subditos habuerunt.' Reg. VII, 25, p. 506 for the pope's responsibility and *ibid.*, n. 2 its Gelasian source.

⁶⁴ Reg. VIII, 21, p. 559: '. . . quid erit de iis, qui multa milia morti tradunt pro huius mundi honore?'

⁶⁵ C. Erdmann, *Die Entstehung des Kreuzzugsgedankens* (Stuttgart, 1935), p. 145 ff.

⁶⁶ Reg. VIII, 21, p. 561.

⁶⁷ Reg. IV, 3, p. 299; IX, 3, p. 574 ff.

⁶⁸ Reg. IV, 2, p. 294, l. 16; VIII, 21, p. 550 f.

⁶⁹ Hauck, *op. cit.*, iii, 759 and 763; Erdmann, *op. cit.*, pp. 156, 188 f., 202. J. Haller *Das Papsttum* (Stuttgart, 1951), ii, 368 f., 379 f.

⁷⁰ Reg. II, 45, p. 184: 'Multo enim melius nobis videtur iustitiam Dei vel novis reedificare consiliis, quam animas hominum una cum legibus deperire neglectis.'

⁷¹ The story is Otto of Freising's. See his *Gesta Friderici I Imperatoris*, S.R.G. (3rd ed., Hanover and Leipzig, 1912), p. 27.

⁷² *Du Contrat Social*, Bk. III, cc. 2, 5, 10, ed. C. E. Vaughan (Manchester, 1918), pp. 54, 59, 74.

⁷³ For the development of the Church's social and political ideology in the twelfth century see Ullmann, *op. cit.*, p. 413 ff. and G. B. Ladner, 'The concepts of *Ecclesia* and *Christianitas* and their relation to the idea of papal *Plenitudo Potestatis* from Gregory VII to Boniface VIII'. *Miscellanea Historiae Pontificiae* (Rome, 1954) xviii, 49 ff.; F. Kempf, S.J., 'Papsttum und Kaisertum bei Innozenz III', *ibid.* xix, 182 ff.; M. D. Chenu, O.P., *La Théologie au Douzième Siècle* (Paris, 1957), p. 252 ff.

Note

For a recent study of this literature of conflict see I. S. Robinson, *Authority and Resistance in the Investiture Contest The Polemical Literature of the Late Eleventh Century* (Manchester University Press, 1978) and Holmes & Meier (New York, 1978).

7

THE GERMAN ARISTOCRACY FROM THE NINTH TO THE EARLY TWELFTH CENTURY

A HISTORICAL AND CULTURAL SKETCH

THE HISTORY OF GERMAN SOCIETY IN THE EARLY MIDDLE AGES IS FOR the most part the history of the German aristocracy, clerical and lay. For no other social group do we possess the materials and the resources to form a coherent picture. The agrarian structure of the East-Frankish regions is known to us in patches only: a few estate surveys, *censiers* and *Hofrechte* here and there reveal classes of dependants ranging from rent-paying free men under their lord's *mundeburdium* (protection and lordship) or advocacy to very much more heavily burdened customary tenants with different names in different regions. But the insights these sources afford do not allow us to speak of these men as part of a German society. Nor is this mere accident. These men belonged to so many smaller regional and local societies centred on great monasteries or bishoprics like St. Gallen, Fulda, Werden, Corvey, St. Emmeran (Regensburg) and Worms. Except for the services and taxes they owed and the *placita* (pleas) which they had to attend, sometimes to be punished and always to be mulcted, the doings of their masters entered but dimly into their horizon. The same cannot, of course, be said of the men who later came to challenge and to enter the aristocracy, the *ministeriales*. But if they, or rather their fore-runners, served in the wars and at the courts of their betters they still belonged to and rose only in their own lord's *familia* and household. Theirs too was an enclosed and confined world. There is little evidence in the early eleventh century that they and their like, for instance the more honoured servants of the abbots of Fulda and Hersfeld formed independent connections, joined forces or nursed common grievances.[1] Until they did, from about 1100 onwards, it is difficult to speak of them as a class.[2] Their self-assertion in the

---

[1] According to the service-code (*Dienstrecht*) of the Bamberg *ministeriales* (1057-64) a man could however seek employment outside the lordship of his master if the latter had no use for him and would not give him a fief. See *Monumenta Bambergensia*, ed. P. Jaffé (Bibliotheca Rerum Germanicarum, v, Berlin, 1869), p. 51. Some of Archbishop Bardo of Mainz's *servientes* deserted him to join the emperor Conrad II (1024-39).

[2] An important, early case of *ministeriales* belonging to various lords joining forces in defence of their status was the murder of Count Sigehard of Burghausen at Regensburg in 1104. He had tried to worsen the rights of his own men. For this incident see G. Meyer von Knonau, *Jahrbücher des Deutschen Reiches unter Heinrich IV. und Heinrich V.* (Leipzig, 1904), v, pp. 195-8.

royal service which so infuriated a Lampert of Hersfeld and the Saxon Bruno could not achieve this in a day. Their new solidarities and corporate rights were at first local. The aristocracy alone formed a political and cultural society (albeit anarchic) in the *Reich* as a whole.

The narrative sources of the tenth and early eleventh centuries were overwhelmingly the work of the more or less privileged inhabitants of monasteries, cathedral communities and courts. When they spoke of the poor, the *pauperi*, they sometimes meant the non-nobles rather than the destitute, but they rarely did speak of them.[3] In the biographies of great personages, like the ladies of the Ottonian house, Henry I's queen Mathilda and Otto I's Adelheid, almsgiving played a large part and in describing it the authors of these works imitated the commonplaces of hagiography and the *vitae* (Lives) of great prelates. But throughout the accent lay not on the social good achieved or on social service, but on the purchasing power in heaven which these charities commanded. Thietmar of Merseburg wrote of Tagino, the archbishop of Magdeburg (1004-1012): "because his weak constitution did not allow him to fast he made amends for this by the lavishness of his alms-giving".[4] Alms and washing the feet of the needy were good for the souls of the donors; where such things are described in the *vitae*, they belonged to a widely accepted devotional repertoire whereby the great could practise humility. They did not denote either a closer relationship to the unfortunate or, on the part of the biographers, any interest in their lot. On the contrary that interest was all self-centred: their own privileged connection with the patron or the subject of their literary toil. When times were dangerous, as they were in the early tenth century during the Hungarian raids, and when monks and clerks had to flee with their shrines to find shelter in some walled city or country hide-out what they resented most was having to mingle with the common herd, the *vulgus*.[5] To return to Archbishop Tagino of Magdeburg: he had

[3] On this see K. Bosl, "Potens und Pauper. Begriffsgeschichtliche Studien zur gesellschaftlichen Differenzierung im frühen Mittelalter . . ." in *Frühformen der Gesellschaft im mittelalterlichen Europa* (Munich-Vienna, 1964), pp. 106-34.

[4] Thietmar of Merseburg, *Chronicon*, vi.64 (ed. R. Holtzmann, Monumenta Germaniae Historica [hereafter MGH], Scriptores Rerum Germanicarum [hereafter SRG], new ser. ix, Berlin, 1955), p. 354.

[5] Adam of Bremen, *Gesta Hammaburgensis Ecclesiae Pontificum*, i.53 (ed. B. Schmeidler [MGH. SRG., Hanover and Leipzig, 1917], p. 54): "clerum vulgo mixtum". Cf. also the *Chronicle of Moyenmoutier*, ch. 6 (MGH. Scriptorum Tomus [hereafter SS], iv, p. 89): "In Mediano autem coenobio . . . vix singuli clerici feruntur resedisse nonnullis mensibus, easdem tantum observantes excubias vulgaris parrochiae"

the gifts of gentleness and compassion but preferred to be on close terms only with nobles and to keep the low-born out of his company.[6]

Annals, chronicles, Lives and *Gesta* were written for an aristocratic audience, whether it was tonsured or belted, a minority, or as shall be seen, a tiny minority among what was a minority of the population in any case. It could not be otherwise for these very few were the only men and women worth influencing or entertaining. The assumption was that nobility had merit and merit again was innate in blood. In the episcopal biographies of the tenth and early eleventh centuries the noble ancestry of the future bishop was set down as a matter of course and always followed by an account of his even nobler virtues.[7] Degeneracy, a problem to most aristocracies, was an individual failing. Noble kins could decay, come to grief in a feud and end up in exile or gradually loose their wealth but this did not shake the confidence and the beliefs of their fellows or the writers who tell us of such misfortunes. Conversely the ascent of a *pauper* into the ranks of the high nobility was, even in the Church, a rare event in tenth-century Germany. The outstanding example was Willigis, archbishop of Mainz from 975 to 1011. Thietmar of Merseburg who should have known, spoke of his "vile" origins but to him almost anyone born below his own high aristocratic circles was less than equal. Willigis's parents seem to have been free and noble but they were poor and lived as peasants. Between mere *nobiles* and *nobilissimi* a wide gulf stretched. Heaven itself had to intervene to point to Willigis's future greatness and so we read that on the night of his birth all the draught-cattle in his mother's house also had male offspring.[8] Prodigies at the birth of saints were a stock-in-trade of hagiography, but Thietmar, though he esteemed the archbishop highly, did not think of him as a saint. Only his career was miraculous. In 1014 and 1019 the Emperor Henry II, for purposes of his own, promoted two clerks of unfree parentage to the small and poor see of Eichstätt. The chronicler of the diocese recorded their

[6] Thietmar, *Chronicon*, vi.65, (p. 354). Conversely Bishop Notker of Liège was praised for his affability towards the *mediocres*. See Anselm's *Gesta Episcoporum Leodiensium*, ch. 30 (MGH. SS., vii, p. 206). The rigoristic Anselm disliked courts and their inhabitants.

[7] A strong protest against this literary convention came characteristically from the circle of the early Lotharingian monastic reformers. See John of St. Arnulf's *Life of John of Gorze* (abbot of Gorze 960-74), ch. 7 (MGH. SS., iv, p. 339).

[8] Thietmar, iii.5 (p. 102). The standing of Willigis's parents has been much in dispute. Thietmar wrote (*loc. cit.*): "Felix mater, quam Dominus pre caeteris contemporalibus suis in tantum visitavit, ut prolem nobilioribus coequalem vel etiam nonnullis meliorem pareret". If Willigis had been altogether plebeian he would have had to say "nobilibus coequalem".

origins with regret, and the subsequent return of noble prelates with relief.[9]

The cultural and political passivity of rural populations in the various German regions was not seriously disturbed, let alone jolted, before the last quarter of the eleventh century.   Before we turn to the question of change it is worth asking whether the townsmen of the earlier middle-ages participated more closely than the peasantry in the life of the great churches, castles and cloisters which formed the core of most urban settlements.   It must be recalled that in many burghs the most active, independent and enterprising section of the population lived in separate quarters, often at some distance from the ecclesiastical foundations.   At Trier the archbishop between 994 and 1008 built a stone-wall round the main clerical citadel to make the segregation more effective.[10]   However important the economic functions and rewards of traders and certain skilled craftsmen in these centres may have been we only meet them occasionally in the writings of their betters.   Before 955 merchants from Mainz and Verdun served Otto I on embassies to Constantinople and Cordoba, later when his kingship had advanced in eminence only bishops and counts were sent on such missions.[11]   At Regensburg, in 983, a royal merchant and his wife can be found to have made considerable grants of buildings and lands, within and outside the city, to the monastery of St. Emmeran for the sake of their souls.   They were by no means the only ones of their kind to have done so.[12]

Merchants were thus men of some consequence in Ottonian Germany and their safety *en route* mattered to their lords and patrons. However, what their world was like we hear from only one and that a hostile source in the early eleventh century, the book which, under the title *De Diversitate Temporum*, Alpert of Metz dedicated to Bishop Burchard of Worms between 1020 and 1024.   Alpert had migrated into the diocese of Utrecht and in his work, an account of contemporary events in the region, he paused to describe the merchants

[9] *Anonymus Haserensis*, chaps. 25-7 (MGH. SS., vii, pp. 260 f.).
[10] E. Ennen, *Frühgeschichte der Europäischen Stadt* (Bonn, 1953), p. 143.
[11] Liudprand of Cremona, *Antapodosis*, vi.4 (*Die Werke Liudprands von Cremona*, ed. J. Becker [MGH. SRG., Hanover and Leipzig, 1915], p. 154). On the Verdun merchant sent with John of Gorze as bearer of Otto I's presents to the Calif Abd ar-Rahman III see the *Life of John of Gorze*, ch. 117 (MGH. SS. iv, p. 370).
[12] K. Bosl, "Die Sozialstruktur der mittelalterlichen Residenz- und Fernhandelsstadt Regensburg. Die Entwicklung ihres Bürgertums vom 9.-14. Jahrhundert", in *Untersuchungen zur Gesellschaftlichen Struktur der Mittelalterlichen Städte in Europa* (Vorträge und Forschungen herausgegeben vom Konstanzer Arbeitskreis für mittelalterliche Geschichte, xi, Konstanz Stuttgart, 1966), pp. 121-5.

of Tiel and their discordant ways.   He looked upon them as a race of
ruffians whose lawlessness was an offence and should be stopped.
Perjury counted for nothing in this trading settlement on the Waal:
a man of Tiel, if he held something in his fist, would swear with the
other hand that it was not there.   Adultery did not rank as a crime
there and Alpert ended his digression with an account of their
drinking-bouts and their common funds — in fact their guild.[13]
That they had one is important but Tiel, the Imperial toll-station on
the way to England, was rather exceptional.   It lay somewhat out of
the local bishop's reach and for at least half a century we have nothing
to echo Alpert's description of these seeming outcasts who were
nonetheless privileged, wealthy and useful.   There is evidence that
prelates worried about the rapid growth of population in unexpected
places where there were as yet few churches and relics and that they
wanted to keep an eye on such developing towns in their dioceses.
Archbishop Brun of Cologne (953-965), Otto I's brother sent the
body of St. Patroclus to Soest in Westphalia because this flourishing
and populous centre was "almost ignorant of worship".[14]

In general the towns too belonged to or were dominated by the
aristocracy and its leaders, especially the bishops, some abbots and, of
course, the kings.   We must now return to them, the *nobiles* and their
cultural roots in early medieval Germany.   Historians of institutions
and critics of writers such as the great Saxon historian Widukind of
Corvey no longer like to contrast too sharply purely Germanic,
Christian and classical elements in this context.   Even the most
heroic saga in the form we possess it confronts us with literacy and
this was only possible through christianization.   When Widukind of
Corvey related the pre-Christian traditions of his people, the Saxons,
he weighed the report of their nordic origins against the story he had
heard in his youth that they were descended from the Macedonians of
Alexander's army and in the end he thought that the latter was nearer
the truth.   Etymological reflections led him to this view, and for all
his family- and Saxon stem-pride he looked back as a scholar.[15]
Again, the famous ox-carts on which the last Merovingian kings, in
Einhard's derisory story, were seen going to the assemblies of the
Franks are now thought to be imitations of the mode of travel used by
late-Roman provincial governors.   Their link with the primeval

[13] Alpert, *De Diversitate Temporum*, ii.20 (MGH. SS., iv, pp. 718 f.).
[14] *De Translatione Sancti Patrocli* (MGH. SS., iv, p. 281): "... locum ...
rebus seculi opulentum, populo plenum, ... sed religionis adhuc pene ignarum".
[15] Widukind of Corvey, *Rerum Gestarum Saxonicarum Libri Tres*, i.2, (ed.
H.-E. Lohmann and P. Hirsch [MGH. SRG., Hanover, 1935], p. 4) and cf.
i.12 (p. 20 f.).

forests is doubtful.[16]   We must therefore be careful also when we speak of a secular aristocratic culture as against that of the Church. The inmates of great monasteries like St. Gallen or Tegernsee were the cousins and brothers of lay nobles whose values and interests in the tenth century they went on sharing — to some extent.   These two houses have been mentioned here because two of Germany's greatest early medieval Latin epics are associated with them, the *Waltharius* and *Ruodlieb*.[17]   Both poems had for their subjects heroes who were forced to serve distant rulers and founded their ascent, fortunes and families by proving themselves in all situations.   They appealed to the day-dreams, if not also the conscience of the lay nobility. *Waltharius* and *Ruodlieb* moreover did not stand alone and the secular clergy were no less interested in this genre of literature than the monks.   Sometime between 1057 and 1064 the *scholasticus* (master of the school) of Bamberg cathedral, Meinhard, wrote to one of his fellow-clerks bewailing the life of their bishop, Gunther, who instead of reading St. Augustine and Gregory the Great spent his time with Attila and Dietrich and may even have composed epics for his court-entertainers.[18]

Charlemagne caused the age-old songs praising the deeds of ancient kings, possibly his predecessors, to be written down.   His son Louis the Pious was anxious to forget all those he had learned as a boy.[19] Of Otto the Great we do not know whether he personally patronised and encouraged the cult of the Saxon stem-saga as Widukind has rendered it but we can be sure that the king, his nobles and the

[16] See J. M. Wallace-Hadrill's review of A. H. M. Jones, *The Later Roman Empire*, in the *Eng. Hist. Rev.*, lxxx (1965), p. 789.

[17] The debate about the origin of the surviving *Waltharius* has not yet closed. If it is Carolingian, then another and now lost version remains connected with Ekkehard I of St. Gallen and the earlier tenth century. See Ekkehard IV, *Casus S. Galli*, ch. 9 (MGH. SS., ii, p. 118). *Ruodlieb* was written at Tegernsee, probably by a monk not long after 1050. For a text with a line by line English translation see *Ruodlieb, The Earliest Courtly Novel. Introduction, Text, Translation Commentary and Textual Notes*, by E. H. Zeydel (University of North Carolina Studies in the Germanic Languages and Literatures, xxiii, Chapel Hill, 1959).   This edition will be referred to here for the sake of convenience.

[18] See *Briefsammlungen der Zeit Heinrichs IV*, ed. C. Erdmann and N. Fickermann (MGH. Die Briefe der deutschen Kaiserzeit, v, Weimar, 1950), no. 73, p. 121; and C. Erdmann, *Studien zur Briefliteratur Deutschlands im elften Jahrhundert*, (Schriften des Reichsinstituts für ältere deutsche Geschichtskunde, i, Leipzig, 1938), p. 102.   For all Meinhard's grumbles Bishop Gunther (1057-65) was also the patron of one of the noblest early German religious songs, the *Ezzolied*.

[19] Einhard, *Vita Karoli Magni*, ch. 29 (6th edn., O. Holder-Egger [MGH. SRG., Hanover and Leipzig, 1911], p. 33) and Thegan, *Vita Hludowici Imperatoris*, ch. 19 (MGH. SS., ii, p. 594).

clerical élite of the bishoprics and royal monasteries nursed common beliefs about the ancestral nobility of their kind. It was to them not the cause — that would have been blasphemous — but at least the necessary condition of their recent successes both in the *militia Christi* and the even more tangible *militia* against Slavs, Hungarians and enemies within, successes which, the victors claimed, supported the *militia Christi* by creating peace and prosperity. These again were measured by the extent of lordship, the size of tribute and the amount of booty gained. The Ottonian empire did not differ very much from the Frankish in the value its aristocracy attached to the wealth and power which might be acquired by successful wars of conquest. They were the rewards of those *nobilissimi mores* of which Widukind had spoken to justify the transfer of kingship from a Frankish house to the Saxon Henry I.[20] We must not be surprised however to find these values looking different in Widukind and the poems from what they looked like in practice.

The aristocracy of early medieval Germany, or rather her disparate and in themselves only half-formed stem-regions — Franconia, Swabia, Bavaria, Saxony and Lotharingia — has been studied from many points of view: all-German political and constitutional as well as local, dynastic and genealogical. Its egotism and unconstructive behaviour towards rulers who were thought to be concerned with German unity in the tenth and eleventh centuries incurred the censures of patriotic historians of the Medieval *Reich*, especially Giesebrecht's.[21] The unpredictability of its feuds and its a-political pursuit of patrimonial aims were held to be responsible for the unfortunate territorial structure of Germany which only blood and iron could mend in 1866. For the constitutional historians again, the most important problem was the transformation of the early medieval nobility into a strictly graded hierarchy with an estate of princes followed by counts and free lords, down to the humblest ranks of *ministeriales*, themselves the vassals of other *ministeriales*. This order, the *Heerschild*, known in the first place from the legal sources of the thirteenth century, seemed to prescribe for the empire a much more immobile and caste-ridden aristocratic society than existed in England or even France. There the initiative of the kings was or came to be greater than in Germany and restricted the autogenous, inherent kind of authority and lordship their vassals claimed. In this school of studies, pioneered by Julius Ficker in the 1860s and holding

---

[20] Widukind of Corvey, *Res gestae Saxonicae*, i.25 (p. 38).
[21] See W. von Giesebrecht, *Geschichte der deutschen Kaiserzeit*, 5th edn. (Leipzig, 1881), i, pp. 284-95 as an example.

its own with Heinrich Mitteis's fine comparative legal and feudal surveys, the idea of the state still held the centre of the stage.[22] Another group of scholars, in particular Walter Schlesinger, has shown that from the start the nobles possessed lordship and powers in their own right, outside the king's reach, and that the *Reich* therefore was born particularistic and did not merely drift in that direction because of mishaps and catastrophes like the extinction of dynasties, royal minorities and the collision with the papacy.[23] However this school too has not quite abandoned the idea of a "central authority" which, in the guise of the kingship, might or should have prevailed.   More recently still a mainly prosopographical approach to the nobility, its functions and achievements in the Frankish and post-Frankish *Reich* has led to a re-examination of the family-structure of the aristocracy in the early middle ages.   The inspiration behind these efforts came from Gerd Tellenbach whose school, especially the work of Karl Schmid, has greatly altered all existing perspectives on the subject and could be important also for the study of the Anglo-Saxon nobility of this period.

Many years ago Tellenbach drew attention to the decisive rôle of a small group of leading families in the ninth-century East-Frankish kingdom whose marriage-alliances with the Carolingians and far-flung connections with one another in his view set them off against nobles with only local roots.[24]   The history and genealogies of these families thus became important in order to understand the workings of the Frankish empire in its good days and bad.   It was Karl Schmid who concluded, in the course of such investigations, that until the mid-eleventh century at least it is quite impossible to look upon these aristocratic clans as dynasties in the modern sense, families which can be traced from generation to generation and identified by their place of residence and high offices like countships and duchies.   In the ninth and tenth centuries the historian is at a loss to find this continuity not because the sources are poorer, but because the very structure of families was different.   The aristocracies of Carolingian Europe were made up of very large family-groups conscious of their nobility by their descent from a great ancestor whose name was

---

[22] J. Ficker, *Vom Heerschilde* (Innsbruck, 1862); H. Mitteis, *Der Staat des hohen Mittelalters*, 4th edn. (Weimar, 1953).

[23] W. Schlesinger, *Die Entstehung der Landesherrschaft* (Dresden, 1941), and reprinted with a new introduction (Wissenschaftliche Buchgesellschaft, Darmstadt, 1964), esp. pp. 261-5.

[24] G. Tellenbach, "Vom Karolingischen Reichsadel zum deutschen Reichsfürstenstand", in *Herrschaft und Staat im Mittelalter* (Wege der Forschung, ii, Darmstadt, 1956), pp. 191-242.

perpetuated in their own and by their membership of the group. Maternal kin mattered as much as paternal and even more if it was deemed to be nobler.   A nice example of its importance is that of Eadgith, the half-sister of the English king Athelstan who in 929 married Otto, already marked out among his brothers as Henry I's successor.   Hrotsvitha of Gandersheim described this match in her *Gesta Ottonis* and dwelt carefully on the ancestry of the bride.   She was the daughter of Edward the Elder by a "most illustrious" mother whereas Athelstan had sprung from an unequal union with a woman of rather indifferent birth.[25]   In some cases we know the mother of a great magnate rather than his father and this is thought to be not merely accidental.   The most important sources which Tellenbach and his school employed with much success to recognize and identify these large families are the *Libri Memoriales* of South German, Lotharingian and Italian monasteries, like St. Gallen, Reichenau, Remiremont and S. Giulia in Brescia.   Thousands of nobles during the ninth and tenth centuries had their names entered on the pages of these books to participate in the benefits which the prayers of the religious community conferred both in life and in death.   Here identifiable individuals and christian names typical of a given family recur in groups of entries each time associated with other names which in turn spill over into further entries.   The persons who caused themselves to be so recorded were thus conscious of belonging to very large kins which through intermarriage blended with other large kins, cognates counting for no less than agnates to make the connection. Some of the individuals we encounter in this way were distinguished — bishops, counts, margraves and, of course kings and dukes; others remained totally obscure and cannot be found in any other source but the *Libri Memoriales*.   We are a long way off from dynasties named after their castles and endowed from father to son with the same lordships — comital, margravial or less — and the same advocacies of monasteries.   The transformation of these *Grossfamilien* into smaller, more circumscribed and close-knit families with a much more continuous history was the real significance of the so-called "rise of the dynasts" which an older generation of historians connected with the long civil wars of the reigns of Henry IV and Henry V and the Investiture Conflict.   The late eleventh and the first half of the twelfth century thus saw a fundamental change in the structure of the German aristocracy.   Only then did it become possible to base

---

[25] Hrotsvitha, *Gesta Ottonis*, ll. 75-97, in *Hrotsvithae Opera*, ed. P. v. Winterfeld (MGH. SRG. Berlin and Zürich, 1965), p. 206 f.

dynasties permanently on the possession of great offices, counties, advocacies, not to mention duchies, landgraviates and margraviates.[26]

These views have won a wide measure of assent, some of it perhaps a little reluctant and weighted with reservations.[27] They invite, however, one general observation. Based as they are so singularly on the *Libri Memoriales*, the religious association of nobles with the prayers of a monastic community, they run the risk, in a rather unusual and intriguing form, of confusing consciousness and being. They assume that, because these men were conscious of being members of a very large and fluid group for the purpose of having their memory kept, they were conscious of this for all other purposes as well. In East-Frankish chronicles, annals, episcopal and abbatial Lives and in the miracles of saints, nobles stand out as individuals, fighting feuds against one another, seizing church lands, restoring them now and again and founding religious houses for complex motives. Kinship and intermarriage between the leading families rather than institutions of government held this world together in the tenth century, and yet the group-consciousness postulated by the new interpretation of the *Libri Memoriales* rarely appears outside them. When men had become rich and powerful agnatic preferences tended to prevail. Fathers strove for their sons and felt the full bitterness of losing them prematurely. They did not relish leaving their *hereditas* to some distant kinsmen but harsh circumstances like the short expectation of life forced them to face this prospect. Even so many preferred to found monasteries and nunneries with the whole of their fortune instead. Otto I's friend, Margrave Gero, is a good example.

When ninth- and tenth-century writers were particularly anxious to mention the maternal rather than the paternal ancestry of a great

[26] K. Schmid, "Zur Problematik von Familie, Sippe und Geschlecht, Haus und Dynastie beim mittelalterlichen Adel", *Zeitschrift für die Geschichte des Oberrheins*, cv (1957), pp. 1-62; "Über die Struktur des Adels im früheren Mittelalter", *Jahrbuch für fränkische Landesforschung*, xix (1959), pp. 1-23; "Neue Quellen zum Verständnis des Adels im 10. Jahrhundert", *Zeitschrift f. d. Gesch. d. Oberrheins*, cviii (1960), pp. 185-232; "Religiöses und sippengebundenes Gemeinschaftsbewusstsein in frühmittelalterlichen Gedenkbucheinträgen", *Deutsches Archiv für Erforschung des Mittelalters*, xxi (1965), pp. 18-81. See also *Studien und Vorarbeiten zur Geschichte des grossfränkischen und frühdeutschen Adels*, ed. G. Tellenbach (Forschungen zur oberrheinischen Landesgeschichte, iv, 1957).

[27] E.g. F. v. Klocke, "Prosopographische Forschungsarbeit und moderne Landesgeschichte", *Westfälische Forschungen*, xi (1958), pp. 196 ff.; and also the *interventions* of K. Lechner, M. Mitterauer and K. F. Werner on the theme "Les classes dirigeantes de l'Antiquité aux Temps modernes", *XII Congrès International des Sciences Historiques*, v, *Actes* (Vienna, 29 Aug.-5 Sept., 1965), pp. 155-8, 158 f., 162-4.

personage they did not always wish to pass genealogical value-judgements but may have had other reasons.   An important example used to demonstrate the possible superiority of *cognatio* (maternal kin) over *agnatio* (paternal kin), is the way in which the Carolingian house-historians spoke of Hildegard, Charlemagne's second wife and the mother of Louis the Pious.   Einhard lauded her Swabian ancestry and Thegan, Louis the Pious's biographer, added that on her mother's side she was descended from the Swabian Duke Godfrid (*c.* 710). Neither Einhard nor Thegan mentioned her father Gerold, a Frank. Yet we know that he was neither a nonentity nor a man to be ashamed of, rather the contrary.   The two biographers had special reasons for being so fussy over Hildegard's Swabian forbears: they wanted to make amends for the Carolingians and heal old wounds which Charlemagne's father Pippin and especially his uncle Carlmann had struck when they ordered the execution of some leading Swabian nobles in 746 and deprived Hildegard's kin of their *ducatus*.   Einhard and Thegan's lines of praise for Hildegard's maternal ancestry discreetly veiled a past feud in the hope it would be forgotten.[28]

The term *cognatio* was not uniformly used by early medieval writers or even by the scribes of charters to mean kinship on the mother's side.   Often it stood for relationship generally as in classical literature.   When in 1014 Hildegundis, the abbess of the Westfalian nunnery of Geseke, placed herself and her house under the *mundeburdium* (protection and lordship) of the archbishop of Cologne she took this grave step because she was, as she declared, the last of her *cognatio* who could rule the convent.   By this she meant her direct descent from her paternal grandfather Haold, through her father Bernhard and this was as it should have been.   For when the Haold family began to found Geseke in the middle of the tenth century they reserved the abbacy to the women of Haold's lineage and the advocacy to his own and his brother's sons.   Otto I's diploma for the foundation (26 October 952) sanctioned all these arrangements and they were remembered in the charter of Archbishop Heribert (999-1021) recording the transfer of 1014.   Here then *cognatio* actually meant *agnatio*, descent from a male ancestor.   Hildegundis

---

[28] K. Schmid, "Zur Problematik...", pp. 22 ff.   Einhard, *Vita Karoli*, ch. 18 (p. 22) and Thegan, *Vita Hludowici*, ch. 2 (MGH. SS., ii, p. 590 f.).   On the relations of Franks and Alemans in the eighth century see I. Dienemann-Dietrich, "Der fränkische Adel in Alemannien im 8. Jahrhundert", *Grundfragen der Alemannischen Geschichte* (Vorträge u. Forschungen, i, 1952 and reprint, 1962), pp. 149-92.

was by no means kinless but her female affinity did not meet the conditions of the 952 settlement.[29]

K. Schmid has rightly questioned the methods of the traditional school of historical genealogists who aimed, at whatever strain to the evidence, at gapless family-trees for early medieval aristocratic society. But the fluidity of the kin-groups found in the *Libri Memoriales* is so great that the excessive certainties of the old school are in danger of being replaced by chaos. The circumstance that nobles entered their kindred and affinity, living and dead, does not prove that they failed to distinguish between nearer and more distant ties of kinship or rule out close agnatic feeling and thinking. The structure of the German nobility cannot be perceived solely from the *Libri Memoriales* which reveal but one facet of its "self-awareness". The situations and enduring necessities which determined that structure must be looked for elsewhere.

We must begin with the customs of inheritance. These, as will be seen, did not draw men together but, on the contrary, divided them and created endemic unrest and tension especially in the more successful and wealthier families of the aristocracy. High blood was a pre-requisite of nobility, but its most tangible expression was the possession of land and lordship. The organization of the Carolingian *Reich*, the methods the Carolingians and their nobles employed to dominate and exploit their conquests had created new kinds of power in the form of high offices, or rather, as far as Germany is concerned, it had transplanted these forms east of the Rhine. Frankish immigré nobles or local friends of the régime in Bavaria, Swabia and Saxony became counts, margraves or even dukes. These positions were much coveted and set new standards for the families whose members held them and, of course, for those who did not. It was not enough to have possessed a high office or a royal connection once; these advantages had to be perpetuated by inheritance. But here the aspirations of successful individuals came into conflict with the

---

[29] For Otto I's diploma see MGH., *Die Urkunden der deutschen Könige und Kaiser*, i (Hanover, 1879-84), no. 158, pp. 239 f. Archbishop Heribert's charter (Staatsarchiv Münster, Geseke 5) reads: "Modo vero ipsa . . . abbatissa cognationis suae quae huic predicto loco praeesse potuerit in se finem conspiciens . . .". For further references see F. W. Oediger, *Die Regesten der Erzbischöfe von Köln*, i, 630 (Publikationen der Gesellschaft für Rheinische Geschichtskunde, xxi, Bonn, 1954-61), p. 188. The text of the charter is silent on the descent of the advocacy and it is possible that this remained with the Haold family for a time at least. Their genealogy and history in R. Schölkopf, *Die Sächsischen Grafen, 919-1024* (Studien und Vorarbeiten zum Historischen Atlas Niedersachsens, xxii, Göttingen, 1957), pp. 141-7 and table, should be treated with caution.

time-honoured principle of division, of treating the *proprietas* of
a family-group as a whole to which brothers, uncles, cousins, lay and
clerk, had a claim.   In tenth-century Saxony women, even nuns were
not excluded, for although custom placed them behind the men, their
better expectations of life — and here nuns excelled themselves —
meant that large inheritances accumulated in their hands.   *Co-
hereditas*, if it was not checked by a high rate of mortality, could lead
to the progressive fragmentation of a great fortune.   It could also
shift possessions from kin to kin or at least bring about a continuous
re-distribution of wealth within an important family.   This was
especially likely to happen when a father died too soon, leaving
behind him a son or sons of tender years.   Their inheritance was
then in jeopardy not because their uncles were proverbially wicked but
because the house needed a head to take charge of its lands and
dependants and the *milites* (vassals) needed a commander whom they
could follow with confidence.

These movements of property did not always take place peacefully
and they suggest that allod was not really a stable base to support
high rank.   The holder of a *ducatus*, a margraviate or comital office
was of course rewarded by lands and revenues which were part of his
fief, but these again set him apart from his less fortunate kinsmen who
could not share them; nor could they always be equally divided
amongst his sons.   The favour Otto I, for instance, showed to
Hermann Billung badly upset the equilibrium within his family: at
first his brother Wichmann became an enemy and when he died his
sons accused Hermann of having cheated them in the distribution of
their father's inheritance.[30]   The dissipation of allods by partition
and marriage made it all the more important to be able to pass on fiefs
of office like countships and to possess as many as possible of these, so
that at least two sons could enjoy honours which, from the tenth
century onwards if not before, came to be identified more and more
with *Hochadel* (high nobility).   Additional sons and occassionally all
but one were placed in the Church where the cathedrals and the royal
chapel offered careers to those with the best connections, ambition
and, not least of all, talent.   This left the monasteries for the
disinherited, but in tenth-century St. Gallen some of the monks were
reported to be rich and to live in affluence.   From the ninth century
onwards a grant of land or revenues from land was expected when
placing a child in a house like Corvey, and the reformed abbeys of the
eleventh did not reject such gifts either.

[30] Widukind, *op. cit.*, ii.4 (p. 70) and iii.24, 25 (p. 116).

Promotion to the highest ecclesiastical honours, archbishoprics, bishoprics and royal abbeys, depended on royal favour; this also mattered more than has been thought in the case of duchies, margraviates and countships.   When kingship was successful and vigilant it could sometimes make the precarious tenure of honours very real.   With so many failures of direct lines and in the newly created eastern marches of Saxony, nephews and more distant kinsmen depended on the king's goodwill to succeed, and the pages of Thietmar of Merseburg reveal what shrewd use the emperor Henry II could make of these opportunities.   If kingship was defective it forfeited control over high appointments as did Henry IV and later Henry V in Saxony and then it also failed to provide the gains in war which increased the fund of land, rewards and honours available for distribution amongst an ever pressing and numerous nobility.   After 1077 Henry IV might advance his followers but it depended on them what they could make of their new positions.   His Hohenstaufen son-in-law survived as duke of Swabia north of the Danube, and Wiprecht of Groitzsch, thanks to his marriage with the daughter of a Bohemian duke, in the valley of the Mulde and the Upper Elbe.

The German aristocracy struggled with these problems generation after generation and they explain most of its perennial feuds, rebellions, outrages as well as its more positive achievements like internal colonization.   Its needs for more lands and lordship were insatiable, given the system of partible inheritances from which neither kings nor dukes nor lesser powers could depart against the pressures of established claims.   In the Ottonian *Reich* only the highest dignities escaped partition, and in the eleventh century *comitatus* at least began to break up inside families.   Even before, they had not been stable and mappable entities.   It is interesting to see the ways in which the family-group was to be reconciled to the outstanding position achieved by one of its members, how cousins or more often brothers were to be made to share the heightened dignity and standing an office-fief represented.   Joint tenures were not uncommon in early as well as later medieval Germany.   For the most part however the lesser kinsmen of a count or margrave or a bishop had to be content with the opportunities such positions might afford them in the future. Soon after Udo of Reinhausen had become bishop of Hildesheim in 1079 his widowed sister Beatrix wrote a long letter to him from Franconia, asking him to see to it that her daughter Sophia who was being pursued by an inferior suitor should be married as befitted her birth.   For the other daughter, Burtgarda, who was "a bride in

Christ" he was to find suitable advancement, no doubt an abbacy. For herself she wanted justice about allods which another brother, by then deceased, had taken from her.   Her sons exiled in Saxony were to be included in any peace the Saxons might make with Henry IV. The great war between the Salian king and Rudolf of Rheinfelden was at its height when this — Carl Erdmann called it the earliest German family letter — was written.[31]   It is arresting because it reveals a situation so very like the one described in *Ruodlieb*.   Here the hero has to go into exile because his lords have let him down and failed to reward him while landing him with many feuds.   Beatrix's sons too had to leave their home because they could not cope with their enemies.   Ruodlieb's mother is left in charge of his lands and house while he seeks better service in exile.   Like Beatrix she had outlived her husband and it was common for aristocratic widows to be left in control of family fortunes and to enjoy great authority.   The "rex maior" (the greater king) of the poem advises his departing *miles,* Ruodlieb, never to marry without his mother's consent and he lets him go home at her request.   Needless to say, he, the mother and Ruodlieb himself all echo their horror about unequal marriages.[32]

Socially the whole kin was meant to share the honour which fell to one of its members.   This is nowhere more poignantly expressed than in the speech which Wipo, Conrad II's biographer places in the mouth of his hero at the most critical moment of his career.[33]   The scene is at Kamba where the archbishops, bishops and princes of all the stemlands of the *Reich* assembled in 1024 to elect a successor to Henry II who had died childless.   Nearness to the Ottonians was the criterion but Conrad shared this equally with a younger cousin also called Conrad.   The younger man, characteristically, had come to possess the lion's share of the Salian family's patrimony simply because the elder Conrad's father died too soon, leaving his son an orphan — a good example of wealth shifting within a kin.   But now the outcome of the *Kur* (election) would mean that one of the cousins must be wholly overshadowed by the other and this is how the older

---

[31] See *Briefsammlungen der Zeit Heinrichs IV*, pp. 64-7 and Erdmann, *Studien*, p. 164.

[32] *Ruodlieb*, v, ll. 476-87; xvi, ll. 14-16 and 55-7 (ed. Zeydel, pp. 74-5, 130-1, 132-3).

[33] For what follows see Wipo, *Gesta Chuonradi Imperatoris*, ch. 2, in *Wiponis Opera*, 3rd edn., ed. H. Bresslau (MGH. SRG., Hanover and Leipzig, 1915), pp. 13-20 and esp. p. 17, ll. 32 ff.   Wipo's *Gesta* are Englished in *Imperial Lives and Letters of the Eleventh Century*, translated by T. E. Mommsen and K. F. Morrison (Records of Civilization, lxvii, New York and London, 1962), pp. 52-100.   The translation here is my own.

Conrad in whose favour events were already drifting tried to prepare his relative for his disappointment:

> The greatest honour and supreme power will now be with us and it comes to us in such a way that it will remain with one of us if we wish it. Therefore it seems to me that if this honour is joined to one of us the other shall not lack a share in it in some way or another (*quodammodo*) . . . . If the kinsmen of kings are honoured for the kings' sake and as all wish to treat us as we treated one another so that really the promotion of one of us depends on the goodwill of the other, well then who can be more fortunate than either of us if the other reigns?

Conrad the Younger was made to feel the sole kingmaker in Wipo's oratory.

> Let us therefore be careful [the future king continues] and not put a stranger before a kinsman, an unknown before one who is known lest this day, so far one of joy, shall bring us lasting misfortune if we deal ill with the goodwill the whole people (*populus*) wishes to show us.

Wipo, like Widukind before him, used the word *populus* when he meant nobles. But what matters most in this homily by which the younger Conrad was to be consoled with the penumbra of participation is the sentiment: better a cousin than a stranger.

By no means all the members of a royal *gens* obeyed the lesson as the bitter feuds in the Ottonian house, the risings of 938-40, 953-4, the 970s and 984 show, nor did the younger Conrad. The existence of commanding heights which could not easily be shared not only had the consequence of disrupting the solidarity of kinsmen which rested on parity.[34] It also meant that the higher nobility did not like to see lesser men, still *ingenui* but not of the leading groups, ride into their midst. During the period of Ottonian military expansion along the eastern borders of Saxony and Thuringia the best opportunities for advancement were monopolized by a few, mainly East-Saxon family-groups. Each clan could thus hope to accommodate more than one of their own in princely positions. Only a handful of comital kins are known for ninth-century Saxony; by the end of the tenth there appear to be at least 27.[35] Not all individual counts can be assigned to a *stirps* but of those who can, very few seem to have belonged to families with no counts in their ancestry and even here

---

[34] The feeling that sudden riches alienated a man from his blood-relations is strongly voiced in *Ruodlieb*, v, ll. 426-9 (pp. 70-1).

[35] The five families listed in S. Krüger, *Studien zur Sächsischen Grafschaftsverfassung im 9. Jahrhundert* (Studien u. Vorarbeiten z. Histor. Atlas Niedersachsens, xix, Göttingen, 1950) might be compared with the twenty-five built up by Schölkopf, *op. cit.* The Billungs and the counts of Stade must be added to her figure whatever its justification. For a critical comment see Schmid in *Zeitschrift für Württembergische Landesgeschichte*, xxiii (1964), pp. 215-27.

it is difficult to be sure.   Countships and burgraviates might come to less important kindreds by way of sub-infeudation and this could mean, from the early eleventh century onwards, through the favour of bishops.   Yet even here they had to meet stiff competition from the second or third sons of the most eminent bloods.   Of Thietmar of Merseburg's four brothers, for instance, two went into the Church as he had done, one, Henry, succeeded his father as count and the other, Frederick, commanded Bishop Thietmar's knights and later became burgrave of Magdeburg.[36]

The distance between great nobles (*primores*) and lesser ones, their *milites* (vassals) was vast and the great took care to keep it that way. To prove this there are some good examples.   In 938 Otto I had to fight against his half-brother, Thangmar, who had resorted to arms because he thought himself cheated of his mother's inheritance.   The king by a rapid march trapped him in the Eresburg.   Thangmar fled into the chapel where he placed his weapons and his golden necklace upon the altar, perhaps as a sign of surrender rather than the symbolic renunciation of a claim to the kingship.   The bastard-son of a noble, Thiadbold, struck at him but was wounded and soon died as he deserved to do.   Then another of the mere *milites*, called Meginzo, killed Thangmar with a lance as he climbed in through the window near the altar.   The king did not know about this; he had not been present, as Widukind is anxious to tell his readers, but when he heard he was outraged by his men's presumption.   Even as an enemy his half-brother was sacrosanct for underlings and nobodies such as Meginzo.   But he could not punish him or his fellows because he needed them.   The wars against the enemies who threatened his precarious possession of the kingship had only just begun and he could not demoralize his *milites*.   On the other hand if Thangmar was immune, even as a rebel, his followers were promptly strung up to make an example.[37]

Another instance of the savage revenge that could await an offending vassal is related by Adam of Bremen.   In 1048 Archbishop Adalbert invited the emperor Henry III to visit Bremen which lay quite outside the usual royal itinerary.   No king had ever been in these regions before.   His very coming was felt to be a threat to the local balance of power between the Billung family and the arch-

---

[36] See R. Holtzmann's introduction to his edition of Thietmar, p. xv.

[37] Widukind, ii.11 (p. 77).   The story of Thangmar's death should be compared with William Rufus's narrow escape from the *vulgus militum* at Mont St. Michael: see William of Malmesbury, *Gesta Regum*, iv. 309 (ed. W. Stubbs, Rolls Series, London, 1889, ii, p. 364).

bishopric.   Count Thietmar, a brother of Duke Bernhard II, seems
to have plotted to ambush the emperor near Lesum, a huge estate
which Conrad II had taken from his widowed aunt Emma, the sister
of Bishop Meinwerk of Paderborn.   It was Billung land and they
feared the archbishop's acquisitive ambitions.   The emperor
escaped, called Thietmar to account and forced him to fight a judicial
duel against one of his own vassals who must have acted as accuser
and champion.   Thietmar perished, but a few days later his son
Thiemo seized this man and hung him by the legs between two
savage dogs until he was dead.   It is true that he paid for his vengeance
with arrest and lifelong exile but by the standards of his caste he had
done the right thing.[38]
   Throughout this period great lords were not squeamish about
hanging or murdering the vassals of their neighbours.   It is as well to
know of such incidents because they show what an idealised world
that of the poem *Ruodlieb* really is: idealised, or seeking to establish
less savage standards of behaviour.   *Ruodlieb* is now dated by
scholars about 1050 and one of its main themes is that of noble
revenge, of forgiving one's enemies with interest rather than
perpetuate hostilities.   Henry III himself preached these ideas and
wished to urge them upon his intractable princes.   The circle of
clerks and writers about him to which the author of the poem may
have belonged, had a task but it was, like the much more ambitious
aims of the Carolingian court school, one they were unable to fulfil
successfully though we are the richer by Wipo's biography and poems,
perhaps *Ruodlieb* and the *Ecbasis Captivi*, thanks to their efforts.[39]
Education alone could not pacify the lay aristocracy or solve its
problems.
   In the very core of the story *Ruodlieb* depicts a world of wishful
thinking, the career of the hero, his ascent from the status of an
unconsidered *miles* who had only his food and clothes to the ranks of
the mighty.[40]   Royal favour was not ubiquitous and the most that his
like could normally hope for was, as has been said, to hold office as

[38] Adam of Bremen, *Gesta*, iii.8 (p. 149).
[39] On the theme of noble revenge in *Ruodlieb* see W. Braun, *Studien zum
Ruodlieb* (Quellen und Forschungen zur Sprach- und Kulturgeschichte der
Germanischen Völker, N. F. vii, Berlin, 1962), pp. 22-4, 29 f.   The connection
of *Ruodlieb* with Henry III's court and of the *Ecbasis* even with his time is
disputed.   At the very least however the creator of *Ruodlieb* wanted to captivate
and exhort a noble lay audience and knew its tastes and resorts well.
[40] *Ruodlieb*, v, ll. 274-7 (pp. 64-5).   On the theme of social ascent in the poem
see K. Hauck, "Haus- und sippengebundene Literatur mittelalterlicher
Adelsgeschlechter", in *Geschichtsdenken und Geschichtsbild im Mittelalter*, ed.
W. Lammers (Wege der Forschung, xxi, Darmstadt, 1961), pp. 187-90.

the vassals of great lay lords or bishops.   Ruodlieb at the end of his
service at the court of the great king is thought worthy of comital
honours, perhaps in imitation of *Waltharius*.[41]   He has conducted
wars and embassies with much skill and yet does not expect a great
deal.   Among the famous councils of wisdom his royal patron gives
him before he leaves we also find a warning, never to lend money to
his lord.   It was better to give outright on demand.   Lending only
caused resentment, some trap would be laid to find him guilty of an
offence so that he would be glad to lose only his money and not life
and limb as well.   The author of course used a biblical source here
(Ecclesiasticus, viii. 15) and advice so couched was all the more
authoritative for his audience.[42]   As a comment on contemporary
lordship it should therefore be taken notice of, although we must not
omit also examples of that *largitas* which in all the sources appears as
a necessary virtue of rulers.   Otto I's brother Henry, duke of
Bavaria, so Widukind tells us, gave his sister-in-law in marriage to
a vassal of modest fortune and so made him his *socius*, his equal and
friend.   Her husband Burkhard can be traced as burgrave of
Regensburg and margrave of the Bavarian Eastern March.   Probably
his marriage raised him to these honours but he seems to have been
"mediocris" only in relation to the *stirps regia* which Widukind
wanted to exalt above all others.[43]

Ruodlieb is important to the historian because the poem seems to
stand between the *Reich* of the Ottonians and the first two Salian
emperors and the cataclysm which later overwhelmed the Salian
dynasty and its inherited, traditional supports.   It is imbued with
all the pre-occupations of the lay aristocracy, including its religious
ones.   There are the embassies and the lavish presents which
denoted the respect in which one ruler and his nobles were held by
another, those gifts which placed fortunes into the hands of a
successful war-lord and which he could then distribute as rewards
to his followers.   Otto I's triumphs followed those of the Carolingians
in this faithfully.   He too received rarities, gold plate, glassware,
ivories, perfumes and exotic animals like apes and ostriches from
Greeks and Moslems after his victory at the Lech, and again the gifts
of half Europe at his last great court at Quedlinburg in 973.   Otto III
and Henry II and their entourage enjoyed no less prestige, we know,

---

[41] *Ruodlieb*, v, ll. 402-4 (pp. 70-1, where however "comitatus" has been
mistranslated).
[42] *Ibid.*, v, ll. 502-10 (pp. 74-5) and see Braun, *Studien zum Ruodlieb*, p. 14.
[43] Widukind, ii.36 (p. 97).

because so many of the gifts they collected ended up in the treasuries of their bishops.   There also, in the poem, are the gestures of self-denial when the "greater king" declines most of what his defeated adversary offers him as compensation.[44]   This could happen occasionally, for we read that neither Otto III at Gnesen (1000) nor Henry II at Ivois in 1023 accepted the riches temptingly displayed for them by their "lesser king", Boleslas and Robert the Pious respectively.   They wanted only relics and took only not to offend.

For the rest the moral in *Ruodlieb* seems to be that aristocratic power and right should be tempered by discretion.   The great king does not advise Ruodlieb to forego concubines chosen from his own bond-women, only they must not become the mistresses of his household.[45]   He also exhorts him to cling to the road, even if it was muddy, rather than ride roughshod through the standing corn but the motive for such self-restraint was prudence and not that nobles owed respect to the toils of the husbandman.   The angered peasants might ill-treat and rob a man of rank who had damaged their crops and given them high words into the bargain.   This counsel faintly foreshadows the provincial peace-oaths of the late eleventh century and the *Landfrieden* of the twelfth which sought to protect cornfields and vineyards against the depradations of armies and travellers.[46]   That we should be led into a village community on Ruodlieb's travels is in itself of great significance.   The households of the old and the young peasant — we can only guess their status — were not poor, and one of them, that of the young man, was accustomed to putting up noblemen on their journeys.   A small present in return for the, perhaps obligatory, hospitality was not unusual.   The behaviour of Ruodlieb's red-headed companion, who mortally wounds his host, also shows the reverse of the medal.   The poet, in what has survived of his work, tells us nothing about the business or the standing of this man and yet, characteristically, makes it clear that evil, by its very nature, was plebeian and not noble.   The red-head is tried on the spot and again it is worth noting that provisions for the instant trial of quarrelsome and noxious travellers can be found in one of the

---

[44] *Ruodlieb*, v, ll. 203-8 (pp. 60-1).

[45] *Ibid.*, v, ll. 476-83 (pp. 74-5).   Examples of eleventh-century German nobles jeopardizing the future of their patrimonies by keeping mistresses and remaining unmarried are not hard to find.   Cf. the case of Count Cuno of Wülflingen below p. 185.

[46] *Ibid.*, v, ll. 457-60 (pp. 72-3); and cf. the *Pax Alsatiensis*, c.9 (MGH. *Constitutiones et Acta Publica*, i, ed. L. Weiland [Hanover, 1893], no. 429, p. 613): "Equi . . . et vinee et segetes sub hac pacis condictione perpetuo permaneant . . .".

peace-oaths of the later eleventh century.[47]   In the village scenes the poem seems to herald the at least partial emergence of the rural population from the cultural passivity and obscurity of the early middle ages.

Its causes were complex.   To say that the growing volume of colonization within Germany and on her Eastern frontiers placed peasant labour at a higher premium and induced lords to grant easier terms to their dependants is to use an argument of convenience. More important was the great movement of ecclesiastical reform, for it looked not only towards the *humiles* and the poor for support but aimed at bettering their religious situation in a church less exclusively aristocratic than in the past.   It sought to provide better parochial services with the help of communities of canons regular, themselves recruited sometimes from the ranks of the *ignobiles*.   The demand for clerical celibacy for the most part concerned them.   The waves of agitation in Southern Germany, especially Swabia and Alsace from about 1075 to 1095 roused them from their obscurity and carried them to the fringes of the monastic reform movement led by Hirsau.   Not all the lay-brethren, Hirsau's most startling innovation, can have been nobles (or even *ministeriales*) whatever the chronicler Bernold wrote in a moment of elation.   In a famous passage he has described how aristocratic converts cooked, baked and looked after the pigs of the monks but he also mentioned the conversion of whole villages and of peasant girls who renounced marriage.[48]   What matters is that nobles as lay-brethren and as part of their new lives in religion, should have imitated the labours of farm-servants, the least privileged class of agrarian dependants.

It is possible also to discover here and there a new relationship between alms-givers and alms-takers in the literature of the late eleventh and early twelfth century, a relationship different from that which spoke so strongly through the pages of early medieval German Lives of royalty and bishops.   The charitable deeds of kings and prelates remained, of course, an essential topic for their biographers

---

[47] *Ruodlieb*, viii, ll. 11 ff. (pp. 94-5) and cf. the *Pax Dei* of 1084, c.8 (MGH. *Constitutiones*, i, no. 426, p. 609).   On these provisions see also J. Gernhuber, *Die Landfriedensbewegung in Deutschland bis zum Mainzer Reichslandfrieden von 1235* (Bonner Rechtswissenschaftliche Abhandlungen, xliv, Bonn, 1952), pp. 206 ff.

[48] Bernold, *Chronicon, a.* 1083 and *a.* 1091 (MGH. SS. v, pp. 439 and 452 f.). On the lay-brethren at Hirsau see H. Jakobs, *Die Hirsauer,* (Kölner Historische Abhandlungen, iv, Köln Graz, 1961), *passim*.   A youth "plebeiae libertatis" and his father are mentioned among the lay-brethren, the "fratres barbati" of Zwiefalten: see Berthold of Zwiefalten's *Chronicon*, ch. 20 (MGH. SS., x, p. 107).

but now a note of personal interest, of real concern for individual
sufferers occasionally appears besides the accepted commonplaces.
Abbot William of Hirsau, on his way to found a new cell, paused to
visit a hovel.   According to Haimo, the author of his Life, he put
aside his dignity and severity, sat by the fire with the very poor woman
he found within and enquired how she could live.   When he discovered that neither she nor her husband knew the creed he taught
them as much as they were able to understand and asked them to come
and see him at his destination next day.   There he received them
kindly and looked after their needs.   William also seems to have
visited the ailing poor in the almonry and even in their villages and to
have taken care that they were decently buried.[49]   Comforting the
sick of any class was normally the task of the parochial clergy and the
critics of Hirsau were not slow to accuse the monks of usurpation.
But these incidents in the "Life of Abbot William" should be judged
in a different light.   Men of his rank and birth had not, in the tenth
century, come so close to the *pauperi* they tried to help.

A like concern for the unfortunate was, surprisingly enough, ascribed
also to Henry IV himself, the man whom all the reformers detested
and damned.   In the anonymous Life of the emperor his care for
the indigent sick is described with exceptionally lurid, if conventional,
details and the author is anxious to show that Henry IV did not merely
order his servants to do good for him.   He also had a fixed number of
pauperi fed and supported at his demesne residences and wanted to
be told when someone had died so that he could keep his obit and
have another appointed in his place.[50]

Necessity forced strange allies upon the king.   Deserted by many
of his princes and nobles and some of his bishops Henry IV sought
friends amongst the lower orders, especially his *ministeriales,* raised
peasant armies and shocked clerical Germany by his close ties with the
burgesses of Worms and his encouragement of their like up and down
the Rhine valley.   The East-Saxon princes too made use of petty
freemen to enlarge their rising in 1073 and to pack their armies, with
disastrous results as it turned out.   Lastly we must not reject
altogether as mere figures of speech the taunts of the pamphleteers
in the long conflict between emperor and pope.   When they tell us

---

[49] *Vita Willihelmi Abbatis Hirsaugiensis*, chaps. 17 and 20 (MGH. SS., xii,
p. 217 and 218.   The value of this source has been underrated in W. Wattenbach and R. Holtzmann, *Deutschlands Geschichtsquellen im Mittelalter*, i, 3
(Tübingen, 1948), pp. 390 f., and also in Jakobs, *op. cit.*, p. xviii.
[50] *Vita Heinrici IV. Imperatoris*, ch. i, ed. W. Eberhard (MGH. SRG.,
Hanover, 1899), pp. 10 f., and the English translation, *Imperial Lives and
Letters*, p. 103.

that the great questions of the day were being bandied about in the women's quarters or that the writings of their opponents had been propagated amongst the crowds, they may have been right for all their rhetoric. Manegold of Lautenbach who amongst others asserted this in his *Liber ad Gebehardum* (1083-1085) was himself a plebeian and sometimes wrote like one. He was also an agitator of genius; his partisans praised him for reviving the revolt against Henry IV in Alsace single-handed. Nobles and knights flocked to him to be absolved from excommunication and promised obedience to Pope Urban II.[51] There is little doubt that the writings and preachings of the anti-Henrician polemicists in the *Reich* reached a much wider circle and, more still, found a much larger and socially mixed audience amongst the laity than any literary "publication" had ever done before.

These upheavals confronted the leading strata of German society with new problems in addition to the age-old ones that were still with them: partible inheritances, the striving for parity between brothers and the rapid flow of estates within families or between them through the claims of affinity by marriage. The long wars in Germany during the last quarter of the eleventh century and the fifty years before Frederick Barbarossa's election if anything aggravated the pressures on noble fortunes. The wars demanded that important families and individuals had to increase their military strength and to keep larger numbers of *milites* than their lands could support. The end of fighting was in itself dangerous. As long as their men were employed they could also hope to maintain them out of the activity of war as such: plunder, foraging, ransoms and any other rewards that successful expeditions and raids might procure. The growing practice of enfeoffing *ministeriales* with fragments of monastic advocacies against which the Church fought in vain, had, according to Ekkehard of Aura, its cause in the need to keep up war-bands. The author of the "Life of Henry IV" described with biting irony the plight of nobles who had lived on a war-footing for too long and were threatened with impoverishment under the emperor's *Landfriede* of 1103. The family historian of the Welfs in the later twelfth century noted that Welf IV (*ob.* 1101) was the first of his house who, in return for great fiefs, deigned to become the vassal of bishops and abbots. He did this because he had given too many estates to his followers

---

[51] In the preface of his *Liber ad Gebehardum* (ed. K. Francke, MGH. Libelli de Lite Imperatorum et Pontificum, i, p. 311), Manegold called himself "genere abiectus". For his activities in Alsace see Bernold, *Chronicon, a.* 1094 (MGH. SS., v, p. 461). A pestilence helped him.

during the time of the troubles.[52]   The Welfs of course were not alone
in trying to recoup themselves for over-enfeoffments by extorting
ecclesiastical fiefs.

The conditions of the late eleventh and early twelfth century thus
did not unequivocally favour, as is usually thought, the consolidation
of noble fortunes and their continuity.   The wars between the last
two Salian rulers, Henry IV and Henry V, and their more implacable
enemies, especially the East-Saxon nobles, only brought it about that
kingship for many years on end was no longer the most important
source of rewards and favours in the northern and eastern regions of
the *Reich*.   This only intensified the endemic feuds amongst
aristocratic contenders for spoils and inheritances.   After 1085 the war
of the East-Saxon bishops and nobles against Henry IV began to
degenerate into a number of murderous vendettas between them.
Yet neither the religious movement with its cautious interest in the
rural *vulgus* nor the rise of the *ministeriales*, the serf-knights, blunted
the initiative of the high aristocracy or changed their caste very much.
It is true that in the expanding society of the twelfth century the
families of the nobility could not man all the positions that had to be
manned and this gave the *ministeriales* their opportunities to invade
spheres of action in government and justice hitherto closed to them.
But the *primores*, the men with important allods, advocacies, countships, not to mention higher honours, at their disposal on the whole
and in most regions remained firmly in control.   The distance which
had always separated a few score individuals and families, the minority
within the minority, from their *milites* was decisive.   It set certain
limits to the advance of the *ministeriales* and made it easier for many of
the less fortunate and economically hard-pressed nobles to merge with
them.   German political society, like the areas settled by its enterprise,
could thus grow larger without experiencing any fundamental shift
in its leading strata or becoming more homogeneous.

There remains the problem of family structure and here the
evidence for the persistent and unyielding habits of the aristocracy in
the management of its most vital concerns, especially inheritances,
must be set against the evidence for change.   The complexity of
claims upon a given estate was at no time more manifest than when it
was proposed to alienate it to the Church.   In the tenth and early

---

[52] On the sub-advocacies as fiefs for warriors see Ekkehard, *Chronicon
Universale*, a. 1099 (MGH. SS., vi, p. 210 f.).   On the plight of the nobles with
overlarge warbands see the *Vita Heinrici IV. Imperatoris*, ch. 8 (*ed. cit.*, p. 28;
the translation, *ed. cit.*, pp. 120 f.).   For Welf IV see the *Historia Welforum*,
ch. 13 (MGH. SS., xxi, p. 462).

eleventh century it had always been difficult to protect proprietary foundations against the importunate resentment of heirs, the kindred of the donor. It was no easier later despite the new *libertas* of monastic houses warranted by papal privileges. Men who wished to found monasteries still had to square their kinsmen in all directions lest their plans should come to grief after their deaths. A good example of the difficulties which even devoted lay patrons of reform had to contend with comes from the foundation history of Zwiefalten, near the Danube in Northern Swabia. It was written in the third decade of the twelfth century by one of the monks, Ortlieb, and completed by Berthold who became abbot of the house. When Counts Cuno and Liutold, commonly called after their castle at Achalm, decided to found a monastery sometime before 1089, they had outlived all their brothers so that most of the family's lands amassed in their hands.[53] Some of them they held jointly, others in severalty. Cuno left behind him three illegitimate sons who became the property of their unfree mother's lord, Count Hartmann of Dillingen, and could not inherit.[54] Liutold was unmarried and childless. To make sure however that Zwiefalten should securely enjoy their gifts they had, first of all, to win over their sister Williberga's son, Count Werner of Grüningen whose claims, Ortlieb declared, came before all the other kin's. He received the castles at Achalm with most of the *ministeriales* as well as half the church and *villa* at Dettingen, half the *villa* of Metzingen and half the church at Endingen.[55] That the brothers themselves only possessed halves in these lands and revenues suggests earlier divisions. Sometime after 1092 when Count Liutold became the sole survivor, two sons of another sister, Mathilda of Horburg, came forward and demanded their shares. Ortlieb thought that custom allowed them no claims whatsoever and that they had already received their due out of their mother's inheritance. But Count Liutold knew better and gave them the castle of Wülflingen (near Winterthur) with all the lands and knights in this region, including an estate already granted to Zwiefalten.[56] This important complex of possessions had come to the family by the marriage of Cuno and Liutold's father, Count Rudolf, with Adelhaid of Mömpelgard. The sons of sisters in this case were merely the most important relations that had to be reckoned

---

[53] Ortlieb of Zwiefalten, *Chronicon*, i, 1 (MGH. SS., x, p. 72).
[54] *Casus Monasterii Petrishusensis*, iii, 3 (MGH. SS., xx, p. 649), the chronicle of the monastery of Petershausen of which one of the sons became abbot.
[55] Ortlieb, *Chronicon*, i.7 (p. 76).
[56] *Ibid.*, i.8 (p. 77).

with, not the only ones.   Five brothers had pre-deceased the founders of Zwiefalten and of these two, Werner, Bishop of Strassburg, and Egino, had reached manhood and received their shares of the family's lands.   Their estates lay partly in Alsace and partly in Swabia and at least one manor, Ebirsheim in Alsace, seems to have been held jointly with Liutold even though Bishop Werner and Egino sided with Henry IV while Liutold and Cuno followed the anti-king Rudolf of Rheinfelden in the great conflict which divided the Swabian aristocracy.   After Egino's death his wife Sophia married again and with her second husband, Count Conrad of Habsburg, had to be given twenty marks as her share out of the sale of Ebirsheim.[57]   The monastery had trouble also with two brothers, named after their seat at Möhringen, who claimed an estate by right of their grandmother, a kinswoman of Count Rudolf.   They too therefore were distantly related to the founders of Zwiefalten.   The abbey however was not always the loser by the endless ramifications of *cohereditas*.   Werner of Grüningen gave a hamlet to Hirsau which had belonged to his mother Williberga and Abbot Gebhard of Hirsau (another kinsman) had to surrender a holding elsewhere to buy out Count Liutold's rights.   The count then gave it to his own monks.[58]

It will be seen that the lands of Zwiefalten's founders lay widely scattered in Northern Swabia, Alsace and Switzerland.   Their parents had lived at Dettingen despite the building of Achalm Castle. Liutold of Achalm himself was occasionally called "of Dettingen".[59] Wülflingen seems to have been regarded as a seat of at least equal importance where Count Cuno took up residence.   The descent of Achalm is especially instructive.   Werner of Grüningen and now also of Achalm seems to have made over his inheritance to the Welf duke, Henry the Black of Bavaria who promptly gave it to his daughter Sophia as a marriage portion when she was joined to Berthold III of Zähringen.[60]   Stem-seats could thus permutate with bewildering frequency within families or change hands so that the traditions of one kin were thrown into the keeping of another and then passed on again to a third.   It was not only the failure of direct male heirs as in the case of Cuno and Liutold which brought about these situations. The proliferation of castles by which individuals and later whole families came to be named thus did not necessarily stand for a more stable and unequivocally patrilineal family structure.   To achieve

[57] *Ibid.*, i.5 (pp. 74 f.).
[58] *Loc. cit.* (pp. 73 f. and 75).
[59] Berthold of Zwiefalten, *Chronicon*, ch. 16 (MGH. SS., x, p. 105).
[60] *Op. cit.*, ch. 18 (p. 106).

this in full measure the German nobles would have had to limit the claims of female heirs and the fragmentation of estates, including lordships, it gave rise to. G. Duby has shown that from the later eleventh century onwards, at least the *droit de commandement* escaped division amongst the families of the castellans in the Maconnais.[61] The development in the *Reich* was not so clear-cut. Perhaps there was more scope for multiplying lordship by colonization and new settlement.

As long as the expectations of life did not improve markedly inheritances remained as fluid as before. For the same reason the powerful and wealthy matron who outlived husbands and brothers, did not disappear from public life. The political history of Saxony in the first half of the twelfth century was dominated by the large inheritances which the great families of the eleventh had to leave to their surviving womanfolk: Wulfhilde and Eilika Billung, Richenza and Gertrude of Northeim, Oda, Kunigunde and Adelheid of Weimar-Orlamünde and most of all Gertrude, the sister of Margrave Ekbert of Meissen, whose wealth, nobility, and power the chroniclers vied in extolling. "Saxony's almighty widow", as the chronicler Ekkehard of Aura called her, was one of the pillars of the conspiracies against Henry V in which her son-in-law Lothar of Supplinburg took the lead.[62] Another bellicose widow, the Welf princess Sophia, whom we have already met as the wife of Berthold of Zähringen, joined her brother Henry the Proud at the siege of Falkenstein (near Regensburg) with 800 knights in 1129 shortly after the death of her second husband.[63] She could safely be left in charge of the operations when her brother was called away to another and more urgent siege by his father-in-law, Lothar, now king. Eilika Billung after the death of her husband, Count Otto of Ballenstedt, settled at Burgwerben on the river Saale where she built up the castle and became the high-handed "advocatissa" of the monastery of Goseck, forcing out one abbot and chosing his successor. From her other castle at Bernburg she was said to tyrannize the countryside.[64] With the exception of Wulfhilde Billung all these noblewomen survived their husbands by at least some years; Kunigunde and Adelheid of Weimar and the Ekbertine Gertrude outlived no less than three.

[61] G. Duby, *La Société aux xie et xiie Siècles dans la région mâconnaise* (Paris, 1953), pp. 277-81, 441, 467.
[62] Ekkehard, *Chronicon*, a. 1112 (MGH. SS., vi, p. 247): "illa prepotens per Saxoniam vidua".
[63] *Historia Welforum*, ch. 17 (MGH. SS., xxi, p. 464).
[64] *Chronicon Gozecense*, ii, 19-28 (MGH. SS., x, pp. 154-6) and *Annales Magdeburgenses*, a. 1138 (MGH. SS., xvi, p. 186).

An over-riding sense of their own powers and rights continued to govern the relations between magnates and their non-noble subjects, not least of all in the cause of monastic reform itself.   The counts of Achalm evicted their tenants from the site of their planned abbey.[65] When Margrave Otakar of Styria in 1107 wanted to turn his secular canonry at Garsten into a Benedictine monastery he dismissed most of the clerks.   Some, however, were his *homines proprii* and these he forced to stay and become monks, and he answered their pleas that vows should not be extorted from them in no uncertain fashion: "You are mine and so you must agree with me and obey my will in everything".   The ringleader of the opposition was beaten until he gave in.   The biographer of Garsten's first abbot recorded this story with only faint embarrassment and ended it on a note even of edification.[66]   The historiography of the revived and new monasteries was as preoccupied with the nobility of their founders as the Ottonian writers had been.   Ortlieb and Berthold of Zwiefalten's devotion to the counts of Achalm was not exceptional.   It is echoed by the Pegau annalist's heroic biography of his founder, Wiprecht of Groitzsch and by the Goseck, Lauterberg and Reinhardsbrunn traditions as recorded by their historians, to mention only a few.[67]   Genealogy was the most personal and abiding concern of the great mid twelfth-century Saxon historian known as *Annalista Saxo*.

What has been said about the early medieval German aristocracy could perhaps be said also about its neighbours further west with whom it shared the Frankish past, and even Anglo-Saxon England. Yet the nobility of the *Reich* differed from them in changing much less. This is not to assert that the development so well set out by K. Schmid did not take place at all, only in Germany it remained incomplete and equivocal.   Nor is it suggested that the German nobles were wholly unreceptive of new ideas whether religious, cultural or in the art of government.   They shared, patronized and used the religious reform movement as their many monastic foundations in the late eleventh and early twelfth century show.   Without them it would have been almost unthinkable.   They were willing to exploit the great opportunities of colonization and towns which the increase of population made possible and also to administer their lordships more effectively.   But all this was compatible with and often subordinated to their age-old

---

[65] Ortlieb, i.2 (p. 72).

[66] *Vita Beati Bertholdi Abbatis Garstensis*, ed. H. Pez (Scriptores Rerum Austriacarum, Leipzig, 1725), ii, col. 90.

[67] On this see H. Patze, "Adel und Stifterchronik", *Blätter für deutsche Landesgeschichte*, c (1964), pp. 8-81 and ci (1965), pp. 67-128.

domestic predicaments and needs: partible inheritances, and how to reconcile parity of status amongst kin and fellows with the uneven distribution of wealth and power.   Their tenacious conservatism moreover proved infectious to their only immediate rivals and challengers, the *ministeriales*.   In this way and because they had to compete with men who were socially so far beneath them, the nobles escaped being swept away or flooded by the ever-growing society of the twelfth century.   They remained its masters and the enduring features of their caste were even more important than the changes.

Note

For the debate which followed this study see *Past and Present*, 45 (Nov., 1969), pp. 3-18 and *Past and Present*, 49 (Nov., 1970), pp. 126-134.
In general see W. Störmer, *Früher Adel Studien zur potitischen Führungsschicht im Fränkisch-Deutschen Reich vom 8. bis 11. Jahrhundert*, Monographien zur Geschichte des Mittelalters, 6, I and 6, II (Stuttgart, 1973). See also my *Rule and Conflict in an Early Medieval Society Ottonian Saxony* (London 1979) and Indiana University Press (Bloomington and London, 1979).

ENGLAND AND THE EMPIRE IN THE EARLY TWELFTH CENTURY

8

THE Norman conquerors of England had at first little cause to seek connexions with the empire of the Salian kings and they had nothing to fear from it. Before William sailed on his expedition, he enlisted, it is true, not only the good-will of the papacy, but also that of the young Henry IV. Henry, who at the age of fifteen had by German custom reached his majority, seems to have made it known that men from Germany could go to host with William, should the latter wish it.[1] Some of the Flemish knights who took part in the venture may have come from those fiefs of the count of Flanders which were held of the empire rather than of the kingdom of France.[2] Bruno, in his *Book on the Saxon War*, would have his readers believe that the Salian king, when preparing his revenge against the Saxon rebels in 1074, sent for help also to William, who is supposed to have replied that he dared not leave England.[3] But in the same year, only a few months earlier, it had been rumoured that the Conqueror was advancing against the Lotharingian frontiers of the *Reich* and about to seize Aachen at the invitation of Archbishop Anno of Cologne.[4]

The very contradictions of these reports have a meaning. The predatory politics of England's new masters and the demoral-ized opportunism of the German princes and of their young overlord did not depend on one another to thrive. Yet few of

[1] Guillaume de Poitiers, *Histoire de Guillaume le Conquérant*, ed. Raymonde Foreville (Paris, 1952), p. 154.

[2] In his treaty with Henry I, in 1101, the count of Flanders stipulated that military obligations to the emperor should count as a legitimate reason for not going to England to help the king against invasion. Henry IV's per-mission was therefore not without moment. *Cf. Actes des Comtes de Flandre, 1071–1128*, ed. F. Vercauteren (Académie Royale de Belgique, 1938), p. 90, § 4, and p. 92, § 13.

[3] *Brunos Buch vom Sachsenkrieg*, ed. H. Lohmann (Leipzig, 1937), p. 38.

[4] Lampert of Hersfeld, *Annales*, ed. O. Holder-Egger, *Scriptores Rerum Germanicarum in usum scholarum*, 1894, p. 195.

the empire's contemporary chroniclers failed to mention the Conquest or its portent, the comet, and at least one later German historian, Giesebrecht, was not a little shocked that a German king should have allowed the Saxons of England to be over-whelmed without stirring a finger; an Otto I or a Henry III would not have done this.[1] The censure may reflect pan-German patriotism of the nineteenth century rather than what was possible or likely in the eleventh, but it contains at least one grain of truth. Between the Old-English kingdom and the empire some community of sentiment and interest had existed ever since 929, when Æthelstan sent to the court of the Liudolfings two of his sisters, one of whom married Henry I's son and successor Otto. Neither the change of dynasty in Germany, in 1024, nor the Danish regime in England altered this. Konrad II married his son to a daughter of Canute. An imperial embassy congratu-lated Edward the Confessor, back on the throne of his ancestors, in 1043. Six years later, Edward concentrated his ships at Sand-wich while Henry III invaded the lands of their common enemy, the count of Flanders. Society and church in later Saxon England on the whole resembled their counterparts in the empire more than those of northern France. Against this, the Norman aristo-cracy and their rulers, a generation after the Conquest, of necessity still looked first towards the courts and vassalages surrounding the duchy: Brittany, Anjou, Blois, the Capetian demesne, Vermandois and Flanders; these were the daily bread of their feuds and alliances. What then led Henry I to accept Henry V of Germany as his son-in-law and to renew connexions with the Salian house which had more or less been forgotten since Edward the Confessor's time? It is now more than sixty years since a German scholar, Rössler, published his work on the Empress Mathilda, and the significance of Mathilda's first marriage was not his chief concern.[2] No systematic study of this alliance, of its purpose and consequences, has appeared since, nor can it be attempted here. But some new evidence has come to light and much of the old may well repay another look, even if there is a danger of making too little go too far.

[1] W. von Giesebrecht, *Geschichte der deutschen Kaiserzeit*, 5th ed., iii, pp. 223 ff.

[2] O. Rössler, *Kaiserin Mathilde, Mutter Heinrichs von Anjou, und das Zeitalter der Anarchie in England* (Berlin, 1897).

In March 1109, Henry I wrote a letter to Archbishop Anselm from Rouen and, amongst other items of news, he told him that the business which had been pending between himself and the emperor of the Romans was now brought to its conclusion 'for the honour of God, our own, that of Holy Church and of all Christian people'.[1] Mathilda's marriage and probably also its terms seem to have been settled by then, at least in principle; for when Henry returned to England and kept his Whitsun court at Westminster on 13 June, imperial envoys arrived 'to complete contracts' and swear the necessary oaths guaranteeing their fulfilment.[2] Henry of Huntingdon described these men as imposingly large and well dressed.[3] A household clerk of Henry V, called Burkhard, later bishop of Cambrai, was most probably one of them, and he certainly helped to escort the eight-year-old princess to her new home in February 1110.[4] Early in March, Mathilda and her large Norman following arrived in Liège, where Henry V received her—in the words of the Paderborn annalist— 'as befitted a king'.[5] For Easter, on 10 April, the court moved to Utrecht and here she was solemnly betrothed to him and assigned dower.[6] On 25 July she was crowned queen at Mainz by Archbishop Frederick of Cologne, assisted by Bruno of Trier; the latter then took charge of her education and saw to it that she was

[1] S. Anselmi ... Opera Omnia, ed. F. S. Schmitt, v (Edinburgh, 1951), p. 410, no. 461.

[2] W. Farrer, 'An Outline Itinerary of King Henry I', Eng. Hist. Rev., xxxiv (1919), p. 353; Two of the Saxon Chronicles Parallel, ed. C. Plummer (Oxford, 1892–99), i, p. 242: 'Daer wurdon þa forewearda full worhte.'

[3] Henry of Huntingdon, Historia Anglorum, ed. T. Arnold (R.S., 1879), p. 237: 'mole corporis et cultuum splendoribus excellentes'. For Suger's impressions of a German embassy at Châlons-sur-Marne, in 1107, see his Gesta Ludovici Regis cognomento Grossi, ch. 9, ed. A. Molinier (Collection de Textes pour servir à l'étude et à l'enseignement de l'histoire), Paris, 1887, p. 26, and infra, p. 201.

[4] Ordericus Vitalis, Hist[oria] Eccl[esiastica], ed. A. Le Prévost, iv (Paris, 1852), p. 296. On Burkhard's career, see F. Hausmann, Reichskanzlei und Hofkapelle unter Heinrich V und Konrad III (Schriften der M[onumenta] G[ermaniae] H[istorica], xiv, Stuttgart, 1956), pp. 87 ff.

[5] Annales Patherbrunnenses, ed. P. Scheffer-Boichorst (Innsbruck, 1870), p. 122; G. Meyer von Knonau, Jahrbücher des Deutschen Reiches unter Heinrich IV und Heinrich V, vi, pp. 116 ff.

[6] Annales Patherbrunnenses, loc. cit., and Robert of Torigny's additions to William of Jumièges' Gesta Normannorum Ducum, ed. J. Marx (Société de l'histoire de Normandie), Rouen, 1914, p. 281.

taught German and the manners of the country.[1] In January 1114, when Mathilda had not yet reached the age of twelve, Henry V, now emperor and at the height of his fortunes, finally married her amidst great festivities.[2] From then onwards she shared the migratory life which the rulers of the *Reich* had to lead to make their authority felt.

The initiative for the match seems to have come from Henry V, though we cannot absolutely trust those Anglo-Norman writers, Henry of Huntingdon, Robert of Torigny and the author of *Draco Normannicus*, who made a point of holding up the Salian emperor as a suitor.[3] They were, for the most part, devout flatterers of the royal house. But there is, in the famous Bamberg collection known as the *Codex Udalrici*, a letter of Henry V to Henry I's queen, Mathilda, in which he thanked her effusively for speaking well of him to her husband and others. Henry V also expected that her goodwill should continue to be of service to him 'in those things which we ask of your lord'.[4] The wording suggests that this letter accompanied one of his embassies and it confirms that the negotiations took some time. But Henry I can hardly have wanted the alliance any less than the Salian king, since he sent him at least 10,000 marks of silver with Mathilda, not to mention other rich presents which she brought with her to Liège.[5] To raise this sum or, more likely, to refill his treasury, he levied an aid of three shillings on the hide.[6] A few anxious prelates and religious can be found to have secured writs com-

---

[1] Robert of Torigny, *loc. cit.* It appears from Suger (*op. cit., loc. cit.*) that Archbishop Bruno was able to speak French.

[2] Ekkehard von Aura, *Chronicon*, ed. Waitz, *M.G.H., Scriptores*, vi, pp. 247–48.

[3] Henry of Huntingdon, *Historia Anglorum* (R.S.), p. 237: 'nuntii . . . filiam regis in domini sui conjugium postulantes'; Robert of Torigny, *op. cit.*, p. 280: 'in conjugem requisivit'; *Draco Normannicus*, ed. R. Howlett, *Chronicles of the Reigns of Stephen, Henry II and Richard I* (R.S., 1884–90), ii, p. 597: 'quaerit consociare sibi'.

[4] *Monumenta Bambergensia*, ed. P. Jaffé (*Bibliotheca Rerum Germanicarum*, v), p. 259, no. 142.

[5] Ordericus Vitalis, *Hist. Eccl.*, ed. A Le Prévost, iv, p. 8. According to the Winchester Annals, the sum was 15,000 marks; *cf. Annales Monastici*, ed. H. R. Luard, ii (R.S., 1865), p. 43.

[6] Henry of Huntingdon, *Historia Anglorum, loc. cit.* In the *Anglo-Saxon Chronicle E*, the aid is mentioned amongst the calamities of the year 1110; see *Two of the Saxon Chronicles Parallel*, ed. C. Plummer, i, p. 243.

manding that this tax was not to prejudice their status under earlier grants or usher in new customs.[1] Very few exemptions can be traced, but one of these acquitting five hides of the abbot of Abingdon's lands reveals incidentally that the king had been granted the aid by his barons.[2] A royal marriage in the twelfth century could not be just the private concern of the ruler. His vassals, his whole kingdom, had to be associated with it. It was their duty to enhance his honour and they shared the pride of a great connexion.

Here is perhaps the idea which prompted, if it did not justify, all the ostentation, the circumstance, the expense of the occasion. The Normans in the early twelfth century were still regarded, not without cause, as dangerous intruders, a threat to established powers and dynasties in a Europe which had not yet acquiesced in the situation created by their conquests. Mathilda's very arrival in Liège furnishes a good example of these suspicions. The large Norman following which escorted her to Germany, especially Roger FitzRichard de Clare, we are told, looked for profitable openings and careers in the empire as their like had done at Salerno and in the Confessor's England. But Henry V who knew his men sent them home again; loaded with presents, they were firmly shown the door.[3] The Norman kings too were newcomers amongst the crowned heads of their time. If their ducal standing was old, their regality was recent. It is true that William I had a crown made for himself by a Greek, which with its arc and twelve pearls resembled that of Otto the Great, the crown of the empire *par excellence*.[4] But these were as yet pretensions, and the possession of power alone could not make them ring true. The most obvious reason for Henry I to give so much in order to marry his daughter into the Salian dynasty was the exaltation

[1] *Regesta Regum Anglo-Normannorum, 1066–1154*, ii, ed. C. Johnson and H. A. Cronne, nos. 946, 963, 968.

[2] *Ibid.*, nos. 959, 962, 964; *Chronicon Monasterii de Abingdon*, ed. J. Stevenson (R.S., 1858), ii, p. 113: 'et nominatim de isto auxilio quod barones mihi dederunt'. It is interesting to note that this, the first aid *pour fille marier*, was levied as a geld and not on the knight's fee.

[3] Ordericus Vitalis, *Hist. Eccl.*, iv, pp. 296 ff. But at least one of her followers, Henry, archdeacon of Winchester, stayed and was later given the bishopric of Verdun; *cf.* Meyer von Knonau, *Jahrbücher*, vii, p. 44.

[4] P. E. Schramm, *Herrschaftszeichen und Staatssymbolik (Schriften der M.G.H.*, xiii, Stuttgart, 1954–56), ii, pp. 393 ff.

of his own house. The emperor was the secular ruler with the highest rank outside Byzantium and, although he had no recognized powers and jurisdiction beyond the western frontiers of the *Reich*, he enjoyed a precedence over other reigning princes which was strengthened if he sprang from a long-established line as Henry V did.[1] He was undoubtedly purple-born, an idea not altogether alien to Germany in the eleventh century, and he defended the dual majesty of his position, the claims of his blood and the imperial name with all the harshness of his nature.[2] When, in October 1119, he entered into negotiations with Pope Calixtus II to be reconciled with the Church, his spokesmen insisted that there should not be another Canossa. Henry V would approach the pope with his boots on and in private.[3] Early in February 1111, on the road to Rome, he demanded that Pascal II should crown him as his ancestors had been crowned, without omitting anything knowingly.[4] This was aimed at the ideology of the reformers, who rejected the older and more theocratic coronation *ordines*.

The enhanced credit and respect which Henry I wanted to derive from his alliance with the Salian dynasty can be found in the writings of his court clerks and biographers. They, on the whole, did not disappoint his expectations. The author of the *Quadripartitus* seems to have counted the imperial connexion as one of the king's triumphs.[5] A more rewarding source, however, is the history of Henry I which Robert of Torigny added as an eighth book to William of Jumièges' *Gesta Normannorum Ducum*. As the date for the composition of this work its editor, J. Marx, has suggested the year 1149, but Robert in the prologue to his later chronicle said that he had written the history of

---

[1] *Cf.* R. Holtzmann, *Der Weltherrschaftsgedanke des mittelalterlichen Kaisertums und die Souveränität der europäischen Staaten* (Wissenschaftliche Buchgemeinschaft, Tübingen, 1953).

[2] Lampert of Hersfeld (*Annales*, p. 270) describes Henry IV as 'in imperio natus et nutritus'.

[3] *Hessonis scholastici relatio de concilio Remensi*, ed. W. Wattenbach, *M.G.H., Libelli de Lite* . . ., iii, p. 26.

[4] See the *Promissio Papae per Petrum Leonis dicta*, *M.G.H., Const[itutiones et Acta Publica]*, i, pp. 138–39, no. 85.

[5] F. Liebermann, *Die Gesetze der Angelsachsen* (Halle, 1898), i, p. 534: 'Teutonicorum maiestatem . . . triumphauit', probably an allusion to the marriage.

Henry I when the king's death was still a recent event, and for this 1149 is decidedly too late.[1] The eighth book carries the story up to the year 1137 and gives an excellent account of Henry I's large, though mainly illegitimate, family. Mathilda, his only surviving legitimate child, has of course pride of place in this assembly and her munificence to Bec, at this time Robert's home, is not forgotten. We learn from this source that the empress after the death of her husband, in 1125, only reluctantly obeyed her father when he sent her to Normandy in 1127 to marry the young count of Anjou.[2] Robert at this point compared her first with her second match and was anxious to console his readers, even the empress herself, for the disparity between them.

'For although the count of Anjou is of far less dignity than the Roman emperor,' he wrote, 'all the same, if anyone consults "the History of the Kings of France", he will discover from how noble a line the counts of Anjou have sprung.'[3]

It was not such a step down after all. There is yet another passage in Robert's continuation of William of Jumièges which shows how the imperial connexion was used to add new material to the Norman dynasty's cult of its own renown. In 1134 Mathilda bore the count of Anjou a second son, Geoffrey, but fell gravely ill during her labour and began to prepare for death by distributing her treasures.[4] Bec received more than many other houses and there she wished to be buried. But Henry I refused to allow this: his daughter, the 'imperatrix augusta', had at Rome walked twice under the imperial crown placed upon her by a pope's hands. It was not fit that she should be buried in any monastery, however famous. She must lie at least in Rouen, the metropolis of the Normans, where her ancestors, Rollo and William Longsword, the conquerors of Normandy, had their tombs. Henry is reported to have yielded to his daughter's wishes in the end; in any case Mathilda recovered.[5]

[1] William of Jumièges, *Gesta Normannorum Ducum*, ed. Marx, p. xxviii; Robert of Torigny, *Chronica*, Prologue, ed. R. Howlett, *Chronicles of the Reigns of Stephen, Henry II and Richard I* (R.S., 1884–90), iv, p. 65.

[2] *Gesta Normannorum Ducum*, p. 300.

[3] *Ibid.*, p. 301: 'Licet enim multo minoris dignitatis sit comes Andegavensis, quam imperator Romanus'.   [4] Robert of Torigny, *Chronica*, pp. 123 ff.

[5] *Gesta Normannorum Ducum*, pp. 303–305, especially p. 304: 'quae semel et iterum in urbe Romulea, quae caput est mundi, per manus Summi Pontificis imperiali diademate processerat insignita'.

The sentiment which Robert attributed to the king becomes the more interesting for being founded on misleading information. Robert did not make Henry I say that his daughter had been anointed and crowned empress. The suggestion is that she had worn the imperial diadem on one of the great feast days, when it was customary.[1] The ambiguity enters with the claim that the pope had placed it upon her head. Robert knew very well that a German king who had not been crowned by the pope at Rome could not properly be called an emperor, for he wrote about Konrad III in his later chronicle: 'he was never crowned at Rome; he is therefore not rightly called emperor, but king of the Germans'.[2] Now, when Henry V and Mathilda advanced on Rome with their forces, early in 1117, Pascal II with most of the *curia* withdrew to the south and would not return.[3] To keep Easter, on 25 March, the emperor had himself crowned at St Peter's by Archbishop Maurice of Braga before the altar of St Gregory which stood in a chapel off the left aisle. The *Vita Paschalis*, our source for this, does not mention Mathilda here, though she may have worn the crown as queen on this occasion.[4] According to the so-called *Annales Romani*, however, Henry V arranged a coronation for her on Whitsun day, 13 May.[5] But only the pope himself could have crowned her empress and, by this time, confused fighting had broken out in the Campagna between his Norman auxiliaries and Henry V's local supporters.[6] These proud solemnities with their *laudes* and *honores* were perhaps intended to serve as a substitute for a true imperial coronation, but this could deceive no-one. Pascal II died on 21 January

---

[1] On the custom in the empire, see H. W. Klewitz, 'Die Festkrönungen der deutschen Könige', *Zeitschrift f. Rechtsgesch.*, lix, Kanon. Abt. xxviii (1939), pp. 48 ff.

[2] Robert of Torigny, *Chronica*, p. 164.

[3] See Henry V's letter to Bishop Hartwig of Regensburg in the *Codex Udalrici*, ed. P. Jaffé, pp. 314 ff., no. 178; *Chronica Monasterii Casinensis*, ed. W. Wattenbach, *M.G.H.*, *Scriptores*, vii, p. 791. On 12 March, Pascal was at Capua, and from 16 March onwards, at Benevento: P. Jaffé and S. Loewenfeld, *Regesta Pontificum Romanorum* (Leipzig, 1885), i, nos. 6545–46.

[4] *Lib[er] Pont[ificalis]*, ed. L. Duchesne, ii (Paris, 1892), p. 304; on the chapel of St Gregory, see E. Eichmann, *Die Kaiserkrönung im Abendland* (Würzburg, 1942), ii, p. 25.

[5] *Lib. Pont.*, ii, p. 344.

[6] *Chronica Monasterii Casinensis*, loc. cit.; *Vita Paschalis II, Lib. Pont.*, ii, pp. 304–305.

1118, and when Maurice of Braga, under the name of Gregory VIII, was set up as a schismatic rival to Pope Gelasius II, the emperor let himself be crowned by him again on Whitsunday, 2 June.[1] This time, he had brought only a handful of knights from northern Italy and it is not certain whether Mathilda was there.[2] But even had she taken part in the ceremony, it would hardly have satisfied either her own or her father's ambitions. Maurice of Braga had already been excommunicated by Pascal II at Benevento in April 1117 for his share in the Roman Easter festivities.[3] He ended his brief pontificate as a captive, humiliated and maltreated by Gelasius II's successors. His acts were anathema, and coronation at his hands was something to keep dark rather than to boast of. These embarrassments Robert of Torigny and indeed Henry I had to gloss over, if Mathilda was to be presented as a true empress.[4] Time alone could cover up the defects of her title, but on the whole it did its work well for the pride of the Anglo-Norman dynasty. As early as 1139, Bishop Ulger of Angers, in the course of defending her rights to the English throne at the Lateran Council, ventured to assert publicly that Mathilda had been anointed empress by Pascal II.[5] In the *Ymagines Historiarum* of Ralph de Diceto the two crownings at Rome have become three, but it must be admitted that Ralph thought it note-worthy, if not odd, that Mathilda, who bore Henry V no children and married again, should have clung to the imperial name as long as she lived.[6] The style of her English charters bears him out. But in Henry V's diplomata, before and after 1118, she is called 'regina' and on the only two which she herself issued in Germany, both after 1118, she appears in the

---

[1] *Chronica Monasterii Casinensis*, p. 792.

[2] *Annales Romani, Lib. Pont.*, ii, p. 346: 'cum festinatione Romam petiit cum paucis militibus'.

[3] See Gelasius II's letter to the prelates, clergy, princes and faithful in France, dated 16 March 1118: Jaffé and Loewenfeld, *Regesta Pontificum Romanorum*, no. 6635, and Migne, *Patrologia Latina*, clxiii, 489.

[4] Robert of Torigny knew that Mathilda up to the time of her wedding, in 1114, was under tutelage and could not have been on the Roman expedition of 1110–11 (*cf. supra*, p.194, n. 1). His carefully chosen words suggest evasiveness rather than error.

[5] John of Salisbury, *Historia Pontificalis*, ed. R. L. Poole (Oxford, 1927), p. 87, and Appendix vi.

[6] Ralph de Diceto, *Ymagines Historiarum*, ed. W. Stubbs, *Radulfi de Diceto . . . Opera Historica* (R.S., 1876), ii, p. 16.

address as *Dei gratia Romanorum regina*.[1] The seal which she brought with her to England bore the same legend.[2]

Much more could be said of the respect which the empire enjoyed in Anglo-Norman historiography, and of the cultural legacy of Mathilda's first marriage. Her treasures included at least two German crowns, a very important relic from the imperial chapel, great mantles of state and books.[3] But when men as hard-headed as Henry I and Henry V concluded alliances, one must ask whether there was not something more at stake than snobbery on one side and admiration for recent success on the other.

The Norman bridal party was not the only embassy to arrive at Liège in March 1110. An imposing German mission to the *curia* returned from Rome at the same time to report, and this was perhaps not just a coincidence.[4] Henry V had come to the throne as the faithful son of the Church, seizing the lead in the last rebellion against his father, in 1105. Probably this seemed to him the only way of saving the kingship for his dynasty, for as long as Henry IV remained unreconciled with the papacy, he was vulnerable and his authority precarious. Absolved from excommunication after leaving his father's camp, the young Henry at once became the hope of many German bishops who desperately wanted peace and the end of schism with its petty local wars which wasted their sees. But he also received the blessing of Pope Pascal II through his legate and in writing. These supports which the young king used with almost repulsive skill to build up his following and force his father to surrender were, however, mutually contradictory. At Rome, it was expected that a more obedient and receptive prince at the head of the *Reich* would at last yield to the demands of the Church. These demands, especially the abolition of lay investiture, as they reverberated from one synod to the next, year in year out, came dangerously near to being mistaken for the ends which they had originally been

---

[1] *Oorkondenboek van het sticht Utrecht tot 1301*, ed. S. Muller and A. C. Bouman, i (Utrecht, 1920), p. 277, no. 302, and p. 291, no. 318.

[2] W. de Gray Birch, 'A Fasciculus of the Charters of Mathildis, Empress of the Romans', *Journal of the British Archaeological Association*, xxxi (1875), pp. 381 f.; P. E. Schramm, *Die Deutschen Kaiser und Könige in Bildern ihrer Zeit*, i, p. 216, and ii, Abb. 118.

[3] See the *Libellus* at the end of the *Draco Normannicus*, ed. Howlett, *Chronicles of the Reigns of Stephen* ... (R.S.), ii, p. 758. The relic was the arm of St James.   [4] G. Meyer von Knonau, *Jahrbücher*, vi, p. 115.

designed to achieve: the *libertas ecclesiae* and reform.[1] It was a far cry from the heroic days of Gregory VII. The German episcopate on the other hand, who looked for security of tenure and a measure of royal protection and peace, accepted the customary method of their promotion even before the new king was firmly established on his throne. Astute and trained in a formidable school, Henry V emerged from the *coup d'état* of 1105-1106 without having granted away any of his rights over bishoprics and abbeys. He had won his reconciliation on fair words, but this also meant that the conflict continued. Faced with stronger and more united opposition in Germany, Pascal II was drawn towards the hospitable Capetians and the reliable hierarchy of France, where papal firmness was backed by the public opinion of the church. In 1107, the negotiations for a settlement between *regnum* and *sacerdotium* took place on French soil and the quarrel at once grew sharper. Henry V's embassy consisting of ecclesiastical and lay princes and of his chancellor Adalbert of Saarbrücken met Pascal II, surrounded by French prelates, at Châlons-sur-Marne in May. Suger's description of the encounter suggests that dislike of the Germans worsened the atmosphere of the public exchanges.[2] Later in the same month, a council held at Troyes again forbade clerks to accept investiture from the laity and bishops to ordain such men.[3]

Henry V had seen to it that his embassy should appear to speak for the *Reich* and not only for himself.[4] It seems also that he tried to win the support of Philip of France before the negotiations with the *curia* began, for, on 2 February 1107, he received envoys from the French king at Quedlinburg to arrange a meeting.[5] But this came to nothing precisely because the Capetians saw their best advantage in allowing Pascal to have the facilities of their kingdom for his stand against the imperial church.[6] The year 1108 passed with the Salian king and his princes waging war in Hungary. When therefore he sent his first and of necessity very discreet embassy to Henry I in Normandy, perhaps soon after the

---

[1] At least one contemporary, Hugh the Chanter, felt this strongly; *cf.* *Historians of the Church of York*, ed. J. Raine (R.S., 1879–94), ii, p. 111.
[2] Suger, *Gesta Ludovici . . . Grossi*, ed. Molinier, pp. 26 ff.
[3] *M.G.H., Const.*, i, p. 566, no. 396.
[4] J. Haller, *Das Papsttum*, 2nd ed. (Stuttgart, 1951), ii, p. 488.
[5] *Annales Patherbrunnenses*, p. 116.   [6] Suger, *op. cit.*, p. 26.

beginning of the new year, the settlement between *regnum* and *sacerdotium* and the Roman expedition for the imperial coronation, for the two had now become joint causes, were still by far the most urgent and serious of Henry V's concerns. They cannot have been left out of his calculations and when he looked for a wife, he also wanted to find an ally for the inevitable trial of strength in Rome.

At this point, it is necessary to turn to the English investiture conflict and the well-known agreement which is by many authorities thought to have ended it, in the first days of August 1107.[1] For its terms, we depend on Eadmer's account of the great assembly at Westminster, which for three days debated the question until in the end Henry I publicly renounced investiture with ring and staff, both for himself and his lay vassals, while Anselm granted that no-one elected to a prelacy should be disappointed of his consecration because he had done homage to the king.[2] Pascal II's letter to the archbishop, dated 23 March 1106, gave authority for this concession.[3] It neither spoke of canonical election nor yet of *electio in praesentia regis*, which is sometimes thought to have been part of the agreement. Eadmer's carefully weighed statement is equally reticent. From this evidence it is difficult to conclude that Pascal II expressly and openly gave Henry I the right to have elections held at his court and in his presence. He preferred to tolerate these evils in silence. What William of Malmesbury and Hugh the Chanter said about the settlement at a later date is not so much a description of its terms as a comment on its results, which seemed to favour the king in everything but a matter of form.[4] Yet despite this, there is

---

[1] *E.g.* A. Scharnagl, *Der Begriff der Investitur in den Quellen und der Literatur des Investiturstreites* (*Kirchenrechtliche Abhandlungen*, lvi, Stuttgart, 1908), p. 66; W. J. Corbett in *Cambridge Med. Hist.*, v, p. 532; Haller, *op. cit.*, ii, p. 482; Raymonde Foreville, *L'Église et la Royauté en Angleterre sous Henri II Plantagenet* (Paris, 1943), p. 8; N. F. Cantor, *Church, Kingship and Lay Investiture in England, 1089–1135* (Princeton, 1958), p. 202.

[2] Eadmer, *Historia Novorum*, ed. M. Rule (R.S., 1884), p. 186.

[3] Jaffé and Loewenfeld, *Regesta Pontificum Romanorum*, no. 6073; Eadmer, *op. cit.*, p. 178 f.

[4] William of Malmesbury, *Gesta Regum*, ed. W. Stubbs (R.S., 1887–89), ii, p. 493; 'retento tantum electionis et regalium privilegio'; Hugh the Chanter, *Historians of the Church of York*, ii, p. 110: 'nihil aut parum amisit, parum quidem regiae dignitatis, nihil prorsus potestatis quem vellet intronizandi'.

good evidence to show that in 1107 and for sometime afterwards Henry I resented the loss of his paternal customs.[1] In the first place, even the concession that bishops elect could do homage to the king for their temporalities was not secure. Pascal II's hope that it should not be so for ever appears in a well-known passage of his letter to Anselm.[2] The king's anger became outspoken in 1108 and the archbishop of Canterbury had to write in some alarm to the Pope that Henry threatened to invest prelates with ring and staff again, under the impression that the German ruler was allowed to do so with impunity.[3] Pascal in his reply announced that the ferocity of the Germans would be tamed and that the sword of St Peter was already drawn against the Salian prince if he persisted in his father's ways.[4] This letter is dated 12 October, just after a synod held at Benevento had in fact decreed that both those who invested and those who accepted investiture should be excommunicate.[5] But Henry I must have remembered an early and notorious incident in his quarrel with Pascal II and Anselm, the allegations of his envoys Archbishop Gerard of York, Bishops Robert of Chester and Herbert of Norwich in 1102. Returning from Rome, they said that the Pope had, despite the uncompromising tone of his letters, told them in private that he would let Henry invest and not exclude him from the sacraments for it, so long as he lived the life of a good prince and chose prelates well.[6] There is another hint of Archbishop Anselm's anxieties and of the king's threats during the early summer of 1108. It comes from Hugh the Chanter's *History of the Four Archbishops of York*. Thomas, the king's chaplain, had, on or just before 24 May, been raised to the archdiocese. For a time at least, his chances of avoiding the profession to Canterbury seemed good, though Hugh was not sure whether the king only favoured the cause of York 'because

---

[1] His extreme reluctance to part with them is well attested; see, for instance, William of Malmesbury, *op. cit.*, p. 489: 'vix tandem ad consentiendum . . . inflexus'.

[2] Eadmer, *op. cit.*, p. 179: 'donec per omnipotentis Dei gratiam ad hoc omittendum cor regium tuae praedicationis imbribus molliatur'.

[3] *S. Anselmi . . . Opera Omnia*, ed. Schmitt, v, p. 399, no. 451.

[4] *Ibid.*, p. 400, no. 452; Jaffé and Loewenfeld, *Regesta Pontificum Romanorum*, no. 6206.   [5] Meyer von Knonau, *Jahrbücher*, vi, p. 90.

[6] Eadmer, *op. cit.*, pp. 137–38; Jaffé and Loewenfeld, *Regesta Pontificum Romanorum*, no. 5928.

he did not love Anselm well', who had forbidden him his investitures.[1]

Henry I was thus not merely a disinterested spectator in the enterprise which his son-in-law was about to set on foot after they had concluded their marriage treaty. He must have known about the *expeditio Romana*, planned for August 1110, which had for its aims the recovery of the Italian kingdom, the imperial coronation and a settlement with Rome which would leave the emperor in possession of his investitures while paying lip service to the demands of the Church. Early in the year, Henry V held a diet at Regensburg, where the expedition was sworn by the south-German princes.[2] At the Easter court in Utrecht, on 17 April, those of the west without exception joined in this oath which bound them to take part with their contingents or at least furnish aid.[3] Mathilda had in the meantime arrived and it is not difficult to see how useful her portion of 10,000 marks was at this moment to Henry V. As they travelled down the Rhine for her coronation at Mainz, the princes and their knights were arming, the age-old and somewhat rusty military machinery of the Roman expedition came to life, oiled by the king's lavish expenditure. According to Ekkehard of Aura, the principal chronicler for the reign, he spent untold sums on the wages of his forces.[4]

The financial resources of a German ruler in the high Middle Ages defy assessment. There is no *Inquisitio Geldi*, no *Dialogus*, no Pipe Roll, to study either the methods used to collect money-revenues or the annual yields from ordinary sources such as tolls, mints, mines and *census*.[5] More certain is our knowledge of the tributes which subject and vassal powers like Poland and Bohemia had to pay when the king's expeditions to these regions compelled their rulers to recognize his overlordship.[6] It is the

---

[1] *Historians of the Church of York*, ii, p. 114: 'an propter hoc quod non bene Anselmum archiepiscopum amabat quia investituras prohibuerat, tunc quidem incertum'.

[2] Ekkehard, *Chronicon*, ed. Waitz, *M.G.H.*, *Scriptores*, vi, p. 243.

[3] *Annales Patherbrunnenses*, p. 122.

[4] 'Regia munificus liberalitate datis ubique inestimabilis pecuniae stipendiis' (Ekkehard, *op. cit.*, *loc. cit.*).

[5] For the history of the *servitia* in kind which bishoprics and royal abbeys owed to the crown, see B. Heusinger, '*Servitium Regis* in der deutschen Kaiserzeit', *Archiv für Urkundenforschung*, viii (1923).

[6] G. Waitz, *Deutsche Verfassungsgeschichte* (Kiel, 1878), viii, pp. 372 ff.

extraordinary exactions, fines, bribes, money paid for having the king's grace or his mercy, ransoms, sums tendered for enfeoffments or bishoprics that chroniclers found worth noting, and from these one can make at least some deductions about the liquid resources available to the *Reich* at a given time. It still remains impossible even to guess how these fitful incidents compared with the ordinary sources of cash. Probably they were always a high proportion of the total and there are grounds for thinking that their importance rose during the first quarter of the twelfth century. It is characteristic of Henry V's aims and methods that the chroniclers from all parts of the empire offer so much and mostly indignant information about his brutal exactions.[1] For his reign was a harsh struggle waged by unscrupulous means to recover possessions that had had to be abandoned during the disastrous civil wars of his father's time or to find compensation and alternatives for what was irretrievably lost. This explains the rumours of new and unheard-of taxes in Lotharingia and Saxony during the years 1114 and 1115 and, above all, Henry V's threat to create a fiscal system on the English model by the advice of his father-in-law.[2] That he had such a plan towards the end of his reign is known from a passage in Otto of Freising's chronicle.[3] Unfortunately, no trace of what the emperor had in mind or how he hoped to assess a general tax has come to light.

As far as can be known, the 10,000 marks from England made up the largest single sum Henry received up to the time of the Roman expedition. In 1106, he forced the men of Cologne to redeem themselves with 5,000 marks for having fought in the cause of his father up to the day of his death.[4] In 1107, it is true, he extorted a promise of 10,000 marks of silver from one of the contenders for the Bohemian duchy, but only 7,000 marks were

---

[1] Ekkehard (*Chronicon*, p. 265) mentions the huge treasure which Henry V was thought to have amassed by the end of his reign; for examples of extortion, see *infra*.

[2] *Annales Rodenses*, M.G.H., *Scriptores*, xvi, p. 698; *Annales Pegavienses*, *ibid.*, p. 251.

[3] Otto of Freising, *Chronica . . . de Duabus Civitatibus*, ed. A. Hofmeister, S[criptores] R[erum] G[ermanicarum] *in usum scholarum*, Hannover–Leipzig, 1912, p. 332 f.

[4] *Chronica Regia Coloniensis*, ed. G. Waitz, S.R.G. *in usum scholarum*, Hannover, 1880, p. 45: 'Colonienses deditionem faciunt, insuper regi pro optinenda gratia sua 5000 marcarum solvunt.'

actually paid.[1] As he fought hard and not very successful campaigns in Flanders, Hungary and Poland during the next few years, a good deal of these reserves must have been spent by 1110. The Roman expedition was by far the most burdensome of the princes' obligations towards the *Reich*. Already in the eleventh century, money was needed to equip the nobles and *ministeriales* and to support them at least until they had crossed the Alps.[2] Once in Italy, the tax known as the *fodrum* and the profits of war maintained the German forces. In the twelfth century, the necessity of finding large sums of money for their contingents often placed a severe strain on the princes. Examples of bishops mortgaging estates for this purpose are not at all rare under Frederick Barbarossa.[3] No such difficulties can be traced in the raising of the Roman expedition of 1110, and this is perhaps most easily explained by Henry V's lavish distribution of pay. Yet he would hardly have been able to spend so much without Mathilda's marriage portion. The army which descended on Italy in mid-August was exceptionally large. That at least can be deduced from the figure of 30,000 knights which Suger, Ordericus Vitalis, Otto of Freising and a Rhine-Frankish source gave for its size.[4] It is not far-fetched to connect its overwhelming strength with the treasure from England. Henry I had a direct stake in the success or failure of his son-in-law's expedition.

The events at and near Rome between 12 February and 13

[1] Cosmas of Prague, *Chronica Boemorum*, ed. B. Bretholz, *M.G.H.*, *S.R.G.*, *nova series*, ii (Berlin, 1955), pp. 187–88.

[2] See the *Dienstrecht* of the Bamberg *ministeriales* of c. 1060 in the *Codex Udalrici*, ed. P. Jaffé, no. 25, p. 52: 'Si expeditio est in Italiam, dominus per singulas loricas unum equum det et tres libras'; see also a Weissenburg *Dienstrecht*, *ibid.*, no. 14.—Henry IV's Italian expedition of 1081 depended largely on paid service (G. Meyer von Knonau, *Jahrbücher*, iii, pp. 352 ff.).

[3] *E.g.* Arnold of Selehofen, archbishop of Mainz, before the Lombard expedition of 1158; *cf.* H. Simonsfeld, *Jahrb. d. Deutschen Reiches unter Friedr. I*, i (Leipzig, 1908), pp. 639–41. In 1166, the bishop of Hildesheim had to pawn an estate to help him raise 400 marks so that he should be quit of service in Italy (*Urkundenbuch des Hochstifts Hildesheim*, ed. K. Janicke (*Publ. aus Preuss. Staatsarchiven*, lxv, Leipzig, 1896), i, p. 322, no. 337). Philip of Heinsberg, archbishop of Cologne, mortgaged his mint in 1174 'ad Italice expeditionis preparationem', and two great manors in 1176 (*Urkundenbuch f. die Gesch. des Niederrheins*, ed. T. J. Lacomblet, Düsseldorf, 1840–58, i, p. 318, no. 452; p. 319, no. 455; p. 328, no. 468).

[4] Meyer von Knonau, *Jahrbücher*, vi, p. 129, n. 40. f.

April 1111 cannot be described here. In capturing Pascal II and a number of cardinals and forcing them to yield an investiture privilege to him, Henry V failed to see where the strength of his opponents really lay. Sixty years of propaganda and agitation had done their work and the churches in southern France, Burgundy, Italy and also in Lotharingia did not accept so damaging a *volte-face* from a pope acting under duress. The Salian king probably knew that his battle was only half won after the treaty of Ponte Mammolo, when Pascal II promised to forgive the injury, grant the investiture privilege and crown him. For Henry had brought with him to Rome a gifted writer with the express purpose of presenting his acts to the world in the most favourable light.[1] David the Irishman had been *scholasticus* at Würzburg cathedral before he was taken into the royal chapel to become the official historian of the expedition and perhaps also draft the emperor's *relatio*, a brief narrative stringing together the documents of the treaty.[2] David's history was known to Ekkehard of Aura, who for a time at least was another of Henry's commissioned historiographers.[3] But besides Ekkehard, only the two Anglo-Norman historians, William of Malmesbury and Ordericus Vitalis, can be shown for certain to have used David's book, which is unfortunately lost.[4] William of Malmesbury has given the most substantial extracts from it together with the documents of the treaty, and he is also our authority for David's later career: in 1120, he became Bishop of Bangor. From Eadmer's account of his election by 'prince, clergy and people of Wales' it would be quite impossible to connect the former imperial chaplain with the Welsh diocesan.[5] Eadmer, though mentioning Henry I's consent to this election, made David appear as a backwoodsman whom Archbishop Ralph instructed for a few days before consecrating him at Westminster and taking his profession of obedience, which has survived in a Canterbury manuscript.[6] Eadmer's indifference to the true background of

[1] For information on David, see F. Hausmann, *Reichskanzlei und Hofkapelle unter Heinrich V und Konrad III*, pp. 83 and 310.

[2] *M.G.H., Const.*, i, p. 151, no. 101.

[3] Ekkehard, *Chronicon*, p. 243, *sub anno* 1110.

[4] William of Malmesbury, *Gesta Regum*, ii, p. 498; Ordericus Vitalis, *Hist. Eccl.*, iv, p. 7: 'Irensis quidam scolasticus'.

[5] Eadmer, *Historia Novorum*, p. 259 f.

[6] Brit. Mus., Cotton MS., Cleopatra E.I., fo. 31r.

the man who made it is not difficult to explain. He wanted to record a telling example of the Welsh bishopric's subjection to Canterbury, recognized in due form. David's promotion was probably not very different from that of most other bishops at that time; the king's will counted for most. He can be shown to have been at court in 1121, to have taken part in episcopal consecrations and in the council held at Westminster in 1127.[1] William of Malmesbury, although he did not approve of David's clever apologia for Henry V's deeds, none the less held him in respect.

Thanks to a discovery and an admirable piece of detective work by Walther Holtzmann there is even better evidence to prove that the results of the emperor's work in Rome were eagerly awaited at Henry I's court.[2] Burkhard, the envoy whom we met conducting Mathilda to Germany in 1110, sent a letter to his Anglo-Norman travelling companion Roger FitzRichard de Clare and a certain Gilbert, one of Henry I's chaplains, shortly after the imperial coronation on 13 April 1111. It was written hurriedly and at night, but he added to it the *acta* of the Treaty of Ponte Mammolo and Pascal II's investiture privilege. The missive ended with the latest news from Rome and southern Italy and the Latin chronicler of Worcester used this source for his account of the peace between *regnum* and *sacerdotium* and of the coronation. The emperor sent the text of his investiture privilege and accounts of his proceedings to all the great churches of the *Reich* but it is clear that England was hardly less well plied with the news and the propaganda than the empire itself.

It could be argued, however, that Henry I after all did not, as far as is known, resume his investitures, and that the case for his being an accessory before the fact is, therefore, at least, not proven. But the protests against the emperor's violence at Rome and the extorted *pravilegium*, as it came to be called, began to be heard even before the Germans had reached home. It soon gained

---

[1] *Regesta Regum Anglo-Normannorum*, ii, nos. 1243 and 1245; *The Chronicle of John of Worcester*, ed. J. R. H. Weaver (*Anecdota Oxoniensia*, 1908), pp. 16, 19, 23.

[2] W. Holtzmann, 'England, Unteritalien und der Vertrag von Ponte Mammolo', *Neues Archiv*, l (1935), pp. 282–301; id., *Beiträge zur Reichs- und Papstgeschichte des Hohen Mittelalters* (*Bonner Histor. Forschungen*, viii, 1957), p. 107.

momentum and took the form of a revolt from below which forced Pascal II to disavow his grant and allow his synods and legates a free hand in attacking Henry V, with whom, however, he himself never quite broke off relations. It would have been dangerous to swim against this torrent anywhere but in Germany, and even there opposition soon rose. But the events of 1111, the recriminations which followed and the confusion they spread in the ranks of the Church's protagonists can only have helped Henry I. For a time at least, they made it easier for him to enjoy his 'customs' in the control of the Anglo-Norman Church. It has already been said that the king's rights over episcopal and abbatial elections, in the case of royal monasteries, were not really secure, but rested on silences at Rome which might at any time be broken. Once the situation created by the *pravilegium* was overcome, Henry I's customs could be challenged and they were. Sooner or later, a new archbishop had to ask for his pallium at Rome and this opened the ecclesiastical regime in England and Normandy to examination and criticism at the *curia*. The letters Pascal II sent to Henry I and the English bishops by his legate Anselm of St Saba, in 1115, after Ralph d'Escures' translation from Rochester to Canterbury, are good examples of this.[1]

From what has been said it might seem as if, of the two rulers, the emperor in his dealings with the papacy gained on the whole more from the alliance than did Henry I. Yet it can be shown that Henry V made common cause with his father-in-law when the latter encountered difficulties at Rome and helped him to defend his interests. The evidence comes from some perhaps neglected passages in Hugh the Chanter's *History of the Four Archbishops of York* and from the *Historia Regum* of Simeon of Durham. On 2 February 1123, Henry I assembled the ecclesiastical magnates of his kingdom and also his earls and barons at Gloucester to fill the vacant see of Canterbury.[2] The Christ Church community, represented by their prior and some of the

---

[1] Jaffé and Loewenfeld, *Regesta Pontificum Romanorum*, nos. 6450 and 6453; the texts are in Eadmer, *Historia Novorum*, pp. 228 and 232.

[2] *Anglo-Saxon Chronicle E*, ed. Plummer, *Two of the Saxon Chronicles Parallel*, i, p. 251; Hugh the Chanter, *op. cit.*, *Historians of the Church of York*, ii, pp. 198 ff.; Simeon of Durham, *Historia Regum*, ed. T. Arnold, *Symeonis monachi opera omnia* (R.S., 1882–85), ii, pp. 268 ff.; *The Chronicle of John of Worcester*, p. 17.

more highly placed members of the chapter, seem to have put forward one or two names of their own order whom they wished to offer to the king and his court for election. But this time, the bishops were determined to have a clerk rather than a monk as their primate, and the king decided in their favour. After two days of dispute, the Canterbury interest had to yield, but to soften this blow against a self-conscious tradition of monastic arch-bishops, the choice fell upon a regular clerk, the prior of St Osyth's, William of Corbeil.[1] Reluctantly accepted by the monks, he was consecrated by his suffragans on 16 February, Thurstan of York having been excluded from this office.[2] The quarrel over his profession to Canterbury remained very much alive.

These details are essential if one is to understand what occurred when William presented himself at Rome to sue for his pallium in May, accompanied by Bishop Bernard of St David's, Anselm, the former papal legate now abbot of Bury, and Seffrid abbot of Glastonbury, to name only the most notable of his following.[3] Bernard of St David's, an experienced man of affairs, acting as William's prolocutor, saluted Pope Calixtus II and handed over a number of letters on behalf of the new archbishop. But when his election came to be considered by the cardinals and the curia, it met with serious opposition on four grounds: In the first place, William had been chosen at court, a place for judgments of blood rather than for the creation of bishops. The Durham writer indulged in an atrocious pun here: 'in curia quae a cruore dicitur'.[4] Secondly, William had not only been elected at the wrong place, but also by the wrong people, that is the bishops and not the

---

[1] That this was one of the reasons for William's election is clear from William of Malmesbury, *Gesta Pontificum Anglorum*, ed. N. E. S. A. Hamilton (R.S., 1870), p. 146, n. 4.

[2] John of Worcester, *op. cit., loc. cit.*; Hugh the Chanter, *op. cit.*, pp. 199 ff.

[3] *Anglo-Saxon Chronicle E*, p. 252; Hugh the Chanter, *op. cit.*, p. 201; John of Worcester, *op. cit., loc. cit.* William and his companions must have reached Rome early in May. The papal privilege confirming his election and announcing the grant of the pallium is dated 21 May (Jaffé and Loewenfeld, *Regesta Pontificum Romanorum*, no. 7136). We know that he was shaken over the pit and kept waiting for at least a fortnight (Hugh the Chanter, *op. cit.*, p. 202). A papal privilege for Seffrid (Jaffé and Loewenfeld, *op. cit.*, no. 7071) is dated 15 May, another for Bernard of St David's (*Ibid.*, no 7073), 25 May.

[4] Simeon of Durham, *Historia Regum*, p. 272.

monks of Canterbury. Thirdly, the archbishop of York who should have consecrated him by age-old prescription had not been allowed to do so. Lastly, William was not a monk.[1] According to Hugh the Chanter, the case took several days to settle, but in the end it was decided that William should not have the pallium, but for kindness's sake, as no-one alleged anything against his person, he might receive a bishopric instead. Calixtus II, on the other hand, seems to have been willing from the start to take a more lenient view and to accept the Gloucester election.[2]

Here it can be seen how precarious Henry I's customs really were and how little the king could rely on acquiescence with his practice when this clashed with the principles, the policies and the pronouncements of so many synods and popes. The irony of the situation was that Henry had taken every precaution to make sure that William's promotion should have a smooth passage. Archbishop Thurstan of York had been detained in England when he wanted to go to Rome to attend the Lateran Council summoned for 18 March. He was to travel with William and had to promise not to intrigue against him at the *curia*. We owe the details of these transactions to Hugh the Chanter's vivid narrative and at least once the author can be detected including himself in the archbishop of York's party, so that he must be regarded as an eye-witness.[3]

What has hardly been noticed and certainly attracted no special comment from historians is that amongst the greetings and letters presented by Bernard of St David's on behalf of William, there were also those of the emperor and they, as befitted his rank, came first.[4] According to the Durham writer, in fact, Henry V had his own envoys there to intercede for the archbishop of Canterbury.[5] Whether these were the men whom the emperor had sent to the Lateran Council or a new mission it is hard to

---

[1] *Ibid.*; Hugh the Chanter, *op. cit.*, p. 202.

[2] Hugh the Chanter, *op. cit.*, *loc. cit.*: 'papa quidem volente'.

[3] *Ibid.*, p. 206, l. 1: 'nobiscum'.

[4] *Ibid.*, p. 201: 'praemissa salutatione domino papae ab imperatore, a rege, ab episcopis Angliae, a capitulo Cantuariae, missas a singulis litteras seorsum obtulit'. It is mentioned in M. Dueball, *Der Suprematstreit zwischen den Erzdiözesen Canterbury und York, 1070-1126* (*Historische Studien*, clxxxiv, 1929), p. 95. The emperor's intervention was noted by T. F. Tout in his article 'Corbeil, William of', *Dictionary of National Biography*.

[5] Simeon of Durham, *Historia Regum*, p. 272.

say. Simeon, who is allowed to be the author of this part of the *Historia Regum*, dealt with the story less fully than Hugh, but his account differs in several important respects from the York writer's and seems to rest on an independent and therefore valuable source. Whichever way the emperor's letter reached Rome, one would give much to possess its text, and fortunately the *History of the Four Archbishops* does not altogether disappoint here. Calixtus II was evidently anxious to honour the formidable joint petition from Henry V and the Anglo-Norman king, and Hugh the Chanter has described how he set to work persuading his cardinals to change their minds 'for the love of the emperor who had but recently been reconciled to the Roman Church'.[1] Now this reconciliation was none other than the exchange of letters known as the Concordat of Worms of 23 September 1122. What Calixtus II said to the *curia* so that the archbishop of Canterbury's election should stand must therefore be connected with the contents of these famous documents, and if one compares Calixtus's privilege for Henry V with the details of William's election, it is easy to see how relevant the Concordat was to his case. The *Calixtinum* granted to Henry V that elections of bishops and abbots in Germany could be held in his presence.[2] William of Corbeil had been chosen at a great council assembled round the king. It provided further that, if disputes arose, the Salian emperor should give his assent and support to the '*sanior pars*' by the advice and judgment of the metropolitan and the bishops of the province.[3] This too Henry I could be argued to have done in William's case. It is true that the English bishops were themselves one of the contending parties, but when were bishops not? Thus under the terms of his own grant Calixtus II could not easily turn down this particular election and one can see why the Anglo-Norman king enlisted the aid of his son-in-law. The terms of the privileges exchanged between the emperor and the pope were no secret and if the English king was one of the first to hear of the Treaty of Ponte Mammolo in 1111, he cannot have been left in the dark about the agreements made at Worms in September 1122.

According to Simeon of Durham, the *curia's* decision against

---

[1] Hugh the Chanter, *op. cit.*, p. 202: 'pro amore imperatoris qui nuper ecclesiae Romanae reconciliatus erat'.

[2] *M.G.H., Const.*, i, p. 161, no. 108.　　　　　[3] *Ibid.*

the Canterbury election was reversed out of respect for the emperor and the king.[1] According to Hugh the Chanter, Archbishop Thurstan did as much as anyone to secure the pallium for William when he might well have stood in his way.[2] It is not necessary to discredit the statement of so disarming a writer as the York historian. Without him next to nothing would be known about the joint representations of Henry V and Henry I. He was certainly at all times anxious to show up Thurstan's good faith and here also William of Corbeil's ungrateful return to the attack in the matter of the profession, but it cannot be said that he succeeded in distorting this incident or even tried to.[3]

Henry I's alliance with the emperor and the Worms Concordat thus made some impression on the uneasy compromises by which the English Church was governed during this period. The Canterbury election of 1123 was really one of the earliest cases to which Pope Calixtus's concessions to Henry V were in a certain measure applied.[4] The two rulers whose relations with Rome differed so markedly from those of the Capetians made common cause. This was one of the chief interests of their alliance and a reason for it which, like Henry I's wish to enhance the dignity of his crown by Mathilda's marriage, has perhaps not been recognized enough.

[1] *Historia Regum, loc. cit.*: 'tandem gratia imperatoris praefati et Henrici regis Anglorum'.

[2] Hugh the Chanter, *op. cit.*, p. 203: 'si vero ei nocere voluisset, hac vice omnino non habuisset', *i.e.* the pallium.

[3] Hugh then described the last, uncompromising, attempt of the Canterbury interest to fight its claim against York at the *curia*; see R. W. Southern, 'The Canterbury Forgeries', *Eng. Hist. Rev.*, lxxiii (1958), pp. 223 ff.

[4] The investiture of an abbot of Fulda with his *regalia* in November 1122 was the earliest (Ekkehard, *Chronicon*, p. 260).

Note

Various problems raised in this, the oldest of the papers collected here, have more recently
been treated in the following publications:

D. L. Bethell, 'English black monks and epicopal elections in the 1120s', *EHR* lxxxiv
(1969), pp. 673-698, including an appendix of texts.

P. Classen, 'Das Wormser Konkordat in der deutschen Verfassungsgeschichte',
Investiturstreit und Reichsverfassung, ed. J. Fleckenstein, *Vorträge und Forschungen*,
Herausgegeben vom Konstanzer Arbeitskreis für mittelalterliche Geschichte, vol. xvii
(Sigmaringen, 1973), pp. 411-460.

M. Minninger, *Von Clermont zum Wormser Konkordat. Die Auseinandersetzungen um den
Lehnsnexus zwischen König und Episkopat*, Forschungen zur Kaiser—und
Papstgeschichte des Mittelalters, 2 (Köln, Wien, 1978).

C. Servatius, *Paschalis II. (1099-1118). Studien zu seiner Person und seiner Politik*
(Stuttgart, 1979).

R. Schieffer, *Die Entstehung des päpstlichen Investiturverbots für den deutschen König*,
Schriften der Monumenta Germaniae Historica, 28 (Stuttgart, 1981).

9

Frederick Barbarossa, Henry II
and the hand of St James

ON 28 September 1157, after a brief expedition against Boleslas of
Poland, the Emperor Frederick Barbarossa opened a well-attended
curia at Würzburg.[1] He could at this moment feel that his campaign
had been rather more successful than it later turned out to be but
there were hostages to ensure that the Piast duke would fulfil his
promises, appear at Magdeburg and pay tribute.[2] He found awaiting
him a splendid array of ambassadors from all quarters of Europe:
there were envoys from Manuel Comnenus, from Henry II of
England, from Denmark, Hungary, Burgundy and the cities of
Lombardy which Milan threatened to incorporate into her *districtus*.
Rahewin in Book III of the *Gesta Frederici* used the occasion to
impress on his readers the large ambit and the even larger horizons
of Hohenstaufen emperorship.[3] The *topos* of many embassies crowd-
ing and elbowing one another to bear gifts to and receive favours
from a supereminent ruler was a familiar one in early medieval
historical writing. We meet it in Einhard, the Frankish Annals,
Widukind of Corvey and the Quedlinburg Annals no less than in
Salian historiography; even the author of the *Vita Heinrici Quarti*
does not dispense with it.[4] It was employed also to sing the praises

1. The story to be told here has been the subject of a study by Professor H. E. Mayer,
'Staufische Weltherrschaft? Zum Brief Heinrichs II. von England an Friedrich Barbarossa von 1157', in *Festschrift Karl Pivec*, ed. A. Haidacher and H. E. Mayer, *Innsbrucker
Beiträge zur Kulturwissenschaft*, xii (Innsbruck, 1966), 265–78. He has very kindly acknow-
ledged my interest in it. Of English scholars Miss B. Smalley has outlined the incident
in *The Becket Conflict and the Schools* (Oxford, 1973), pp. 59–61 and p. 163. Dr B. Kemp
has questioned some of Mayer's conclusions in his 'The Miracles of the Hand of St.
James. Translated with an Introduction'. *The Berkshire Archaeological Journal*, lxv (1970),
1–19. It was when working on Anglo-Imperial relations in the early twelfth century
that I first came to connect Henry II's letter to Frederick in 1157 with the relic of St
James which Mathilda brought back from Germany in 1125. My debts of gratitude for
interest, advice and help generously given are numerous. I owe them to Sir Richard
Southern, Professors C. R. Cheney and R. H. C. Davis, Dr P. Chaplais, Mr J. Campbell,
Dr H. Mayr-Harting, Mr R. T. Reuter and Mr D. Corner. For the Würzburg *curia* of
Sept. 1157 see H. Simonsfeld, *Jahrbücher des Deutschen Reiches unter Friedrich I*, 1152–8
(Leipzig, 1908), pp. 557–64.   2. Simonsfeld, pp. 541–51.

3. *Ottonis episcopi Frisingensis et Rahewini Gesta Frederici*, iii. cc. 6–9, ed. F.-J. Schmale,
Ausgewählte Quellen [*zur deutschen Geschichte des Mittelalters, Freiherr vom Stein-Gedächtnisausgabe*], xvii (Darmstadt, 1965), 404–8.

4. For Einhard see *infra*, p. 234. *Annales regni Francorum*, *sub anno* 814, ed. F. Kurze,
S[*criptores*] *R*[*erum*] *G*[*ermanicarum in usum scholarum*], (Hanover, 1895), p. 140. *Die
Sachsengeschichte des Widukind von Korvei*, iii. cc. 56 and 75, ed. H.-E. Lohmann and P.
Hirsch, *SRG* (Hanover, 1935), pp. 135, 152. *Annales Quedlinburgenses*, 991, *M*[*onumenta*]
G[*ermaniae*] *H*[*istorica*], Scriptorum Tomus [=*SS*], iii. 68, one of many good examples.
Vita Heinrici IV. Imperatoris, c. 1, ed. W. Eberhard, *SRG* (Hanover, 1899), p. 12.

of the imperializing Anglo-Saxon and Anglo-Norman kings of the tenth and eleventh centuries.[1] For Rahewin it gave substance to the imperial rhetoric of his former master, Otto of Freising: the *patrocinium*, the protection of the whole world belongs to the emperor. He echoed these sentiments when he described how a brother of the Hungarian king fled to Barbarossa early in 1158 and sought his help because he knew that the Roman Empire was the refuge of all the world.[2] Later, W. Giesebrecht saw events in this way too. The embassies of the September court at Würzburg to him spoke for Barbarossa's new universal emperorship.[3]

The two passages, the one from Otto of Freising's *Chronica*, the other from Rahewin's part of the *Gesta Frederici*, both belonged to the Hohenstaufens' dealings with their south-eastern neighbours, the Magyar kings whose family feuds (like those of the Piasts) often presented the *Reich* with opportunities to impose satellite status upon them in varying degrees. But on this occasion, the September diet of 1157, Rahewin and the Hohenstaufen panegyrists had a much better card to play: the letter presented by Henry II's ambassadors. It is quoted in full and so preserved for us in the *Gesta Frederici*. Let us look at the text:

To his cordial friend Frederick, by the grace of God unconquerable emperor of the Romans, Henry King of England, Duke of Normandy and Aquitaine and Count of Anjou greetings and the harmony of true affection. We thank your excellency and best of rulers as much as we are able for that you have graced us with your envoys, greeted us in your letters, were the first to send gifts and, what we cherish even more, that you began to forge compacts of peace and love between us. We rejoiced and our spirits rose as your promise wherein you gave us hope in dealing with our kingdom's affairs filled us with alacrity and pleasure. We rejoiced, I say, and with all our heart we have risen to your highness to make this answer to you in all sincerity: whatsoever we know to pertain to your honour we are prepared to do to the best of our ability so that it shall be accomplished. We place our kingdom and everything subject to our rule anywhere at your disposal and entrust it to your power so that all things shall be arranged at your nod and that the will of your command (*imperium*) shall be done in everything. Let there be then between us and between our peoples an indivisible unity of peace and love and of safe commerce, yet in such a way that the authority to command shall go to

1. E.g. William of Malmesbury, *Gesta Regum*, ii. c. 135, ed. W. Stubbs, (R[olls] S[eries], 1887–9), i. 149 f. on Aethelstan and v. c. 409 (ii. 484) on Henry I. For Eadgar see Florence of Worcester's *Chronicon*, ed. B. Thorpe (Eng. Hist. Soc., 1848), i. 139 and more elaborately Goscelin of St Bertin's *Vita Sancte Edith virginis*, c. 10, ed. A. Wilmart, *Analecta Bollandiana*, lvi (1938), 62 f.

2. *Ottonis Frisingensis Chronica*, vii. c. 34, ed. A. Hofmeister, *SRG* (Hanover and Leipzig, 1912), p. 367: '. . . quatinus auctoritate imperiali, ad quam tocius orbis spectat patrocinium, ei subveniatur', (the Hungarian claimant Boris in 1146) and cf. Rahewin, *Gesta Frederici*, iii. c. 15, p. 424: 'quod Romanum imperium totius orbis esset asilum'.

3. W. von Giesebrecht, *Geschichte der deutschen Kaiserzeit*, 5th ed. (Leipzig, 1880), v. i. 119.

you who holds the higher rank and we shall not be found wanting in willingness to obey. And as the bestowal of your gifts keeps our remembrance of your highness fresh so we wish that you remember us as we send you the most beautiful things we had and such as would most likely please you. Pay heed therefore to the fondness of the giver and not to the things given and accept them in the spirit in which they are given. As to the hand of St. James about which you wrote to us, we have charged master Heribert and our clerk William to reply for us by word of mouth. Witnessed by Thomas the chancellor at Northampton.[1]

Historians have done Rahewin's propagandistic intentions proud and in the continuing debate about the place and ideal content of the medieval empire amidst the rising kingdoms of western and southern Europe, Henry II's letter has been much cited.[2] It became the crown-witness for the view that the *imperium* had, if not a direct lordship, at least some kind of indefinable ascendancy over all the *regna*, something that was expressed in the word *auctoritas*, and that their rulers recognized and accepted this. Here we find an 'auctoritas imperandi' and in response a 'voluntas obsequendi' and *obsequium* meant service. Many years ago Robert Holtzmann thought that he had found in the terms of Henry's missive the evidence to reconcile Hohenstaufen claims to world-wide rule with the realities of Angevin and Capetian power and independence.[3] The empire enjoyed an ideal superiority that was founded on classical political traditions, the *auctoritas* of the Roman *princeps*. More recently Robert Folz concluded similarly: the emperor possessed a universal patronage over the other rulers and his political primacy, if at times disputed, was real.[4] In his fine studies of papacy and empire F. Kempf, without directly referring to the letter, held that the emperor had a dignity above all others, a precedence which in turn Holtzmann had compared with the hierarchical gradation of states in the byzantine political system.[5] And had not Henry, in his letter, derived the emperor's *auctoritas* from his pre-eminent *dignitas*? Lastly, the Austrian scholar Heinrich Appelt, after a close examination of Frederick's early diplomata, thought that while not much could be gained by applying the classical Roman

1. *Gesta Frederici*, iii. c. 8, p. 406. The translation is mine.

2. For a thorough survey and discussion of the literature on Henry II's letter see F. Trautz, *Die Könige von England und das Reich 1272–1377, Mit einem Rückblick auf ihr Verhältnis zu den Staufern* (Heidelberg, 1961), pp. 64–8. That a universal imperial lordship was not recognized in the Anglo-Saxon and Capetian kingdoms of the late tenth and eleventh centuries nor claimed by the Ottonian and Salian emperors is shown by H. Loewe, 'Kaisertum und Abendland in Ottonischer und Frühsalischer Zeit', H[istorische] Z[eitschrift], cxcvi (1963), 529–62. For France especially see K. F. Werner, 'Das hochmittelalterliche Imperium im politischen Bewusstsein Frankreichs,' HZ, cc (1965), 1–60.

3. R. Holtzmann, 'Der Weltherrschaftsgedanke des mittelalterlichen Kaisertums und die Souveränität der europäischen Staaten', HZ, clix (1939), 251–64 and separately (Tübingen, 1953).

4. R. Folz, *The Concept of Empire in Western Europe from the Fifth to the Fourteenth Century*, translated by S. A. Ogilvie (London, 1969), p. 109 f.

5. F. Kempf, 'Das mittelalterliche Kaisertum', in *Das Königtum, Vorträge und Forschungen*, iii (Lindau and Konstanz, no date), p. 237 f. and nn. 42, 43. R. Holtzmann, *ubi supra*.

conception of *auctoritas*, another Roman political idea, that of *amicitia* which bound the peoples beyond the Roman frontiers to the Roman state and its rulers, could explain both real and ideal relationships between twelfth-century kings and emperors. We certainly hear much about *amicitia* in early medieval imperial diplomacy, both western and byzantine, but it was an ambiguous word which might or might not imply a shadowy form of dependence. It cannot therefore help us a great deal with the interpretation of the letter.[1]

Now for whatever reason Henry II wished to please or placate Frederick in the autumn of 1157, he was known to harbour very different thoughts about his and his kingdom's place in the world at other times. John of Salisbury reported in 1168 how Henry boasted that he had at last regained his grandfather's privileges who was king, apostolic legate, patriarch, emperor and all he wished in his land.[2] Here it is worth remembering that the author of the *Quadripartitus* had called Henry I *augustus* and *cesar* and when he recited the king's triumphs, he numbered the Empire among them, as if Henry had overcome the 'Teutonicorum majestas' by giving his daughter in marriage to the last Salian emperor.[3] Henry II too spoke of Barbarossa merely as 'imperator Alemannorum' in his famous angry scene with Herbert of Bosham at Angers in 1166 when Herbert sneered at the *intitulatio* 'Romanorum imperator augustus'.[4] It is therefore not impossible to dismiss Henry II's letter of 1157 as empty verbiage, as historians who felt sceptical about Hohenstaufen ambitions and especially their recognition outside the *Reich*, have done. They were anxious to show that Henry II was no miser with his flatteries but had them dealt out with a lavish pen.[5] Towards Louis VII of France he struck similar notes when it suited him and he wrote in 1164 that he was prepared to obey his will in everything (*obsequendum* again) and him also he called, quite correctly, his lord – a title he deftly avoided in his address to Frederick.[6] His letters to Louis in 1164, claiming the vassalage of the counts of Auvergne, made the most of the Capetian's obligations as overlord and they are

1. H. Appelt, 'Die Kaiseridee Friedrich Barbarossas', *Oesterreichische Akademie der Wissenschaften Philosophisch-Historische Klasse, Sitzungsberichte*, cclii, Abhandlung 4 (1967), 24 f. and *cf. infra.* p.234, n. 3 and p. 235.

2. *Joannis Saresberiensis . . . opera omnia*, ed. J. A. Giles (Oxford, 1848), ii. 114, no. 239 and W. Holtzmann, 'Das mittelalterliche Imperium und die werdenden Nationen', *Arbeitsgemeinschaft für Forschung des Landes Nordrhein Westfalen*, Heft 7 (1953), 18 f. and n. 20 who cited this passage against R. Holtzmann's view.

3. *Die Gesetze der Angelsachsen*, ed. F. Liebermann (Halle, 1903), i. 533 f. and K. Leyser, 'England and the Empire in the Early Twelfth Century', *Transactions of the Royal Historical Society*. 5th ser., x (1960), 66. *Supra*, p.196.

4. William Fitzstephen, *Vita Sancti Thomae*, c. 97, *Materials for the History of Thomas Becket*, ed. J. C. Robertson (R.S., 1877), iii. 99–101. Mayer, p. 267 f. and B. Smalley, p. 63.

5. H. J. Kirfel, *Weltherrschaftsidee und Bündnispolitik Untersuchungen zur auswärtigen Politick der Staufer (Bonner Historische Forschungen*, xii (1959)), 178 and Trautz, p. 67.

6. *Recueil des Historiens des Gaules et de la France*, xvi. 111, no. 342 and *cf.* no. 339, p. 110. Neither of these two letters though was ornate with rhetoric.

therefore not strictly comparable with the one sent to Barbarossa in
1157. In general, it is true, the language of twelfth-century diplomacy
was sonorously grandiloquent. When Henry the Lion wrote to the
king of France to thank him for a small favour he too offered him
his wholehearted service.[1]

There appears to be almost no tangible matter in the context of
Henry II's letter. Giesebrecht thought that he wanted to make sure
Frederick would not ally himself with Louis VII but these manoeuvr-
ings of a realistic *Aussenpolitik* barely begin to make sense in the
twelfth century.[2] Henry II when he sent off his envoys was planning
a campaign against the Welsh which ended at least as successfully as
did Frederick's against the Polish duke. The chroniclers at this
moment were impressed by the solidity of his not yet three-year-old
regime. One or two hints, however, can be wrested from the ornate
fretwork of the letter-writer's prose. In the first place the initiative
for this exchange of compliments and messages seems to have come
from Frederick Barbarossa and not the Angevin king. Apparently
it was he who sent letters and presents first. This has even a certain
formal significance since in early medieval diplomacy at least, the
first despatch of an embassy to another court was an honour paid to
that court.[3] It raised the prestige of the receiver more than the sender.
Frederick's ambassadors in England moreover can be traced in the
Pipe Rolls of Henry's fourth year. This would be the period from
19 December 1157 to 18 December 1158 but the two sheriffs of
London were behindhand with their account at the Exchequer and
it is under their expenses for Henry's third year that we find £12 6s. 8d.
spent on four gyrfalcons to be given to the 'emperor of Germany'.
The ambassadors themselves received a present of over £25.[4] The
four falcons are the only English evidence for the gifts 'the most
beautiful things in our possession' mentioned in Henry's letter. The
present which impressed the Germans most must occupy us later.
It was Barbarossa therefore who had requests to make and perhaps
something to offer in return but even this is not unequivocally clear.
For in June 1156 the emperor had celebrated his marriage to Beatrix
of Burgundy, also at Würzburg and the Würzburg Annals mentioned
that 'at this very time' the English king sent presents that befitted the
imperial *magnificentia*.[5] More impenetrable still is the allusion to a
promissio by which Barbarossa gave Henry some hope and help in the
governance of his own kingdom. No one has as yet advanced even a

1. *Recueil des Historiens des Gaules et de la France*, xvi, p. 42, no. 137.
2. Giesebrecht, v. i. 119.
3. The honour is alluded to and Frederick thanked for it in Henry II's letter. *Supra*,
p. 2.
4. *The Pipe Rolls of 2-3-4 Henry II* (London, 1930), p. 112: 'Et pro iiii Girfalc ad opus
imperatoris Alemannie. xii. l. et vi. s. et viii. d.' He is not called 'imperator Romanorum'
here either.
5. Annales Herbipolenses, 1156, *MGH. SS.* xvi. 9. It is conceivable that the Würzburg
annalist misdated the embassy from England by a year.

guess what this meant or whether it meant anything. Lastly there is a mention of mutual protection for the merchants trafficking between England and the *Reich* and here we are on firmer ground. For in July 1157 Henry issued two writs in favour of the merchants of Cologne granting them general protection and the right to sell their Rhine wines as advantageously as French ones were sold on the London market.[1]

Of English commentators on Henry II's letter it was A. L. Poole who made as much sense out of it as it will bear. He saw in it an attempt to renew the alliance which Henry V's betrothal to Mathilda had brought about in 1109.[2] It had served Henry II's grandfather, Henry I well not only in his dealings with the papacy but also in the defence of Normandy in 1124. When the Salian emperor advanced to invade France he diverted Louis VI so that he could not come to the rescue of the Norman rebels who had been crushed at Bourg Théroulde earlier in the year. But A. L. Poole also thought Henry II's letter quite needlessly effusive and humble and was a little cross with the great Angevin ruler for sending it. It smacked perhaps too much of a more recent sin of English foreign policy towards the *Reich*: appeasement.

Until recently the last phrase of our text with its reference to a hand of St James has received no attention whatsoever from historians who have weighed every word of its portentous ideological passages.[3] It has usually only been mentioned by the way and it is characteristic that Robert Folz in his *L'Idée d'Empire dans L'Occident* and the English translation published in 1969, has omitted the passage as irrelevant from the translation of the letter amongst the illustrative sources.[4] Yet any acquaintance with the practices of early medieval diplomacy and methods of communication should have suggested that it was much the most important statement in the whole document. Very often the letters given to ambassadors or confidential agents served only to accredit them or to create the right mood for the business they had come to transact by word of mouth.[5] They informed the addressee that he was to believe what the envoy told him as the true and authentic intent or wishes of the mandatory. It was often dangerous to entrust more than generalities to paper as

---

1. *Hansisches Urkundenbuch*, ed. K. Höhlbaum (Halle, 1876), i. 8, nos. 13 and 14. The writs are translated in P. Dollinger, *The German Hansa* (London, 1970), p. 380 f.
2. A. L. Poole, *From Domesday Book to Magna Carta* (Oxford, 1951), p. 326 f. R. W. and A. J. Carlyle, *A History of Medieval Political Theory in the West* (Edinburgh and London, 1915), iii. 173–9 saw in Henry II's letter vestigial remains of beliefs held in the early middle ages but *cf.* Loewe, *supra*, p. 217, n. 2. It received no mention in W. L. Warren, *Henry II* (London, 1973).
3. Trautz, (p. 65), clearly saw the importance of the last sentence for judging the letter as a whole.   4. As Mayer (p. 270) points out.
5. On these 'clauses of credence' in Henry II's correspondence see P. Chaplais, 'English Diplomatic Documents to the end of Edward III's reign', in *The Study of Medieval Records Essays in Honour of Kathleen Major*, ed. by D. A. B. Bullough and R. L. Storey (Oxford, 1971), pp. 22 ff. and esp. p. 24.

the adherents of Alexander III were to discover during the schism. Written instructions for envoys may have become more common in the twelfth century. In the west they were rare before that time. We hear of them once in the case of Liudprand of Cremona's famous mission to Constantinople in 968 for which the suspicious Otto I (who more than once repudiated engagements made on his behalf) had given him a sealed brief.[1] What then had Henry II asked Master Heribert and the *clericus* William to tell Barbarossa about the hand of St James?

The religious life of the early middle ages would be unthinkable without the cult of relics.[2] The *virtus* and merits of saints gave victory in war, averted disasters of all kinds, restored health, protected local interests and served as legal sanctions and the possession of their relics ensured the presence of the saints. It was the one element in christianity which could be shared between the aristocratic church of kings, nobles, bishops and monks on one side and the *vulgus*, the *pauperi* of peasant society on the other. If the rural population of ninth-century Saxony was slowly won over from its tenacious heathenism it was done largely by the translation of relics and by their wonder-working powers.[3] The *pignora sanctorum* were the most precious possessions of monastic houses and in bad times the monks fled with them and could hope to survive as a community if they were not deprived of their relics. The question what did the Otto-nians and their following gain by the acquisition of the Italian kingdom and their precarious hold on Rome, is often asked. It invites the answer: first and foremost relics. Amongst the treasures they carried away with them the evidence for the bones and bodies of saints bulks largest. The spoliation of Italian shrines and the assi-duous collection of relics was one of the marked pre-occupations of German bishops and, not least of all, royal chaplains.[4] For from an early time, at least the ninth century onwards, the presence of a powerful saint was thought to ensure the survival and well-being of not only individuals and local societies but of whole kingdoms. When Louis the Pious's regime began to show signs of strain and failure Einhard caused the relics of Saints Marcellinus and Petrus which had been secured for him rather adventurously at Rome, to be brought to Aachen in order to restore the *Reich* to political

1. Liuprand, *Legatio*, c. 26, Die Werke Liudprands von Cremona, ed. J. Becker, *SRG* (Hanover and Leipzig, 1915), p. 189. F. L. Ganshof, *Histoire des Relations Inter-nationales*, i, *Le Moyen Age* (Paris, 1953), p. 123 f. and D. E. Queller, *The Office of Ambas-sador in the Middle Ages* (Princeton, 1967), p. 122 f.

2. For an excellent introduction to this subject see H. Fichtenau, 'Zum Reliquien-wesen im früheren Mittelalter', *Mitteilungen des Instituts für Österreichische Geschichts-forschung*, lx (1952), 60–89.

3. K. Honselmann, 'Reliquientranslationen nach Sachsen', *Das erste Jahrtausend*, Textband, i, ed. V. H. Elbern (Düsseldorf, 1963), pp. 159–93.

4. Some of the evidence for this is noted by R. Köpke and E. Dümmler, *Kaiser Otto der Grosse* (*Jahrbücher der Deutschen Geschichte*, Leipzig, 1876), pp. 343, 378 f. and nn. 2, 3.

health.[1] The acquisition of *pignora sanctorum* was a competitive pursuit and the arrival of the Holy Lance with a nail from the cross in Liudolfing Saxony or the despatch of a St Maurice banner to Aethelstan were seen to alter the balance of power in western Europe and to mark the way to success for rising rulers and their warlike following.[2] There is no evidence that the veneration felt for relics and the urgency to possess them diminished in the twelfth century. If anything the demand proliferated and reached new dimensions.[3] One of the most popular forms of lay piety and penance, the pilgrimage, usually reached its goal and climax at a great shrine, notably that of St James of Compostella. Well might a Guibert of Nogent utter misgivings and warnings against exploitation and abuses in the cult of sacred objects when, for instance Otto of Freising, no less learned than the abbot of Nogent, brought home relics from his studies at Paris of which the very identity remained undisclosed. They were however solemnly received by his father, Margrave Leopold III of Austria and kept in his foundation, Klosterneuburg.[4] We tend to be more interested in the twelfth century's intellectual triumphs, its humanism and new forms of religious sensibility than this abiding belief in the protection of the saints secured by the possession of their relics. Reform does not seem to have changed much in this sphere. Byzantium, for many centuries the greatest treasure house of these miracle-working agents of faith, continued to furnish of her riches to the courts and travellers of western Europe and presents of relics remained amongst the most valued gifts the emperors used in their diplomatic relations with the West.[5] As before royal chapels contained especially rare and holy objects which it was essential to preserve or to give only to the most privileged churches and above all to royal sanctuaries. Here their veneration by the many could help to propagate loyalty and gratitude to the founders and rulers who had bestowed the presence and *virtus* of a great saint on the locality.

1. *Translatio et Miracula SS. Marcellini et Petri*, ii. cc. 3–8, iii. cc. 13, 14, iv. c. 10, *MGH, SS*. xv. i. 247, 252–3 and 259 and H. Fichtenau, *Das karolingische Imperium* (Zürich, 1949), p. 263 f.

2. K. Leyser, 'The Tenth Century in Byzantine-Western Relationships', in *Relations between East and West in the Middle Ages*, ed. D. Baker (Edinburgh, 1973), p. 42 and nn. 78, 79. *Cf. supra*, p. 116 and nn. 78, 79.

3. The discovery by divine revelation of a *cappa Salvatoris* at Argenteuil and the body of St Bartholomew the apostle after a flood at Rome, both in 1156, can be cited to illustrate this. See *The Chronicle of Robert of Torigni* in *Chronicles [of the Reigns of Stephen, Henry II, and Richard I]*, ed. R. Howlett (R.S., 1884–9), iv. 187, 189.

4. On these misgivings see C. Morris, 'A Critique of Popular Religion: Guibert of Nogent on *The Relics of the Saints*', in *Popular Belief and Practice*, ed. G. J. Cuming and D. Baker, *Studies in Church History*, viii (Cambridge, 1972), 55–60 and K. Schreiner, 'Discrimen veri ac falsi. Ansätze und Formen der Kritik in der Heiligen- und Reliquien-verehrung des Mittelalters', *Archiv für Kulturgeschichte*, xlviii (1966), 1–53 and esp. 31–33. For Otto of Freising's acquisitions in France see *Urkundenbuch zur Geschichte der Baben-berger in Österreich*, iv. i, *Ergänzende Quellen 976–1194*, ed. H. Dienst and H. Fichtenau (Vienna, 1968), p. 71, no. 653.

5. Leyser, 'The Tenth Century', p. 42 and n. 80. *Cf. supra*, p. 116 and n. 80.

We can now embark on the story of the hand of St James, the Apostle. When Archbishop Adalbert of Hamburg-Bremen died on 16 March 1072 his treasury was found to be nearly empty except for books, vestments and relics. His friend and erstwhile protégé, King Henry IV seized all these. It is one of the earliest examples of a royal *jus spolii* in Germany about which Frederick Barbarossa's and Henry VI's bishops were to complain so much. Adalbert, although in failing health, followed the itinerant court to the last. He died at Goslar and this may explain Henry's opportunity to take advantage of his old mentor's end. He carried off the charters of the arch-bishopric – it is interesting to note that the archbishop travelled about with them – and the hand of St James. Our source, Adam of Bremen, moreover tells us that his master had acquired it from a Venetian bishop, Vitalis, probably during the Roman expedition of 1046/37.[1] Vitalis presided over the see of Torcello and according to Andrea Dandolo his cathedral had in 640 received an arm of St James which, together with the bodies of other saints and treasures had been ferried to the safety of the island from Lombard-ridden Altino on the mainland. Archbishop Adalbert, it is clear, acquired only part of this relic. The arm remained in Torcello but the hand now came into the possession of the Salian king and was most probably kept in his itinerant court chapel, guarded and looked after by the small staff of *capellani* who served there.[2] Nothing more is heard of it until 1125 when the emperor Henry V died childless, leaving the *insignia* and his treasures in the hands of his wife Mathilda, Henry I's daughter, and her in the care of his nephew, Frederick, the second Hohenstaufen duke of Suabia and Barbarossa's father. Frederick and his brother Conrad were the heirs of the Salian patrimony, Mathilda as widow was entitled to dower and a share of the movables, the huge treasure left behind by the ruthless and unloved last Salian emperor.[3]

When Henry recalled his daughter shortly after her husband's death and the frustration of Duke Frederick's hopes for the succes-sion, Mathilda had to abandon her German lands. It is worth noting that some of these lay on the Lower Rhine in the diocese of Utrecht;

1. *Magistri Adam Bremensis Gesta Hammaburgensis Ecclesiae Pontificum*, iii. 67, 3rd. ed., B. Schmeidler, *SRG* (Hanover and Leipzig, 1917), p. 214. For the bishops of Torcello in the eleventh century see H. Kretschmayr, *Geschichte von Venedig* (Gotha, 1905), i. 406.

2. *Andreae Danduli Ducis Venetiarum Chronica*, ed. E. Pastorello, *Rerum Italicarum Scriptores*, XII. i (Bologna, 1938), pp. 95, 106. Adam of Bremen's seems to be the earliest reference to the St James relic in the cathedral of Torcello. The arm was still thought to be there in the seventeenth and the mid-eighteenth century. See Flaminio Corner's *Ecclesiae Torcellanae antiquis monumentis . . . illustratae* (Venice, 1749), i. 50–52 and the *Menologium Torcellanum* under VIII Kal. Augusti (25 July, the feast of St James) in Corner, iii, *in fine*. Legend connected the arrival of the relic with a visit of Bishop Heliodorus of Altino, (late fourth century) to Jerusalem. It does not seem as if a great deal was made of it at Torcello and Dandolo cited the *pignora* of several local saints, including the body of St Heliodorus, before the arm of St James in his account of their deposition.

3. *Ekkehardi Chronica*, ed. F.-J. Schmale and I. Schmale-Ott, *Ausgewählte Quellen*, xv (Darmstadt, 1972), 374.

that is, along the safest line of communication between Henry V's *Reich* and England.[1] The emperor had spent most of his last years trying to enlarge his foothold in these regions. Of the treasures he left behind certain *insignia*, a sceptre, an orb, the Holy Lance, the cross and the crown now in Vienna, were essential for the coronation and legitimate rule of a future king. They soon fell into the grasp of Archbishop Adalbert of Mainz, a bitter enemy of the Hohenstaufen who identified the cause of the church's *libertas* very much with the enlargement of the Mainz temporalities at the expense of the *Reich*. He had somehow persuaded Mathilda to part with them before forcing the election away from Duke Frederick. On what terms she relinquished them and whether it was with or without the consent of the Hohenstaufen claimant, we do not know. Otto of Freising later maintained that the archbishop of Mainz had given her false promises, perhaps to make her believe that Duke Frederick would carry the election.[2] The disposal of Henry V's treasure raised problems similar to those which beset the descent of his lands and the succession as a whole: the distinction between Salian house property and imperial demesne. Even if it was clear what objects must go to the emperor's successor there had to be a further division of treasure between Henry's wife and his kin, the Hohenstaufen brothers and their mother, Agnes.

Be that as it may, Mathilda returned from Germany with an astonishing quantity of precious things. There were at least two crowns. One, of solid gold with a frontal cross and large jewel, must have resembled the very *Reichskrone* which she had surrendered. It weighed so much that it had to be supported by two silver rods when worn. The other was smaller and lighter and had been used by the emperor for crown wearings on solemn feast days. We know all this from a *Libellus* listing Mathilda's gifts to the abbey of Bec and Roger of Howden too wrote of an imperial crown brought back by the 'empress' which Henry I kept in his treasury.[3] According to the *Libellus* Henry II was crowned with the heavy diadem in 1154 and it is possible that Richard I wore it at his coronation in 1189 when

1. She made two grants there: see *Oorkondenboek van het Sticht Utrecht tot 1301*, ed. S. Muller and A. C. Bouman (Utrecht, 1920), i. nos. 302, 318.

2. *Gesta Frederici*, i. c. 16, p. 156. It is noteworthy that Otto here called her *imperatrix* (and *cf.* p. 90). That Mathilda had been given the *imperii insignia* by her dying husband and that the archbishop of Mainz took charge of them before taking charge of the election was known also to Ordericus Vitalis. See *Historia Ecclesiastica*, xii. 43, ed. A. Le Prévost (Paris, 1838–55), iv. 467. On the issues raised by the election of 1125 see E. Wadle, *Reichsgut und Königsherrschaft unter Lothar III (1125–1137)*, *Schriften zur Verfassungsgeschichte*, xii (Berlin, 1969).

3. The *libellus* at the end of the *Draco Normannicus* completes the author's panegyric of Mathilda as the benefactress of Bec. See *Chronicles*, ii. 758 f. and *Chronica Magistri Rogeri de Houedene*, ed. W. Stubbs (R.S., 1868), i. 181. What Roger wrote about the *corona imperialis* contradicts the *libellus* which listed it as the foremost of Mathilda's gifts to Bec. Henry II may have borrowed and then not returned it after his coronation. See J. Deér. *Der Kaiserornat Friedrichs II.*, *Dissertationes Bernenses*, ii. 2 (Bern, 1952), 35–37.

two earls had to help sustain its weight on his head.[1] The Bec inventory of gifts is lengthy and it may not always specify whether an item had come from Henry V's chapel but there were at least two 'pallia imperialia'. Very likely the empress's haul included the autograph copy of a chronicle written for her husband. The manuscript with a picture of their wedding feast in 1114 is now in Corpus Christi College, Cambridge.[2] Mathilda had brought Henry V a jointure of at least 10,000 marks and many treasures besides and it seems reasonable to assume that she was allowed to depart with so much of his hoard to compensate her for the dower lands she would enjoy no more. She was entitled to a larger share and this is important for the understanding of later events.

She also carried off the hand of St James. We know this from three sources: a dubious writ of Henry I's, Roger of Howden writing much later and a far more valuable German annal which seems to have escaped the historians who have followed the history of the relic. The *Annals of Disibodenberg*, a monastery by the river Nahe (diocese of Mainz), were compiled about the year 1147 out of varied ingredients including local notices. Under the year 1125 they record: 'Queen Mathilda' – in the *Reich* she was rarely called anything else – 'travelled to her father in England taking the hand of St James with her and by this she did irreparable damage to the "regnum Francorum".'[3] Disibodenberg lay not very far away from the Trifels, the castle in the Palatinate where the dying Henry V had wished the *regalia* to be kept until the princes met. In this neighbourhood the departure of the relic could be known, resented and blamed for the restless and feud-ridden times that followed. That it was stored in the Trifels as if it belonged to the *regalia*, is again significant for what happened later.[4]

Mathilda joined her father in Normandy and spent the better part of a year with him there. They crossed the Channel in September

1. Roger of Howden, iii. 11: 'coronam. . . quam duo comites sustinebant propter ponderositatem ipsius.' H. G. Richardson, 'The Coronation in Medieval England', *Traditio*, xvi (1960), pp. 181 ff. questioned the authenticity of Roger's account of Richard's coronation in 1189 on the grounds that he merely adapted, and that clumsily, a directory from the early years of Stephen's reign but he did not discuss crowns and this passage. The mention of so many of the participants should warn us against hypercriticism. Roger was an eyewitness, wrote close to the event he described and knew how to combine the use of a document with his own experience. (I owe this information to Mr D. Corner.) P. E. Schramm in *Herrschaftszeichen und Staatssymbolik, Schriften der MGH*. 13/iii (Stuttgart, 1956), iii. 759–65 suggested that Mathilda herself had the two silver rods made so that she could wear her former husband's crown.

2. MS. C.C.C. 373 fo. 95ᵛ and Schramm, *Die deutschen Kaiser und Könige in Bildern ihrer Zeit*, i (751–1152) (Leipzig, 1928), pp. 3, 145 and *Tafeln*, Abb. 124. For the text of the *Kaiserchronik* written for Henry V see *Ausgewählte Quellen*, xv. 212–65.

3. *Annales Sancti Disibodi*, 1125, *MGH. SS*, xvii. 23: 'Mathildis regina in Angliam ad patrem proficiscitur, manum sancti Iacobi secum deferens; per quod irreparabile dampnum regno Francorum intulit.' The appellation 'regnum Francorum' for the German kingdom was becoming rarer in the twelfth century but some writers very deliberately clung to it.   4. Ekkehard, p. 374.

1126. At some time after this date the hand of St James was given
to Henry I's foundation, Reading Abbey, the house which he had
built and where he came to be buried.[1] The question is: when?
Reading had been peopled at first by monks from Cluny and Cluny's
English dependency, Lewes Priory and it was given the Cluniac
observance. Yet it was also Henry I's most ambitious monastic endowment by far and from the very beginning Reading enjoyed a
highly prized 'regia libertas'.[2] However close the abbey's links with
Cluny were throughout the twelfth century it did not join the
Cluniac family as a subject.[3] Its abbots often rose higher and made
brilliant ecclesiastical careers.[4] Important royal servants like Robert
de Sigillo, Henry I's *magister scriptorii*, retired there while out of office
and before being advanced to the see of London by Mathilda in 1141.
Peter the Venerable himself, always pleased with a prominent recruit,
wrote Robert a fulsome letter and wished he would come to Cluny.[5]
Some of the great men of Henry I's circle, like King David of Scot-
land, Robert II, earl of Leicester and Brien fitz Count duly made gifts
to their lord's foundation.[6] Reading was thus a fitting home for a

1. On the foundation and building of Reading Abbey see Dom David Knowles,
The Monastic Order in England, 2nd. ed. (Cambridge, 1963), p. 281 f., H. M. Colvin
(General Editor), *The History of the King's Works* (London, 1963), i. 49–50 and J. B.
Hurry, *Reading Abbey* (London, 1901).
2. The expression is Pope Eugenius III's in a letter to Archbishop Theobald of
Canterbury (*c.* 1150). See W. Holtzmann, *Papsturkunden in England*, iii. no. 86 (Göttingen, 1952), p. 218.
3. This is *communis opinio* among English monastic historians. See Knowles, p. 281
and now B. Kemp, 'The monastic dean of Leominster', *ante*, lxxxiii (1968), 511 with
good evidence but Mayer (p. 273 and n. 43) maintains that the dubious foundation
charter of Reading sought to suppress the abbey's original subjection to Cluny. There
are however in the Reading Cartulary, B[ritish] M[useum] MS. Egerton 3031, fos.
48ᵛ–49ʳ three *cartae* which set out the relations between the two houses. The first was
addressed by Peter the Venerable to Abbot Hugh (1123–30), the second to Abbot
Anscher (1130–35) while the third was sent by one of Peter's successors to Abbot Hugh II
(1189–99). The bonds between Reading and Cluny were here defined by the term
societas, a *societas* of judicial parity and shared spiritual benefits. According to the *cartae*
the monks of Reading made profession to their own house and had the right to elect
their abbot from their own number or from Cluny. All this was said to have been
instituted by the 'will and command of the lord king Henry (I)' and the consent of the
abbot and convent of Cluny. The *cartae* are not without their problems and await a
critical edition but Hadrian IV's confirmation of the *societas* and fraternity between the
two houses which referred to a sealed *scriptum* of the abbot of Cluny (Papsturkunden,
iii. no. 127) though cited by Mayer, does not support his hypothesis. In general there
are strong grounds for thinking that Reading's independence went back to the reign
of its founder. Henry I was far too important a direct benefactor to Cluny for his wishes
to have been slighted by Peter the Venerable. On the king's gifts of badly needed cash
see G. Duby, *Hommes et structures du moyen âge* (Paris and the Hague, 1973), p. 72.
4. For examples see Knowles, p. 282, n. 2. Abbot Hugh, before becoming archbishop
of Rouen in 1130, had been called to the *curia* by Pope Honorius II who wished to
retain him in his service. Henry I protested strongly and forbade him to go. See the
letters in *Papsturkunden*, iii. nos. 15–22.
5. *The Letters of Peter the Venerable*, no. 77, ed. G. Constable (Cambridge, Mass.,
1967), i. 211 f. and ii. 149 f.
6. *Early Scottish Charters*, collected by Sir Archibald C. Lawrie (Glasgow, 1905), no.
clxi, pp. 123, 390 and G. W. S. Barrow, *The Kingdom of the Scots* (London, 1973), pp. 177,

relic of such importance as the hand. Unfortunately, however, some of the early charters of the abbey preserved in its cartularies (notably the Egerton MS. 3031 in the British Museum (*c.* 1200)) are suspect and not least of all the writ announcing the gift of the St James relic. It was addressed to the abbot and convent and commanded them to receive, revere and display the hand 'which my daughter Mathilda the empress gave me when she returned from Germany'.[1] In Roger of Howden the very foundation of the abbey is linked with the coming of the relic. 'King Henry for sheer joy of the hand of the blessed apostle St James founded the noble abbey of Reading . . . and placed the hand of the blessed Apostle James there.'[2] The writ is dated at Portsmouth where Henry had just arrived from Normandy (September 1126) and the gift thus purports to be one of the first things he did on his return but it has a faulty witness list. It would be rash, however, to conclude as Professor Mayer has done that the hand was not given to Reading in Henry I's reign. It is true that in the early fourteenth-century *Chronicle of the Kings of England* copied into a Leominster Priory cartulary – Leominster was part of Reading's initial endowment – there is an entry suggesting that the relic came to the mother house only in 1156, a year before Frederick Barbarossa's letter.[3] The same notice found its way into Higden's *Polychronicon* and the *Eulogium Historiarum*.[4] Moreover, neither the scanty *Reading Annals*, edited by Liebermann, nor the so-called *Annales Radingenses Posteriores* which Previté-Orton found in a former Reading manuscript now in St John's College, Cambridge, contain any mention of the hand being given to the abbey by Henry I.[5] Still this argument *e silentio* cannot be pressed very far.[6] Both these annals are no more than marginal jottings and omit other important events in Reading's early history nor do they give any countenance to the tradition that the hand arrived only in 1156.

It is time to look at the positive evidence. There are in Mathew Paris's *Chronica Majora* three entries which make it possible to follow

185 f. The earl of Leicester's grant is in BM. MS. Egerton 3031, fo. 36ʳ. Brien fitz Count's *obit* was kept at Reading on 5 March according to an entry in the calendar of the thirteenth-century almoner's cartulary, BM. MS. Vespasian E. v, fo. 12ᵛ.

1. *Regesta Regum Anglo-Normannorum*, ii. ed. C. Johnson and H. A. Cronne (Oxford, 1956), no. 1448, p. 198. For the text see Dugdale, *Monasticon Anglicanum*, new ed. (London, 1846), iv. 41, no. iii.

2. Howden, i. 181.

3. BM. MS. Domitian A. iii, fo. 31ᵛ: 'Eodem anno (1156) delata est manus sancti Iacobi Radinges.' B. Kemp, 'Miracles', p. 1, discusses this entry and rejects Mayers's view.

4. *Polychronicon*, ed. J. R. Lumby (R.S., 1863), viii. 38 f. and *Eulogium*, ed. F. S. Haydon (R.S., 1863), iii. 68.

5. F. Liebermann, *Ungedruckte Anglo-Normannische Geschichtsquellen* (Strassburg, 1879), p. 10 f. and C. W. Previté-Orton, '*Annales Radingenses Posteriores*, *Ante*, xxxvii (1922), 400 f. For the MSS. of these annals and their associations with Reading and Leominster see N. R. Ker, *Medieval Libraries of Great Britain*, 2nd. ed. (Royal Hist. Soc. Guides and Handbooks No. 3, 1964), pp. 114 (Smaragdus) and p. 155 (Bede).

6. As in Mayer, p. 274. The point is well made by Kemp, p. 3.

the relic's history during the last years of Henry I's and the troubles of Stephen's reign. Whereas most of the older sources embodied in this portion of his work are known these Reading notices cannot be identified and here Mathew must have drawn on some Reading history now lost. That such a one existed, can moreover be proved. The Egerton MS. 3031 is more than a cartulary. It contains also a list of treasures, of relics and a catalogue of the abbey's books towards the end of the twelfth century. Here we find an entry: 'Gesta regis Henrici et ystoria Radingis in uno volumine'.[1] Already Previté-Orton observed that Mathew Paris's Reading items were not borrowed from the *Annales Radingenses Posteriores* he printed nor did they stem from the annals edited by Liebermann.[2] Under the year 1133 we read in the *Chronica Majora*: 'King Henry crossed over (to Normandy) for the last time and sent the hand of St James to Reading.'[3] It was thus a parting gift. 1133 as the year when the relic first came to Reading would at once explain why Henry I had, at an earlier date (*c.* 1129–33), granted to the monks a fair, not on the feast of St James but on St Lawrence's day. Before 1133 a specially close connection between the apostle and the monastery did not yet exist.[4] The next of our three entries reveals why the monks were so anxious to prove their possession of the relic for the earliest possible date. *Sub anno* 1136 we read: 'Bishop Henry of Winchester took the hand of St James away from Reading.'[5] Henry I had died in Normandy on the first of December 1135, but his mortal remains were hazardously brought over to England to be buried before the altar of the abbey church on 4 January 1136 in the presence of Stephen, already king, and his brother, Henry of Blois. He may have seized the relic there and then.[6]

In his *Gesta Regum* and the *Gesta Pontificum* William of Malmesbury described Henry I's foundation when it was still in the making. The king, he thought, had located it on one of the busiest thoroughfares of England, between the Thames and the Kennet, so that it could offer shelter to travellers. William praised the Cluniac monks for

1. MS. Egerton 3031 fo. 9ʳ in the margin. The catalogue was edited by S. Barfield, *Ante*, iii (1888), 113–25. For this entry see p. 119 but the transcription is faulty. By omitting the *et* the editor turned one volume into two. Reading very rightly possessed a history of its founder, perhaps Robert of Torigny's addition to William of Jumièges. See Leyser, 'England and the Empire', p.196 f.

2. Previté-Orton, *ubi supra*, p. 400.

3. *Chronica Majora*, ed. H. R. Luard (R.S., 1874), ii. 159: 'Rex Henricus extremo transfretavit, et manum Sancti Jacobi misit Radingas.'

4. *Regesta*, ii, no. 1864. Mayer regarded this and the grant of a St James's day fair in Henry II's reign as positive evidence for the view that the relic did not come to Reading before about 1155.

5. *Chron. Maj.*, ii. 164: 'Henricus Wintoniensis episcopus abstulit manum Sancti Jacobi de Radinges.' The two entries are also found in the *Flores Historiarum*, ed. H. R. Luard (R.S., 1890), ii. 56, 58 together with some Reading notices (pp. 58, 69 and 72) not in Mathew Paris. That Henry I sent the hand to the abbey in 1133 was mentioned also in the *Worcester Annals* (*Annales Monastici*, ed. Luard, R.S., 1869, iv. 378). Mayer has disregarded all these passages.

6. Kemp. p. 3, n. 15 draws attention to Henry of Blois's presence.

their exemplary hospitality and this was indeed the special raison d'être of the abbey.[1] That the *susceptio* of guests, especially *pauperes Christi* and pilgrims had been the avowed aim of the founder is asserted in a charter of Abbot Hugh II (1186–99) which recorded the endowment of a hospital and guesthouse for the poorer visitors.[2] In the very problematic foundation charter of Reading, dated 1125, the charitable purpose is expressed in a clause which warned the abbot elect against squandering the alms of the monastery on his lay kinsmen and charged him to take care of the needy, the visitors and pilgrims. This *passus* occurs again and again in royal confirmations of Henry's charter and it is embodied also in a long series of papal privileges, all transmitted in the abbey's cartularies.[3] Reading was a *regale monasterium*, a royal monastery, and wanted to be.[4] Its abbots were high franchisers who ruled over a considerable ecclesiastical empire. They were *personae regni* like the heads of older royal foundations but for good reasons they wished to escape the burdens of such a position, especially knight-service and the harder forms of custody during vacancy. The unusual exemptions they claimed were in part justified by the continuous *susceptio* of guests, high and low.[5]

1. *Gesta Regum*, p. 489 and *Gesta Pontificum Anglorum*, ed. N. E. S. A. Hamilton (R.S., 1870), p. 193.

2. Monasticon, iv. 42, no. xiii.

3. It was repeated throughout the twelfth century. For Henry I's charter see *Regesta*, ii, no. 1427 and *Monasticon*, iv. 40, no. ii. For Stephen's confirmation *Regesta*, iii, ed. H. A. Cronne and R. H. C. Davis (Oxford, 1968), no. 675. For Henry II's, Richard's and John's confirmations see MS. Egerton 3031 fos. 20^v–21^r, 22^r, 27^v, 29^v and BM. MS. Harley 1708, fos. 21^v, 31^v, 34^r, a mid-thirteenth-century Reading cartulary. The papal privileges which embodied this formulary are in *Papsturkunden*, iii, nos. 12 (Honorius II), 28 (Innocent II), 85 (Eugenius III), 126 (Hadrian IV) and 278 (Alexander III).

4. So Herbert of Bosham called it, like Westminster, in his *Vita Sancti Thomae*, iii. c. 21 (*Materials . . . Becket*, iii. 260 f.).

5. Mayer's interpretation of the Reading charters must be seriously questioned. He noted (p. 272 and n. 38) that in a shorter version of the foundation charter, the *carta gestatoria*, a purported original of 1127, now BM. Add. Ch. 19571 (*cf. Regesta*, ii, no. 1474 and also C. Johnson, 'Some Charters of Henry I', in *Historical Essays in Honour of James Tait*, ed. J. G. Edwards, V. H. Galbraith and E. F. Jacob, Manchester, 1933, pp. 137 ff.) there is no mention of the duty to look after travellers and pilgrims and so he concluded that the forger wished to do away with this tiresome commitment ('lästige Verpflichtung'). Yet the document is described on the dorse as a *carta . . . gestatoria de libertatibus*. It was a detailed statement of Reading's judicial rights and fiscal exemptions and nothing else. It cannot possibly be adduced to prove that the abbey sought to evade its obligations to travellers and pilgrims. We have already seen that these were spelt out again and again in the confirmations of the larger foundation charter of 1125. In the almoner's cartulary and calendar of the thirteenth century (BM. MS. Vespasian E. v, fo. 17^v) the hospitality clause is especially picked out as might be expected. The *carta gestatoria* moreover omitted some of the most important provisions in the foundation charter: the exemption from knight service, the right of self-administration during vacancies, the injunction against creating fees, employing hereditary lay officials and admitting child oblates. These clauses really constitute a programme of reform, if not a new model for an Anglo-Norman royal abbey. It is noteworthy that much of this material appears also in one of the spurious foundation charters of Battle Abbey and some of it elsewhere, for instance at Alcester. (*Monasticon*, iii. 245, no. x and iv. 175, no. i.) The Reading text therefore cannot be studied in isolation. It defined a constitution

For a centre of monastic hospitality a great saint and his cult which might make a visit to the abbey an end in itself, were of course highly desirable. Reading had possessed its most compelling relic for perhaps less than three years before Henry of Blois removed it. He was the king's brother and one of the most formidable Cluniac grandees of his time. It would have been difficult to resist him. The founder's death almost certainly created an atmosphere of insecurity for the monks and the need to please new masters. What Henry intended to do with the relic is not clear. Perhaps Winchester was to have gained what Reading lost but for the moment, it seems, the hand joined the bishop's renowned treasure of works of art, jewellery and plate.[1] During the later phases of the war between Stephen and the Angevins, now led by the young Henry of Anjou, the Thames Valley became a frontline and the abbey suffered severely. Amongst its papal letters there is one suggesting that not only adulterine castles but also adulterine churches had to be put down.[2] Gilbert Foliot, already bishop of Hereford but also a former monk of Cluny, wrote to Pope Eugenius III on Reading's behalf and Eugenius ordered Archbishop Theobald of Canterbury to proceed against anyone building fortresses on the abbey's lands.[3] From the lost Reading history as reflected in Mathew Paris and the *Flores Historiarum*, it appears that Stephen himself raised a castle at Reading in 1150, evidently on the monastery's grounds, 'contra jus fasque' as Robert of Torigny indignantly reported. Two years later Duke Henry's garrison at Wallingford came and destroyed it.[4]

If the house of Blois made very free with Henry I's inheritance his Angevin grandson was adamant in seeking to regain what he could. The bishop of Winchester attended his coronation but before many months he had to face the cold demands and threats of the new regime. He fled the country secretly in the middle of 1155 and saved his treasure by misusing the diplomatic immunity of his friend, the

---

for the abbey markedly different from that of other royal houses with their abbots' baronies and vassalages. The experience of at least fifty years of Anglo-Norman monasticism lay behind the aspirations expressed in these clauses. Reading's Berkshire neighbour, Abingdon, owed the services of thirty knights and not so distant St Albans had suffered much from its abbots' nepotistic transactions. If Reading's foundation charters were tampered with in the 1170s, the time favoured by Mayer, the object of the forger was not to eliminate the duty of furnishing hospitality but to shield the abbey's franchises against the mounting surge of royal justice and the exchequer's prying. It is unlikely moreover that all the ingredients of the Reading formulary – as we might call it – were latter-day falsifications.

1. For his collection of relics see 'Gifts of Bishop Henry of Blois . . . to Winchester Cathedral', *Downside Review*, iii (1884), 33–44 and Adam de Domersham's *Historia de rebus gestis Glastoniensibus*, ed. T. Hearne (Oxford, 1727), ii. 316 f.

2. *Papsturkunden*, iii. no. 131.

3. *The Letters and Charters of Gilbert Foliot*, ed. Dom. A. Morey and C. N. L. Brooke (Cambridge, 1967), no. 85 and *Papsturkunden*, iii. no. 86.

4. *Chronica Majora*, ii. 184, *Flores Historiarum*, ii. 69 *sub annis* 1150 and 1151, Robert of Torigny, *Chronicles*, iv. 174.

abbot of Cluny who removed it for him.[1] The hand of St James, however, remained behind and was returned to Reading. We do not know the details but there is some evidence that Henry of Blois did not hand it over willingly or with a good grace.[2] The last of our three Mathew Paris passages, *sub anno* 1155, reads thus: 'Frederick (Barbarossa) was sacered emperor by Pope Hadrian; the hand of St James was restored to Reading.'[3] The juxtaposition of the two events is odd. Did Mathew Paris find more in his Reading source than he chose to include in his text?

The Angevins, anxious as they were to appear as the founder's true heirs, ostentatiously patronized the abbey and it became for a time their family mausoleum. What Fontevrault was to them on the continent, Reading was to be in England. In 1156, when Henry II lost his eldest son, an infant boy called William, he had him buried at Henry I's feet in Reading.[4] The monastery here played an important role in exhibiting the rightfulness of the Angevin succession to the crowds of pilgrims who came to visit the repository of St James's hand. For the monks lost little time now in propagating their exalted relic and making it work for the restoration of their house and the repair of war damage. There are in the Egerton manuscript no less than sixteen episcopal letters of indulgence for those who visited Reading Abbey on the feast of St James, 25 July, or within the octave. They were given remission of penances that had been enjoined on them, ranging from fifteen to forty days. The originals of some of these letters have survived, including Archbishop Theobald's.[5] Most suffragans of Canterbury followed suit: the bishops of Salisbury, Hereford, Lincoln, Bath, Ely, Chichester, Norwich, St David's and Llandaff. All these were enthroned by 1157 (the date of Henry II's letter to Barbarossa), as was Hugh de Puiset, bishop of Durham who also issued an indulgence. Some bishops of later appointment, including Thomas Becket, Bartholomew of Exeter, Richard of Coventry and Gilbert Foliot as bishop of London, must be added to the list. Joscelin of Salisbury as Reading's diocesan

1. Robert of Torigny, p. 186 and L. Voss, *Heinrich von Blois Bischof von Winchester 1129–71*, *Historische Studien* ccx (1932), 40.

2. See *infra*, p. 232.

3. *Chronica Majora*, ii. 210: 'Frethericus consecratus est in imperatorem ab A(driano) Papa; manus Sancti Jacobi restituta est Radingo.'

4. Torigny, p. 189. In 1175 Earl Reginald of Cornwall, a natural son of Henry I, was buried in Reading. See (Howden's) *Gesta Regis Henrici Secundi*, ed. W. Stubbs (R.S., 1867), i. 105. For Eleanor of Aquitaine's confraternity with the abbey see C. R. Cheney, 'A Monastic Letter of Fraternity to Eleanor of Aquitaine', *Ante*, li (1936), 488–93. For Fontevrault see T. S. R. Boase, 'Fontevrault and the Plantagenets', *Journal of the British Archaeological Association*, 3rd. ser., xxxiv (1971), 1–10.

5. MS. Egerton 3031, fos. 57ᵛ–60ʳ. Archbishop Theobald's letter is edited in A. Saltman, *Theobald, Archbishop of Canterbury* (London, 1956), p. 435, no. 213. The date should be narrowed down to 1155–61. For Hilary of Chichester's indulgence see *The Acta of the Bishops of Chichester 1075–1207*, ed. H. Mayr-Harting, *Canterbury and York Society* (1964), no. 45. For Gilbert Foliot's, both as bishop of Hereford and as bishop of London see *Letters and Charters*, nos. 339, 430.

welcomed and approved his colleagues' grants. These letters of indulgence have on the whole been seen as preparations for the dedication of the abbey which Thomas Becket himself performed in the presence of Henry II and a great throng of bishops and nobles on 19 April 1164.[1] Yet some of them were probably issued earlier following the restoration of the hand. Archbishop Theobald's (ob. 1161) must have been and it is unlikely that not a single one of his suffragans should have followed his lead. The monks in the thirteenth century compiled a record of the total number of days remission for the feast of St James and from this it is clear that new letters were granted from time to time.[2] Almost alone in the province of Canterbury Henry of Winchester does not seem to have offered an indulgence for the St James pilgrimage to Reading. No letter of his appears in the Egerton collection, an eloquent testimony of his resentment. His successors for at least a century failed to make good his omission.[3]

The new cult soon gained momentum and became very popular. Henry II helped it by granting to the abbey a fair on the feast of St James and the three days after.[4] That Thomas Becket had dedicated the church and commended the pilgrimage with his indulgence was not forgotten after his martyrdom and canonization.[5] The monks also saw to it that the miracles wrought before their relic or by the water into which it had been dipped, should be recorded. A collection of these dating from the last decade of the twelfth century has survived in a Gloucester Cathedral manuscript.[6] The origins of those who experienced the wonder-working *virtus* of the apostle were usually mentioned. They came from the vicinity and from distant parts of the country and it is noticeable how neatly, not to say purposefully, all ranks and orders of Anglo-Norman society from the king down-

---

1. *Annales Radingenses Posteriores*, p. 400. Among the bishops present was Henry of Winchester. (See *Acta of the Bishops of Chichester*, p. 109.) Dr Mayr-Harting linked the indulgences wholly with the dedication. The editors of Gilbert Foliot's letters allowed for the possibility of connecting them with the earlier date.

2. BM. MS. Harley 1708, fos. 186ᵛ, 187ʳ. Among the later grantors of indulgences were the papal legate Nicholas of Tusculum (1213/14) and Archbishop Boniface of Savoy.

3. But Bishop Godfrey de Lucy (1189–1204) contributed 40 days 'In festo Sancti Philippi specialiter', (MS. *cit.*, fo. 186ᵛ) and there were relations of confraternity between the convents of St Swithun and Reading (BM. Add. MS. 29436 fo. 44ᵛ). Besides Henry, only the bishops of Worcester and Rochester do not appear on the list of those who added to the *dies indulgentiarum*. Worcester was vacant from 1157–8 and again from 1160–3. Bishop Roger (1163–79) was only consecrated in Aug. 1164. Rochester was but the assistant of Canterbury.

4. *Monasticon*, iv. 42, no. x.

5. See Pope Alexander III's letter addressed to all the faithful in the Province of Canterbury exhorting them to visit Reading on the anniversary of the dedication and on the feast of St James (*Papsturkunden*, iii. no. 312, 1173–81).

6. On MS. Gloucester Cathedral no. 1 see N. Ker in S. M. Eward, *A Catalogue of Gloucester Cathedral Library* (Dean and Chapter, 1972), p. 1. It probably belonged to Leominster. In general see Kemp, 'Miracles', *passim*. I am grateful to Mr D. Bethell who very kindly gave me a copy of his transcript of the *Miracles*.

wards, were represented in these incidents. Reading was to be not merely the poor man's Compostella. In the list of relics owned by the abbey towards the end of the twelfth century the hand of St James appears behind the relics of Christ and the Virgin.[1] These most awe-inspiring objects of the Reading treasury were characteristic of a royal sanctuary and reflected the far-flung diplomatic relations of the Anglo-Norman and Angevin rulers. Some of them had been sent to Henry I from Constantinople by the Emperors Alexius and John Comnenus and others came from the chapel of the exiled Henry the Lion. Before the end of the century the abbey had established a feast for its collection as a whole, a 'festivitas sanctarum reliquiarum'. Here St James headed the list.[2]

It is time to return to Frederick Barbarossa's *curia* at Würzburg and the letter presented by Henry II's envoys accrediting them to speak on the king's behalf about the hand of St James. From the evidence that has been assembled it is now fairly clear what passed between the emperor and Henry in 1157. Frederick must have requested that the hand of the apostle be returned to him as a sacred possession of the imperial chapel. It is equally clear that Henry II refused to part with it. This is what his ambassadors had been charged to convey to the Hohenstaufen as tactfully as possible. If one of them was, as has been suggested, Herbert of Bosham, the tact might not have been very noticeable. What the emperor really wanted he was denied but instead he received the letter which in the light of his rebuff might be regarded as a sham or, because of its very solemnity, a piece of bland irony. Henry II's unwillingness to meet Frederick's wish had respectable reasons. There were his mother's rights to be considered. Reading Abbey moreover, as has been shown, had a part to play in strengthening the Angevin regime's roots in England. The pilgrims who flocked expectantly to the apostle's relic might also thank the king who had caused it to return to the Thames Valley. The cult was by now under way, already backed perhaps by the archbishop's and some of the bishops' letters of indulgence. It would have been practically impossible to interfere. Henry II's envoys, of course, had not come to Würzburg empty-handed. Rahewin wrote of their many and varied presents and he took pains to describe the most important one, a huge tent, superbly made from the finest materials. It was so large that it could only be raised mechanically. It seems as if Otto of Freising's secretary was at Würzburg and saw it. As Frederick Barbarossa was to spend the next few years more or less under canvas campaigning in Italy this turned out to be a very useful gift. It was seen and admired later by Vincent of Prague, pitched outside Milan and large enough for a

1. MS. Egerton 3031 fos. 6ᵛ–8ʳ and D. Bethell, 'The making of a twelfth-century relic collection', in *Popular Belief and Practice*, p. 69.
2. See the twelfth-century Reading *Martyrologium*, BM. MS. Harley 82, fo. 23ʳ.

coronation ceremony. Here on 8 September 1158, the emperor had mass celebrated by the archbishop of Milan as a sign of reconciliation.[1]

It would thus be unsafe to lean too heavily on the text of Henry II's letter in order to construct a general theory of imperial ascendancy over the kingdoms of the West in the twelfth century. It would be equally mistaken, however, to dismiss the whole episode now as unimportant and the pomp of the phrases: 'authority to command' matched by a 'willingness to obey', as wholly barren. Henry II's letter had its uses for the Hohenstaufen and was not allowed to fall into oblivion like Barbarossa's own *scripta* to which he had entrusted his request for the return of the hand. Rahewin not only quoted the text, he also harnessed it to the main theme of his work in a very ostentatious way. At the very end of the *Gesta* he devoted a long chapter to the *mores* of his hero, Frederick, and he enhanced its solemnity and resonance by closely imitating Einhard.[2] Anyone who in the twelfth century knew Einhard's *Life of Charlemagne* – and it was a deeply implanted text – would instantly recognize the sentences and vocabulary which Rahewin here used. By clothing Frederick's relations with other rulers in the language and thought of Einhard, Rahewin made them appear to match Charlemagne's example. They became thus part of an established and known imperial tradition and he authenticated this literary manoeuvre by evoking the most beguiling phrases from Henry II's letter: on one side Frederick Barbarossa's 'auctoritas imperandi', on the other the foreign kings' 'voluntas obsequendi'. With the help of these words he was able to prove his point. Henry II's letter here found its first echo and Rahewin moreover employed it to generalize about Frederick's relations with other rulers. What Henry had written only for himself, the court historian would have his readers believe, applied also to the emperor's dealings with the kings of Spain, France, Denmark, Bohemia and Hungary.[3]

This stance was not entirely new. Early in 1142 Conrad III informed the emperor John Comnenus that he had made peace in all parts of the *Reich* – there was a shortlived détente in the Welf-

---

1. *Gesta Frederici*, iii. c. 7, p. 404 f., *Vincentii Pragensis Annales*, 1158, MGH, SS. xvii. 675 and Mayer, p. 277 and n. 65. For some of the other presents see *supra*, p. 219.

2. *Gesta Frederici*, iv. c. 86, pp. 708–12 and esp. p. 712.

3. *Gesta*, p. 712: 'Reges Hyspanie, Anglie, Francie, Datie, Boemie atque Ungarie, quamvis *suspectam semper eius haberent potentiam, sibi adeo* per *amicitiam* et *societatem devinxit* et *ad suam voluntatem sic inclinatos habet, ut,* quotiens *ad eum litteras vel legatos miserint,* sibi cedere auctoritatem imperandi, illis non deesse voluntatem obsequendi denuntient.'

Einhardi Vita Karoli Magni, c. 16, ed. O. Holder-Egger, SRG (Hanover and Leipzig, 1911), p. 20: 'Erat enim *semper* Romanis et Grecis Francorum *suspecta potentia'* and (p. 19) '*Adeo* namque Hadefonsum Galleciae atque Asturicae regem *sibi societate devinxit, ut* is, *cum ad eum vel litteras vel legatos mitteret* . . . Scottorum quoque *reges sic habuit ad suam voluntatem* per munificentiam *inclinatos* . . .'

Einhard also used *amicitia* here. Kirfel (p. 172) ignored Rahewin's literary debt.

Hohenstaufen conflict – and that the kingdoms adjoining the empire were sending frequent embassies to him affirming their willingness to carry out: 'imperii nostri mandata'.[1] He named France, Spain, England and Denmark. There is no evidence for this in the case of England. It is just possible that Mathilda, during her brief moment of regality in 1141, sent Conrad whom she must have known from her days in the *Reich*, a letter. She was his aunt by marriage. What matters in this bold and inflated claim is that Conrad who, though not crowned, styled himself emperor in his correspondence with the Comneni, wanted to be seen as the spokesman of the West towards Byzantium. The Greeks of course took good care to maintain independent and direct relations with western rulers whom they thought to be important and influential. Yet it should be remembered that there were byzantine ambassadors at the Würzburg *curia* in autumn 1157 and the presence of so many other envoys from England, Denmark, Hungary and Italy could be arranged and used to impress them. When Barbarossa opened his diet at Besançon a few weeks later there was once again an array of embassies to overawe the bishops and nobles of the Burgundian kingdom. Rahewin spoke of Romans, Apulians, Tuscans, Venetians, French, Spaniards and, surprisingly, Englishmen. Since it is very unlikely that Henry II sent yet another mission the emperor must have ordered the two envoys to accompany or precede him from Würzburg to Besançon so that they became unexpectedly eyewitnesses of his calculated outburst against Pope Hadrian IV's legates.[2]

There is some evidence that even before this date Frederick had worn an air, not only of superior *dignitas* but also of *auctoritas* in his dealings with Henry II. We possess a letter he wrote to him, dated Aachen 6 May 1157 to which the missive brought by Master Heribert and the clerk William in September cannot have been the reply. Barbarossa's letter has been preserved in the collection of Abbot Wibald of Stavelot and Corvey who also drafted it. In the protocol Henry was addressed as *frater* and *amicus*, that is to say as an equal, but Frederick was given an unusually solemn *intitulatio*.[3] The text was more pointed still. Here the emperor interceded for an Abbot Gerald of Solignac (diocese of Limoges) and commended him and

1. Otto of Freising, *Gesta*, i. c. 26, p. 172 and MGH, *Die Urkunden Konrads III und seines Sohnes Heinrich*, ed. F. Hausmann (Vienna, Cologne, Graz, 1969), no. 69. Of the large literature on Conrad III's exchanges with the Comneni only G. Koch, *Auf dem Wege zum Sacrum Imperium* (Vienna, Cologne, Graz, 1972), pp. 221 ff. shall be cited here. The discussion has concentrated on the *intitulatio* he used rather than the claims advanced in this passage.

2. *Gesta Frederici*, iii. c. 10, p. 408. Ambassadors needed formal leave to depart again and the emperor may have adjourned his reply to Henry's messages to the next *curia*.

3. *Wibaldi Epistolae*, no. 461 in *Monumenta Corbeiensia*, ed. P. Jaffé, *Bibliotheca Rerum Germanicarum*, i (Berlin, 1864), p. 594. 'Fredericus Dei gratia Romanorum imperator augustus, magnus et pacificus, a Deo coronatus . . .' and R. M. Herkenrath, *Regnum und Imperium Das Reich in der frühstaufischen Kanzlei*, Oesterreichische Akademie der Wissenschaften Philosophisch-Historische Klasse, *Sitzungsberichte*, ccliv, 5 (1969), 52.

his house to Henry's protection.[1] He was to defend it against the hostilities of evil persons. Abbot Gerald had come to Aachen to solicit this letter under Wibald's patronage, for Stavelot and Solignac shared the *patrocinium* of St Remacles and were linked by bonds of confraternity. The Limousin monastery had continuous trouble with the nobility of the region and the abbot must have felt that Barbarossa's intervention with the king-duke was worth trying and less likely to offend than Louis VII's. The letter stressed that Solignac lay in Henry's *principatus* and the Angevin was exhorted to do his royal duty. The *arenga* dwelt on the imperial propriety of holding out a helping hand to churches and convents so that they could pray God's mercy for the emperor's and the people's well-being. These were commonplaces which might occur in any diploma granted to a German or Italian church. It was not unusual in the twelfth century for the greater subjects of one ruler to enlist the good offices of another in dealings with their own king but a certain note of *hauteur* is unmistakable in Frederick's text. Perhaps Thomas Becket deliberately played on this vein of imperial rhetoric when he authorized the draft of Henry II's letter for the Würzburg embassy in July 1157.[2]

It remains to ask whether the obliging phraseology of the Angevin chancery had any consequences. Henry II certainly did not wish to subject his empire to the Hohenstaufen's but his words could still be interpreted and remembered in that sense by the audience for whom the *Gesta Frederici* were written. His letter, as we saw, had been received into the foremost work of Hohenstaufen historiography. Now it is symptomatic of Germany's development under Frederick Barbarossa that the *Gesta* did not carry all before them. Their historical perspective was only one amongst many but their influence, though circumscribed, should not be underrated. The exemplar sent to Barbarossa's chancellor Ulrich and the notary Henry in 1160 was kept at court and soon disseminated from there to the Hohenstaufen monasteries in Alsace.[3] Frederick kept a good library in his palace at Hagenau filled with saints lives, histories,

1. Not 'Solesmes' as in Mayer (p. 270) and Kirfel (p. 177), both following Simonsfeld (p. 527). At about this time Abbot Gerald of Solignac significantly sought and obtained also a papal privilege of protection for his house. See W. Wiederholt, *Papsturkunden in Frankreich*, vi (*Nachrichten der Königl. Gesellschaft . . . Göttingen, Philol.-Histor. Klasse*, 1911, Beiheft), p. 66, no. 29. On the relations of *societas* and *fraternitas* between Stavelot and Solignac see J. Halkin and C.-G. Roland, *Recueil des Chartes de l'Abbaye de Stavelot-Malmedy*, *Academie Royale de Belgique, Commission Royale d'Histoire* (1909), i. 321, no. 158 and F. Baix, 'Saint Remacle et les Abbayes de Solignac et de Stavelot-Malmedy', *Révue Bénédictine*, lxi (1951), 202–7. Solignac suffered again badly at the hands of Brabancon and German mercenaries during the wars between Henry II and his sons in 1173/4 and the ensuing pacification. (*Recueil*, i. 506, no. 268.)

2. Trautz, p. 67 and F. Böhm, *Das Bild Friedrich Barbarossas und seines Kaisertums in den ausländischen Quellen seiner Zeit*, *Historische Studien*, cclxxxix (1936), 17 and 81 who argued for Becket's authorship on somewhat specious grounds.

3. On the transmission and circulation of the *Gesta* see Schmale's introduction to his edition, pp. 48–71.

leges, philosophical and medical works.[1] By 1200 the *Gesta* had also
spread in Bavaria from the copy Rahewin took with him when he
retired to Freising. Hohenstaufen propaganda hung fire during the
schism despite the archpoet but it revived after the Peace of Venice
in 1177. Much poetry attended the great occasions of Frederick's
later years. The most ambitious of these seasonal works, the *Ligurinus,* has survived, albeit precariously, and here the matter of the
Gesta Frederici from 1152 to 1160 was set to verse. The author,
Gunther of Pairis (in Alsace), dedicated his long poem to the
emperor and his sons, not least of all Henry VI who had just married
Constance of Sicily (1186). Gunther used the court version of the
Gesta and he knew the Hohenstaufen circle. At one time he tutored
Frederick's son Conrad, one of the black sheep of the family. In the
Ligurinus, Book vi, the whole episode of Henry II's embassy in 1157,
the tent, the messages of compliance and service, was retold and
embroidered on.[2] Even more than in Rahewin the letter here served
to buttress the panegyrical theme of Hohenstaufen world rule.
Henry II's power, wealth and success were extolled only to enhance
the value of his supposed offer of obedience. Gunther, writing in
1186/7, wanted to connect Barbarossa's early triumphs with his
present good fortunes passing over the embarrassing schism with as
few words as possible. His work fell into oblivion but it evidently
wanted to please by saying welcome things about the past.

A rather less gifted poet, Gottfried of Viterbo, the long-serving
chaplain and notary of the Hohenstaufen, also knew and used Otto
of Freising's and Rahewin's *Gesta Frederici* although he does not
allude to the embassies of 1157 in his own.[3] Barbarossa took pains
to have his sons well educated as was the way of unlettered newcomers to the German kingship. The young Henry VI to whom
Gottfried dedicated some of his works almost certainly knew the
Gesta Frederici or their verse echos, or both. It is not far-fetched to
regard their carefully selected topics, including the king of England's
gratifying offers of *obsequium,* as part of a Hohenstaufen house consciousness while the loss of the hand was forgotten. However hard-
faced, downright and unpoetic Henry VI's dealings with Richard I
were in 1193/4, the compromising tenor of Angevin rhetoric in 1157
may have served as a useful precedent when Richard I was persuaded

1. It was described and praised by Gottfried of Viterbo in a poem entitled, *Denumeratio
regnorum imperio subjectorum.* For the text see L. Delisle, *Literature latin et histoire du Moyen
Age* (Paris, 1890), p. 48.

2. *Guntheri Poetae Ligurinus,* vi. 22. 168–229, ed. C. G. Dümgé (Heidelberg, 1812), i.
114 ff. Only the reference to the hand was omitted. Instead the poet concluded with a
peroration asking Barbarossa to accept the tent:

> 'Semper habe scenam, quae te, Dux optime velis
> Protegat expansis, qui totum protegis orbem'.

On Gunther see Kirfel, p. 96 and refs.

3. Gottfried's *Gesta* was edited by G. Waitz in *MGH, SS.* xxii. 307–34.

to surrender his kingdom to the emperor 'sicut universorum domino' – the words are Roger of Howden's – and to do homage for it.[1]

Not even the eclipse of the *Reich* after the dual election of 1198 altogether obscured the memory of earlier Hohenstaufen attitudes and Henry II's obliging response to them. Only a few years ago S. Kuttner and A. Garcia y Garcia edited and introduced a new and hitherto unknown account of the Fourth Lateran Council. The author was a German clerk writing home to a prelate waiting for news and he described an extraordinary incident during the last solemn plenary session on 30 November 1215. Innocent III told the bishops of his hopes for the crusade and how much might now be expected from King John who had become a vassal of the Roman Church and, by making his kingdom tributary to it, had singularly advanced the *honor* of the apostolic see. 'But', the author of the letter continued, 'because the kingdom of England belongs, as is said, to the imperial power and lest the princes of the Empire hereafter should lose their right in this', the archbishop of Mainz, Siegfried von Eppenstein, rose and attempted to assert and prove 'that the aforesaid kingdom pertained by right to the emperor and the princes of Germany.' The pope raised his hand and bade him be silent: 'Will you please listen to me now and I may listen to you later.'[2] The incident, almost timeless in its details, reveals the princes as partners in the *Reich* sharing the honour of the English kingdom's alleged subjection with the emperor and also the profits which might accrue. The very vagueness of the author's statement, 'ut dicitur', brings it into the vicinity of Henry II's letter. It was perhaps not wholly immaterial either in 1193/4 or in 1215 when it could have been one of the archbishop's proofs as the editors suggested in their commentary.[3]

The attitudes of Frederick and Henry II are very understandable. It must be apparent that both came to their kingship with the sense of a lost past that needed regaining. Henry was nothing if not an injured heir who looked back to his grandfather's reign. Mathilda too clung to her father's name in the style of her charters as if this entitled her to act as she did. Before Barbarossa succeeded to his Suabian duchy in 1147 he spent his young years in the time-honoured practice of feuds for which it is hard to discover any 'political' purpose. He did not then expect to be king but when he was he had to look backwards, past his uncle and predecessor Conrad III, to the

---

1. Howden, iii. 202 f. *sub anno* 1193. On the date and motives of Richard's homage see Poole, p. 366, Kirfel, pp. 139–42 and Trautz, pp. 88–92.

2. S. Kuttner and A. Garcia y Garcia, 'A new Eyewitness Account of the Fourth Lateran Council', *Traditio*, xx (1964), 115–78 and esp. p. 128 and the commentary p. 159 f.

3. *Cf.* also the questionable report in Howden (iv. 37) that after Henry VI's death Richard was summoned as a *princeps imperii* to attend a meeting for an imperial election at Cologne on 22 Feb. 1198.

grandfather whose alliance with Agnes, the daughter of Henry IV, had raised the Hohenstaufen from the penumbra surrounding them for most of the eleventh century. The Salians were Barbarossa's imperial forbears and it was their traditions which as an inexperienced, if determined novice, he wanted to renew:[1] The St James relic had belonged to their *capella*. Both Frederick and Henry, at the beginning of their reigns were sensitive about ancient neglected rights and honours and if they had a programme it was to recover lost possessions, tangible and intangible, which they felt belonged to their kingships. They did not always know what they were. Barbarossa's demand for the hand is of a piece with his earlier refusal to hold Pope Hadrian's stirrup at their meeting in Sutri in 1155. Henry's 'no', whatever the rights of the case or the practical reasons behind it, is equally characteristic of his jealous concern for an inheritance that had, as he saw it, been tampered with by intruders.

The letter which the two ambassadors took to the emperor from the great council held at Northampton in July 1157 was an unusual product of the Angevin chancery. There are not many genuine pieces like it in Henry II's diplomatic and other correspondence.[2] We do not know who drafted it. If Thomas Becket and his *dictator* deliberately played upon the imperial sensibilities of the Hohenstaufen which they had come to know from Barbarossa's letters they did not render their master a particularly good service.[3] Their 'honeyed words', as Rahewin who probably knew the real purpose of their embassy called them, could be exploited. Henry II was to hear more of Frederick's exhortations, not to say instructions, when the emperor wanted to settle the papal schism in his own way.[4]

1. On the changes in the Hohenstaufen conception of their own traditions and inheritance see the searching study of O. Engels, 'Beiträge zur Geschichte der Staufer im 12. Jahrhundert', (i), *Deutsches Archiv.* xxvii (1971), 432–56. During Frederick's early years the link with the Salians was all-important.

2. Biblical commonplaces embellished the message of goodwill Henry II sent to the Patriarchs of Antioch and Jerusalem and the Prince of Antioch in 1188. (Howden, ii. 342 f.). It was clearly meant for wider circulation. In 1173 Henry directed plaintive letters to 'all emperors and kings whom he believed to be his friends' (Howden, ii. 47) lamenting his misfortunes over his rebelling sons. Their ringing literary style can be inferred from William of Sicily's reply (*ibid.* p. 48). The startling missive addressed to Alexander III in the letter collection of Peter of Blois (*Petri Blesensis . . . Opera Omnia*, ed. I. A. Giles, Oxford, 1847, ii. 19–21, no. 136) purported to belong to this genre. Here also Henry professed himself bound to the pope as his overlord 'quantum ad feudatarii juris obligationem'. Poole (p. 458) seems to have regarded this letter as genuine. R. Foreville, *L'Eglise et La Royauté en Angleterre sous Henry II Plantagenet* (Paris, 1943), pp. 349–56 thought it to be a latter-day confection to justify King John's vassalage to Rome. But the letter, even if fictitious, belonged to the first recension of Peter's collection in 1184. I owe this information to Sir Richard Southern.

3. It is not impossible that Frederick Barbarossa's own envoys were consulted in preparing a draft which might soothe their master's displeasure about the refusal of his request.

4. *Cf.* Frederick's letter to Henry II, dated 28 Oct. 1159 asking him to send bishops to the planned *conventus* at Pavia. It ended with the instruction not to recognize either pope in the meantime: 'Interim autem in neutram partem predicte scissure assensum tuum declines nec tamquam iustam et rationabilem aliquatenus recipias.' This mandatory

Nor is this all. The letter of 1157, as has been seen, furnished welcome supporting evidence for the Hohenstaufen chancery rhetoric which proclaimed, in more or less ringing tones, the empire's ascendancy over other kingdoms and even over Byzantium. Historians have read the manifestos inserted into the text of the *Gesta Frederici* mainly as puzzling and contradictory statements about Barbarossa's intentions towards his neighbours. The contradictions are resolved if it is understood that these manifestos were directed inwards rather than outwards. They sought to create a body of common sentiment amongst the princes and counts who thronged to Frederick's assemblies, their entourages and the imperial *ministeriales*. They wanted to generate solidarity and the sense of belonging to a very privileged and exalted institution. Frederick Barbarossa's problem was how to counter the increasingly centrifugal interests of his leading men, how to make his solemn courts still their most important social meeting ground and to attract them to his enterprises which did not necessarily concert well with their own. He did this by flattering them and to some extent he succeeded as the Archbishop of Mainz's unexpected outburst at the Lateran Council proves.

Let us remember finally also the words of the Disibodenberg annalist. By taking away the hand of St James Mathilda 'did irreparable damage to the *regnum Francorum*'. The loss of especially sacred relics brought calamities and the twenty-five years since Henry V's death could be regarded as a bleak period for the *Reich* and its ideology. Barbarossa was not doing more than his duty if he wanted to banish the spell by pressing for the return of the hand and so announce to his following that better times had not only come but would stay.

---

phrase was taken almost literally from Barbarossa's encyclical to the German bishops of 23 Oct. Both sets of letters claimed for the emperor the right to summon the disputants and settle their dispute. Kirfel, (pp. 111–13) does less than justice to what was common ground between them. See *MGH, Constitutiones*, i. ed. L. Weiland (Hanover, 1893), nos. 182, 183. Arnulf of Lisieux writing to Alexander III, could not deny that Frederick's injunction had had some effect on Henry II. See *The Letters of Arnulf of Lisieux*, ed. F. Barlow, Camden 3rd. ser., lxi (1939), p. 33, no. 24.

10

SOME REFLECTIONS ON TWELFTH-CENTURY KINGS AND KINGSHIP

The rulers of the early middle ages are known to us mainly through the writings of historians and poets who did not see their task to lie first and foremost in individual characterisation.[1] Every description of a king was also a discussion of kingship. The *vitae* and *res gestae* of rulers sometimes reflected the vows found in coronation *ordines* or they likened their subject's way of life to the rule of St. Benedict. Helgaud, the author of the *Epitome on Robert the Pious*, a monk of Fleury writing circa 1030, left the task of writing about his *militia secularis* to others and he dwelt only — and this by choice — on the sacred functions graced and enhanced by the king by which he manifested his regality. He had much to say about royal alms-giving at the various palaces: Paris, Soissons, Orleans, Senlis, Dijon, Auxerre, Avallon, Melun and Etampes where three hundred and more poor men were fed on bread and wine. On Maundy Thursday the king himself distributed vegetables, fish, bread and a penny to three hundred poor at tierce, to one hundred clerks twelve pence each and prebends of bread and fish at sext. Robert the Pious in Helgaud's text is described as a very rich king — it won't do to belittle the early Capetians — and alms were a means of consuming demesne produce which itineracy could not always use up and do so in a way that strengthened the king's hold on these localities. Charity as an attribute of the *ministerium regis* was in Robert's case made to be even more demonstrative and effective. Twelve poor men on stout asses followed his marching train all the time, praising God, looking cheerful and praying for the soul of their benefactor as they rode along. The vivid spectacle of ritualised charity and gospel lesson displayed the king as the fulfiller of God's commands and as their teacher in Christ's place. Here also we first hear of royal healing miracles.[2]

1   In presenting this study comparing early with high medieval kingship and their literary images I am venturing on certain themes which have recently been treated in two capital works: C. Morris, *The Discovery of the Individual 1050-1200*, Church History Outlines, 5 (London, SPCK, 1972) and A. Murray, *Reason and Society in the Middle Ages* (Oxford, 1978). All I can hope to do is to illustrate some of these themes in novel and unexpected ways.

2   *Epitoma Vitae Regis Rotberti Pii*, ed. R.-H. Bautier and G. Labory, Sources d'Histoire Médiévale, 1 (Paris, 1965), c. 21 (almsgiving), cc. 11, 27 (healing), 15 ('rex ditissimus').

This is not how Einhard had set forth Charlemagne, the Astronomus Louis the Pious, let alone Widukind of Corvey, Otto I. Yet they too typefied, exemplified and built their subjects' personalities round dominant and quintessential qualities. For Einhard these had been *magnanimitas, animositas, constantia animi* and a piety which showed itself in deeds rather than heart-searching and self-torments: so many churches built, ornaments installed, so many acts of piety, of forbearance really, towards sometimes troublesome kinsmen. Above all there was the end result: he, Charlemagne, had nobly enhanced and enlarged the *regnum Francorum* and enriched his Frankish followers.[3] It is not as if Einhard conceals from us the living man altogether: his high-pitched voice, his dislike of fasting and preference for roast game, his swimming bath, riding and concubines are all there but let it not be imagined that they did not serve a didactic and even polemical purpose. To give but one example: the *barbara et antiquissima carmina* which Charlemagne caused to be written down in the vernacular and seems to have ordered his sons to learn, Louis the Pious detested and did not want either to read or to hear recited, let alone be taught. When he feasted he listened in unsmiling silence to what the mimes and players performed. There is little doubt that Einhard approved of the songs and lays and that Thegan wrote at him when he described Louis's personal style and made it clear that a very different conception of the duties of a king really lay between father and son.[4] For the anonymous biographer of Louis his central qualities were forbearance, patience, *temperantia* and forgiveness towards his rebellious sons (except in the end Louis the German). He was however Carolingian enough never to neglect his riding even during holy seasons when religious devotions and almsgiving pre-dominated. There were also long and regular bouts of hunting.[5]

3   Eginhard, *Vie de Charlemagne*, 3d. ed. L. Halphen, Les Classiques de l'Histoire de France au Moyen Age (Paris, 1947), cc. 7, 8, 11, 18, 21, 26, 28, 31 and S. Hellmann, 'Einhards literarische Stellung', in *Ausgewählte Abhandlungen zur Historiographie und Geistesgeschichte des Mittelalters*, ed. H. Beumann (Wissenschaftliche Buchgesellschaft, Darmstadt, 1961), pp. 210ff.

4   Cf. Einhard, *ed. cit.*, c.29, p.82 and *Thegani Vita Hludowici Imperatoris*, c. 19 in *Quellen zur Karolingischen Reichsgeschichte*, ed. R. Rau (Freiherr vom Stein-Gedächtnisausgabe, Darmstadt, 1955), p. 226.

5   *Anonymi vita Hludowici Imperatoris*, c.62 'ita ut vix uno aut duobus diebus propter exercitationem equitationi indulgeret', in *Quellen, ed. cit.*, p. 374. For his hunting see *Annales regni Francorum*, ed. F. Kurze, *Monumenta Germaniae Historica*, henceforth cited *MGH, Sciptores Rerum Germanicarum*, henceforth cited *SRG*

Widukind of Corvey, like many others, drew deeply upon Einhard and the notion of what a king should be like and how he ought to conduct himself, remained under Einhard's influence also in the twelfth century, especially in a conservative aristocratic society like that of the German kingdom but also in France where the Capetians insisted more and more, and successfully too, that they and they alone were Charlemagne's heirs and true successors. To return to Widukind: Otto I's person too was sculpted out of dominant qualities. In a chapter that concludes the account of the murderous feuds dividing the Liudolfing kin between 938 and 941 Widukind described the victor, Otto. He had survived, partly thanks to luck but contemporaries did not see it that way. Victory against the odds was a manifestation of divine might, for God could defeat the many through a small host. Otto stood out in the *res gestae Saxonicae* by his piety — he is said to have fasted always before crown-wearings — his *constantia* and *iocunditas*. Kings must be cheerful but this quality was tempered by the power to inspire fear. Lastly and above all there was clemency. Elsewhere Widukind spoke of his endurance of toils and hardship. It is only by studying Otto's career and the impression he made on other contemporaries and on posterity that we can understand the *res gestae Saxonicae* and what they wish to tell us about Otto's achievement in the segmented society he had to rule.[6] He was in fact the very reverse of forgiving but inflicted more forfeitures and severe punishments than almost any other Ottonian ruler as his *diplomata* prove. Yet by the qualities Widukind set out, Otto was deemed to have made his leading Saxon nobles rich, respected and the equals of Frankish, Bavarian, Lotharingian and Suabian princes. Before they had not been.[7]

It is a commonplace of school-essay writing to attribute the disasters as well as the prosperity of medieval kingdoms to their rulers —there are strong kings and weak ones — but what the authors of this genre of explanation do not realize, is that contemporaries did exactly the same, only not in so rationalistic a vein. Kings were sacral and the qualities inherent in them were

(Hanover, 1895, 1950), *e.g.* 819 (p.152), 820 (p.154), 821 (p.155), 822 (p.159), 823 (p.162), 825 (p.167).

6   *Widukindi Monachi Corbeiensis Rerum Gestarum Saxonicarum Libri Tres*, 5th ed. by P. Hirsch and H. E. Lohmann, *MGH, SRG* (Hanover, 1935), ii, c.36, p.96f. See also K. J. Leyser, *Rule and Conflict in an Early Medieval Society: Ottonian Saxony* (London, 1979), pp. 35ff.

7   Widukind, *op. cit.*, i, c. 36, p. 48 and ii. c. 36, p. 117f.

tested by events and their outcome: good harvests, health, fertility, victory of the host, booty, prestige and foreign embassies with presents, all these were divine gifts but they accrued through the *virtus* and *bonae mores* of kings. Writers had all the difficulties in the world to reconcile the successes of some rulers with their vicious qualities, *e.g.* in the case of William Rufus. Historians, with the exception of William of Malmesbury, had to content themselves with lurid descriptions of his end and the presages of it and this was how, for instance, Gerald of Wales handled his story, as a kind of match to the dark portraits he had painted of Henry II and Richard I.[8] Here too exaltation was followed by decline and a disastrous end. As we have stumbled into the twelfth century let us make one point immediately: we must not think that its modernities, the things we recognise and regard as germane and related to ourselves, *i.e.* individuality, sensibility, lyrical feelings, naturalness and a more empirical approach to government, that all these swept away the past and existing traditions. No, they lived on, strong and assured side by side with the new capacity for abstraction and self-realisation.

What is the meaning of these typifying characterisations which seem to brush aside or to ignore so much we can infer about early medieval kings from other sources? Where institutions were weak and ill-defined, administrations fragmentary as was the case in Ottonian Germany and other post-Carolingian kingdoms, a commanding, charismatic, sacral ruler or a failing one was an obvious substitute and on his qualities the outcome of important issues would be seen to depend. Rigid conventions therefore governed the characteristics of kings and kingship. There was in fact little room for individuality and genius in the modern senses of these words. The more a ruler approached or could be represented to fulfil the categorical imperatives of kingship the better were his chances of doing what was expected of him. Personal monarchy was thus, *pace* the school essay-writer, paradoxically much less possible to an Otto I than, say, Frederick II of Prussia because the person of a Saxon king carried these normative qualities about with him. Max Weber distinguished between patrimonial, charismatic and bureaucratic authority as successive stages of social development.[9] Our early medieval

---

8   Giraldus Cambrensis, *De Principis Instructione Liber*, ed. G. F. Warner, *Giraldi Cambrensis Opera*, VIII, *Rolls Series*, henceforth cited *RS* (1891), pp. 315, 322-26.

9   Max Weber, *Economy and Society*, ed. G. Roth and C. Wittich (Berkeley, 1968), I, pp. 215, 231f., 235f., 241f., 251f., II, pp. 1006ff., 1013ff., 1111ff., 1141f.

royal biographies mirror the first and second of these stages. One of their favourite classical tropes may serve to show this. Einhard wrote of Charlemagne that he interrupted his nightly sleep four or five times and not only awoke but rose from his bed.[10] Widukind went further and said of Otto I that he slept little and talked in his sleep so that you might think he was always awake.[11] The ever-vigilant king, released almost from the needs of natural man, was the image behind these passages. In another form the king's sleep was likened to that of a lion with an ever open eye. The primitive wholeness of this vision belongs to the patrimonial and household form of governance and its resources. In the last but one chapter of the *res gestae Saxonicae* Widukind described the ritual lament of Otto's following at his death. The *populus* (his men) recalled that he had ruled those subject to him with fatherly piety.[12]

Kingship in the twelfth century is, as has already been said, characterised by the continuity of these traditions, side by side with quite new attitudes towards it and wholly new literary representations of its facets. We must at once beware to call these attitudes and characteristics more realistic and rational, because, as anthropologists warn us, to a more primitive and archaic orientation its magical beliefs are as real and logical as those with which we can identify ourselves.[13] We must also quote chapter and verse for the strength and unabated hold of the older didactic over historians and indeed political theorists of the twelfth century if the anachronistic word can pass muster. Not only Alfred was described by Asser in some of the conceptual moulds and once also in the language of Einhard.[14] This was done also to William the Conqueror, Henry I and above all Frederick Barbarossa in the last chapter of Rahewin's portion of the *Gesta Friderici*:[15] Robert de Torigny in his *Gesta* of Henry I used the

---

10   Einhard, *Vie de Charlemagne*, c.24, p.72.

11   Widukind, *Res Gestae Saxonicae*, ii, c. 36 (p. 96): 'dormiendi parcus et inter dormiendum semper aliquid loquens, quo eum semper vigilare aestimes'.

12   Widukind, iii, c. 75, p. 153.

13   E. E. Evans-Pritchard, *Witchcraft, Oracles and Magic among the Azande* (Oxford, 1937), p. 540f.

14   *Asser's Life of King Alfred*, cc. 73, 75, ed. W. H. Stevenson (Oxford, 1959), pp. 54, 57f. and A. Gransden, *Historical Writing in England c. 550 to c. 1307* (London, 1974), p. 52.

15   For William I see *De Obitu Willelmi* in *Guillaume de Jumièges, Gesta Normannorum Ducum*, ed. J. Marx, Société de l'Histoire de Normandie (1914), p. 147f.

very words of Einhard's renowned prologue: 'Vitam et conversationem et ex parte non modica res gestas nobilissimi regis...' and to a schooled ear this at once indicated the example with which the king would be ranged.

Let us now, however, consider how twelfth-century kings were seen, described and judged by their entourages and more distant viewers and wherein the novelty of these observations and the things observed lay. For the writers of the twelfth century were interested in the individuality of rulers, their idiosyncracies and eccentricities even, without interpreting these traits symbolically or figuratively, e.g. like Otto I talking in his sleep.[16] We must not think of this as sheer gain for the art of biography. There were also losses. The concentrate aims and methods of some early medieval writers achieved personality portraits of intense literary power and conviction. Nithard in his *History of the Sons of Louis the Pious* gave a pretty penetrating view of the Emperor Lothar. Even if the real Lothar was not quite like that, his unscrupulousness and respect only for the language of *force majeure* here lack nothing in clarity and vividness. Moreover a memorialist like Thietmar of Merseburg, revealed himself fully as a person: his doubts, anxieties, hesitations and remorse, are all there but his *Chronicon* stands by itself. Even an age much greedier for the use of the pen than was the tenth century and glutted with letters, knew only one Duc de St. Simon.

Kings then were in the twelfth century presented as individuals. The world of experience superseded the world of categorical imperatives. Men and what they were meant to embody parted company and observed behaviour replaced the vision of lived or disregarded norms. Comparisons between the habits of early medieval royal biographers and later ones will illustrate this. Einhard regaled us with very few anecdotes and sayings of Charlemagne. There is but the story that he would not have gone to St. Peter's on the holiest of days, Christmas 800, had he known of the pope's plan.[17] The *Lives* of Louis the Pious

On Henry I see Robert of Torigny in *op. cit.*, p. 266. On Frederick Barbarossa see *Ottonis et Rahewini Gesta Friderici I. Imperatoris*, iv, c. 86, 3. ed. B. v. Simson, *MGH, SRG* (Hanover, Leipzig, 1912), p. 344f. but there were also many novel traits.

16   Einhard and Widukind's descriptions of their heroes' light sleep should be compared with William of Malmesbury's story that Henry I was a heavy sleeper but was often woken up by his own snoring. William here seems to challenge and to reject the ancient symbolism with deliberate irony. See William of Malmesbury, *Gesta Regum Anglorum*, v, c. 412 ed. W. Stubbs, *RS* (London, 1889), ii, p. 488.

17   Einhard, *op. cit.*, c. 28, p. 80.

were equally sparing. This does not mean that there were no anecdotes but we have to wait for Notker's *Gesta Karoli* of c. 886 to be entertained by a large collection of tales which enlarged the memory of Charlemagne and began to turn it into legend. These stories dwelt on the shortcomings of bishops, clerks and their servants. They magnified the ruling qualities we have come to expect and they sought to demonstrate their efficacy in action. Now if we turn to the writers of the twelfth century, they revel in anecdote and even Otto of Freising in his *Gesta Friderici* has quite a few.[18] Here anecdote becomes the means to illuminate personality and also the new relationships between rulers and the intelligentsia of clerks, of the elite careerists who could make and break reputations —at any rate among themselves.

At this point it may well be asked why some important descriptions of rulers in the twelfth century should have differed so much from those we owe to writers like Einhard or Wipo in his *Gesta* of Conrad II. What was it that made it possible for individuality and humanity to be valued in their own ways rather than serve as vehicles for general qualities and ethical norms embodied in the living man but transcending him. Paradoxically it went with a new capacity for abstract thinking, for detaching the attributes of kingship from its temporary incumbent, with the ability to analyse the timeless and objective as against the contingent and subjective in the exercise of royal power. In the twelfth century it became more general and customary to think of the crown as an institution and not just as the most exalted *insigne* of a given king. [19] This form of transpersonal reflection and discussion had, of course, roots in the past. One of the most cited examples is the Emperor Conrad II's famous indignation after the Pavese had demolished the ancient royal palace inside the city. They pleaded that they had not broken their fealty to the emperor since they had none when they destroyed the *palatium*. It was done during the interregnum after Henry II's death. Conrad argued that although they had not broken the house of their king because at the time they had none they could not deny that they had torn down the royal residence. 'When the king dies, the kingdom

18   *Gesta Friderici I. Imperatoris, ed. cit.* pp. 23, 27, 67, 144. That Notker's *Gesta Karoli* circulated widely and gained literary success in the twelfth century was no accident.

19   E. H. Kantorowicz, *The King's Two Bodies* (Princeton, 1957), pp. 336ff. and P. Classen, 'Corona imperii, Die Krone als Inbegriff des Römisch-Deutschen Reiches im 12. Jahrhundert', *Festschrift Percy Ernst Schramm*, ed. P. Classen and P. Scheibert (Wiesbaden, 1964), I, pp. 80- 101.

remains as the ship remains whose steersman perishes.' The buildings were public not private. They were another's right not theirs.[20]

The word *regnum* was sometimes used to designate royal demesne rather than the super-personal idea of the kingdom. The men of Pavia had invaded property which did not belong to them and so rendered themselves liable to the king's justice. Moreover royal demesne, as against the patrimony of a *stirps regia*, could not become lordless and it is this idea which Wipo already advanced during the 1040-ties. In a faint way his use of Roman political vocabulary anticipated the great shifts of the twelfth century when the language of Justinian's *Corpus* was received and began to shape the utterances of Conrad II's Hohenstaufen successors. Here too the idea of a lasting institution, its characteristics, appurtenances and rights pushed their way into pronouncments of policy and into diplomata. The Roncaglia Diet of 1158 and its legislation could not be understood without the idea of state power vested in the emperor. Here the three last laws, discovered by Colorni, have given cohesion to what would otherwise seem to be only a bundle of partly traditional rights found now and again in earlier charters. Here it is also laid down – and this put paid to the claims of the Pavese – that the emperor may build palaces in any one of the towns. 'Omnis jurisdictio et omnis districtus apud principem est et omnes judices a principe administrationem accipere debent et iusiurandum prestare, quale a lege constitutum est.' The *Corpus* also entitled and encouraged Frederick to demand taxes on a regular footing and his Bolognese lawyers, Bulgarus, Martinus, Jacobus and Hugo were the experts who furnished the professional knowledge for the emperor's policies.[21]

When we turn to the narrative sources of the twelfth century it is noticeable that the Anglo-Norman and Norman-Sicilian milieus were particularly rich in the new genre of anecdote and beyond

20   Wipo, *Gesta Chuonradi Imperatoris* in *Wiponis Opera*, c. 7, 3rd. ed. H. Bresslau, *MGH SRG* (Hanover, Leipzig, 1915), p. 29f. and H. Beumann, 'Zur Entwicklung transpersonaler Staatsvorstellungen', in *Das Königtum, Seine geistigen und rechtlichen Grundlagen*, ed. T. Mayer, *Vorträge und Forschungen III* (Konstanz, 1956), pp. 185-224 and H. Beumann, *Wissenschaft vom Mittelalter* (Cologne, Vienna, 1972) pp. 135-174.

21   V. Colorni, 'Le tre leggi perdute di Roncaglia (1158) ritrovate in un manoscritto parigino (Bibl. nat. cod. lat 4677), *Scritti in memoria di Antonino Giuffrè* (Milano, 1966), cited here from G. Fasoli, 'Federico Barbarossa e le città lombarde', *Probleme des 12. Jahrhunderts, Vorträge und Forschungen*, XII, herausgegeben vom Konstanzer Arbeitskreis für mittelalterliche Geschichte (Konstanz, 1968), p. 130. For the four Bolognese jurists see *Ottonis Morenae et Continuatorum Historia Frederici I.*, ed. F. Güterbock, *MGH, SRG, nova series*, VII (Berlin, 1930), p. 58f.

that, incisive, businesslike comment on kings and their doings. This is not fortuitous. Nowhere else had institutionalised rule, the distinction between the personal and the objective, the abstract, advanced so far and creatively re-modelled so many existing traditions as in these two kingdoms. It is not surprising therefore that Walter Map, Gerald of Wales, Roger of Howden, William of Newburgh, Peter of Blois, Romuald of Salerno, Alexander of Telese, and Hugh Falcandus belong to the most illuminating commentators we have.[22] And here it must be noted that some of these writers, especially Walter Map, Gerald, Peter, Roger and Romuald were international figures, i.e. they knew and had much to say about rulers other than their own. In the case of Walter and Gerald the wealth of their references to the Capetian kings of France, especially Louis VII, is very striking.[23] They seem to share a profound respect for him and what Gerald had to tell is in part borne out by Walter or confirmed by other sources, for instance the letters of John of Salisbury. Here we read that Louis appeared to his entourage often as a 'civilian', as we would say, rather than a warrior. It was held against him by the Germans that he did not always surround himself with armed men but lived 'civiliter' among his people.[24] More famous still is the story that he slept in the open attended by only two *milites* and when rebuked for this by the Count of Champagne he replied: who would be after his life anyway.[25]

The anecdote is revealing of its genre. It proclaims the profound security of Capetian kingship. Unlike Barbarossa, the Hautevilles and Henry II, a Capetian did not have to look over his shoulders too anxiously or wonder whether the ground was still underneath his feet. This is also the point of the celebrated comparison between the resources of the French kings and those of their European contemporaries, related by Walter Map as a conversation between himself and Louis VII and adapted by Gerald of Wales in his 'De Principis Instructione'. 'We in France', Louis is reported to have said, 'have only bread, wine and joy'.[26]

22   On Hugo Falcandus and Romuald of Salerno see H. Hoffmann's illuminating article, 'Hugo Falcandus und Romuald von Salerno', *Deutsches Archiv für Erforschung des Mittelalters*, 23 (1967), pp. 116ff.

23   Confirmed by or derived from him. See Walter Map, *De Nugis Curialium*, distinctio V, c. 5, ed. M. R. James, *Anecdota Oxoniensia* (Oxford, 1914), pp. 221-232 and Giraldus Cambrensis, *De Principis Instructione*, distinctio III, c. 30, pp. 317-322.

24   *The Letters of John of Salisbury*, No. 277, ed. W. J. Millor, S. J. and C. N. L. Brooke (Oxford, 1979), II, p. 592.

25   Walter Map, *op. cit.*, p. 226.

26   Walter Map, p. 225. The story was much enlarged upon by Giraldus, *op. cit.*, p. 317f. and see also R. W. Southern, *Medieval Humanism* (Oxford, 1970), p. 147f.

The deceptively modest boast led Gerald to sing the praises of the French court, almost certainly to contrast it with the Angevin régime he had come to dislike. Not only did the French not pack themselves with arms and the military in times of peace but they did not have a host of marshalls and tipstaffs with rods and sticks to drive away suitors and plaintiffs. The Capetians also forbore from swearing as abominably as other princes and invoked only the saints of *Francia*. Even that their device was a flower rather than a wild beast is praised.[27]

This vision of a 'civilian' king must be set against the iconography of the Bayeux Tapestry. There the princely presence is signalled usually by armed men round the seat of state whether we are looking at Edward the Confessor, Duke William or merely at Guy, count of Ponthieu.[28] What is more, a recent study of Capetian government in the twelfth century, by Éric Bournazel, particularly stressed the importance of lesser knights in the Capetian entourage and pieced together the careers of some of these men of the sub-structure.[29] In other words, historians must beware of anecdotes seeking to convey a manipulated vision of a régime. We know from less friendly sources, Guibert of Nogent and the Chronicle of Morigny, how receptive the Capetians, especially Louis VI, were for money and profits and the same is occasionally admitted also for Louis VII.[30] Favours were for sale. But even if anecdotes, echoed in more than one source, seek to convey one impression, one certain image of a king and his régime, it is a human and observed reservoir of experience rather than a calendar of virtues which speaks. Louis VII is still a king with a central quality in Gerald of Wales: *mansuetudo*, mildness, and it was one men remembered and missed under his successor, Philip Augustus.[31] Gerald's account of Louis also proves how

27   Giraldus, *op. cit.*, p. 318f. For the device see p. 320f.

28   See *The Bayeux Tapestry A Comprehensive Survey*, General Editor, Sir Frank Stenton (London, 1957), plates 11, 14, 18, 29, V, 50. The exceptions are No 1 (Edward the Confessor, but cf. plate V), No. 35 (where Harold is told of the comet) and No. 37 (William in council with Odo of Bayeux).

29   E. Bournazel, *Le Gouvernement Capétien au XII Siècle 1108-1180* (Limoges, 1975), pp. 29-91.

30   *Guibert de Nogent, Histoire de sa Vie*, (1053-1124), iii, 6, iii, 7, iii, 14, ed. G. Bourgin, Collection de Textes pour servir à l'Étude et à l'Enseignement de l'Histoire (Paris, 1907), pp. 153, 162, 197, 201 and English translation, *Self and Society in Medieval France, The Memoirs of Abbot Guibert of Nogent*, ed. J. F. Benton (New York and Evanston, 1970), pp. 164, 171, 200, 203. *La Chonique de Morigny*, (1095-1152) ii, 8, ii, 12, ed. L. Mirot, *Collection de Textes* (Paris, 1912), pp. 29, 46.

31   *De Principis Instructione*, pp. 318, 319, 320. See also Walter Map, *op. cit.*, p.

successful Abbot Suger had been when he proclaimed God's
rewards to this good and kind man and his father. Yet these
characteristics, mildness and piety, were anchored in a new
realism, an eye for social conventions and their importance.

Kingship has become a job. It was a profession in a world
which experienced the rise of a good many organised professions
as the early Middle Ages had scarcely known them, at least in
Western, North Western and Central Europe: lawyers, doctors,
academics and, not least of all, administrators.[32] The appearance
of institutionalised and *sui generis* professional government − I
hesitate to fall in with Max Weber and call it the bureaucratic state
− here and there relieved kingship of some of the ideological
burden it had had to carry in the early Middle Ages. We must now
look for evidence of its new professionalism.

Walter Map in his *De Nugis Curialium* has left a much- quoted
description of Henry II's person and régime: 'He was the subtle
inventor of obscure and unaccustomed judgement'.[33] This is
matched by what Romuald of Salerno and others, like Alexander
of Telese, had to say about Roger II of Sicily. 'He used reason
more than force' and spent much time inspecting the books to see
that his revenues flowed in smoothly.[34] His harsh and often
savage methods, according to Hugh Falcandus, were dictated by
diligence and necessity, almost *raison d.état*, his kingship being
new.[35] In Alexander of Telese we meet the time-honoured
exhortations that Roger must serve God for the things he holds of
him and the means by which the earthly kingdom should be
rightly governed were justice and peace. Yet Alexander − and here
lies the novelty − also endorsed the relentless government
programme of the Norman king, those determined and terroristic

221. On Philipp Augustus see A. Cartellieri, *Philipp II. August König von Frankreich*
(Leipzig, 1922), IV, ii, p. 585f.

32   C. Morris, *The Discovery of the Individual 1050-1200* (London, 1972) pp.
46ff.

33   *De Nugis Curialium* dist. V, 6, *ed. cit.*, p. 237 cf. Peter of Blois, *Epistolae*,
LXVI, J. -P. Migne, *Patrologiae*, CCVII, 198: 'nemo est argutior in conciliis.'

34   *Romualdi Salernitani Chronicon*, ed. C. A Garufi, L. A. Muratori, *Rerum
Italicarum Scriptores*, Nuova Edizione, VII, i (Città di Castello, 1909-1935), p. 237 and
*Alexandri Telesini Coenobii Abbatis de Rebus Gestis Rogerii Siciliae Regis Libri
Quatuor*, iv, c. 3, *Cronisti e Scrittori Sincroni Napoletani*, I, ed. G Del Re (Naples,
1845), p. 147.

35   Hugh Falcandus, *Liber de Regno Siciliae*, ed. G. B. Siragusa, *Fonti per la
Storia d'Italia* (Rome, 1897), p. 5f. and esp. p. 6: 'ego sic existimo virum utique
prudentem....in novitate regni ex industria sic egisse'. and see H. Hoffmann, *art. cit.*, p.
128.

actions which had made the Rogerian kingdom. 'So that this boon of peace and justice can be perpetuated in your realm, it will be useful if you alone have the stronger and less easily conquerable fortresses and towns under your lordship'.[36] Roger is shown as the master of the *Blitzkrieg* and we are told also of his insistence that military wages must be promptly paid. All had to be written down. We even learn that Roger was good at press-conferences or at any rate had the gift of the wise answer to the sudden question.[37]

To return to Henry II: Walter Map describes the lessons Mathilda taught her son. He was to delay all the business of all men and should keep in his own hands anything that reverted into his patronage and to receive the revenues thereof and by such means keep the hopes of those aspiring to these things in suspense. She used to back this advice with a cruel parable: an insolent hawk if it is offered meat frequently which is then taken away or hidden becomes greedier and much more serviceable and clinging. She also taught that Henry should be much in his chamber and rarely in public and that he should confer nothing on anyone, however good his repute, unless he saw and knew the person.[38] Walter Map did not approve of these shifts but they were a recognisable form of man-management. We have a description of Frederick Barbarossa by Burchard of Ursberg (1229/30) in which the catalogue of commonplace virtues, like 'strong in arms, sharp in mind, warlike, robust, provident in council and staunch against the overmighty', is rounded off by the observation that he had an excellent memory: whomever he had seen and met only once in his life, when they came back to him, even if it was years later, he instantly greeted them by name, as if they had been in his company all the time.[39] For an ever itinerant ruler whose government contented itself with a modicum of written communications and continued to function without elaborate fiscal, judicial and administrative records, this was a useful gift to

36   Alexander of Telese in his *Alloquium ad regem Rogerium, ed. cit.*, p. 85f.
37   Alexander of Telese, iv, c. 4, p. 147
38   *De Nugis Curialium*, p. 238. and *cf.* R. B. C. Huygens, 'Dialogus inter regem Heinricum secundum et abbatem Bonevallis, un écrit de Pierre de Blois réédité, *Révue Bénédictine*, 68 (1958), p. 104: 'et omnia differuntur in futurum, que tamen brevi deliberatione poterant expediri.'
39   *Burchardi Praepositi Urspergensis Chronicon* 2nd ed. O. Holder-Egger and B. v. Simson, *MGH, SRG* (Hanover, Leipzig, 1916), p. 23. Henry II had the same gift, an excellent memory for persons. See Giraldus Cambrensis, *Expugnatio Hibernica* i, 46, *Opera*, V, p. 306.

possess. Barbarossa, we also know, was an excellent speaker in his native tongue.[40]

Like modern business executives twelfth-century kings needed a lot of calming down. There is a well-known story about Henry II and Bishop Hugh of Lincoln, the Carthusian. Hugh had no sooner been made a bishop when he excommunicated a chief forester of the king's and he also refused to bestow a vacant canonry on one of the *aulici* at Henry's request. The bishop was summoned to Woodstock and when he was about to arrive the king with his company of nobles and courtiers withdrew to an open space in the forest. Hugh appeared, no one rose to greet him and the tension was unbearable. To fill out the void Henry asked to be given a needle and thread to sow up a piece of cloth he wore as a bandage round his fingers. He did this just to fill the time and the author of the *Magna Vita* explains that this is how people who are in a speechless rage, behave. [41]

The most common characteristic of twelfth-century rulers, however seems to have been chicanery. It was like their *ira* and *gratia* institutionalised and a well-recognised practice. Walter Map's story of Mathilda's advice to her son bears this out but to find royal chicanery in action we must turn to the accounts of men who had business to transact and interests to defend. There are two that spring to mind: Hugh the Chantor's narrative of Archbishop Thurstan of York's struggle against Henry I and Romuald of Salerno's masterly report of Frederick Barbarossa's conduct of the negotiations, which after many crises led to the peace of Venice in 1177.

In each case the last ounce of advantage was to be wrested from the situation. For Henry I the methods of imposing delay, of throwing difficulties — we would call them red herrings — into an argument, were habitual and what Hugh the Chantor had to describe was no isolated incident. Henry had used such tactics before against the pressures to abandon investiture and episcopal homage. When he had already been persuaded to accept the surrender of the ceremony but to retain the practice of exacting homage, he suddenly wrote to Archbishop Anselm that it had come to his knowledge there were two popes in Rome and he did

---

40   Rahewin, *Gesta Friderici I. Imperatoris*, iv, 86, *ed. cit.*, p. 344. The passage is modelled from Einhard, *op. cit.*, c. 25.

41   *Magna Vita Sancti Hugonis*, iii, 10, ed. D. L. Douie and H. Farmer (Edinburgh, 1961), I, p. 116f. The date was 1186 or early in 1187.

not know whom to regard as the rightful one. True, there was a schismatic backstreet pope but the issue had only been raised to foment confusion and delay. False rumours during the next few years and further delays, in the hope that the aged archbishop might die before anything was formally settled, surround the so-called Concordat of London in 1107.[42]

The story of Thurstan's promotion and struggle to escape having to make a profession of obedience to the Archbishop of Canterbury, begins in 1114.[43] In every respect the royal nominee for the vacant see was all a Henrician bishop should be: a royal chaplain, *familiaris* of William Rufus and Henry I who transacted much business for the king. However, after meeting his chapter he decided to resist having to make the profession although his clerks warned him of what the consequences might be. At first, it seems, Henry was in two minds about the profession but very soon Ralph d'Escures, Archbishop of Canterbury, prevailed. It was a *consuetudo* going back to the Conqueror and hence the king was engaged. It is not his purposes but the means by which he sought to attain them which concern us here. After having refused to make profession to Canterbury and hence to be consecrated by Ralph — without profession no consecration — Thurstan wanted to place himself in the pope's judgement over the contested issues. The king neither allowed him to go nor even to find out by his agents what was to be done next. It took a year before a letter from the canons announcing Thurstan's election, reached Rome. At Rome, of course, Pope Pascal II at once supported the York case which was more consistent with the Holy See's primacy than an intermediate profession of obedience by one archbishop to another, albeit in the same kingdom. By 1116 the breach between the king and the archbishop elect had become open. Remembering whose creature he was Thurstan in fact accepted that he could not enter his charge against the king's ill-will and resigned his see *per manum*, a kind of

42   *S. Anselmi Cantuarensis Archiepiscopi Opera Omnia*, ed. F. S. Schmitt (Edinburgh, 1951), V, p. 320, letter No. 377. On Henry I's reputation for vexatiousness see also Henry of Huntingdon, *Historia Anglorum*, viii, 1, ed. T. Arnold, *RS* (London, 1879), p. 255: 'Pauperes...delatoriis hamis intercipiebat'.

43   For Henry I's dealings in the Canterbury—York dispute over the profession of obedience Hugh the Chantor, *The History of the Church of York 1066-1127*, ed. and translated by C. Johnson (Edinburgh, 1961), pp. 33ff. has the fullest and most rewarding evidence which will be followed here. Eadmer's *Historia Novorum in Anglia* ed. M. Rule, *RS* (London, 1884) and Symeon of Durham's *Historia Regum*, ed. T. Arnold, RS (London, 1885), II, are important sources for the dispute but less revealing about the king's part in it than is Hugh.

self-disinvestiture.[44] He had however received his chapter's promise, long ago, that they would not elect another prelate if Thurstan was displaced because he refused to profess to Canterbury nor did Henry regard the see as vacant. Instead he took Thurstan with him to Normandy and retained him in his service while the bishop of Exeter went to Rome to try and bend Pascal II over the matter. The purpose of keeping the elect in Normandy was to prevent him going to Rome to seek consecration there and also to deprive him of the support of his clerical *familia* in York. When they sent for him, a mission of two archdeacons, a canon of Beverley and a monk of St. Mary's York, they at once exposed themselves to the charge of having come without the king's leave.[45] In the discussions that followed they pointed out that Thurstan could only resign to the king what had been given to the Church by the generosity of kings and others, *i.e.* temporalities and nothing else. Their election, confirmed by the pope — and here lay the rub — remained valid.

Henry appears to have given them fair words. His main object was to see them go home again while keeping Thurstan away from Rome. He would allow him to go after the Archbishop of Canterbury had come back from there, for he now set out to see what he could do at the curia. Another year passed. The papal letters Ralph brought back did contain the phrase that he was to have whatever his predecessors were known to have held justly and canonically.[46] Litigation and judgement at the *curia* were evidently invited but once again leave for Thurstan to go to Rome to clinch his case, was refused but he was restored to the *status quo ante* his disinvestiture. Papal letters ordering Ralph to consecrate Thurstan without profession remained unheeded until Pascal II's death on Jan. 21, 1118.[47] The situation now changed and the chances of the elect of York improved when the new Pope, Gelasius II, came north across the Alps to visit the *regnum Francorum* but he too died and was buried at Cluny and Calixtus II, hitherto Archbishop of Vienne, succeeded him. The parties were summoned to attend the Council of Reims in 1119 for the determination of their case. By this time Thurstan had decided to risk all, if need be, and leave the lordships of his king to visit the

---

44   Hugh the Chantor, (1116) *ed. cit.*, p. 43.
45   Hugh the Chantor, p. 47.
46   *op. cit.*, p. 51.
47   *op. cit.* (1117), p. 56f.

pope even without permission and Henry saw that he could not keep him any longer but at once demanded a promise that the elect would not accept consecration from the Pope.

Consecrated however he was, saving the rights of Canterbury if it had any.[48] Characteristically, for fear of the king, the party of Norman and English bishops who had come to attend the Council of Reims, including the bishop of Durham, did not dare to have open communion with the Archbishop of York. As they left they forbade him to enter the *terrae regis*. A friendly interview between Calixtus II and Henry followed between Gisors and Chaumont. The king barricaded himself behind a vow that Thurstan should not enter England by his leave unless he made a personal and temporary profession to Archbishop Ralph — none to be made in future. Letters to this effect were to be exchanged. The Pope saw through this and pointed out that an oath against justice should not be observed and as St. Peter's successor he would absolve him. Henry then withdrew from this position and said that he could not proceed without consulting his bishops and *primores*, the lay magnates of England. He also asserted that the Pope had been wrongly informed and Thurstan had not been disseized of his archbishopric. Hugh the Chantor commented that technically this was true but it meant only that the letters already engrossed to that effect, had not yet been published.[49] In the meantime some of the king's men went round to see Thurstan nearby and urged him for the love of the king and the peace of the Church to do as his predecessors had done. Calixtus II had to be cautious. He had been elected, so to say, en route, by the cardinals and to pick a quarrel with a ruler of Henry I's power, wealth and influence was impolitic. Without achieving anything for Thurstan they parted friends. Thurstan was disappointed. Moreover, no sooner had the king returned from the interview, he sent off his men to disseize the archbishop taking care however not to injure the canons who were with him. The Bishop of Orkney and an archdeacon who had attended his consecration had a hard time to regain the king's grace and offered to swear that they had not for this reason gone to the Council of Reims.[50]

In the end Henry had to give in. It was the papal legate, Cuno of Palestrina (a German) who by the threat of an interdict forced

48   Hugh the Chantor, p. 72
49   Hugh, p. 79.
50   Hugh, p. 81.

the king to retreat but even so he bargained successfully for delay and it took still more time before Thurstan was allowed back to England. Even then the archbishop of Canterbury fondly demanded his profession and when William of Corbeil succeeded Ralph d'Escures the suffragans of Canterbury would not admit Thurstan to the office of consecrating him. 'The churches are now divided', they said.[51] It was victory at a price and perhaps for Rome as much as for the See of York. Fear of the king to the last exacted a heavy burden of return-services and delays from the archbishop of York. The case at Rome was not yet over by any means, eight years after Thurstan's promotion. It is true, of course, that Hugh the Chantor's is a partisan's account but where it touched the king the writer's attitude was one of resigned acceptance of his dealings rather than pronounced animosity. The men of Becket's circle, writing about Henry II, were to be less patient and restrained.

We may ask what lay behind this relentless pressure. Ultimately it was not the *consuetudo* so much as loss of face or the fear of it. We know that Henry was touchy about personal asides. 'Despectus' and 'maliloquium de eo' was one of the misdeeds that placed a man into the king's judgement and no one else's. One of the prisoners taken at Bourgthéroulde in 1124, was blinded because he had written lampoons about him.[52] Henry of Huntingdon has left us a description of Henry's body's perilous last journey from Normandy where he died, to Reading Abbey where he wished to be buried. The details are quite repulsive. The man who had been hired to entomb his entrails, brains and eyes at Rouen died, probably of septicaemia. 'He is the last of many Henry killed', the archdeacon grimly commented. He goes on to describe the journey of the body, wrapt in ox-hides, to Caen where it lay for some time. The topoi of decay and the impermanence of earthly honour were habitual and often repeated but here their rhetoric rose to a shrill climax:

'Behold how horribly the body of the mighty king rolled whose head was crowned with gold and pearls and shone with

51   Hugh the Chantor, p. 110.

52   *Leges Henrici*, 10, 1 and *cf.* 13. F. Liebermann, *Die Gesetze der Angelsachsen* (Leipzig, 1903), I, pp. 556, 558. Was it significant that 'despectus' and 'maliloquium de eo' were cited immediately behind infidelity and treason as causes in which the king had sole justice over all men in his land? For the blinding and death of Luc de la Barre, the author of the lampoons, see *The Ecclesiastical History of Orderic Vitalis*, xii, c. 39, edited and translated by Marjorie Chibnall, vol. VI (Oxford, 1978), p. 353f.

almost divine splendour, from both whose hands sceptres glittered, whose exterior sparkled with cloth of gold, whose mouth used to taste the most exquisite foods, to whom all were wont to rise, whom they dreaded, applauded and admired.'[53]

The theme, as has been said, belonged to a repertoire but it being so long drawn out here suggests the wholly disagreeable and unpleasant atmosphere of fear, sycophancy and intrigue round Henry I's person and his court.

With Henry of Huntingdon it is for once possible to pierce the veil of conventionality in twelfth-century judgements of kings. Henry drew an utterly disillusioned portrait of the mighty, and not least of all Henry I, in his tract *De Contemptu Mundi* of 1135-45. The king's crimes are bluntly and pithily set out: avarice, murder and bestial cruelty towards his own kin. 'He seized many men by treason and killed them by guile'.[54] Kings were looked up to and admired by the crowd and also by men of understanding and deemed fortunate. They would think differently if they but knew the secrets of their ruler's mind. Kings were haunted and obsessed by vexation and above all, by fear. Nobody in their realms could equal them in misery and crime. The stress on fear is particularly pointed and perceptive. Henry I, the author asserted, had been very frightened indeed when his brother Robert landed in England, when the Count of Anjou and Count Baldwin of Flanders threatened Normandy and especially when his nephew William Clito became Count of Flanders.[55] The archdeacon admitted that he had praised Henry I in his *Historia Anglorum*: 'Yes, I have called him great in wisdom, profound in council, renowned in arms' and more such *epitheta ornantia* but the things he had now added were all too true.[56] Henry of Huntingdon's frank confession of the panegyric sham as against the all too repulsive actuality by the seat of power, is very startling. The moralistic commonplaces, however exaggerated, coupled with the warning not to envy the great, were shot through with formidable

53   Henry of Huntingdon, *Historia Anglorum*, viii, 2, *ed. cit.*, p. 256f. I cannot follow D. Lohrmann's interpretation of these passages in his 'Der Tod König Heinrichs I. von England in der mittellateinischen Literatur Englands und der Normandie', *Mittellateinisches Jahrbuch*, 8 (1973), pp. 90-107. He called them 'Phantasievoll' and 'moralisierend', (p. 94) without perceiving the point they wanted to make about the living king's person and presence.

54   Henry of Huntingdon, *Epistola de Contemptu Mundi*, 12, , in *ed. cit.*, p. 311: 'Multos proditione cepit; multos subdole interfecit'.

55   *de Contemptu Mundi* 12, p. 312.

56   *op. cit.*, 14, p. 313 and *cf. Historia Anglorum*, vii, 26, p. 236 and viii, 1, p.255 where however the *notatio* is divided and eulogy balanced with condemnation.

insight, understanding and detachment. Men knew that they served such masters as Henry I or Roger II of Sicily at their peril, however great the rewards might be.

Let us now turn to Frederick Barbarossa on the eve of the Peace of Venice. Romuald of Salerno who has left us the fullest account of the transactions, was himself one of the plenipotentiaries of King William II of Sicily.[57] There were four parties to these negotiations, the pope, Alexander III, the emperor, the Lombard cities and the Sicilian king. The first point Frederick gained was the site of the proposed peace, the place of reconciliation. Bologna had already been agreed upon but it was too hostile and stood close to the Lombards. Venice promised to be more neutral ground. The emperor's principal negotiator was Christian of Buch, archbishop of Mainz, and it became clear at once that a quick peace with the Lombard cities was out of the question and that much more time would be needed to reach any kind of agreement on the disputed questions, *regalia*, consulships and others. Alexander therefore changed his plans and prepared a six-years truce for the Lombards and he also insisted that the *regno* (Sicily) must be included in the peace since he did not want to expose the papacy again to the situation before the Schism. Without the king of Sicily's inclusion, no peace with the Roman Church and he suggested a temporary accomodation for fifteen years.

As these were new proposals Archbishop Christian, Archbishop Wichmann of Magdeburg, Arnold of Trier and Bishop Werner of Worms replied that they had to seek new instructions from their lord, the emperor.[58] They found him at Pomposa. On the face of it Barbarossa bridled at these suggestions and berated his ambassadors for having entertained them at all. They were told to return and say: peace with the Roman Church, yes, fifteen

---

57   Romuald of Salerno, *Chronicon, ed. cit.*, pp. 2 271-288 For a less detailed narrative of the negotiations leading up to the reconciliation see Boso's life Alexander III in the *Liber Pontificalis*, ed. L. Duchesne (Paris, 1892), II, pp. 437-441. The relevant documents are in *MGH, Constitutiones et Acta Publica Imperatorum et Regum*, I, ed. L. Weiland (Hanover, 1893), Nos. 259-273. For a recent comment see D. Abulafia, *The Two Italies*, Cambridge Studies in medieval Life and Thought, 3rd series, vol. 9 (Cambridge, 1977), pp. 145-147 and R. M. Thomson, 'An English Eyewitness of the Peace of Venice, 1177', *Speculum*, I (1975) with another text.

58   Romuald, *Chronicon*, p. 277. The proposals were new only in their specific details about time-limits. In the preceeding negotiations at Anagni in autumn 1176 (see *Constitutiones*, I, No. 249) Barbarossa had bound himself in principle that the would make peace with the Lombards and give peace also to the king of Sicily.

years peace with Sicily and six years truce with the Lombards, no. When they had been to Alexander III and gone again — and Frederick knew that the pope was anxious for a settlement and had come too far north to leave without one — he sent, unknown to his first embassy, another, headed by his chancellor Gottfried, with some secret proposals to be made 'caute et privatim'. The new envoys were to accept the fifteen years peace and the six-year truce if the pope agreed to an imperial request which they would not communicate to him but to two of his cardinals (presumably friendlier towards the *Reich*.) Alexander allowed this strange procedure, the cardinals heard the request and advised him to grant it but then the pope took fright and wanted to know what he was agreeing to. Upon this Gottfried indignantly returned but the bishop of Clermont and abbot of Bonnevaux who had come with him remained behind to tell Alexander what had been demanded. It was nothing less than that the revenues of the Mathildine lands which in the preliminaries at Anagni (1176) had been yielded to the Roman Church, were to remain for the duration of the fifteen years peace with the Normans in Barbarossa's hands.[59] Thereafter he would enter into a plea with the Roman Church for their possession. Alexander, for the sake of including William of Sicily, accepted the retention of the revenues but in the end the Church must have seisin though it would be willing to do the emperor justice if he could make a case.

When the abbot and the bishop returned with these proposals they had a cold reception. In the meantime Christian of Buch was sent back to urge Alexander to allow the Germans to come nearer Venice, to Chioggia in fact, so that the peace negotiations could proceed on a better footing. To Chioggia Barbarossa now went when a solemn legation of cardinals, William of Pavia, bishop of Porto, John of Naples, Peter de Bona, Dietwin, cardinal priest and Iacinth, cardinal deacon, together with Christian of Buch, visited him at Alexander's behest. They were to ask that he should allow the envoys of the king of Sicily and the Lombards to appear before him and that in their presence he would have an oath sworn on his own behalf by some of his princes: that he would observe permanent peace with the Roman Church, peace with the king of

---

59   At Anagni Frederick had agreed that the Roman Church should have possession. See *Constitutiones*, I, No. 249, c. 6 and No. 250, c.1. These clauses disappeared at Venice (*op. cit.* No. 260) so that the emperor retained possession of whatever he effectively controlled but Alexander III and his successors kept pressing for restitution.

Sicily for fifteen years and a truce with the Lombards for six.[60]
The purpose of this solemn arrangement was security. Only when
the oath had been sworn should Barbarossa come to Venice. If he
came without it it was clear that he could treat the representatives
of the cities and of King William II as enemies. In the meantime
however Barbarossa had received overtures from a group of
Venetian *populares* to come to Venice at once without Alexander
III's permission and they promised they would see to it that peace
was made between him and his enemies. The possibilities of a *coup
de main*, of imposing negotiations under duress, loomed on the
horizon. It was a threat particularly for the Lombards who
withdrew hastily to Treviso and the Sicilians, feeling equally
threatened, made preparations to leave by sea. The Pope was
invited to join their galleys but could not do so because some of
his cardinals were with the emperor still at Chioggia.[61]

The proposed coup, *i.e.* the emperor's sudden arrival, was
stayed by the fears of the Doge. His responsibilities as host and the
city's hostages' in Southern Italy and Sicily thwarted the plot.[62]
The Sicilians were appeased. Hearing that his game had failed
Frederick, at Chioggia now began to humour the cardinals and to
talk peace more seriously. Once again, it seems that his
arrangements with the Venetian plotters were underhand so that
his official negotiators, the archbishop of Mainz and the other
ecclesiastical princes, did not quite know what was afoot. Fearing
to loose their sees as schismatics if they did not come to terms
with Alexander and were seen to do so, they made a démarche and
declared that he was their pope from now on and not Calixtus III
'his (Frederick's) idol in Tuscany'.[63] At this Barbarossa thought
it wise to retrace his steps and offer to have the required oaths
sworn on his behalf by Count Dedo of Groitsch. With this gesture
peace proceeded. He had however gained the Mathildine lands for
fifteen years and the fact that this was not set down in any of the
written instruments only enhanced the uncertainties of the Roman
Church.

Here again then chicanery and the determination to extort the
utmost advantage by fair means or foul! The Barbarossa we see
here is a very different man from the one described by either his

60   Romuald of Salerno, *Chronicon* p. 279.
61   Romuald, p. 280f. D. Abulafia (*op. cit.*, p. 145f) has the *populares* storm the
doge's palace of which Romuald, our sole source for their plot, said nothing.
62   *op. cit.*, p. 281. The Venetians feared reprisals against their fellow-citizens who
happened to be staying and trading in the Sicilian king's lands at the time.
63   Romuald, p. 283.

Italian or German panegyrists and poets. In the *Reich* especially the Einhard tradition of rulers embodying transcendant qualities remained strong. It was a much more conservative institution than the Angevin and Norman kingdoms and even Capetian France. It is only if we can see kings at their business through the eyes and the pen of a close observer and *homme d'état*, like Romuald, that generalisations become possible and worth while.

We must now turn to another trait of twelfth-century kings which distinguished them and those who wrote about them from their early medieval predecessors. The court-life of Charlemagne was graced by a literate circle but we do not hear in the writings of Alcuin or even the monk of St. Gallen, of any risqué conversations. To his intimates Charles was David. He ceaselessly admonished his bishops and if he had histories read out to him at table, so was St. Augustine's *City of God.* [64] The rulers of the twelfth century and their courts talked much more freely and with less regard for clerical proprieties. We know how blasphemously free the Emperor Frederick II is represented to have been in the pages of Salimbene. Yet already in the twelfth century the laity of the highest rank indulged in easy and sometimes alarmingly unconstrained conversation about *spiritualia*. William of Tyre when attending King Amalric I of Jerusalem during a tertian ague suddenly found himself confronted with questions about the resurrection of the body. The king professed to believe all the Church taught but could William please explain.[65] From Giraldus Cambrensis we have the family legends of the Angevins, the story of the countess of Anjou who rarely went to church and never remained there until the *secretum* of the mass but left after the reading of the Gospel. When four of the count's knights at his orders wanted to prevent this she disappeared with two of her sons through the window. Richard I often told this story and said it was not surprising that, coming from such ancestry, sons fought fathers and brothers one another. They had all sprung from the devil and, he added, would return there.[66] Another Plantagenet, Count Geoffrey of Brittany, is reported by Gerald to have claimed

64   Einhard, *Vie de Charlemagne*, c. 24, p. 72.

65   William of Tyre, *Historia rerum in partibus transmarinis gestarum*, xix, c.3, *Recueil des Historiens des Croisades, Historiens Occidentaux* (Paris, 1844), I, p. 87f. The conversation between Philip Augustus and Petrus Cantor recorded by Stephen of Gallardon, belongs to the same genre. Petrus's covert criticism of the king evoked the question why saintly bishops were so rare now, a tart royal comment on canonical elections. See A. Cartellieri, *Philip II. August*, IV, ii, p. 590f.

66   Giraldus Cambrensis, *De Principis Instructione, dist*. iii, c. 27, p. 301.

fratricidal and patricidal strife as his birthright, his *jus hereditarium*.[67] To give another example, in the slightly later, ironical *chante-fable, Aucassin and Nicolette* the hero is told that he would not enter paradise if he made the girl his mistress. He replied: 'What have I to do in Paradise. I don't want to go there unless I have Nicolette, my beautiful girl whom I love so much. For into paradise go none but such people as I will tell you: aged priests and old cripples who all day long and night cough before the altars .... those who go in old clothes full of sores and the miserable. All these go to Paradise. I'll go to hell where there are handsome clerks and knights killed in tournaments and profitable wars'. Fashion and breeding were to be found there.[68]

The progressive secularisation of kingship and its new professionalism was a consequence of that separation of spheres which was the often desired but ominous outcome of the papal reform movement. Its zealots were by no means silent in the twelfth century. If Gregory VII had any successors they did not so much sit on the papal throne where his memory and legacy were troubled enough but could be found prominently among the learned, climbing and resentful men of Thomas Becket's entourage and stamp, especially, say, Herbert of Bosham.[69] Some of the academically educated clerical élite believed that they had a right, indeed a duty to stamp on the dignity and pride of kings, to rub their noses in their dirt, so to say, for their own good. The new power of abstraction and the already impressive judicial apparatus by which it was given expression in secular government, alarmed them and took them by surprise. This lay behind the vehemence and agitation of the clash between Becket and his circle and Henry II. They were alarmed that the royal government too resorted to having everything written down. It could even be argued that the archbishop and his clerks were really the reactionaries in this quarrel or rather that they claimed a monopoly of righteousness and enlightenment for their milieu which they did not possess. The secular world which their opponents inhabited — and it enlisted the services of many of their clerical colleagues   and former friends — was more mature, sophisticated and even moral than they were prepared to admit.

67   Giraldus, *op. cit.*, p. 302.
68   *Poétes et Romanciers du Moyen Age*, ed. A. Pauphilet (Bibliothèque de la Pléiade, 1952), p. 457.
69   On Herbert see B. Smalley, *The Becket Conflict and the Schools* (Oxford, 1973), pp. 59ff.

It would be wrong to isolate these observations about kings and their doings from their context. The men who recorded them in their writings were for the most part still engaged in the age-old search for a *Herrscherethos* and the genre of writing, later known as the Mirror of Princes, had much success. Yet in the twelfth century authors like Hugh of Fleury who addressed his treatise on *Royal Power and the Sacerdotal Office* to Henry I, came to include more mundane rules of conduct in their advice to kings. [70] They struck a much more pragmatic note than their predecessors, say the high homilies of a Jonas of Orleans in his *'De Institutione Regia'* had done. Moreover Hugh wanted to see the four royal virtues of *sobrietas, justicia, prudentia* and *temperantia* backed by literacy. The king's mind should be sharpened every day by reading in the divine books. Above all he should be informed and strengthened by the examples of the ancients and the moderns. In other words: kings must study history. It seems that twelfth-century rulers did this more systematically and thoroughly than their forbears had done, at least since the later ninth century. We know for instance that Frederick Barbarossa had a splendid library at Hagenau in Alsace, filled with historical works, not to mention that he commissioned his uncle Otto of Freising and furnished him with a brief for the *Gesta Friderici*.[71] The Stederburg Annals tells us that Henry the Lion spent whole nights — it was admittedly after his fall — in having the manuscripts of chronicles collected, copied and recited.[72] Hugh of Fleury, to go back to him, dedicated his *Historia Ecclesiastica* to Henry I's sister, the Countess Adela of Blois with another letter eulogising her father, the Conqueror, in 1110, and in 1114 he indited a historical work, the *Modernorum Regum Francorum Liber* to Mathilda, Henry I's daughter, then married to Henry V.[73]

---

70   *Hugonis monachi Floriacensis tractatus de regia potestate et sacerdotali dignitate*, i, cc. 6, 7, ed. E. Sackur, *MGH, Libelli de Lite Imperatorum et Pontificum* (Hanover, 1892), II, pp. 473-75: Literacy (p. 473), 'risumque modestum' (p. 475), 'victus habundans' (p. 475). William of Tyre (*loc. cit.*) mentioned Amalric I's gross laughter as a blemish, evidently.

71   *Ottonis et Rahewini Gesta Friderici I. Imperatoris*, pp. 1-5. On Frederick's library see K. Leyser, 'Frederick Barbarossa, Henry II and the hand of St. James' *above*, p. 237, n. 1.

72   *Annales Stederburgenses, MGH, SS*, XVI, p.230. Amalric I of Jerusalem though not very literate was an assiduous student of history. See William of Tyre, *loc. cit.*

73   *MGH, SS*, IX, pp. 349, 376 and see H. Jedin, 'Zur Widmungsepistel der "Historia ecclesiastica" des Hugo von Fleury', in *Speculum Historiale*, ed. C. Bauer, L. Boehm, M. Müller (Munich, 1965), pp. 559-566.

History was felt to be part of the professional equipment of kings and princes.

The last word must belong to John of Salisbury, the author of the twelfth century's most consummate and influential treatise on the governance of Christian society, its morals and manners.[74] His critical poise, a certain detachment and independance in the service of truth, as he saw it, mark him out and set him apart in the Becket circle. The fame of an ass and of an emperor, John had said in the prologue of his *Policraticus*, were the same after a while unless the memory of one or the other of them was preserved by the boon of the written word.[75] Here as elsewhere John wanted to remind his readers that men of letters and scholars were now a force to be reckoned with. His *Policraticus* sums up much about rulers, rulership and government that was new in the twelfth century and new also in the way of thinking about these topics. His huge wealth of story and anecdote appealed to a growing public and taste. Gluttons for anecdote, twelfth-century historians and moralists shared with their patrons the need to exemplify and illustrate what they had to say on the largest possible canvas, much larger anyway than had sufficed to their predecessors. John's book, however, was much more than a work of entertainment, edification, warning and guidance for an élite. Unlike any other thinker before the re-emergence of Aristotle's *Politics* in the West, John of Salisbury came close to endowing the secular state with an ethic of its own while at the same time denying categorically that it could have one. For he endorsed the full rigours of the doctrine of Hugh of St. Victor and St. Bernard which made kings but the policemen of the *sacerdotium*.[76] Their functions of bloodshed and punishment were, it is true, exalted by John. He saw them as part — albeit an inferior part — of the holy ministry of the priesthood. The king's gruesome business, *pia crudelitas* as he called it, was legitimated from this source.[77] Yet at the same time John accepted, welcomed and

74   C. C. J. Webb, *John of Salisbury* (London, 1932). C. Brooke, *The Twelfth Century Renaissance* (London, 1969), pp. 53ff., B. Smalley, *The Becket Conflict and the Schools*, pp. 87ff., R. W. Southern, *Medieval Humanism*, pp. 174ff., W. Ullmann, *Law and Politics in the Middle Ages* (Cambridge, 1975), pp. 255ff. and 'John of Salisbury's Policraticus in the later Middle Ages', in *Geschichtsschreibung und geistiges Leben im Mittelalter Festschrift fur Heinz Löwe*, ed. K. Hauck and H. Mordek (Cologne, Vienna, 1978), pp. 519ff. G. Stollberg, *Die soziale Stellung der intellektuellen Oberschicht im England des 12. Jahrhunderts, Historische Studien*, 427 (Lübeck, 1973), pp. 18ff.
75   *Policraticus*, ed. C. C. I. Webb (Oxford, 1909), I, p. . 13
76   *Policraticus*, iv, 3, *ed. cit.*, I, p. 239.
77   *Policraticus*, iv, 8, I, p. 262.

breathed the very air of the enriched life of courts and of greater rationality in government.

The *Policraticus* expounded rulership in terms of Roman public law. The prince bore the *persona publica* who procured the *utilitas* of the *res publica*, the state. He was 'utilitatis minister et aequitatis servus'.[78] *Utilitas* and *aequitas* had been preached also by the mentors and critics of Carolingian kings but they now acquired a sharpness of definition and fullness of scope which reflected the growing and ever more elaborate and sophisticated judicial and administrative substructures of Angevin England compared with their own past or even the precocious decades of Charlemagne and Louis the Pious. It was a development the Angevins and the Hautevilles of Sicily led but did not monopolise. It can be traced also in Capetian France and even in Hohenstaufen Germany for the rise of the princes and the gravitational pull of their courts and patronage were as novel as, say in their different sphere the *baillis* of Philip Augustus. Yet judging by the amount of literature, the Anglo-Normans seem to have been more bothered about their kings than their neighbours. The reason for this must have been the close-meshed system of government under which they experienced their rulers more acutely and harshly than most, even when these rulers were absentees. In France general assemblies of the whole kingdom were relatively rare in the first half of the twelfth century, rare enough for Suger to make the most of the occasion of 1124.[79] In the *Reich* they were more frequent but although the princes had to attend *Hoftage* and knew their man, the structure of the German kingdom was already many-centred enough for the *primores* not to be absorbed, their time not to be filled wholly or even mainly by the affairs of the *regnum Teutonicorum*. This was the age of the regional charter, an immense increase in the output of episcopal and monastic chanceries and *scriptoria* and also of lay princes chanceries, the Welfs and the Babenbergs in the first instance.

Like Hugh of Fleury, John of Salisbury wanted his king to be literate and, if they were not, to be advised by *litterati*, men of his own stamp.[80] He was indeed a useful and very employable councillor, a man of integrity who, but for the accidents of his

---

78   *Policraticus*, iv, 2, I, p. 238.
79   É. Bournazel, *Le Gouvernement Capétien au XIIe Siècle*, pp. 134-143, 157-161.
80   *Policraticus*, iv, 6, I, p. 254.

career, might have served the *regnum* and was not wholly averse to doing so.[81] Yet there lay embedded in his *Policraticus* not so much contradictions as incompatibilities even though these were seemingly rare in his own make- up. The Roman legal concepts he fastened to kingship were echoed faintly also in the prologue of the *Dialogue of the Exchequer* and of Glanvill. They gave to a ruler like Henry II and his entourage their self-possessed political stance. The gap that opened between the tutelary teaching of an Honorius, St. Bernard and Hugh of St. Victor on the subject of the secular arm and the intelligence and know-how which now supported, justified and enhanced royal government, could not be closed in the twelfth century. It was a legacy charged with dynamite.

81   John's integrity might be questioned if he was the author of the fictitious letter, allegedly written by Plutarch to the Emperor Trajan (*Policraticus*, v, 1, I, p. 281) but even then he must be judged by the literary conventions of his day and not ours.

NOTE

p. 262 and n. 4: Jonas of Orleans (†842/3) in his *De Institutione Regia*, c. xi (ed. J. Reviron, Paris, 1930, p. 168) denounced shocking talk and questionable entertainment at meals in the spirit of Louis the Pious's preferences. The writers of the twelfth century now and again tell us what was said on such occasions (e.g. Walter Map, *op. cit.*, p. 38). I should like to thank Professor Johannes Fried of the University of Cologne for the reference to Jonas.

On Gerald of Wales see now R. Bartlett, *Gerald of Wales* (Oxford, 1982).

On Romuald of Salerno see now D. J. A. Matthew, 'The Chronicle of Romuald of Salerno', *The Writing of History in the Middle Ages Essays presented to Richard William Southern* edited by R. H. C. Davis and J. M. Wallace-Hadrill (Oxford, 1981), pp. 239-74. Professor Matthew would allow Romuald to have been the author of that part of the *Chronicon* which dealt with the Venice peace negotiations. He seems to me (p. 270) to underrate the acuteness of his vision in the portrayal of men and events before the more solemn occasions with their rituals and lengthy addresses in Venice.

11

THE EMPEROR FREDERICK II

Few medieval rulers hold a place in the literary and historical imagination of contemporary man outside the lecture rooms of academies and the craft-guild of professional historians. In this country it might be King Alfred and William the Conqueror, perhaps also Richard Coeur de Lion and Henry V who now and again find an echo or rouse a popular response. France has St. Louis, a holy king who can still work miracles. By comparison the Germans stand perhaps a little closer to their medieval past and they have had a way of cultivating it in the light of a changing political present. If any medieval ruler besides Charlemagne can and perhaps should appeal to modern Europeans at large it is Frederick II, the last Hohenstaufen emperor. He died in 1250 and during the first half of the thirteenth century his lordship ranged, with varying degrees of intensity, from the Baltic to Sicily. He was also king or at least regent over the remnants of the crusading states on the eastern mediterranean seaboard. Norman, Suabian, French and Italian by descent, he belongs to no single national tradition. If Lombardy and Central Italy became his chief battle-grounds, his conflict with an unrelenting papacy compelled him to try and be understood also in England, France and Hungary. His great manifestoes were sent in all directions and, as has often been observed, the struggle he fought out knew no frontiers. The figure of Frederick II moreover has not only captivated historians. Since the last century it has also haunted the philosophers of culture and the prophets of new values. Frederick fills the opening pages of Jacob Burckhardt's book on the culture of the Italian Renaissance: he is the first modern ruler, objective and calculating, forging his state as a malleable instrument, a work of art. For Nietzsche the Hohenstaufen emperor belonged to an age of dissolution. Full of inner contradictions — and here Nietzsche got his Frederick right — he was one of those enigmatic men destined either to conquer or to lead astray. He was, so the philosopher wrote, the first European entirely to his taste.

A new, large-scale biography of Frederick II, the recently published work of Professor Van Cleve, is therefore something of an event, all the more so as the last full-scale study of him created a furore. I mean the *Life* of Frederick by Ernst Kantorowicz, first published in 1927 and translated into English in 1931.[1] Kantorowicz only just escaped from Hitler's Germany in 1938 but before that he had been an ardent patriot of a strongly nationalist cast. At Heidelberg he belonged to the gifted and elevated circle of the poet Stefan George. The somewhat misty aspirations of this group included biography: the true life of a great man must be seen, felt and experienced from within by the would-be biographer. Kantorowicz's Frederick II was created in this mood. But in seeing the emperor as he wished to be seen, through the preambles of his letters, his constitutions, his charters, his book on falconry and the iconology of his buildings, Kantorowicz also practised, if he did not invent, a new historical method. The person and the horizons of the emperor were fashioned out of the solemn prose of his chancery clerks and their reflexion was caught in contemporary and later chronicles. In this way the whole cultural and spiritual climate of his court came to life. Kantorowicz had in fact broken with the positivist school of history which treated the ideology and the messianic tone of Frederick's manifestoes as empty rhetoric and mere propaganda concealing his real intentions. The historian has the duty, so the early critics of the book argued, to state the facts first; in this case to find out what Frederick's political aims really were. Only then was it worth while asking what symbols these aims had used as a disguise. Kantorowicz, it was said, went wrong because he had turned 'realities into symbols and symbols into realities'. The flaw in this censure lay in the assumption that the politics of a Frederick II were like our own or, at least, shared with ours a rationality which the positivist historical school believed to be timeless. The critics also sought to discredit Kantorwicz's method by identifying it with the mythology of the George-circle when it had in fact grown out of a deep and dedicated understanding of the sources. Kantorowicz wanted to present his emperor whole, not only as a political schemer.

Yet some of the misgivings about his Frederick II seem in

(1)   T. C. Van Cleve, *The Emperor Frederick II of Hohenstaufen* (Oxford, 1972); E. Kantorowicz, *Kaiser Friedrich der Zweite*, 2 vols. (Düsseldorf und München, 1927-31) and reprints, 1963, 1964. English translation, *Frederick II, 1194-1250*, by E. O. Lorimer (London, 1931).

retrospect to have been quite justified. When he wrote the book Kantorowicz appears to have believed in the world ruler as a transcendant historical phenomenon, perhaps even as a kind of saviour. Such rare personalities, he thought, were the true generators of change and not for nothing was Frederick called by his contemporary, the Englishman Mathew Paris 'the greatest of all princes', the 'stupor mundi' and the 'wondrous changer'. Frederick in Kantorowicz's pages all too often leaves his own century and setting and is likened to, for instance Napoleon, at least twenty times. He is the first absolute ruler who finds in his Sicilian and South-Italian subjects a willing and receptive people, ready to be shaped to his purposes.

Against this heady wine Professor Van Cleve's Frederick II is sobriety itself and yet, ironically, the older book has cast a kind of spell over his. In arrangement and sometimes also in their foibles they can come surprisingly close to one another. Like his predecessor, for example, Van Cleve greatly exaggerates Frederick's share in the transmission of Aristotelian and Arabic science to the learned centres of the west. The exotic court of Sicily rendered useful services to this cause but it did not lead, let alone monopolise it. Like all good biographers of Frederick II Van Cleve is fiercely partisan. To him the emperor was culturally and intellectually superior to his age. His detractors were hirelings bent on character assassination. He has a marked distaste for the papacy's efforts to retain lands it had recently acquired by imperial gift. Occasionally he shakes an angry fist at the pope's local representatives, men like the Cardinal-Legates Rainer of Viterbo or the suave Ottaviano Ubaldini who campaigned, intrigued, bribed, excommunicated and wrote pamphlets with few holds barred. There was too much foul play but he forgets that it was foul play on both sides. Against Pope Innocent IV's cold determination to destroy him, the emperor's resistance and counter- attacks, it is true, have a certain harsh pathos.

The time has come however for historians to be less spell-bound by Frederick II and his deeds. He was for all his gifts neither likable nor reassuring. For this he must not be blamed too much for his personality had been scarred for ever by the experiences of a long and particularly unfortunate minority. He was born in 1194 at Jesi in the March of Ancona. His father, the

Emperor Henry VI died in 1197, his mother Constance of Sicily in 1198. Royal minorities were times of crisis and unrest in the kingdoms of the Early and High Middle Ages, a calamity for which their ruling strata knew no remedy. The child-king's acts had full validity. He represented the royal lordship in its plenitude as if he were an adult, yet what he did was done at the bidding of those who happened to be in charge of him. In the case of Frederick these were a succession of German military bosses, high dignitaries of the Sicilian kingdom and papal emissaries, grasping insecure and ambitious men who had to use their favourable moment. The losses of castles, royal lands and rights were serious but with luck they could be regained. More serious in such situations was the psychological damage done to the fatherless and motherless youth on whose exploitation the whole system depended. The conditions of his childhood explain much about the later Frederick: his boundless selfwill, his deeply suspicious, distrustful and callous make-up, not to mention his notorious cruelty. He knew how to charm but he knew how to terrorise even better. His experience was not unique, that of the Salian emperor Henry IV springs to mind who in 1062 was kidnapped from his mother. Like Henry IV Frederick was bent on revenge for injuries suffered during the years of helplessness. In later years he could not forego it even when it would have been wise to do so. Altogether he learned the rigours of the game of ruling in a sordid school. We are often given an idyllic picture of his boyhood and education in the back-streets of Palermo meeting all sorts of people, Germans, Italians, Moslems, Greeks and Jews. He was, so Kantorowicz and others enthusiastically wrote, 'schooled by life'. Here Van Cleve is surely right when he dismisses the idyll as nonsense. If the men who controlled the boy-king had let him out of their sight he might well have been kidnapped and they were done for.

Frederick's life presents a paradox. His Norman predecessors in Southern Italy and Sicily had been adventurers who succeeded in creating a measure of lawful and law-backed royal authority. Frederick was the rightful heir of his Hohenstaufen father, Henry VI and his Norman mother, Constance but his early career with its narrow escapes and hairbreadth turns of fortune resembled that of an adventurer. Later, not surprisingly, he was filled with a sense of his providential, divinely ordained mission and in his letters he pressed this belief to its furthest limits. For him therefore emperorship assumed more sacredness and divinity than ever before. It would be dangerous to think that he remained personally aloof from this cult of his own messianic role. Also, when Frederick lifted the first stone from the tomb of his recently canonised kinswoman St. Elisabeth at Marburg in 1236, he was not, as Van Cleve thinks, acting out of character. That he took a leading part in the translation of the saint's body and died wearing the grey habit of a Cistercian monk does not rule out the risqué and scoffing remarks attributed to him of which his enemies made so much. In the thirteenth century it was no longer enough to excommunicate a ruler. He had to be branded as a heretic as well before opinion, men and resources could be mobilised against him. Even so St. Louis of France and Henry III of England remained remarkably aloof from the struggle waged by the papacy and its allies, the Lombard cities, against the emperor.

What was that struggle about? No more really, in the first place, than Frederick's attempts to regain the rights of his ancestors in the Sicilian kingdom, in Germany and finally in Northern and Central Italy, as he saw them. The effort to restore something which had already been overtaken and by-passed by events in the end broke him. The Empire belonged to and made sense in an earlier period, between the ninth and the twelfth century perhaps, when Europe had been less populous and the ever itinerant emperors provided certain cultural and political communications between distant centres. By the 1230ies Frederick's most formidable opponents, the great Italian city republics, Milan, Bologna and Florence for instance, had enjoyed another generation of massive and untrammelled growth. Their control over their environment, their population, wealth and military potential continued to increase and to outdistance the South, the base from which the emperor sought to re-impose his authority. Every corner of this crowded city-state world was struggling with its own complex problems and the same is true of the German lands north of the Alps. For their solution Frederick II was less relevant and still less acceptable than his grandfather Frederick Barbarossa had been. His refusal to come to terms with these half-landed, half-trading urban societies leagued against him, overtaxed the strength of his Italian supporters and his Sicilian subjects. It was not a wholly barren refusal. Some of the institutions imposed by the emperor long survived him though the whole edifice remained a shell, soon to become a ruin.

There remains the admiration lavished on Frederick's South-Italian state, his legislation, his bureaucracy, his economic policies and the rational, utilitarian ideas on which they are thought to have rested. Here Van Cleve and Kantorowicz are once again on common ground. They share it with Jacob Burckhardt, only the Swiss historian was less ready to admire. 'Let no one have any liberal sympathies for this great Hohenstaufen', he wrote. Frederick inherited from his Norman predecessors the traditions of a self-centred and *dirigiste* regime, as we would call it. A comparison with royal government elsewhere may help us to understand his own a little better. In the High Middle Ages sophisticated officialdom, advanced financial administration and centralisation tended to develop mainly in societies which for various reasons lacked solidarity and inner cohesion. In these societies the ruled had no cause to be particularly loyal to their rulers and very often the opposite. The Anglo-Norman and Norman-Sicilian kingdoms were of this kind. They began with conquest and usurpation in contrast to, say, France and Germany. In France the kingship of the Capetians had by the twelfth century struck deep roots. It could go from strength to strength without the expensive machinery of controls needed so badly by a Henry II of England and by Roger II, Frederick's Norman grandfather, the very founder of the Sicilian monarchy. In Germany too such clever devices seemed superfluous and were suspect.

This said we can now turn to Frederick II's government of his South Italian and island kingdom. It professed exalted aims but they clashed with its day-to-day needs. For the last fourteen years, from 1236 to 1250, as the costs and tensions of the Italian war mounted, there was a state of emergency. Yet even in peaceful times the legislation and the activities of royal officials from the Grand Justiciar, a kind of chief executive, down to the meanest bailiff, were stifling. They left no sphere of life unvisited. We are able to see this government at work through the eyes of a minor official the chronicler Richard of San Germano. San Germano lay near the northern frontier of the kingdom, not far from Monte

Cassino, an important place on an important route where Richard could observe the comings and goings of higher dignitaries. He tells us of taxes imposed year after year, confiscations of church treasures, the sudden removal of officials, arrests, endless inquests and levies of military service. Some of these things are very reminiscent of Angevin England. Frederick's Lombard wars were no more popular in the *Mezzogiorno* than, let us say, Richard I's French campaigns were in Yorkshire. Even more than in Angevin England the officials and those close to government were the main beneficiaries of this type of rule. They could enrich themselves in ways not open to other members of their society. Frederick's most powerful office-holders, the justiciars of provinces, imperial vicars and captains were usually nobles and knightly but just below them there were large numbers of lawyers, as befitted a system that worshipped paper-work. The regime was therefore literate and skilled with accounts but its structure remained remarkably narrow: at the top a handful of aristocratic families and their offspring whom Frederick characteristically educated at his court so that he had always hostages for the loyalty of their elders. Police spying and denunciations flourished. The narrow base of Frederick's rule almost invited treachery and the fear of it became the dominant theme of his reign. In the end only his illegitimate sons and his sons-in-law filled the key positions. The conspiracy of 1246 struck deep into the emperor's entourage. The punishment of those unlucky enough to be caught constituted a propaganda of terror; some of their wives were publicly burnt. The suspiciousness and cruelty of the emperor matched the subversive intrigues of those close to him who were losing faith in his future. The centralising regime Frederick II had developed in Sicily was therefore not an unequivocal source of strength to him. On the contrary it made him vulnerable. Legally the Sicilian kings were vassals of the Holy See and the popes therefore their feudal overlords. When Gregory IX excommunicated the emperor and Innocent IV deposed him, it was as the tyrant of Sicily and the oppressor of its inhabitants that Frederick stood condemned. Historians have taken these charges to be mere pretexts but pretexts had to be good on such occasions and the popes chose their ground carefully. Their reproach that in Frederick's kingdom no one dared to move a hand or a foot without his orders, went home.

Yet what of the emperor's personal aura, his works of art and the enlightened interchange of ideas between the representatives of otherwise hostile cultures at his court? With the multi-racial and multi-lingual Norman kingdom of Sicily the Hohenstaufen rulers had inherited also a tradition of cosmopolitan learning. They needed Greek and Arab secretaries. In general, however, the situation of the religious minority groups in the kingdom had deteriorated. Persecution drove the Arab elite out of Palermo and Frederick himself dealt harshly with the rebellious Saracens on the island whom he forced to settle in Lucera on the mainland. The educated Moslems at his court were really a few privileged survivors. The centre of gravity shifted from Sicily to the north and especially to Apulia. A Latin culture and the Latin Church advanced steadily at the expense of Greek and Arab. It would be absurd to deny Frederick, the first ruler to found a state university, his intellectual vision and gift for patronage. But his greatest subject by far, St. Thomas Aquinas left Naples and the kingdom although his family belonged to the foremost nobles of Frederick's circle. He was glad to escape. The scholars of the Sicilian court had, unlike Charlemagne's, no wider mission. They served their master's own tastes and inclinations. Here as elsewhere the self-centred emperor wanted to control and impose too much.

One of his greatest buildings was the portal flanked by two massive towers on the bridge across the Volturno at Capua. Only fragments of it survive but high over the entrance the statue of Frederick, seated in majesty, showed him as the new Caesar Augustus, the restorer of concord. A visitor in 1266 noted the stern, admonishing gesture of the emperor's left hand and the verses which could be read somewhere on the gateway. Their message contained more menace than comfort: they threatened waverers and traitors with retribution to come. It was the time-honoured duty of medieval kings to do justice and punish the wicked but here, in the most conspicuous place possible, these verses echo once more the haunting fear of treachery, so characteristic of Frederick and his circumstances. We must not expect him to have risen above them too often.

INDEX